BATTLE IN ANTIQUITY

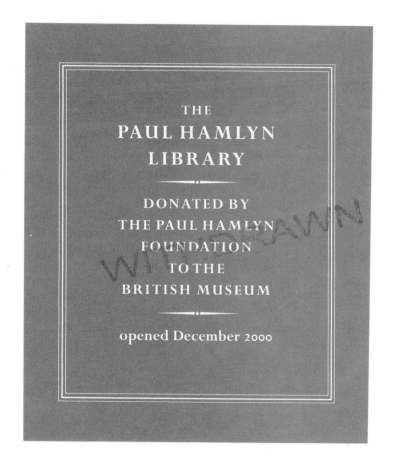

Battle in Antiquity

edited
by
Alan B. Lloyd

Contributors:
Catherine Gilliver, A.D. Lee, Alan B. Lloyd,
Stephen Mitchell, Daniel Ogden, Ian Shaw,
Hans van Wees

Duckworth
in association with
The Classical Press of Wales

First published in 1996 by
Gerald Duckworth & Co. Ltd.
The Old Piano Factory
48 Hoxton Square, London N1 6PB
Tel: 0171 729 5986
Fax: 0171 729 0015
in association with The Classical Press of Wales

Originated and prepared for press by
The Classical Press of Wales
15 Rosehill Terrace, Swansea SA1 6JN
Tel: 01792 458397

ISBN 0 7156 2695 7

A catalogue record for this book is available from the British Library

Printed and bound in Great Britain by Antony Rowe Ltd.,
Chippenham, Wiltshire

CONTENTS

Preface   vii

1. Heroes, Knights and Nutters: Warrior Mentality in Homer   1
   Hans van Wees (University College London)

2. Hoplite Warfare in Ancient Greece   87
   Stephen Mitchell (University of Wales Swansea)

3. Homosexuality and Warfare in Ancient Greece   107
   Daniel Ogden (University of Wales Swansea)

4. Philip II and Alexander the Great: the Moulding of   169
   Macedon's Army
   Alan B. Lloyd (University of Wales Swansea)

5. Morale and the Roman Experience of Battle   199
   A.D. Lee (University of Wales Lampeter)

6. The Roman Army and Morality in War   219
   Catherine M. Gilliver (University of Wales Cardiff)

7. Battle in Ancient Egypt: the Triumph of Horus or   239
   the Cutting Edge of the Temple Economy?
   Ian Shaw (University College London)

Index   271

PREFACE

This volume has its origins in a day-school entitled *Battle in Antiquity* run by the Department of Classics and Ancient History at the University of Wales Swansea on April 24, 1993, under the auspices of the University of Wales Institute of Classics and Ancient History and Swansea's Department of Adult Continuing Education. The rationale behind this day-school lay in a seminal work of John Keegan entitled *The Face of Battle. A Study of Agincourt, Waterloo and the Somme*, published in 1976, which provided a highly original and penetrating analysis of the ways in which men confront the problems and trauma of battle and succeed or fail in such confrontations. Under Keegan's influence Victor Hanson has already produced distinguished work which analyses the evidence of the ancient Greek experience of battle, and the Swansea conference was concerned to carry this research forward either by further enquiry in areas covered by Hanson himself or by broadening the time-range to which the method was applied. Given this brief, the speakers covered 'Homeric' battle and hoplite warfare but also extended the analysis to include Ancient Egypt, Hellenistic warfare, and the Roman battle experience, focusing on the factors which determined who won and who lost in ancient warfare. This involved investigating in varying degrees such issues as technology, the workings of morale, ideology of warfare, professional versus amateur, mechanisms for bonding fighting men into effective military units, and the ways in which such matters affected the outcome of military action.

The success of the day-school suggested that a volume should be produced which encapsulated the results of this research, and most of the papers published here have sprung from lectures delivered on that occasion, though the intervening time has inevitably seen modifications both in thought and points of emphasis. However, we have been particularly fortunate in that the day-school stimulated two other scholars in the University of Wales to offer studies in areas directly germane to the aims of the conference, and the result has been the addition of the papers of Dr Daniel Ogden (Swansea) and Dr Catherine Gilliver (Cardiff).

Most of the papers published here deal with a comprehensive range of issues raised by the evidence of ancient battle at particular periods. Those of Hans van Wees and Lloyd are in-depth analyses of the image of battle projected by Homer and the historians of Philip and Alexander respectively and apply in detail the perspectives gained from reading Keegan and Richard Holmes' *Firing Line* (1985) in elucidating the psychology of battle. Not the least intriguing of van Wees's results is that 'Homeric warrior mentality is neither particularly heroic nor particularly primitive'. He finds it as easy to find counterparts of much of the modern battle experience in Homer as Lloyd does in his Hellenistic and Roman sources on the creation of the Macedonian Empire. Lee casts a similarly wide net in dealing with the Roman army over an unusually generous time-range and emerges with a rich crop of points of contact with modern research. Mitchell's canvas is rather less broad. He is rightly concerned to derive fundamental aspects of hoplite warfare from its socio-political origins but in developing this point is able to isolate illuminating evidence of the psychological motivation of the hoplite soldier which lay pre-eminently in the imperative to show courage and solidarity in a common cause. In dealing with battle in pharaonic times Ian Shaw is forced to grapple with major source problems, but he succeeds in defining incentives to battle which are sometimes entirely of a piece with the results yielded by other papers but which stand apart in the very low priority placed on honour, glory, and heroism as part of the soldier's psychological apparatus. Ogden and Gilliver take a different path and concentrate on one specific topic: the former investigates the evidence for the effects of homosexual relationships in the context of battle whilst Gilliver analyses how the concept of rules of war affected Roman military behaviour. However, whether the essays deal with one theme or many, they constitute *in toto* the most comprehensive attempt yet made to elucidate ancient responses to the experience of battle.

As editor of this volume I have been unusually fortunate in my contributors and collaborators. I must thank all authors both for the quality of their work and the exemplary speed with which it was delivered. I should also like to express my deep gratitude to Dr Anton Powell, Secretary of the University of Wales Institute of Classics and Ancient History, for taking on the burden of copy-editing and seeing the volume through the press.

Department of Classics and Ancient History   A.B. Lloyd
University of Wales Swansea

HEROES, KNIGHTS AND NUTTERS
Warrior mentality in Homer

Hans van Wees

An egotistical pursuit of personal glory is generally regarded as characteristic of so-called primitive warriors. A modern soldier may have hopes of a medal, and small dreams of fame, like Philip Caputo who on the eve of his first operation in Vietnam fondly imagined making the local papers back home ('A Chicago-area marine has been awarded the Silver Star'), but such incentives are marginal to his motivation.[1] His main concern is to do what he sees as a job he is paid to do, defending his country while protecting his comrades and trying not to get himself killed. The soldier, moreover, is supposed to do his job efficiently and in a disciplined manner, whereas the warrior who lives and dies for fame is believed to be prone to 'irrational' behaviour, ranging from practising war magic to cannibalism, and from ritualized duelling to running amok.

Homer's heroes are traditionally placed firmly at the primitive end of the spectrum and contrasted with their more modern and disciplined successors, the hoplite soldiers of Archaic and Classical Greece. Marcel Detienne's classic portrait of the Homeric warrior is distinguished from that of the stereotypical warlike savage only by the absence of warpaint:

> Two features characterize the behaviour of the warrior in epic and in mythological tradition: the single-handed exploit, and the state of *furor*. The epitome of warlike activity is the individual feat of arms in combat between two champions vying in challenges, a parade of nobility and a proof of valour. The exploit is accomplished in a state of exaltation in which the warrior, beside himself so to speak, is possessed by a furious madness... A good deal of room is allowed for an element of spectacle: challenges, insults, spell-binding mimicry, gesturing, fearsome shouts, flashing of arms, so many means of striking terror into the opponent.[2]

More recently, the role of mass combat in Homer has come to be recognized, and the supposed centrality of the single-handed exploit is no longer widely accepted. Such a reassessment of combat tactics, bringing Homeric warfare much closer to Classical warfare, demands a re-examination of the traditional image of warrior mentality as well. We shall see that, while there is some evidence for each of its features, the composite picture is seriously misleading. The heroes at times do span the range from chivalrous restraint to berserk fury, but behave for the most part in a far less exotic manner, and fight in a frame of mind similar, though not identical, to that of the hoplite, and indeed the twentieth-century soldier.

1. The battlefield and the army

'If I'd known I was going to do this much lying down I would have brought a fucking pillow', one British paratrooper joked during the Battle of Goose Green in the Falklands War,[3] putting his finger on a central feature of life on the modern battlefield. Machine-gun, sniper and artillery fire force soldiers to keep their heads down constantly, and dash from one cover to the next. In consequence, the enemy is largely invisible and the battlefield seems empty. A new recruit may find it hard even to identify the frontline.

> Howell was puzzled. It was his first time in the lines. 'What is the front like?' he asked Hahn. 'You're it', said Hahn. 'Didn't you know it?' 'But what do you do?' Hahn replied: 'You just keep going until you see someone shooting at you. And you keep looking all around.'[4]

That seems as good a summary as any of the basics of modern infantry combat, and it highlights the very different nature of ancient warfare. In most ancient battles, hand-weapons predominated, and such missiles as were used had a shorter range than bullets or mortars and were, of course, less lethal. There was thus much less use of cover and much more face-to-face combat, as opposed to shooting in the general direction of a barely discernible enemy. Such differences in military technology and tactics are bound to affect battlefield psychology. If we are to understand fully the mentality of the Homeric warrior, therefore, we must begin by considering the tactics, equipment and organization that shaped his experience of war.

The battles of the *Iliad* combine fighting at close quarters with rather more missile warfare than is found in Classical Greece. Homer's mass armies fight in the open plain and in open formation, which allows the combatants a good deal of space for individual mobility towards, away from, and across the front line. At any one time, the bulk of the army keeps its distance from the enemy, while a minority stride or run forward into enemy range to shoot an arrow, throw a spear or stone, or engage an opponent in hand-to-hand combat with spear or sword. No one is expected to stay in the killing zone constantly, and no one is supposed to stay in the rear throughout the battle. Every man in the mass must go forward at least once in a while to join the 'foremost fighters' (*promakhoi*/πρόμαχοι), then drop back out of range and rejoin the 'multitude' (πληθύς) or 'crowd of comrades' (ἔθνος ἐτάρων). Although normally the combatants are separated from one another by a considerable distance, there are times when warriors gather in much denser clusters, as battle intensifies and more men move up to the front, or as a struggle for possession of the corpse of a fallen hero brings fighters flocking together from across the battlefield. Eventually such localized clusters break up as the men scatter again.[5]

Battle continues all day, and in its course there will be a number of breakthroughs. Time after time, one side will panic and run until someone manages to rally them; the other side will pursue closely, but retreat to a safer distance when the enemy turns round to face them once more. Then regular 'stationary battle' (σταδίη ὑσμίνη) resumes, until dark. Later Greek battles are decided the moment one side breaks and runs, but the constant ebb and flow of Homeric warfare need produce no clear winners at the end of the day.

Occasionally, a tactical manoeuvre is improvised, but otherwise the heroic style of combat is unsophisticated, reminiscent of the street battles fought between rioters and police, or between rival groups of football supporters, and very similar to the 'tribal' warfare practised by politically simple communities, such as those of the Highlands of Papua New Guinea.[6]

Leadership is loosely organized. We find a hierarchical structure of sorts in operation immediately prior to battle, but during the engagement itself this structure dissolves. The basic unit is a band formed by a leader, usually an aristocrat (*basileus*/βασιλεύς:'prince'), and his personal followers (*therapontes*/θεράποντες: 'retainers'). The size and number of such bands is a matter of speculation, but since the average Greek contingent at Troy consists of 40 ships with crews of 50 rowers, a 'standard' Homeric army of at least 40 war bands of at most 50 men may be implied. Followers are recruited from among a prince's close kin and friends, who may include exiles from abroad receiving shelter in his household, and also from among men of lower standing who are obligated to the prince, or wish to gain his support, or indeed are coerced into following him.[7] The aristocratic leaders are notionally one another's peers, but some are inevitably more equal than others.

3

Commander-in-chief is he who is of the highest birth or has the largest number of followers – the two criteria coincide happily in Homer – and he is charged with exhorting and drawing up the troops before battle. This process more than once involves dividing the army into five columns with designated leaders, presumably for the purpose of expediting the advance into battle. Once the troops are engaged, their mobility is such that soon there is no trace of advance columns or indeed any kind of formation or centralized command. Apart from *ad hoc* exhortation and advice, the only form of leadership available in combat is that exercised by princes over the retainers who follow them about the battlefield.[8]

Military organization in Homer may be rudimentary by modern standards, but it should be borne in mind that the heroic army is nevertheless a more hierarchical body than the above-mentioned tribal forces of football hooligans or New Guineans, these being commanded merely by informal 'fight leaders', whose authority is based on public recognition of their suitability to the task and does not extend beyond the battlefield.[9]

The equipment available to the Homeric warrior, finally, is quite advanced. The heroes usually carry a sword and one or two spears, though references to masses of arrows being shot imply that many men carry bows instead. Strikingly, the heroes are described as clad in bronze armour from head to shin. Homer gives the impression that the full panoply – consisting of a plumed helmet, a plate corselet reaching down to the waist, a metal belt, a pair of greaves, and a round, bronze-faced shield – is widely worn. It is certainly in general use amongst the leaders, but it is probably to be taken as read that many of their followers are less well protected. The leading men enjoy the additional advantage of having at their disposal a chariot and driver. In the normal course of battle, the warrior dismounts to fight, leaving his charioteer and horses in relative safety, though there are rare instances of chariots driving right up to the enemy lines. The chariot really comes into its own during flight and pursuit, when speed is a matter of life and death.[10]

It is in this context of well-equipped but loosely-organized war bands practising simple tactics that we must try to understand the mentality of warriors in the *Iliad*.

2. Combat stress: happy heroes and shell-shocked soldiers
The degree of danger and discomfort to which a man is exposed will naturally shape his experience of combat. Taking calculated risks,

even with one's life, can be a stimulating experience, as indicated by the euphoric comments of American fighter pilots in the Gulf returning from dangerous, but not too dangerous, bombing raids on Iraq:

- I feel like a young athlete after his first football match!
- I was gung-ho the whole way. It was kinda neat!
- Q: Are you looking forward to doing it again? A: Absolutely![11]

Similarly, in some forms of tribal warfare the number of casualties is so low and the physical and mental effort so undemanding by the standards of modern infantry combat that to a Western observer it might seem that 'they fight for fun'.[12] The more hazardous the form of warfare, and the more discomfort it involves, the less likely it is to afford any kind of pleasure: fear and exhaustion become the predominant experiences of battle. A surprisingly large number of Second World War veterans admit to having at some point literally shat themselves with fear – 10% in one American infantry division – and prolonged exposure to the dangers and hardship of the modern battlefield has at times produced staggering proportions of psychiatric casualties as men have snapped under the strain.[13]

The Homeric warrior could experience either extreme of emotion. The *Odyssey* features one character so keen to fight that he becomes restless barely a month after returning home from a ten-year war. 'For I did not like work or household management,' he says, 'but I always loved oared ships, and battles and polished javelins and arrows, miserable things which others find horrifying' (14.222–6). It is quite clear, however, that he sees himself as an exception (227–8), and the *Iliad* confirms that a positive liking for war is generally disapproved of (I.176–7; V.889–93). Still, even for those who are not unduly keen on combat, a rush of self-confidence may inspire the odd moment of pleasure in action. Aias, certain of his superiority (VII.186–232), enters a formal duel with energetic strides and a smile on his face (212); Paris, 'trusting in his speed', runs laughing towards the battlefield (VI.505–14). Several times a divinely inspired sense of strength causes the Greeks to discover the 'joy of battle' (XIII.82), 'sweeter' than the prospect of going home (II.445–54; XI.3–14).[14] To balance the more warlike characters, we also meet a rich man prepared to pay for the privilege of not going to war (XXIII.295–9), a few men so paralysed with fear that they allow themselves to be slaughtered without resistance (XIII.394–6, 434–8; XVI.401–3), and a large number of Greeks who withdraw from battle physically exhausted and burst into tears at the sight of the Trojans breaching their defences, 'for they thought that there was no escape from coming to grief' (XIII.85–9). It is

5

impossible to generalize from either set of instances, and we must look for more general indications of how stressful Homeric battle is, and how the heroes cope with the strain.

Judging by its epithets, the epic battlefield is a very grim place indeed. It is commonly called destructive (δήϊος or ὀλοός), dreadful (αἰνή), abominable (στυγερός), a cause of tears (δακρυοεις or πολύδακρυς), or simply bad (κακός). Occasionally, it is also described as bloody, wretched, baneful, cruel, harsh, piercing and 'burning hot'. To counter this, there are a very few neutral epithets, and but a single positive one: glory-bringing (κυδιάνειρα).[15] The narrative adds to the less than pleasant picture with regular references to pain, exhaustion, sweat, dust and noise. At times, the sound of thudding missiles, clashing arms, and shouting men is louder than a raging forest fire or the wind screaming in the trees (XIV.393–401), too loud for shouted commands to be heard (XII.336–42). Noise is a particularly harrowing feature of the modern battlefield, and that it was so for Homer is indicated by his use of yet another standard epithet for war, 'ill-sounding' (δυσηχέος), and of a common metonymic expression for battle, 'the dreadful din' (φύλοπις αἰνή).[16]

It emerges, however, that this is a picture of combat at its worst, its most intense. Battle is not always equally taxing. The fighting over the corpse of Patroklos is so fierce that

> all the time they relentlessly dashed forward with their spears...and killed one another [while] the sweat of exhaustion constantly, relentlessly streamed into the eyes and down the arms of those who fought, and down their knees and shins and feet below (XVII.385–7, 412–13).

They throw up a cloud of dust thick enough to blot out sun and moon (XVII.366–8, 375–6). But elsewhere on the battlefield, 'the other Trojans and Greeks fought *in comfort*, under a clear sky... They fought intermittently, avoiding one another's pain-inflicting missiles, standing far apart' (XVII.370–5). Apparently, Homeric combat becomes physically and mentally draining at times of crisis, but much of the time it need not be particularly demanding. Given that, up to a point, it is left to the individual warrior to decide how far and how frequently to venture into enemy range, the experience of battle is only as hard as one chooses, or feels obliged, to make it for oneself.

The heroes cope with the physical discomforts of battle in a manner more pragmatic than we tend to associate with 'heroic' behaviour in the colloquial sense of the word. To begin with, they insist on taking a substantial breakfast to sustain them through the day's fighting. When

Akhilleus, as a gesture of mourning for Patroklos, proposes to fight without food or drink, a lengthy debate ensues in which Odysseus tries to explain to him that fighting on an empty stomach is courting disaster, and that common sense should prevail over grief (XIX.154–72, 198–237). Even the gods get involved as Akhilleus persists in refusing to take food himself: they fill him with divine sustenance, nectar and ambrosia, 'so that grim starvation may not weaken his knees' (340–54). Some commentators find the episode banal and betraying a lack of appreciation of a magnificent heroic gesture, but surely it must rather be taken as evidence for a Homeric concern that powerful emotions should not blind the warrior to the practicalities of warfare.[17]

Attitudes to wounds and injuries are equally down-to-earth. There is not the slightest suggestion that brave men should be impervious to pain. Sarpedon faints in agony, while Hektor loses consciousness no fewer than three times. When he comes to, he vomits up blood, breathes with difficulty, sweats, and takes some time to begin recognizing his friends. Agamemnon's injured arm causes him pains famously said to be as sharp as those of a woman in labour.[18] As in modern armies, wounded, but not wholly incapacitated, men are expected to leave the battlefield rather than make a brave but ineffectual attempt to fight on. Glaukos, however much distressed he is at the fall of Sarpedon, 'could not help him', since he had earlier been hit by an arrow (XVI.509–12). It requires instant healing by a god before he can come to his friend's aid. Even more strikingly, Agamemnon, Diomedes, Odysseus, Makhaon and Eurypylos all withdraw as soon as their wounds start hurting, and, although they remain ambulant, they do not return to the fray even when disaster threatens. For, as Nestor emphasizes, and Diomedes agrees, 'there is no way for a wounded man to fight' (XIV.62–3, 128–30). In other heroic traditions the greatest warriors may be expected to sustain horrific injuries and battle on regardless, but Homer seems to make a point of rejecting the very idea.[19]

Nor do the heroes of the *Iliad* often push themselves to the limits of their physical endurance. As has been explained, at any particular moment the majority of men are taking it easy beyond enemy range, not because there is no room for them at the front, but because they 'shirk the fight of their own free will' (XIII.234). They 'stand off and fight not, doing as they please' (XIV.132). Even great heroes may stand back from the action for quite a while: Hektor spends the first part of both his last two battles out of danger, 'among the multitude and out of the turmoil' (XX.376–8; XI.163–4), and Aineias, for reasons of his own, may often be seen 'at the very back of the crowd' (XIII.459–61). When Paris finds himself magically transported home, he is in no hurry to return to the battlefield but has sex with his wife first (III.380–448; VI.313–VII.12), and Nestor, having left the field to look after a wounded man, takes his time drinking wine and telling stories until the ever-louder roar of battle begins to worry him (XI.596–804; XIV.1–15). Admittedly, Paris is exceptionally off-hand about his duties, and Nestor is an old man, but even so it is clear that lengthy absences from the front are by no means unusual.[20] The first thing Homeric warriors tend to do when momentarily out of action is to dry their sweat in the breeze, and where possible have a wash. Fighting in heavy armour under a hot sun is of course sweaty work, but such immediate concern with personal hygiene does confirm that the heroes are not prepared to suffer anything like the degree of exhaustion and physical discomfort regularly faced by modern soldiers.[21]

More severe than any other form of combat stress is fear, and Homeric warriors do have much to be afraid of. For the individual there is the prospect not only of pain and death, but also of mutilation and non-burial of his corpse. For army or community, the ultimate fate is not merely defeat but annihilation.[22] The symptoms of fear are vividly depicted.

> The skin of the coward keeps changing colour, and the spirit within him will not let him sit still, but he fidgets and squats first on one leg and then the other, and his heart in his chest pounds hard as he contemplates the demons of death, and his teeth chatter (XIII.279–83).

The brave man, by contrast, is not wholly fearless, but a steady man who 'does not fear *too much*' (284–5). As with pain, so with fear: no one in Homer is immune to it. Even Akhilleus is afraid once, when for an instant he believes that his shield is about to be penetrated by Aineias's spear (XX.261–3). The three next bravest Greek heroes all experience a 'shudder' of fear at least twice, while their opponents display the more extreme symptoms. Face to face with Aias, Hektor's heart 'pounds'; the Trojans at large tremble and change colour.[23]

The mobility in combat that allows men to retreat from the enemy when wounded or tired also allows men to retire when scared. Hektor defends his retreat before Aias as follows:

> I certainly do not shudder at the sight of battle, or the thundering sound of chariots, but the will of aegis-bearing Zeus always prevails; he can

make even a strong man frightened and easily rob him of success, and at another time he too can spur him on to fight. But come here, friend, stand beside me and see what I shall do, whether I shall be a coward all day (XVII.175–80).

The comment on how Zeus can make brave men lapse into moments of cowardice is repeated elsewhere (XVI.688–90), and clearly the feeling is that a man can occasionally give in to fear without thereby necessarily disgracing himself. Certainly, no man is expected to fight against the odds. Retreating into safety, or calling for help, is regarded as an excusable, indeed advisable, course of action. Menelaos, although initially shamed into trying to take on Hektor in person, is put right by his friends: 'You are crazy, Menelaos! There is no need for this madness... Do not seek, out of rivalry, to fight a man better than yourself' (VII.104–21). Later, in an interesting sequence, Deiphobos, challenged by Idomeneus, decides after a moment's hesitation to retreat and fetch help from Aineias (XIII.455–9); it is then Idomeneus's turn to call for help, admitting freely that, as an older man, he is 'terribly afraid' of young Aineias (476–86). Aineias, for his part, while not scared of any single person, does not dare to stand up to two opponents at once: 'although he was a nimble warrior, Aineias did not stand his ground when he saw two men making a stand side by side' (V.571–2). Several heroes declining to engage an enemy assure their friends that they *would* fight – if only the contest were somehow more 'equal'.[24]

Whereas for an army fighting in a rigid and close formation a general panic means defeat, since it is impossible to restore order once the ranks have been broken, fighting in open formation means not only that individuals can succumb to fear and beat a temporary retreat without necessarily endangering their comrades, but also that the army as a whole can afford to suffer an occasional panic and still rally with relative ease. Hence Homer tends to treat panic as an unfortunate fact of life rather than as something to be avoided at all costs. Fear personified, *Phobos*, son of the god of war, 'makes afraid even a brave warrior' (XIII.300), and however hard a man like Aias or Hektor may try to resist joining a general stampede, there will come a moment when Zeus suddenly causes him to panic, too (XI.544–5; XVI.656–7). When the situation is hopeless there is no disgrace in running. Hektor, in fact, orders his entire army to flee, 'since he knew the fate lying in Zeus's sacred balance' (XVI.657–8). So too, Meriones encourages an already fearful Idomeneus to join the general retreat: 'you can see for yourself that force is no longer with the Greeks' (XVII.620–5).

9

Rare instances of heroes choosing to stand their ground against superior enemies must be judged in the light of the norm that no warrior need feel obliged to fight when outnumbered or merely outclassed by someone younger or stronger, and that no one can be blamed for being swept along in a general panic. Hektor believes he can salvage his reputation only by facing Akhilleus, but receives a warning rather than praise from his father: 'Do not stand up to that man by yourself, without others, my son, ...for he is a much better man' (XXII.38–40). There is no hint of criticism as Hektor after all loses his nerve and runs, not stopping until he is tricked into believing that help is at hand. Diomedes calls Odysseus a coward for failing to face Hektor, only to be told by Nestor that he, too, would be better advised to retreat (VIII.137–44), and that no one would seriously regard him as a coward for doing so (151–6). He takes some persuading, but does eventually yield. Finally, Odysseus, about to panic at the prospect of being surrounded, catches himself with the thought:

> But why does my spirit tell me such things? For I know that cowards leave battle, but a man who seeks to excel in fighting must by all means stand his ground strongly, to be struck down or to strike down his opponent (XI.401–10).

He does stand his ground and fights successfully, but in the end a wound forces even him to shout for help and retire. These words and deeds sometimes are singled out as representing an alleged strict 'heroic code' which allows no sign of fear and no retreat. It should be clear by now that they represent no such thing. The norm for behaviour on the battlefield is far less demanding: Hektor, Diomedes and Odysseus set themselves an admirable but exceptionally high standard – and ultimately fail to live up to it.[25]

There is, then, scope for yielding to fear by avoiding danger. How do the heroes cope with fear when escape is or seems impossible? Some display a quiet resignation to death. Above all, this is characteristic of Akhilleus, who chooses, first, to go to Troy, and then to kill Hektor, in the full knowledge that each of these moves is destined to bring him closer to his own death. This is untypical insofar as other heroes do not have foreknowledge of their fate, but it is not far removed from the fatalistic philosophy attested generally and best expressed by Sarpedon in his address to Glaukos:

> My friend, if the two of us were to be ageless and immortal forever once we escaped this war, I myself would not be fighting at the front, nor would I be sending you into glory-bringing battle. But since, as it is,

countless demons of death are hanging over us, and no mortal can escape or avoid them, let us go and see if we will hand victory to someone, or someone to us (XII. 322–8).

Modern critics have had much to say in appreciation of Homeric attitudes to death, and justifiably so.[26] It may be noted, however, that in essence the sort of fatalism shown by the heroes is fairly common-place among those used to risking their lives, from the Kapauku of New Guinea, who tell anxious young warriors 'that the manner of every man's death is ordained ("it is the work of the sun") and that hiding from the enemy is no guarantee of longevity', to modern Western soldiers telling one another that there is no escaping a bullet or shell 'with your name on it'.[27] Furthermore, equanimity in the face of death may be the ideal in Homer, but it is not imperative. Quite a few courageous men break down and cry when the situation seems desperate; quite a few others beg for mercy, pleading with their conquerors not to kill, but capture and ransom them instead. Neither response is regarded as undignified, though pleas for mercy are not always granted.[28]

Fortifying oneself with alcohol or drugs, and placing one's trust in supernatural forces, two means of muting the psychological strain of fear and exhaustion common to many cultures including our own, are remarkably marginal in Homer. The heroes do drink rather a lot of (heavily diluted) wine as part of their regular diet. Yet the idea that alcohol could work as a stimulant in combat ('Wine greatly boosts the spirit of a tired man' VI.261) is formulated only to be rejected. 'Do not bring me wine...or you may rob my limbs of force, and I will lose courage,' Hektor tells his mother (VI.264–5). Again, the heroes do pray to the gods for help, and take inspiration from 'signs', but rely much less on the supernatural than one might have expected. The course of war may be influenced by a variety of meteorological phenomena – thunder and lightning, storm, a rainbow or shooting star – and by bird omens, which encourage or dishearten armies according to the meaning attributed to them. Although it is recognized that some men have the gift of reading the signs correctly, it is noteworthy how haphazard in Homer the process of interpretation is. Every man draws his own conclusions, and twice the Trojan army mistakenly draws new strength from an omen which in truth, as the poet makes clear, presages success for the Greeks. What is more, several reliable augurs are scolded for offering unwelcome interpretations, and then ignored.

You are telling me to be guided by the omens of long-winged birds, which do not concern or trouble me in the least, whether they fly to the

11

right towards the dawn sun, or to the left towards the dark west... There is *one* excellent bird omen – the defence of the fatherland (XII.237–43).[29]

The role of the supernatural is not all that much more pronounced than it is in the armies of our own society. Secularized as the military is, still 'the whole world goes religious on you' when war approaches. 'It started on the boat down. The nearer we got, the higher the attendances. By the time we got to the service before the service before the service before we landed, God was playing to a full house.'[30] Unofficially, soldiers may indulge in the reading of signs, too:

> On the bottom of the trench was a book; I picked it up... The book was called *Just William*. The soldier in the trench with me was called Bill. I took this to be a bad omen and threw the book away.[31]

If the religious element in Homeric combat-psychology is rather more prominent than this, it certainly is far removed from the level of institutionalization found in Classical Greece, where designated soothsayers read omens before every battle and armies were supposed to remain passive under enemy assault rather than fight while the signs were unfavourable.[32]

Missing altogether is any sign of magical protection, whether in the shape of lucky charms as carried by many Western soldiers, or in the shape of the more sophisticated amulets and talismans which ensure the invulnerability of, say, the Liberian guerrillas who happened to make the news at the time of writing. 'They proudly display magical fly-whisks. A long slender one in brown leather will protect a hundred men standing behind it, they say, while a short, thick, yellow whisk will deflect a missile.'[33] It is significant that there is no hint of such magic in Homer, although Greek myth did know of supernatural invulnerability. Legend had it that Akhilleus's entire body, except the notorious heels, had by immersion in the river Styx been made impenetrable to weapons. The *Iliad*, however, refers only to the near-impenetrability of Akhilleus's *armour* (XX.261–72; XXI.164–8). The shift of emphasis may be suggestive of the extent to which Homeric warriors are content to put their trust in their heavy armour. A bronze panoply offers better protection against arrows and spears than flakjackets and helmets do against bullets and shells, and this may be a case of superior defensive technology reducing the need for protective magic.

In short, the experience of combat is portrayed as grim and frightening, and the occasional thrill enjoyed by a successful warrior is no reason to conclude that Homer's heroes generally are 'happy' fighting, or that war for them is a pleasurable 'pastime'.[34] Yet the degree of hardship endured by the heroes is not such as is likely to induce the state of shell-shock associated with modern warfare. Combat tactics allow scope for periods of mental and physical relaxation, while attitudes towards coping with the various strains of battle are pragmatic and not notably exacting. The Homeric warrior goes into battle well-fed and well-armoured; he is not expected to fight on when wounded or exhausted; he is not expected to stand his ground against a superior enemy; he is permitted to express fear and yield to it, occasionally even to panic. All of this contributes to making battle bearable, and perhaps reduces the need to find solace in alcohol or the supernatural. Such are the requirements of Homer's 'heroic code', and the most renowned of warriors earn their reputations, not by living up to the code, but by performing feats of courage and endurance well beyond its modest demands.

3. Combat drives: glory and discipline

Survival is a prime concern of warriors everywhere. Homer's heroes, who have no Valhalla or Heaven but an afterlife less appealing than an existence of abject poverty and subordination to look forward to (11.488–91), have all the more reason for wanting to stay alive. Before going into combat, they accordingly pray for nothing more ambitious than 'to escape death and the mêlée of war' (II.400–1). Even Akhilleus is at one point driven to assert that he will give up fighting because nothing can compensate for the loss of life (IX.398–409), and, as we have seen, the Homeric code of behaviour in battle allows considerable leeway for the urge to survive. But the instinct of self-preservation must of course be overridden by some positive drive to fight.

Studies of modern warfare suggest that 'discipline is the stick which drives men on in battle', whether it be 'the discipline enforced by the officer's pistol or the firing-squad's volley', or the discipline 'produced by mutual respect and affection'.[35]

> Man in battle...is a being in whom the instinct of self-preservation dominates, at certain moments, all other sentiments. Discipline has for its aim the domination of that instinct by a greater terror... Discipline in battle becomes the more necessary *as the ranks become more open*, and the material cohesion of the ranks not giving confidence, it must spring from a knowledge of comrades, and a trust in officers, who must always be present and seen.[36]

The common view of Homeric warfare and the stereotypical view of primitive warfare, by contrast, as we saw at the outset, posit that a desire for personal glory is the main force driving men on into the fight. It is true that fame is a significant issue in the *Iliad*, particularly in the lives of Akhilleus and Hektor, but a survey of motivation in battle will show that striving for individual glory is only part of a wider concern with reputation, which in turn is no more important than the various Homeric forms of discipline, springing from leadership, from a general concern to protect and avenge comrades, and from a sense of patriotism.

Patriotism: in war and in battle

In many twentieth-century wars, there has been a striking discrepancy between the prominence of patriotism as a motivating factor during mobilization, as well as in retrospect once the war is over, and its marginality as a motive on the battlefield itself. American, British and German soldiers of the First and Second World Wars commented, respectively:

– Ask any dogface on the line. You're fighting for your skin on the line. When I enlisted I was patriotic as all hell. There's no patriotism on the line. A boy up there 60 days in the line is in danger every minute. He ain't fighting for patriotism.
– I suppose we were fighting for our country but I'm doubtful if we gave it much thought.
– Lofty feelings of patriotism, love of country and so forth did not play a role. Nobody I knew thought in these terms.

Some groups of soldiers actually rejected patriotism 'as fit only for civilians or prisoners', and created a 'taboo against talk of a flag-waving variety'.[37] In view of this, the relative scarcity of appeals to patriotism in Homeric scenes of battle need not mean, as some scholars have thought, that the notion of country or state as something worth fighting for is little developed in Homer.[38]

The 'fatherland' (*patris gaia*/πατρὶς γαῖα, or *patrê*/πάτρη) is a concept which pervades both the *Iliad* and the *Odyssey*, being used nearly a hundred and fifty times in all. Most often it is the 'dear fatherland', and not merely home or family, to which men hope to return from abroad, and from which exiles are banned. Regularly, it is noted that Greeks and Trojan allies fight and fall 'far from their people and their fatherland'. Conversely, Hektor dies and is mutilated 'in his own fatherland'.[39] By comparison, exhortations to *fight* for the fatherland are few. We have Hektor's rallying cry, cited earlier, 'There is *one* excellent bird omen – the defence of the fatherland' (XII.243), and an equally stirring declaration elsewhere: if a man should fall in battle, 'Let him die! It is not unseemly for him to die in defence of the fatherland' (XV.496–7). Later, it is Hektor's turn to be reminded that what is required of the Trojans is 'an unshakeable, fearless spirit, such as enters men who make enemies toil and struggle when fighting for their fatherland' (XVII.156–8). He, of course, obliges, and is killed 'defending his fatherland' (XXIV.500). That is all, and even bearing in mind that such appeals can only be expected among the Trojans, since the homelands of neither their allies nor their enemies are under threat, it is not, perhaps, very much.

We should add, however, the rather more frequent references to the defence of the community which do not use the term fatherland, but urge warriors to protect 'the women and children' and, less often, parents and property. It would be unfair to comment, as some have done, that such references show that to Homeric heroes 'fatherland' is an empty phrase, which really means 'household' and little more. Of course a man may be concerned about the safety of his own household whilst fighting for his country, but it is not implied that this is his only or main concern. Each of the passages in question refers to a *collective* defence of *all* the Trojans' wives, children, parents and property. And clearly, with all the men of fighting age constituting the army, the Trojans' collective wives, children and parents *are* the community.[40] A Homeric hero may not have anything more abstract to fight for – since the outcome of war is either survival or destruction, political autonomy is not an issue, nor is the defence of a political system or of a 'way of life' – but this does not make him any less of a patriot, in the sense of someone who is driven by a desire to fight for his country. Even if Hektor is only once said explicitly to have defended his 'fatherland', there is a string of other phrases which portray him as defender of the community:

> 'Hektor by himself protected Troy', 'by himself he protected their gates and great walls', says the poet (VI.403; XXII.507). 'You have worn yourself out defending your fellow-townsmen', 'you were the protector of all the Trojan men and women in the city', says Hektor's mother (VI.262; XXII.433–4). 'You were the overseer who protected the city itself and held in your hand the wives and little children', says his wife (XXIV.729–30).
> 'I, who defend the Trojans from the day of slavery', says he (XVI.835–6).

Evidently the defence of one's city is a prominent theme in the *Iliad*.[41] Since this is so, and since emotional attachment to one's fatherland is abundantly attested in other contexts, we should not conclude that the relative scarcity of direct appeals to fight for one's country indicates a low level of patriotism among Homeric warriors. More probably, as in modern warfare, love of country is an important motive, but one which recedes into the background during combat itself, when more immediate concerns take precedence.

Comradeship: emotional and contractual solidarity

A high priority is given to the protection of one's comrades or 'companions' (*hetairoi*/ἑταῖροι). Most wounded men in the *Iliad* receive instant attention from their friends, who offer cover, carry or escort the wounded to the rear, and sometimes provide basic medical care.[42] A man in trouble who calls for help can generally count on at least a couple of friends, and more often a whole crowd, to come running up and 'stand close by him, leaning their shields against their shoulders, their spears levelled'.[43] Quite often, friends are seen to keep an eye out for one another, rushing to the rescue without waiting to be asked. The most impressive example of this is the self-sacrifice of Koiranos, who spontaneously drove into the thick of battle to help Idomeneus, 'to whom he came as a [saving] light, and he warded off the inexorable day [of death], but lost his own life' as a spear intended for Idomeneus hit him in the neck.[44] The bodies of the dead, too, need protection – from being despoiled or mutilated – and fights over corpses are common, indeed pivotal, in the narrative of the *Iliad*. They often act as catalysts, escalating from one-to-ones between killer and defender to intense mass struggles, as increasing numbers of men join in the attempt to save their dead comrades. Failure to offer such protection in death is commented upon by the poet.[45]

Ideally, one should not merely safeguard the body of a friend from humiliation, but also exact revenge for his death. Akamas retaliates for the death of Arkhelokhos,

> so that compensation for my brother would not long remain unpaid. Surely it is for this reason that a man prays to leave at his death a full brother in the house as a defender in war (XIV.483–5).

Accordingly, Euphorbos hopes to silence the laments of his parents by bringing home his brother's killer's head (XVII.34–40), and many others take instant revenge for a relative, close companion, fellow-countryman, or simply for someone who happens to fall right in front of them.[46] The poignancy of lying unavenged is highlighted in the case of a father who carries his son from the battlefield, and weeps: 'but there was no compensation at all for his dead son' (XIII.658–9).

16

Even more telling than the long catalogue of men defending and avenging individual comrades is the prominence of the concept that a man's efforts in battle may, and indeed must, benefit his comrades at large. Glaukos is thought of as 'protecting his comrades in war' (XVI.512) when he makes an assault on the Greek wall. Idomeneus is described as determined to kill or die in battle, 'warding off disaster from the Greeks' (XIII.426). The Aiantes are told: 'You two must save the Greek troops' (XIII.47, cf. 95–6). The feats of prowess of several heroes, including Akhilleus, are said to 'bring a saving light to their companions', allowing tired warriors to 'breathe' again.[47] Hektor is highly conscious of what is expected of him in this respect. Just as he is the great protector of his community, so he is the great defender of his comrades in the field, eager to rejoin battle 'to defend the Trojans, who miss me mightily when I am away' (VI.361–2; cf. XIV.391). At a later stage, knowing that all is lost, 'he stood his ground nonetheless, and saved his loyal companions' (XVI.362–3). Akhilleus for a long time remains impervious to reminders that his prowess ought to be of 'benefit' to others, and that he ought to 'defend the Greeks', but ultimately even he realizes with distress that 'I did not bring the least light to Patroklos, nor to my other comrades...but I sat here by the ships, a useless burden on the earth, although in battle I am a man who has no equal among the Greeks' (XVIII.102–6). He makes amends at once.[48]

Leading figures may be expected not to be preoccupied solely with their direct opponents, but to retain a grasp of developments elsewhere on the battlefield, and to throw themselves into the fight at whichever point the threat to their troops is greatest.[49] But the protection of others is a concern by no means restricted to leaders and outstanding heroes. A series of exhortations and gnomic utterances leave no doubt that the ideal is for *all* men to support one another. We will not miss Akhilleus very much, the Greeks are told, 'if the rest of us rouse ourselves to defend one another' (XIV.368–9); accordingly, they go into battle 'in silence, breathing force, eager in their hearts to protect one another' (III.8–9). The tactical advantage enjoyed even by a mere two men fighting side by side is repeatedly brought home. One man remarks: 'We may do some good even if there are only two of us; joint prowess comes even from very poor fighters' (XIII.236–7). We have already seen that the enemy is unlikely to stand his ground when he encounters 'two men standing together' (παρ' ἀλλήλοισι μένοντε, V.565–72; cf. XVII.721). Nestor's advice tends the same way. He tells chariot fighters to cooperate ('Let no man think of fighting the Trojans

17

alone, ahead of the others...nor let him retreat, for you will be weaker', IV.303–5), and even envisages that 'phratry might help phratry, and tribe help tribe' (II.363). The most spectacularly successful defence in all of the *Iliad* is staged by Aias, who, like Nestor, tells the men to stay close together rather than retreat or run forward to fight (XVII.356–9). The initial effect is that the enemy cannot penetrate the Greek defence at all (354–5). Even when the struggle does resume, the poet comments, of the Greeks *'far fewer died – for in the mêlée they always remembered to protect one another from the sheer slaughter'* (364–5). The moral could not be clearer or more emphatic, and it is hard to understand why modern scholars have virtually ignored it, along with the rest of the evidence cited above, in favour of a notion of uncooperative heroes driven by purely selfish ambitions.[50]

The importance of comradeship in modern battle is very well attested. 'For the key to what makes men fight – not enlist, not cope, but fight – we must look hard at military groups and the bonds that link the men within them', says Richard Holmes. Many soldiers bear witness to the power of such bonds:

– Those men on the line were my family, my home... Men, I now know, do not fight for flag or country, for the Marine Corps or glory or any other abstraction. They fight for one another.
– It's a closeness you never had before. It's closer than your mother and father, closer than your brother or your sister, or whoever you're closest with in your family.
– I became the mother hen... I was watching the other five guys like they was my children.

Jonathan Shay stresses the 'thousands of unambiguously sacrificial deaths in war' inspired by the devotion of soldiers to their friends, and notes how often veterans continue to suffer a sense of guilt for failing to protect comrades, even when they could not possibly have saved their lives, just as Akhilleus blames himself for the death of Patroklos.

I didn't do my job. I didn't bring him home... When it come the time, Doc, I didn't take care of him. When he needed me, I wasn't there... I should've took the fucking round myself.[51]

Like the modern military 'buddy' relationships which attain such importance in battle, the ties that bind Homer's heroes to their friends are emotionally charged. The sight of a wounded comrade makes men 'groan deeply', and the fall of a friend in combat inspires grief, compassion and anger. Mostly, these emotions are plainly stated: 'he felt pity', 'they felt sorrow', 'his soul was stirred', 'he shuddered', or 'he was very angry in his heart'.[52] Sometimes stronger feelings are expressed in colourful phrases such as 'his heart raged within him' (V.670), 'a black cloud of sorrow covered him' (XVII.591), or 'a powerful grief covered his eyes as his brother fell' (XI.249–50; cf. XX.421). The extremes of emotion are reserved for Patroklos's best friends, Antilokhos, who cries and loses control of his voice on hearing the bad news (XVII.694–6; XVIII.17, 32), and of course Akhilleus, who defiles himself with dust, groaning and lamenting so passionately that Antilokhos thinks it advisable to hold his hands to prevent him from stabbing himself (XVIII.22–35).

The relationship between Akhilleus and Patroklos is exceptionally close, and later Greek tradition indeed presented them as lovers. Homer, however, makes a point of informing us about their separate sleeping arrangements – in opposite corners of the 'hut', each with a woman by his side (IX.663–8) – so as not to leave any doubt that, in his view, their relationship is *not* a sexual one. The rather heavy-handed hinting in this and another passage may suggest that views of homosexual relations varied in Homer's day, as they continued to do, with Homer obliquely supporting an early version of platonic ideals – thereby tacitly acknowledging that there were others who felt that sex between warriors was acceptable.[53] With or without a sexual element, strong feelings of friendship and love spur the Homeric warrior on to defend and avenge his comrades, and drive him into battle.

Homeric comradeship has its contractual aspects, as well as an emotional content. A warrior regards himself as doing his leader and community a 'favour' (*kharis*/χάρις) by serving in the army, and expects gratitude in return. He also expects his comrades, leader and community to give him 'honour' or 'respect' (*timê*/τιμή) commensurate with his status and his performance in battle. Not only military service generally, but also the performance of a particular feat in combat may be seen as a favour bestowed: two men who get themselves killed, one after throwing himself into the thick of the fight, another after attempting to drag an enemy corpse into Trojan lines, are both described as having wanted 'to do Hektor and the Trojans a favour' (XV.449; XVII.291). The expected return favour might take the form of protection in battle, or a fair share of the spoils afterwards. When such forms of gratitude are not forthcoming, warriors may respond by withholding, or threatening to withhold, their services.[54] Similarly, a warrior who feels treated with insufficient respect will be reluctant to fight. Akhilleus's anger at being 'dishonoured' and his refusal to defend the Greeks any longer are central to the *Iliad*, and there are

19

several other references to insulted heroes retaliating by 'shirking', among them Aineias, who hangs back resentfully 'because Priam used not to honour him at all, although he was a fine man among men' (XIII.459–61).[55]

The fact that, when reciprocity in granting respect and favours is lacking, men may withdraw from battle shows that the motives of Homeric warriors are not, of course, wholly selfless. More importantly, it also demonstrates that the bonds within Homeric armies are conceived of as essentially egalitarian and voluntary. Despite clear differences in status and power, a leader is no more than a 'companion' to his followers, and he owes them, just as they owe him, support and protection. There is never any question of a feudal-style hierarchy which demands unilateral sacrifice from retainers for their lords.[56]

Reciprocal obligations thus combine with emotional attachments to create the discipline 'produced by mutual respect and affection' referred to earlier. If this is, as was suggested, a vital element in modern warfare, it is more vital still in Homeric warfare, because the heroes' rules of reciprocity are more exacting than ours. In twentieth-century warfare, soldiers will try to protect one another, but there is no clear expectation that they will also protect comrades' corpses or avenge comrades' deaths. If they do, it is purely a matter of personal inclination. Two incidents from the same Second World War battle in the Pacific illustrate the unpredictable range of the modern soldier's responses, from sad resignation to ferocious retaliation. First, when Sergeant Hartl's closest comrade was shot dead, a soldier who had seen it happen came up and 'said to Hartl, "Your buddy's dead." Nothing else was said' – or done. Shortly afterwards, enemy fire damaged the radio carried by Private Morgan. His furious reaction could not have contrasted more sharply with that of the sergeant:

> 'Those bastards!' Morgan yelled. '...the sons of bitches. Kill them all. Kill every goddam one of them.' ...Morgan was still shaking, unable to control himself, when a few minutes later [he spotted a Japanese machine gunner about to open fire on another squad]. Morgan grabbed an M1 from one of the other men and ran a few yards to where he could get a bead on the Jap and shot him dead with the first bullet. When he came back to Avery he was perfectly calm and cheerful. The account had been squared.[57]

In Homer, by contrast, it is not merely a matter of spontaneously feeling like protecting and avenging comrades, or not feeling like it, as the case may be: one has an *obligation* to do so. Conversely, a lack of mutual affection and respect may diminish the morale of a modern military unit, but demotivated though they might be, its members would not have the option of overtly withholding their services. In Homer, the rules of reciprocity actually *require* a man treated with insufficient respect to retaliate with blatant shirking, or, if he is angry and powerful enough, with total withdrawal from battle. As Akhilleus puts it, a man who allowed himself to be denied due respect would not be a real man, but 'a worthless one, a nobody' (I.293). Reciprocal respect and friendship, therefore, are absolutely essential; without them a Homeric army would fall apart. Yet where they exist, these relationships do much more than merely keep men together: they inspire a great deal of mutual support from comrades, and create a powerful solidarity in combat.

Reputation: masculinity and shame

This solidarity is reinforced by fear of the criticism and ridicule that would accompany failure to fight for one's friends. Here a concern with reputation, and more specifically shame at losing reputation, comes into the reckoning.

In contemporary warfare, the fear of being shamed before one's comrades is, if anything, a still more powerful and pervasive motive to fight than is friendship. To quote Richard Holmes once more:

> The letters and diaries of soldiers, and interviews with veterans, leave no doubt as to the pervasive nature of fear of failure... 'My main hope,' said Geoffrey Stavert, an artillery officer in Tunisia in 1942–3, 'was not to do anything which would let myself or my family down, and to put up a good appearance in front of the troops.' ...Raleigh Trevelyan [in 1944] begged God not to let him disgrace himself, and, later, wrote: 'I remember father saying on embarkation leave that the worst part of battle was wondering how you were going to behave in front of other people.' ...Most of the [Falklands War] soldiers I interviewed acknowledged that they were very frightened indeed before the battle started, and for many of them the greatest fear was not of being killed or wounded, but of 'bottling out', of showing cowardice.[58]

It is much the same in the *Iliad*, where all the talk is of the shame (*aidôs*/ αἰδώς) incurred if one fails to meet expectations, whether as an individual or as a group. Appeals to the troops' sense of shame are constant.

> – My friends, be men and put shame in your hearts. Feel shame before one another in hard battles. Of men of shame more survive than die; from men who flee there issues no fame or force (XV.561–4; cf. V.529–32).
> – Ah, you boasters, you Greek women, men no more! It will be a worse than terrible disgrace if no Greek now goes to face Hektor. May you all

turn into water and earth, sitting there, all of you just as you are – without spirit, without reputation (VII.96–100).
– Shame on you Greeks! You bad disgraces, you are all looks. Where did they go, our boasts, when we said we were the best… Each one of you was going to take his stand in battle against a hundred, no, two hundred, Trojans, but now we are no match for just one of them… (VIII.228–34).

Exhortations to 'be men' and taunts of being 'women' or 'little boys' are common and indicate that a prime cause of shame is to fall short of standards of masculinity.[59] A rather more individual and demanding standard is that of expectations raised by a warrior himself, whether by his appearance, his previous performance in combat, or his boasts; the shame of not living up to the boasting claims and promises one has made to friends and companions is cited particularly often.[60] A man may also be shamed by an unfavourable comparison with his father or another warrior of an older generation, or even with one of the enemy, but this, the highest standard of performance, is invoked less frequently than the others.[61]

Sensitivity to shame is even more developed in Homeric warriors than it is in modern soldiers. It has been found that in modern armies anxiety about fighting like a man is strongest amongst fresh recruits, and wears off with growing experience of battle, when fear of being wounded or killed comes to predominate.[62] In Homer, by contrast, seasoned fighters continue to worry about their reputations as well as about danger. They expect cowardice to be met with ridicule by the enemy, and with reproaches by their friends; they will have to hang their heads in shame, but say that they would rather sink into the ground. These emotions are probably felt more keenly than they are by modern soldiers, and are experienced not merely before comrades in the field but also before the entire community. Hektor 'would feel most terrible shame before the Trojans and the Trojan women' if he did not fight well (VI.441–3; XXII.105), and Nestor sets up Akhilleus's father, Peleus, as a father-figure to all the Greeks, to shame them into action when they fail to deliver.

Oh popoi! Great sorrow comes to the land of Greece! Loud would be the lamentations of the old horseman Peleus…who once felt great joy as he questioned me in his house, enquiring after the descent and parentage of all you Greeks. If he now heard that all these men were cowering before Hektor, he would raise his hands to the gods time and again, [praying] for his spirit to leave his body and enter into the house of Hades (VII.124–31).[63]

Shame, then, impels men, individually or collectively, to preserve their reputations by fighting back when the Homeric code requires a response to an attack or challenge. It must be stressed that shame is *not* likely to drive people positively to enhance their reputations by performing outstanding feats of prowess. The same is true of the other drives analysed thus far. Both patriotism and friendship between comrades stimulate essentially *defensive* action.

Reputation: personal and collective fame

For a motive that may inspire acts of *aggression*, we must turn to the love of fame (*kleos*/κλέος) and glory (*kudos*/κῦδος). The fact that 'glory-bringing' is the only positive epithet of war ever used in the *Iliad* is telling: glory is one of the few compensations for the misery of war, and as such features heavily in the psychology of Homeric warfare.

Before jumping to conclusions about a self-interested pursuit of fame, however, one should stop to reflect that there is such a thing as *collective* glory, and that in Homer armies as often as individuals are said to earn themselves a reputation. Throughout the narrative, collective success is described not merely as a victory or triumph but as 'glory' won collectively by the Trojans or Greeks, in phrases such as 'the Greeks through their own force and strength would have taken glory even beyond the destiny set by Zeus' (XVII.321–2) or 'the ranks of the Trojans which stood round Patroklos, intending above all to drag him back to their city and win glory' (XVII.285–7).[64] Moreover, it is acknowledged that the collective success of an army is reflected in the fame of its commander. Agamemnon says that his army's sack of Troy would be a 'great glory' for him (VIII.236–7) and Diomedes affirms that Agamemnon 'will trail a cloud of glory, should the Greeks destroy the Trojans' (IV.415–16). Similarly, much of the *kudos* won by Hektor is due to the efforts of his troops, and more than once glory is said to be won by 'the Trojans and Hektor'.[65] Thus at least part of the quest for fame consists in gaining glory for the group, and by the group.

Should anyone doubt that the thought of collective glory is much of a spur to action, one need only consider modern soldiers' well-known pride in the reputation of their regiments and battalions, perfectly illustrated by a Falklands veteran's account of how a newly appointed colonel turned the troops' hostility into instant popularity by demonstrating that 'everyone back home now knew the name of 2 Para'.

> From his jacket he pulled a stack of telegrams and messages that the battalion had received... The colonel read words from the Queen, praise from Prince Charles, and 'That's my boys,' from Margaret Thatcher. The boys loved that one: we were famous... One by one the colonel held up editions of the British newspapers for the day after Goose Green. He

read aloud the headlines from each one. They all referred to us as heroes. We were heroes... As the colonel read aloud from the *Sun*, people just couldn't restrain their joy any longer... By the time the colonel got to the Page Three girl that had always wanted a paratrooper boyfriend, soldiers were clapping and cheering aloud at the end of each sentence.[66]

Although personal fame as a goal is not actually mentioned signifi-cantly more often than collective glory, it enjoys greater prominence as a theme. Akhilleus's choice of a short life rewarded with 'imperishable fame', when he could have had a long but obscure one (IX.410–16; cf. XVIII.120–1), and Zeus's bestowing 'honour and glory' upon Hektor 'and upon him alone among many men, for he had but a short while to live' (XV.610–14), highlight the centrality of fame in the lives of these outstanding heroes. And it does require someone of outstanding abil-ity to attain fame, for it is not every victory in combat which brings glory. The only feats which Homer says, in so many words, merit fame, are highly conspicuous achievements: slaying a rival in single combat before the assembled army, or being the first to breach the wall in an assault on fortifications; slaughtering not one, but a string of enemies, with hardly a pause for breath, in a display of bravery known as an *aristeia*; or killing a warrior of great stature, an Aineias, Diomedes or Hektor. The simple killing of a less distinguished opponent does not register sufficiently to add perceptibly to the victor's reputation. It would barely be noticed in the mêlée, and Homer never mentions fame in such contexts. Even Aias, the greatest warrior after Akhilleus, the man who in practice leads the Greeks through the main battle of the *Iliad*, is never said to win glory, or even to want to win it – except when he fights Hektor in a formal duel.[67] The prospect of becoming famous for individual deeds of prowess is therefore an incentive only to the very strong and the very brave. The mass of ordinary warriors does not and cannot aspire to this type of personal glory.[68]

The select few capable of becoming famous warriors do not seek glory exclusively for themselves. A couple of men at least are motivated by the thought that their performance in battle will give their fathers a good name (VI.444–6; VIII.281–5). Beyond the immediate family, an individual's glorious feats also reflect on his community. Hektor is 'a very great glory' to the Trojans, according to his mother (XXII.435). Akhilleus may make sure that no one but he can take credit for the killing of Hektor (XXII.206–7), but he still proclaims:

Come, let us sing a paean, young men of Greece...
We have won great glory – *we* have killed Hektor (XXII.391–3).[69]

The pursuit of private glory can thus quite happily contribute to the reputation of the community. In fact, Sarpedon believes that the community *demands* that its leaders seek fame. We must fight hard, he tells Glaukos, 'so that some well-armoured Lykian may say: "They are certainly not without fame, our princes who rule over Lykia"' (XII.316–19).

It has been claimed that, at the culmination of the *Iliad*, Hektor ultimately chooses personal glory at the expense of the common good. This is hardly a fair summary of his motivation. True, Hektor decides that his reputation is best served by fighting Akhilleus outside the town gate, despite his father's plea for him to come inside and 'save the Trojans' (XXII.56–7). Hektor's reason for facing Akhilleus, however, is not that he wants a chance to show off his bravery regardless of the risk to his country. On the contrary, he fights Akhilleus because he feels that his community expects him to: he has boasted that he would stand up to Akhilleus, but failed to protect his comrades from his onslaught; as he sees it, the only way to compensate and salvage his reputation is to make a last-ditch attempt at saving the city by facing the enemy as promised. Shame and a sense of responsibilty, not an inordinate love of fame, cost Hektor his life.[70] In short, while it is quite conceivable for an individual's pursuit of fame to be at odds with the common good, neither in this episode nor anywhere else does such a clash of interests feature in Homer.

Profit and prestige: spoils and prisoners
The profit motive is another, potentially very powerful, drive to aggressive action. In modern warfare, of course, looting is not officially tolerated, but the temptation is too strong, and surreptitious, small-scale plundering is widespread. As one soldier put in charge of an occupied shop put it, 'I can remember walking amongst the shelves and feeling that I should take something. Almost as if it was my duty to.' Boots and batteries, bayonets and binoculars are cited as prize items of booty.[71] In heroic warfare, taking plunder is a legitimate practice, and the prizes are far greater – cattle, slaves, precious metal treasures.

When a captured city or camp is destroyed, plundering is under central control. All booty is brought together for commander-in-chief or king to allocate to his troops according to status and merit. The heroes are anxious to obtain their fair share and may quarrel about the distribution, but they tend to cast their arguments in terms of honour and respect rather than material gain.[72] During battle, on the other hand, spoils are acquired privately, as men strip the enemy dead of their valuable bronze armour, and take prisoners whom they hope to sell or release for a ransom. This private accumulation does have materialistic motives. Although pieces of armour and weapons taken from the enemy sometimes serve as personal trophies, most apparently do not. Hektor at one point cries out to his men to continue their advance against the Greeks and to 'Leave the gory spoils!' (XV.347). Nestor explains the rationale of this command, when he encourages the Greeks to keep pursuing the Trojans: 'Friends, ...let no one now stay behind to throw himself on the spoils, in order to return with the most. No, let us kill men. Afterwards you may despoil at your leisure the dead bodies on the plain' (VI.67–71). The implication is clearly that the bulk of the spoils is gathered up by whoever happens to come across them during pursuit of a fleeing enemy. Spoils acquired in this way, or taken after the battle, as Nestor suggests they should be, can have little prestige value as personal trophies, and we must assume that they are sought primarily for their material value. The profit motive is thus a major, but problematic, incentive. While it no doubt encourages men to take part in war, it may become counterproductive if it comes to predominate in battle.[73]

Disapproval of undue acquisitiveness is implied also by the poet's attitude towards taking prisoners. That prisoners were commonly taken and sold is clear from the large-scale bartering of slaves for wine (VII.472–5), and from Akhilleus's claim that, in the past, he 'took many alive and sold them' (XXI.101–2). We are told of an episode in which he took Lykaon prisoner 'and then sold him to Lemnos' (XXI.40–1). One might therefore have expected that during the battles of the *Iliad*, too, warriors would occasionally decide to take prisoners. Yet this never happens. Aias, son of Oileus, does once capture a Trojan alive, but kills him on the spot (XVI.330–4). We do find, however, five occasions on which a Trojan takes the initiative and asks to be taken alive. They touch the victor's knees – a formal gesture of supplication – and promise him a ransom. Sometimes there is an appeal for pity, but the emphasis is always on the wealth of one's family and the excellent prospects of an 'infinite' ransom in gold, bronze and iron. The tone is strikingly different from what John Gould has described as the Greek suppliant's normal strategy of 'total self-abasement', and is suggestive of the heroes' materialism.[74] Yet, once more, there is not a single instance of the evidently common custom of taking prisoners with an eye to ransom in the *Iliad*, where every suppliant is killed.

Diomedes kills Dolon, on the grounds that a prisoner ransomed may come back and rejoin battle, as indeed a couple of Trojans have done (X.446–53; cf. XI.101–6). Agamemnon insists that rules of revenge demand that no Trojans should be spared (VI.55–60; cf. XI.138–42), and after the death of Patroklos, Akhilleus agrees (XXI.99–105). This has seemed harsh to modern readers, but the poet himself approved of the hard line taken by these heroes. He calls Tros a fool for thinking that Akhilleus might spare him, 'for [Akhilleus] was certainly not a man of sweet disposition [γλυκύθυμος] or of mild mind, but he was most eager [to fight; μάλ' ἐμμεμαώς] XX.466–8). The unique reference to a 'sweet disposition' must have much the same ironic force as the English phrase does in such a context: it is hinted that sparing Tros would have shown undue softness. And if that is not clear enough, Homer calls 'proper' (αἴσιμα, VI.62) Agamemnon's advice to kill all Trojans, even the unborn.[75]

The reason why the poet excludes from his narrative, and indirectly even counsels against, the common practice of taking prisoners is no doubt that the custom may become just as counterproductive as the taking of spoils. Manpower is required to bind captives and conduct them out of battle, and this manpower is of necessity taken out of combat. A preoccupation with taking prisoners for the sake of material gain, therefore, is bound to hamper the war effort. The poet may disapprove, and his leading heroes may try to prevent it, but Homeric warriors are apparently in some danger of being distracted from their common goals by greed, rather than glory.

Leadership: enforcement and encouragement

In Hektor's attempt to deal with this threat to the Trojan war effort, we find evidence of a coercive kind of discipline, 'enforced by the officer's pistol'. He threatens to kill and deny burial to anyone who fails to obey his order to leave the spoils (XV.348–51). Earlier, he had threatened Poulydamas: 'If you hang back from the fight, or if you persuade someone else to turn away from battle, you will die at once, struck by my spear' (XII.248–50; cf. XVI.722–3). In the Greek camp, too, Nestor and Agamemnon issue death threats to those unwilling to fight (II.346–9, 357–9, 391–3). The bark of these leaders is worse than their bite. The most severe punishment actually inflicted, in a serious crisis of discipline, is a hard blow with a staff. Even this is applied only to the rank and file: those of higher status are politely asked to get a grip of themselves (II.185–210, 243–69). When order has been restored, the poet stresses the extent to which the Greeks normally obey their leaders:

> Each of the leaders commanded his people, and they advanced silently. It seemed as if that whole mass of troops which followed had no voice in it, [as they went] in silence, in fear of their commanders (IV.427–31; cf. III.8; XII.413–14).

Although coercive discipline plays its part and is approved of, it is rare for leaders to threaten and bully. Normally, they exhort, encourage and persuade their men, even plead with them, to fight, by stressing the chances of victory, warning of the consequences of defeat, and appealing to all the things that are supposed to motivate the troops. This kind of leadership is remarkably diffuse. The commander-in-chief features prominently, but a wide range of other leaders also take it upon themselves to encourage the army at large, as indeed they are expected to do. Thoas, for instance, is reminded that 'in the past you have been one to stand your ground in battle, and you would encourage other men when you saw them shirking. Do not stop now, but spur on every man' (XIII.228–30). In fact, not only recognized commanders, but anyone in the ranks may provide leadership of this sort. The masses of Greeks and Trojans call out encouragement 'to one another' (VIII.346; XV.368), 'in the crowd' (XI.460; XIII.332), 'to their companions across the lines' (XI.90). Sometimes exhortations are put in the mouth, not of a named commander, but of an anonymous, 'someone', who 'would raise the spirit of his comrade' (XVII.414–23). Despite an element of coercion and hierarchy, Homeric leadership is thus largely decentralized and based on persuasion. In other words, it is constituted essentially by mutual encouragement among comrades; the leaders merely play a more active role than most.[76]

While exhortations in combat cover the full range of motivations, they do not appeal to all of these in equal measure. We saw earlier that patriotism is relatively rarely invoked. Direct appeals to the prospects of fame and riches are rarer still. In several dozen speeches of exhortation, I can find only three that hold out the prospect of material reward and personal glory. All the others invoke instead a sense of responsibility for fellow-warriors and, overwhelmingly, a sense of shame at not living up to expectations.[77] The poet may speak of booty and fame to be won, but in the heat of battle the heroes do not appear to act primarily from such aggressive motives, nor are they to any great extent driven by fear of their leaders. What motivates them most is their sense of affection and obligation towards their comrades, and their concern to avoid the shame of failure before their friends and communities. In adopting this egalitarian and essentially defensive form of discipline, the heroes are much closer to the twentieth-century soldier than to the stereotypical primitive warrior. With respect to combat motivation, the main difference between modern soldier and Homeric warrior, important as it is, is one of degree: discipline owes even less to coercion and even more to a powerfully developed sense of solidarity and shame in the armies of the *Iliad* than in our own.

4. Combat etiquette: knights or nutters?

The 'impersonalization' of modern combat, as John Keegan called it, makes it easy to forget that pitched battle is in its way a social occasion. The battlefield is a setting for hostile interaction with an etiquette of its own, as Homer's heroes recognize when they ironically refer to combat as the 'tender conversation' (ὀαριστύς) of warriors (XIII.291; XVII.228), using a term otherwise applied to relations between lovers and spouses.[78]

The rules governing relations between enemies in combat are by no means always dictated by military expediency. Among the Kapauku of New Guinea, for instance, in consequence of a strict taboo against a man killing a woman, even by accident, women wander freely through enemy lines, gathering up spent arrows and shouting tactical advice to their husbands on the other side. 'The annoyed and embarrassed enemy could only try to chase the women away by pushing them or beating them with bows or fists... [Since] the women wielded walking sticks, usually much longer than a bow...it was sometimes the men who received the pushing and beating'.[79] It is tempting to classify as 'primitive' or 'ritual' combat fought according to rules such as these, in contrast to 'pragmatic' and 'rational' modern Western behaviour on the battlefield, but that would be a gross oversimplification.

Consider for example the norm, still in force in the nineteenth century, that soldiers under fire should remain at their station without budging or even ducking.

> Men who flinched were reproved: when a shell passed over a column of the 52nd, the men 'instantly bobbed their heads'; Colborne, the commanding officer, shouted, ' "For shame, for shame! That must be the 2nd Battalion (who were recruits), I am sure". In an instant, every man's head went as straight as an arrow'.[80]

Such extreme demands on soldiers' courage may have contributed to maintaining discipline, but contain a prominent element of display, a gratuitous show of bravery for the benefit of friend and foe. Even if this particular kind of display has now also been abandoned, the contemporary soldier still does more than merely kill: he acts out a role in combat, much as one acts out roles in social life. Ken Lukowiak's account of the Falklands War again provides a good illustration. He recounts how, at the risk of his own life, he carried a wounded Argentinian into British lines to receive medical attention, and continues:

> As we were leaving I shouted at the boy who we had just saved...and then I kicked hard at one of his wounded legs. You should have heard him scream...
> I have often wondered why I kicked the boy. Which is strange because I always knew – others were watching. I may have helped save him but I wasn't soft, I was still hard. See, I just kicked him. I was still a man.[81]

Rather than make categorical distinctions between ritual and pragmatic, or primitive and modern, warfare, it may be better to look at battle as a violent social occasion on which the behaviour of men differs from one society to another, depending, partly of course on military technology, but no less on what image of themselves and of their enemies their culture encourages them to project.

Let us look in this light at the way Homer's heroes conduct themselves towards their opponents. In order to see more clearly what is peculiarly Homeric about their behaviour, and to raise our awareness of how they might have behaved but do not, we shall throughout compare and contrast the heroes with warriors and soldiers from a range of other cultures.

Picking an enemy: social class on the battlefield

If battle is considered a social occasion, it is of prime importance whether warriors know their adversaries personally or deal with anonymous opponents, as modern soldiers do. In some cultures, it is customary to announce one's identity prior to combat, in order to ensure that one is matched with a worthy opponent, or to draw the attention of one's comrades to one's subsequent feats of prowess, or both. According to *The Tale of the Heike*, twelfth-century *samurai* habitually declared themselves in this manner.

> He rose in his stirrups and cried out in a thunderous voice:
> 'Men in the distance – hear me! Men near at hand – behold me! I am Matatarô Tadatsuna, aged 17, the son of Ashikaga no Tarô Toshitsuna, tenth-generation descendant of Tawara no Tôta Hidesato, the warrior who long ago won great fame and rewards for destroying the enemies of the emperor... Here I stand, ready to meet any among the men of...Yorimasa [the enemy commander]. Who dare fight me? Come forward and fight!'

Often such declarations are followed, not by a duel, but by a seemingly indiscriminate charge into enemy ranks, which suggests that, in spite of being framed as challenges, they serve equally to alert friends to the deeds one is about to do. The inclusion of boasts such as 'I am the first rider in the charge on Uji River' or 'We are the first in the assault on Ichi-no-Tani', less relevant to the enemy than to rivals on one's own side, tends to confirm this. At the same time, the need to select suitable adversaries is made quite explicit. 'Know that your fame depends on your opponent. A worthless opponent gives you no chance of increasing your fame.' Accordingly, men are reminded that 'the slaughter of many men of little fame will only add to your sins', and, conversely, that it would be shameful to be 'slain at the hand of a low, worthless retainer of some unknown warrior'. If the opponent is found to be of suitable status, he may be told, 'Your sword deserves a fight with mine.' Interestingly, if circumstances force two warriors of unequal status into a confrontation, he who enjoys superior status may decline to reveal his identity, and fight anonymously, as in the famous story of a young courtier, Atsumori, caught alive and asked by his captor to give his name.

> 'Declare yourself! Then I will spare your life!'
> 'You? Who are you?' replied the youth.
> 'I am a warrior of little importance. A native of Musashi province... Naozane, that is who I am.'
> 'I cannot declare myself to such as you. So take my head and show it to others. They will identify me.'
> 'Ah, you must be a great general, then', replied Naozane [and cut off Atsumori's head].

On the medieval Japanese battlefield, a social etiquette is thus in force, which dictates that one should seek to fight primarily men of one's own social status, just as one would associate mostly with one's peers in daily life, and that, faced with inferiors, one should deal with them without granting them the courtesy of an introduction, just as in daily life one would only introduce oneself to those whose status warrants some degree of respect.[82]

It has been asserted that Homeric heroes, too, when they fight 'important' enemies, declare their names and lineages as a matter of course, to make sure that their opponents are 'worthy' and 'prestigious'. 'When the genealogy of the adversaries is not mentioned in their speeches, it is because they know one another already.'[83]

In fact, with two exceptions, it is assumed throughout the *Iliad* that *all* the Greeks and Trojans know one another's names and lineages,

31

thus obviating the need for introductions.[84] The exceptions are Akhilleus, who does not know Asteropaios, who explains that he has only recently arrived at Troy with a fresh contingent of allies, and Diomedes, who does not know Glaukos, which is explained by the plot-requirement that they should only now recognize the hereditary ties of guest-friendship between them. The context shows that Akhilleus's and Diomedes's question 'Who are you?' is not part of a regular procedure of mutual identification. It is explicitly inspired by curiosity at the audacity of Asteropaios and Glaukos, who are the only men to put up any resistance when the two Greek heroes are sweeping all before them, rather than by a general need to know one's adversaries: 'Who are you...who *dare* come against me?' (XXI.150; cf. VI.123–6). Both times, the answer is 'Why do you ask about my lineage?' (VI.145; XXI.153). Evidently, the question is unexpected; by implication, introductions are *not* thought to be essential even between strangers who find themselves face-to-face in relative isolation from the mass. And indeed, when Sarpedon makes a stand against the onslaught of Patroklos, specifically in order to find out who is this warrior who wears Akhilleus's armour but is not Akhilleus himself (XVI.423–5), he does not stop to ask. At once, 'as two vultures...fight on a high rock, shrieking loudly, so they rushed at one another shouting' (428–30). They fight without exchanging a word.

Since warriors do not normally *say* who they are, they can only be identified by their equipment. Diomedes is recognized 'by his shield and his helmet...and [by] looking at his horses' (V.181–3), while one can tell Aias by his shield alone (XI.526–7). Even Akhilleus is recognizable only by his armour, so that another man wearing it is indistinguishable from him (XI.798–800; XVI.40–2, 278–82). Given the importance of armour as a means of identification, as well as an item of 'treasure' and an object of gift-exchange, one might expect it to receive detailed attention, as it certainly does in the Japanese tradition, where every warrior of any significance is introduced with a precise description of his accoutrements.[85] Not so in Homer. Only two sets of armour are described in detail – Agamemnon's (XI.17–42) and Akhilleus's new set, forged by Hephaistos (XVIII.478–613) – while an epithet used once refers to Deiphobos as having a white shield (XXII.394). Otherwise, we hear no more than that a few men have equipment of gold rather than bronze, that some helmets have double or quadruple rather than single plumed crests, and that some shields are larger than others, Aias's shield being broader and thicker than anyone else's. Horses are sometimes named but never described, other than to say that some are of divine stock.[86] This does not add up to much by which to identify a man, and it is therefore not surprising that the heroes are sometimes slow to recognize their opponents. Aineias, for one, fails initially to identify Diomedes (V.174–8); Agamemnon cannot tell Isos and Antiphos by their armour, though he knows their faces once he has killed and stripped them (XI.110–12). It is difficult, then, to tell the heroes apart in combat, and Homer's comparative lack of interest in identifying features of equipment suggests that to his mind it does not matter a great deal.

If heroic equipment has few identifying features, its real-life counterparts would have fewer still, since several of the most notable characteristics are clearly fantastic. In reality, no warrior wore golden armour, no shield could be as large and heavy as Aias's – and no horse would be immortal. This would leave all those in heavy armour looking pretty much the same, wearing near-identical bronze cuirasses and helmets, and carrying shields which differ but marginally in size and are only rarely adorned with distinctive decoration. It seems all the more unlikely, therefore, that warriors of Homer's own day would be as familiar with their enemies as the heroes are. Among the élite, there might well be some knowledge of the enemy, through ties of kinship and friendship across community boundaries. Some might have guest-friends in communities with which they find themselves at war, as Diomedes and Glaukos do, or sporting rivals whom they might meet on the battlefield as well as at funeral or festival games, as Nestor does (XI.750–2; XXIII.638–42). Some might even learn to recognize a few of the more prominent foe in the course of a campaign. But without regular battlefield introductions and with hardly any physical features to identify a warrior, even well-informed aristocrats could surely recognize only a small number of opponents. If the heroes do seem to know almost everyone they kill, this must be due to the narrative convention that the characters know everything the poet knows; it can hardly reflect contemporary practice.

Nevertheless, there is evidence of a certain selectiveness in the choice of adversary. At the start of the first battle, Paris challenges 'all the best men of the Greeks' to face him (III.19–20; cf. VII.50, 73–5), and during the last battle Akhilleus exclaims that, if he must die, he would prefer death at the hands of Hektor, 'who is the best man here' (XXI.279–80; cf. XXII.108–10). Being 'the best' (ἄριστος) is in Homer a matter of social status as much as of personal merit, and several passages imply that the heroes seek to fight primarily other *basileis*, fellow-leaders and members of the élite of princes.

> Whom did he kill first, whom last, Hektor son of Priam? ...First Asaios and Autonoos and Opites and Dolops...and Opheltios, as well as Agelaos, Aisymnos, Oros and Hipponoos... These *leaders* of the Greeks he killed, *and after them the multitude* (XI.299–305).

The poet pictures how in flight and pursuit 'footsoldiers killed footsoldiers and horsemen killed horsemen' (XI.150–1), while elsewhere it is assumed that in 'stationary' combat, too, chariot-fighters will fight one another (IV.306–7). Since chariots do not form a separate arm but fight in the midst of the infantry, the implication is that those who own horses – men of wealth and high status – tend to seek out one another. Unlike identification of an opponent by name, identification by status is thus feasible by 'looking at the horses'. The panoply, too, may allow identification by status. While it may not have sufficient distinguishing features to allow identification of individuals, its use as such, even if more widespread than that of chariots, is probably confined to those of some wealth.

The evidence, scanty as it is, suggests that, even in the physical proximity of the mêlée, Homeric aristocrats try to keep their normal social distance from commoners. This may be hard to achieve in practice, but as a norm such differentiation by status is known not only from European and Japanese feudal society, in which retainers are not supposed to attack noble lords, but also from the scarcely stratified society of the Mae Enga of New Guinea, where the rule is that 'ideally, when in action, fight leaders should fire at their counterparts, and ordinary warriors should not strive to injure them.' Ambitious 'rubbish men', as those of low standing are known, are deterred from taking 'advantage of the confusion to dog and shoot an opposing fight leader or Big Man' by the knowledge that the victim's clansmen will make every effort to slay and mutilate them.[87] The *Iliad* mentions no such prohibition or deterrent, but it is probably significant that a commoner simply never kills a prince. In sum, the identity of a man's opponent matters only insofar as he should ideally be of one's own social class. Homer does not elaborate on such class-distinctions, but he may be taking their importance for granted.

Performing prowess: three styles of combat

The etiquette of combat itself is as telling as that of mutual identification. As suggested, a fight involves not merely an attempt to defeat an opponent, but an attempt to project a certain image of oneself. Bravery must always be part of that image, but the degree of bravery expected, and the proper manner of displaying it in action, are culture-bound.

The ideals of medieval Japanese culture, for instance, encourage the *samurai* or warrior-monk to demonstrate his courage by seeking out impossible odds. He charges into the opposing ranks and kills many; whether he emerges victorious or dies a hero, he sustains a severe battering. Thus, the monk Jômyô distinguishes himself as follows:

> He loosed twenty-three arrows in the twinkling of an eye. He killed twelve of his enemies and wounded eleven more. Then...he sprang barefoot onto the beam of the bridge. No other man dared walk there... With his long sickle-bladed halberd he mowed down five of his opponents, but when he encountered the sixth, the shaft of his halberd snapped in two. He threw the weapon away and drew his sword. Enclosed on all sides, he wielded the sword like a spider's legs, like twisted candy, then in the form of a cross, and finally like a somersault and a waterwheel. In an instant he had cut down eight men.
>
> [Eventually,] Jômyô managed to crawl back to the Byôdô-in temple... Then, stripping off his armour, he counted the dents that the weapons of the Heike had made. There were sixty-three in all, but his armour had been pierced through in *only* five places.

In death-defying courage, Jômyô is matched by Yoshinaka, who rallies the 300 survivors of a defeated army of 800, and on being told that the nearest enemy force has 6,000 men, cries 'Just right!' and charges again and again until his forces are reduced to fifty, to four, and finally to a single retainer.[88]

Such near-suicidal bravery, displayed by seeking confrontations against the odds, contrasts with the chivalric bravery of medieval Europe, displayed ideally in a 'fair and equal' fight. A notorious early example is the decision of Earl Byrhtnoth of Essex, 'in his pride', to stop defending a causeway across the river at Maldon so that an army of Danish raiders might cross it freely and fight the Earl's forces on equal terms.[89] The story of *Sir Gawain and the Green Knight* represents this ideology pushed to fantastic extremes: Gawain is allowed to deal the Green Knight a single blow and must then present himself after a year and a day to receive a single blow in return. The legend highlights the extent to which a knight must give his opponent a chance to fight back: when the Green Knight, decapitated with one blow, simply picks up his head and departs, Gawain knows that he will be decapitated in turn, but nevertheless in all 'fairness' presents himself on the appointed day. Great stress is laid on the importance of accepting the challenge without any sign of fear.

> Gawain glanced up at the grim axe beside him as it came shooting through the shivering air to shatter him, and his shoulders shrank slightly from the sharp edge.

35

The other suddenly stayed the descending axe, and then reproved the prince with many proud words: 'You are not Gawain,' said the gallant, 'whose greatness is such that by hill or hollow no army ever frightened him; for now you flinch for fear before you feel harm. I never did know that knight to be a coward.' ... Said Gawain, 'Not again shall I flinch as I did before; but if my head pitch to the plain, it's off for evermore.'

After this, the Green Knight's attempts to frighten Gawain find him 'unswerving, with not a wavering limb'.[90]

The bravery displayed by Homeric warriors is often assimilated by scholars to either the chivalrous model of rule-bound single combat, or the *samurai*-style killing spree of the warrior gone berserk, or a combination of both, as in Marcel Detienne's portrait of the hero in action, with which this paper began.[91] One must be wary, however, of uncritical application of familiar models, and one fundamental difference to be noted at the outset is that Homeric standards of bravery are *lower* than those of the knight, not to mention those of the *samurai*. We have already observed that Homer's heroes are comparatively free to express and yield to fear, and we shall see that, since the Homeric warrior is under less pressure to display courage, he does not normally adopt either of the feudal styles of combat, European or Japanese, though sometimes he comes close.

(i) Hit-and-run attack: destruction without display

A minority of battlefield confrontations could be described as 'duels', and an even smaller number as 'sustained assaults', but most combat action in the *Iliad* takes the form of one-sided and very brief attacks. One man kills another with a single shot or blow; the victim generally appears to have been taken unawares.[92] The pattern may be illustrated by the very first sequence of fighting in the *Iliad*.

First Antilokhos killed a Trojan man...Ekhepolos; he hit him...in the forehead... When he fell, Elephenor took hold of his feet...and pulled him away from the flying missiles with the intention of plundering his armour as soon as possible. [But when] Agenor saw him dragging the corpse, he struck him with a spear in the flank exposed beside his shield as he bent down.

A hard fight developed over his body... They jumped at one another like wolves, and man overthrew man. There Aias hit...Simoeisios... As he was coming forward, Aias hit him in the chest... Antiphos cast his sharp spear through the crowd at Aias; he missed him but hit Leukos, Odysseus's fine comrade, in the groin as he was dragging the body to the other side...

Odysseus was very angry at his death and made his way through the foremost fighters, took his stand very close by, looking all around him, and cast his spear. The Trojans fell back before the man as he took aim...but he hit Demokoon, bastard son of Priam (IV.457–99).

The deeds described are evidently no more than selected highlights from the action; unnamed 'foremost fighters' and an anonymous 'crowd' surround the protagonists; missiles are flying. The crowd, which is dense enough for a spear which misses its target to hit another, may afford a degree of anonymity to attacker and victim. Antiphos attacks Aias from within the crowd, rather than openly presenting himself and giving his intended victim a chance to fight back. Odysseus casts his spear into a group of men to hit an apparently random target. Elephenor, his attentions otherwise engaged, never even sees his killer. The overall impression is one of quick, opportunistic attacks.

In the form of assaults on opponents who are defenceless, at a disadvantage, or simply unaware of danger, opportunism characterizes the action throughout. In each of the many episodes of flight and pursuit, men are continually hit or stabbed in the back without the least attempt to make them stand their ground and fight. In long-range combat, every advantage is taken of the element of surprise as archers jump out from cover to shoot at unsuspecting victims. Even in medium-range and hand-to-hand combat, where the element of surprise is necessarily limited, no opportunity is missed. Men who, like Elephenor, try to take possession of a corpse are not challenged but attacked from all sides and killed without warning as soon as they take their eyes off the enemy. A man may be hit while still in the process of dismounting from his chariot. Other men engage in a struggle with one opponent only to fall victim to a second opponent who creeps up on them unnoticed. A few are simply slaughtered while in a helpless state of shock.[93] Scholars have sometimes regarded such actions as 'striking violations' of a supposed Homeric code of chivalry governed by 'an implicit notion of fairness', allowing 'no ambush, no stratagem, no diversionary or dilatory tactic'. There is not a hint of disapproval in Homer's narration of these deeds, however, and a couple of them are in fact committed by the most 'gentle' of his heroes, Patroklos and Menelaos. The admiration expressed for the brave man who does not lose his nerve in an *ambush* confirms that the poet finds nothing wrong in creating and exploiting opportunities to eliminate enemies in an unchivalrous but efficient manner.[94]

Equally unchivalrous, but efficient in terms of self-preservation, is the frequency with which the heroes back out of man-to-man confrontations even when these are offered. Their habit of shunning younger and stronger opponents has already been commented upon, and the extent to which verbal challenges to combat fail to provoke a response will be discussed shortly. Add to this the tendency of warriors to duck spears flying at them, most of which end up hitting someone else. One might have thought that such a failed assault would constitute an implicit challenge, but none of the heroes who have a narrow escape of this kind apparently feels any need to respond.[95] Nor do those who have tried and failed to kill an enemy often try again, or give him a chance to fight back: men who have struck an unsuccessful blow tend to give up immediately and run back to safety.[96]

The brevity of fights is as remarkable as their lack of chivalry. From a total of 170 battlefield encounters described and a further 130 referred to, only 18 involve more than one blow, and a mere 6 of these involve more than a single exchange of blows. The only fight to go beyond a second exchange of blows is not part of a battle, but a specially arranged formal duel.[97] It has generally been assumed that fights are so short because in Homer almost every shot, cast or blow that hits its target is lethal. No one has failed to note that such an extremely high rate of instant fatalities is unrealistic; in life as opposed to literature, the wounded would outnumber the dead, and a slow death would be more common than a quick end. 'Perhaps the tradition developed in this way to avoid tedium, though one would think that much longer description could be enjoyed' is one scholar's explanation; 'the Homeric poems are interested in death far more than they are in fighting' is another.[98] However, while it is true that the fatality rate is fantastically high, this is *not* the cause of the brevity of the fights. As has just been pointed out, even in the few cases when the first blow does not at once despatch the enemy, the attacker often retreats at once, rather than trying again. In other words, individual assaults are always short, whether or not they are immediately fatal. I would suggest that encounters are brief simply because hit-and-run tactics are the Homeric norm. Such tactics fit well with an opportunistic attitude to combat, and seem plausible enough. It is only their extraordinary deadliness which is unrealistic.

Instant death when hit is a narrative device obviously akin to the modern cinematic convention that a single punch or shot eliminates the extras from fist- and gunfights, while it takes much more to dispose of the chief villains, let alone of our heroes. Neither in film nor in epic is the function of this device merely to 'avoid tedium', or to focus attention on the experience of death. Rather, it serves to bring home to us the prowess of the protagonists and their vast superiority to the multitude.

In the *Iliad*, as in some films, that message is reinforced by occasional close-ups of the devastating damage done by the heroes' weapons. A favourite is the jab in the belly which makes a man's entrails spill out ('all his guts gushed on the ground'), several times bursting right through the metal cuirass. Also popular are the stone which splits in two a skull inside a helmet, and the spear in the head which not only makes blood spurt everywhere and brains slither out, but even causes eyeballs to pop out of their sockets and fall to the ground. Blows land with such force that victims fall off walls and chariots 'like divers', one of them landing head first in deep sand and standing rigid, upside-down, until knocked over by his own horses. The penetrative power of some men's weapons is astounding. Akhilleus's spear once passes straight through a man's corslet and body to exit on the other side, and on another occasion goes in one ear and out the other. A single blow from his sword sends a head flying through the air, marrow spurting from the vertebrae. Aias goes one better and decapitates a man with a *spear*.[99] Most of this is physically impossible. The gory detail is not inspired by acute observation of the horrors of war. It is there to illustrate the superior force of the ideal warrior.[100]

Such, then, is the dominant image of the warrior in the *Iliad*. He is a man who does not court danger, but attacks without taking more chances than strictly necessary, seeking favourable odds whenever possible. The fact that he is prepared to enter the fight at all is sufficient proof of his bravery. In combat itself, he aims to kill efficiently. If there is an element of display, it is in the narrative rather than in the action, and it is a demonstration of destructive physical strength, rather than of courage or fighting skill.[101] The image, in short, is much like that of the twentieth-century soldier, who aims 'to get the job done' while exposing himself only to the minimum necessary danger – and we shall see that the Homeric warrior tends to agree with the modern soldier in regarding those who exceed this brief as 'mentally unbalanced'.[102]

(ii) Face-to-face fight: chivalry?
About one in six battlefield confrontations in the *Iliad* conforms to a minimal definition of a duel, insofar as it involves adversaries who mutually agree to fight. The agreement is mostly tacit, and evident only from the fact that a warrior stands his ground as an enemy

approaches, or that both warriors deliberately move towards one another. Rather less often, words are exchanged before the fight.[103] Without the element of surprise, these 'duels' tend to take slightly longer than hit-and-run assaults, but brevity remains their hallmark and the very first blow still settles nearly half of them.[104]

Does this type of combat reflect a chivalrous mode of conduct? Those who believe that it does, point to the self-restraint practised by Aias and Hektor in the formal duel which they fight at dusk one day, after the battle has ended. The combatants begin with an informal agreement that the body of whoever loses is not to be mutilated. In the end, they decide that it is not even necessary to fight to the death: they call it a draw and exchange gifts (VII.55–305). Moreover, in his precombat speech Hektor boasts of his *skill* as well as his valour (237–41), while both men insist on fair play. Aias invites his opponent to make the first move ('Begin combat and battle!' 232), thereby giving away an advantage important enough to be awarded by lot on an earlier occasion, when a trial by combat is fought.[105] Hektor accepts the offer but warns Aias to be on guard: 'I do not want to hit a great man like you by stealth, looking for my chance, but openly, if I can' (VII.242–3). Martin Mueller has been particularly eloquent in arguing that 'the ethos of fighting is perfectly embodied' in these last words, and that Homer 'presents a spectacle of war at once brutal and innocent.'[106]

As a matter of fact, however, in none of the other face-to-face confrontations in the *Iliad* do adversaries reach the kind of agreement, or express the kind of sentiment, found in this passage. The heroes' actions in combat show no sign of any form of chivalrous self-restraint, least of all a concern to offer an opponent equal odds. In the climactic fight of the *Iliad*, Hektor wants odds of two against one in his favour before he is prepared to face Akhilleus (XXII.226–53).

Scrutiny of the poem's fourteen pre-combat dialogues and monologues equally fails to bring to light further expressions of chivalry.[107] Except for two conversations which are implausibly long, exchanges of words are brief and their contents not necessarily unrealistic. No speech is longer than fourteen lines and the shortest one consists of a single verse: 'Come closer, so that you may meet your end sooner' (XX.429; cf. VI.143). This one line contains two of the chief components of these speeches: a challenge and a threat. Threats are the single most common feature. The warrior who speaks first invariably tries to intimidate his opponent with a straightforward 'You will meet your death here' (XXI.588), a sarcastic 'Fall back and join the crowd...before something nasty happens to you' (XX.196–8; cf.

XVII.30–2), or a heroically oblique 'Children of unfortunate parents are those who stand against my force' (VI.127 = XXI.151). When the enemy replies – the challenger does not always wait for a response – he either issues a counter-threat, or asserts that he will not be intimidated 'like a silly boy', and could easily reciprocate, 'for I myself, too, am expert at uttering biting and violent words' (XX.200–2, 431–3).[108]

Boasts reinforce threats. A couple of times, a warrior brags of his past victories over the opponent or his family, and declares that this time, too, he will win (XVII.20–30; XX.187–96). Another couple of times, a warrior boasts of the collective prowess of the Trojans or Greeks, no doubt to demoralize his enemy (XIII.810–11; XXI.585–8). Rather more often, a man boasts of his ancestors. The purpose of this becomes evident during Akhilleus's encounters with Aineias and Asteropaios.[109] Aineias is reluctantly persuaded by Apollo to face Akhilleus, on the grounds that, as grandson of the old sea god Nereus via his mother Thetis, Akhilleus is descended 'from a lesser god' than Aineias, whose maternal grandfather is Zeus himself (XX.105–7). When Akhilleus challenges Aineias, he declares that at a previous encounter 'Zeus and the other gods' had saved Aineias's life, but will not do so now (194–5). Aineias counters by reminding Akhilleus of their respective parentage, implicitly advancing his claim to superior descent. He then traces at length his descent from Zeus through seven generations in the paternal line as well (203–41) and adds that it is Zeus who grants or denies success (242–3). In the sequel, the gods do in fact save Aineias's life again, and Akhilleus is left to exclaim: 'So Aineias, too, is indeed dear to the gods – and I thought his boasts were vain and empty' (347–8). Clearly, the point of reciting genealogy here is to impress upon the enemy one's chances of divine support and victory. It is the same when Asteropaios declares that he is a grandson of the River Axios, a statement described by the poet as 'threatening' (XXI.157–61). Akhilleus kills him and retorts that the support of a river god can never be as powerful as the support of Zeus, and he, Akhilleus, is after all a great-grandson of Zeus via his father Peleus (184–99). Two of the remaining three genealogies recited at the enemy are also traced back to Zeus, and they too seem intended primarily to frighten the enemy and make him despair of his chances of winning.[110]

Challenges and insults are relatively uncommon. We find: 'Come closer!' (VI.143; XX.429), 'Come here!' (XIII.809), 'Stand and face me!' (XIII.448), and 'Let us fight!' (XXI.160), as well as 'Bragging ox!' (βουγάιε, XIII.824), 'Silly child!' (νηπύτιε, XXI.585), and 'Why does a

41

raw recruit like you have to come here to skulk?' (V.633–4). Challenges are regularly merely rhetorical, in that they are addressed to men who already stand prepared to fight the challenger, and serve to reinforce the confident and dominant image projected by boasts and threats. The rarity of insults, coupled with the occasional use of complimentary epithets in addressing the enemy, confirms that the main purpose of pre-combat speeches is intimidation, not humiliation or provocation.[111]

Speaking loudly and talking too much may of course serve also to relieve and mask one's own anxiety. It has been attractively suggested that the excessive length of the speeches of Glaukos and Aineias is meant to indicate to the audience their nervousness at facing superior enemies.[112] Accordingly, if Akhilleus tends to be laconic – Asteropaios gets a two-line threat (XXI. 150–1), Hektor initially only one line (XX.429), and Agenor nothing at all (XXI.581–96) – this may be a deliberate indication of his anger and lack of fear.

Verbal exchanges prior to combat are thus largely aimed at gaining a psychological advantage over the enemy by persuading him of one's superiority, and in this respect they are merely elaborate and more articulate versions of the wordless threatening behaviour commonly displayed by the heroes, who raise and shake their spears, walk with long strides, and 'scream piercingly'.[113] The element of display intended to intimidate the enemy is plain, but it is hard to follow Detienne and others in seeing here a substantial degree of ritualization and 'primitive' histrionics. The Homeric warrior behaves fundamentally like, say, the modern American soldier who 'kept yelling: "Come on out and fight, you bastards, you bastards, you" ', or the one who, while throwing a grenade, 'screamed at the top of his voice, just to release his pent-up nerves', and who had Japanese troops shout back at them, in English, 'You damn fools!', 'You going to die!', 'You surrender!'[114] The main difference, apart from the literary embellishment of such threats in Homer, is that in modern combat threats are addressed to the enemy at large, distant and invisible as he normally is, whereas the much more open and close-range confrontations of the Homeric battlefield invite man-to-man exchanges.

Only rarely do the heroes trade anything other than threats before combat. Three times, a man lets his opponent know that he means to avenge upon him the death of a brother (XI.431–3; XVII.34–40) or friend (XXII.271–2), thereby investing their fight with special significance. Three times, a man tries to negotiate terms with his opponent. Only one of them is successful: Diomedes persuades Glaukos not to fight him since there are hereditary ties of friendship between their families (VI.212–36). On the other hand, Euphorbos's 'arrogant' demand to be allowed to strip his victim of armour, without interference from the dead man's comrades (XVII.12–16, 19), and Hektor's suggestion to Akhilleus that he who wins should strip but not mutilate the loser's body (XXII.254–9), meet with exasperation and black looks (XVII.18; XXII.260) and are utterly rejected. Finally, three of the challenges issued in the course of pitched battle are not merely rhetorically addressed to an opponent with whom one is already face to face, but genuine challenges aimed at provoking an enemy to come forward for a contest of prowess. Striding forward, Paris challenges 'all the best men' (III.19–20) and Aias challenges Hektor (XIII.809–10), while Idomeneus, 'shouting loudly', invites Deiphobos to come and face him (XIII.445–8). Only Paris's challenge is taken up – by Menelaos, who sees an opportunity for revenge, rather than a chance to display his prowess – but Paris himself loses heart and retreats (III.21–32). Neither Hektor nor Deiphobos responds to the challenge, though later in the course of battle Deiphobos, 'nursing resentment', without warning casts a spear at Idomeneus (XIII.516–17), and Hektor, too, takes a shot at Aias (XIV.402).

This is the full extent to which Homeric warriors try to reach some verbal agreement with their opponents about the conditions on which they are to do battle. The paucity of such attempts, and their almost complete failure, leaves no doubt that this kind of ritualization at any rate plays only the most marginal of roles in Homeric warfare.[115]

It is not difficult to account for the gap between, on the one hand, the attitudes displayed by Hektor and Aias in single combat, and, on the other hand, the attitudes displayed by these two, along with everyone else, in pitched battle. Firstly, the formal duel is fought before a wider audience. In battle, one fights amidst a crowd of 'foremost fighters', and one's actions are accordingly less conspicuous than they are when performed in isolation before two assembled armies. Secondly, and more importantly, whereas battle has an ulterior goal in the capture of the enemy's city, in the formal duel the main thing at stake is a reputation as a good fighter. The duel therefore demands an element of show, a display of courage and skill, and need not be fought to the death, provided the combatants are satisfied that they have acquitted themselves well.[116] Enemies meeting in the mêlée, by contrast, not only stand to gain less from showing off and taking unnecessary risks, but must make it their first priority to eliminate their opponents by any means.

While less conspicuous than formal single combat, 'duels' in battle, particularly when preceded by a shouted challenge or an exchange of words, are bound to be rather more visible to friend and foe than hit-and-run attacks, and they inherently involve greater risk and thus greater courage. Face-to-face combat, therefore, involves some show of bravery. But the element of display is slight: there is no suggestion that 'duellists' deliberately draw attention to themselves. Homeric challenges and boasts, unlike those of the *samurai*, are not designed to show off to one's comrades, but are wholly addressed to the enemy and almost exclusively devoted to frightening him. Nor is there any suggestion of a conscious display of skill or bravery. Apparently, a show of *strength* continues to be the first priority, and hence these 'duels' are not governed by a code of chivalry, but follow the pattern of hit-and-run attacks insofar as they rely on unrestricted use of force to kill the enemy – compensating for the element of surprise lost with opportunities for intimidation gained.

(iii) Sustained combat: madness?

Some heroes fight harder than others. One man may attempt a single hit-and-run attack or engage in a single duel and then withdraw from combat for a while, while another may take on a string of opponents without a break. In *Iliad XIII*, for example, we find Meriones and Idomeneus re-entering battle – one having recovered from earlier exertions (83–93), the other having looked after a wounded comrade (210–15) – and attacking four Trojans each. But whereas Meriones runs back and forth, launching four separate, brief assaults,[117] Idomeneus kills his opponents one after the other, without leaving the killing zone. Initially he appears set to emulate Meriones's methods as he kills a man and immediately drags off the body towards the ships (370–84). While he is doing so, however, he is attacked by two Trojans in quick succession; he kills the first (384–93) and ducks the spear of the second (402–10). At this point, the audience might have expected Idomeneus to complete his retreat to safety and stay out of battle for some time, but the poet explicitly counters this:

> Idomeneus did not call a halt to his great spirit [μένος/*menos*], but his desire was always either [to kill] some Trojan or to fall himself defending the Greeks from disaster (424–6).

He proceeds to kill a dazed and defenceless Trojan (427–44) and to challenge Deiphobos (445–56). When Deiphobos responds by getting Aineias to help him, one might again have expected Idomeneus to retreat, as Aineias himself had done in a similar two-against-one situation (V.571–2), but the poet emphatically comments that

> fear did not seize Idomeneus…but he stood his ground, like a wild boar in the mountains, confident of his strength… Thus did the famous warrior Idomeneus stand his ground, and he did not retreat (470–6).

Instead, he calls for help, ducks Aineias's spear (502–5), kills another Trojan, retrieves his own spear, then finally retreats step-by-step, forced by a barrage of missiles (506–18).

Such uncommon persistence is otherwise found only in the most intense fights over a corpse, in the most desperate defensive stands, and in the fiercest of assaults. We may recall that, although most of the time men fight 'intermittently [μεταπαυόμενοι], avoiding one another's pain-inflicting missiles, standing far apart' (XVII.370–5), in the struggle to gain possession of Patroklos's corpse 'they relentlessly [νωλεμές] dashed forward with their spears all the time [αἰεί]' while 'the sweat of exertion constantly, relentlessly [νωλεμὲς αἰεί] ran down their faces and bodies' (XVII.412–13, 385–7). The narrative is less explicit about other corpse-fights, but these presumably involve a higher degree of persistence, too.

The desire to protect fleeing comrades sometimes leads men to expose themselves to danger for longer than usual. Thus Odysseus calls upon Diomedes to join him and his followers[118] in putting up some resistance so that the rest of the Greeks may 'breathe more freely and flee more easily' (XI.310–27). At first, they keep interrupting their attacks to despoil their victims (333–4, 368, 373–5), but when Diomedes withdraws wounded, Odysseus, having made his famous decision to carry on fighting (404–10), fights without pause. He kills six men in quick succession before he calls for help (420–63) and himself retires hurt. For the rest of that day of battle, it is Aias who leads the Greek defence, but not even he fights without interruption. First he reluctantly retreats before the Trojans (XI.544–95), 'occasionally' (566) turning round to fight. Later, when the Greek fortifications have fallen, he forms the rallying point for resistance, but despite his divinely inspired 'powerful spirit' (*menos*), which lifts his battle-weariness and makes him keen to fight (XIII.59–82), he still retires from combat to plunder a corpse (197–202) and to take regular breathers, handing over his enormous shield to his followers 'whenever tiredness and sweat came upon him at the knees' (710–11). It is not until the Trojans are about to burn the Greek ships that Aias finally fights without pause (XV.674–88, 727–46):

The bright helmet around his temples produced a fearsome clanging sound as it was hit, and its solid plates were hit constantly. His left shoulder was tiring from holding the shining shield continually without a break [ἔμπεδον αἰέν]... He was always gasping for air, and much sweat was pouring down his limbs all over, and he had no chance to catch his breath (XVI.104–11).[119]

As well as prolonged defensive action, we encounter several sustained charges into enemy ranks, some of them specifically aimed at the point where these are densest (XI.148–9; XV.615–16; XVI.285). Although such assaults are superficially reminiscent of the near-suicidal charges of the *samurai*, there are major differences. The Homeric charge – conventionally known as the *aristeia* ('outstanding performance') of the hero involved – is never a solo attack. Although Akhilleus, for example, is the only Greek warrior to feature in the narrative of the final battle of the *Iliad*, the rest of the Greeks fight anonymously alongside him, as he himself reveals when he appeals to his comrades: 'Do not stand at a distance from the Trojans any longer, you Greeks. Come! Man must face man, intent on combat. It is hard for me, strong as I am, to tackle so many men and fight them all' (XX.354–7).[120] A second difference is that an *aristeia* is rarely aimed at a body of men prepared to fight back, but targets a group of men in panic and confusion. Diomedes, Agamemnon, Patroklos and Akhilleus in turn pursue fleeing Trojans, slaughtering large numbers without meeting much resistance. Unlike the badly bruised *samurai*, they emerge with hardly a scratch. As soon as the enemy rallies, the hero normally kills only one or two more men, and may himself fall victim to a counterattack.[121] Moreover, despite the emphasis on the relentlessness of their charge, none of these heroes is above occasionally interrupting pursuit to indulge in the common Homeric habit of plundering one's victims.[122]

Only Hektor appears prepared to mount a prolonged attack against troops actively defending themselves, when he attempts to break the Greeks' defence of their ships. Backed by the Trojans, 'he tried wherever he saw the largest crowd and the best equipment' (XV.615–16), trying so hard that 'he began to foam at the mouth, his eyes blazed under his grim brow, and as he fought his helmet shook fearsomely around his temples' (607–9; cf. XIII.802–7). When he finally reaches a ship, he refuses to retreat from it (704–6, 716–26).

There is a remarkable discrepancy in attitudes towards sustained fighting according to whether it is defensive or offensive. The sturdy defence put up by Idomeneus, Odysseus and Aias is clearly regarded as admirable, but there is ambivalence towards the aggressiveness of the others. Their prowess inspires awe, and they themselves, unlike those who fight defensively, fully expect that their onslaught will bring them fame and glory.[123] Yet it is felt that these men are liable to go too far in their aggression. Both Diomedes and Patroklos ignore the specific instructions issued to them, and both need to be reminded of their limitations by Apollo, who tells them to 'Think and retreat!' A Trojan, watching Diomedes in action, acknowledges that he is currently even more lethal than Akhilleus, but simultaneously criticizes him for being 'a savage warrior' (ἄγριος, VI.97 = 278), commenting that 'he is too crazed' (λίην μαίνεται, VI.100–1). Akhilleus, too, is 'filled with a savage spirit' (XXII.312–13), and said to be possessed by 'rabid rage' (λύσσα/ *lyssa*, XXI.542–3), while the Greeks speak of Hektor with disapproval as 'that savage man', 'that rabid dog', 'who stinks of *lyssa*...who [falsely] claims to be a son of Zeus' (VIII.96, 299; XIII.53–4). Odysseus goes so far as to say that Hektor 'has gone utterly crazy [μαίνεται ἐκπάγλως], and, relying on Zeus, has no respect at all for men or gods' (IX.238–9).[124] His enemies are right to believe that Hektor in his fury rates himself too highly, as is almost comically obvious when he grandly announces that he will jump the Greek trench in his chariot and that their walls cannot stop him, but in the event is reduced to wheeling his chariot back and forth behind the trench, impotently glaring at the Greeks 'with the eyes of a Gorgon or of murderous Ares' (VIII.178–9, 348–9). He later makes fatal mistakes, as he will ultimately come to realize, in wilfully ignoring sound advice, as well as an omen, driven by an unjustified trust in his own strength.[125]

The term 'berserk' might describe a warrior in the grip of such 'madness' or *lyssa*, provided one is thinking of the state of mind of the modern soldier going berserk, rather than of the howling and shield-biting antics of the original Norse berserkers, let alone of the hideous transformations of Cú Chulainn in his warp spasm. Physical symptoms are minimal in Homer: apart from flashing eyes, they are limited to Akhilleus grinding his teeth in anger (XIX.365–7) and Hektor foaming at the mouth – which, despite the suggestive association with rabies, need be nothing more sinister than the result of extreme physical exertion. When one scholar asserts that a raging hero also 'becomes hot, fiery...and shakes all over', he is already going well beyond the evidence.[126] The emotional and behavioural symptoms are reminiscent of those reported by American soldiers who went berserk in Vietnam.

I just went crazy. I pulled [a dead Vietcong soldier] out into the paddy and carved him up with my knife... Even then I wasn't satisfied. I was fighting with the [medical] corpsmen trying to take care of me. I was trying to get at him for more... I just couldn't get enough. I built up such hate, I couldn't do enough damage.

Along with an uncontrollable hatred, these soldiers developed a sense of invulnerability.

– I felt like a god, this power flowing through me. Anybody could have picked me off there – but I was untouchable.
– I started standing up on ambushes... Instead of letting them have it from the brush, I'd stand up and let [them] see me and then let them have it. I'd use my knife... They couldn't kill me. No matter what they'd do.
– Got rid of my helmet, got rid of my flakjacket. I just wanted to kill.

Finally, they lost their ability to discriminate and might not only turn on civilians as well as combatants, but also put their comrades at risk ('You know, I was endangering five other people. But I wasn't worried about that'), and even attack them. Nevertheless, other soldiers apparently felt a certain admiration for the strength and bravery of a soldier gone berserk and sometimes volunteered to go on patrols with them.[127]

Since in the modern army running amok in this way is abnormal behaviour, triggered by traumatic events, whereas among Homeric heroes it is evidently a more regular phenomenon, a closer parallel in some ways is the fighting style of the 'nutter', who is a fixture of fighting in the streets and on the terraces, and plays an almost institutional role. Amongst football hooligans, beyond the mere bravery of the 'aggro leader',

total fearlessness, the issuing of challenges against impossible odds is the prerogative of the *nutter*. And fans are in no doubt as to where bravery ends and sheer lunacy begins. There are usually about five or six nutters in [a gang] at any one time... Typical of their behaviour would be 'going mad', 'going wild', or 'going crazy'. Attempting to beat someone to a pulp would be described in these terms... To call someone a nutter, however, is not to use what they would see as a term of abuse. It is simply a comment on their style of doing things.

The nutter, like the berserker, is regarded with some ambivalence: although useful in a fight, too often he puts himself and his friends at risk. He is 'constantly being caught by the police because part of being 'nutty' is the absence of any real form of self-preservation.'[128]

These comparisons show that there is nothing particularly 'primitive' or 'ritualized' about Homeric battle-madness. On the contrary, they show that by modern standards, not to mention Norse or Celtic standards, the hero, even at his wildest, is a sane and unadventurous sort of berserker. He certainly has no difficulty distinguishing friend and foe. He takes risks, but these are limited by the fact that he tends to swoop down on panicking troops whose capacity for self-defence is seriously undermined. He feels superior, even invincible, and may, counter to normal Homeric practice, fight on even after being wounded, but he does remain aware of his vulnerability: during their *aristeiai*, Diomedes, Agamemnon and Akhilleus all experience a *frisson* of fear.[129] Characteristically, whereas 'berserking American soldiers invariably shed their helmets and flak jackets', Akhilleus, however furious, is happy to obey his mother when she tells him not to fight until she brings him a new set of armour to replace the one captured by Hektor. When he is urged to join the fight, he replies: 'How could I enter the fray? *They* have my armour.'[130]

'Rabid rage', *lyssa*, is neither an altered state of consciousness nor an ingrained trait of character, but merely the normal warrior 'spirit', *menos*, temporarily intensified and hardened. Akhilleus's *lyssa* is otherwise described as an 'iron spirit', and Diomedes is urged on simply by 'a spirit three times greater' than normal.[131] Bearing in mind that Homeric norms make relatively modest demands on the spirit of a warrior, we can understand why even a spirit thrice as fierce still seems comparatively restrained; 'mad' heroes are only mad because they are measured against low expectations of courage and stamina.

In sum, sustained combat is rare, which is perhaps not surprising given the burden of bronze armour weighing down the fighters. The poet's few descriptions of non-stop action certainly reveal an acute awareness of the physical effort required, particularly the strain of holding up a shield for any length of time.[132] Those few who do engage in it obviously demonstrate greater courage than those who confine themselves to brief assaults or duels; a sustained defensive effort against an advancing enemy requires great courage indeed. However, no hero matches Homer's mosquito, memorably praised as a model of 'daring' since it *persists* in its attempts to bite, however often one may try to brush it off (XVII.570–3). Sustained assaults on a panicking enemy are by comparison low-risk and opportunistic ventures, and tend once again to highlight the destructive force of the warrior and his terrifying impact on the enemy, rather than his bravery. The fact that it is primarily the assault, not the defence, which earns fame and glory, confirms that, as suggested by the tactics of hit-and-run and face-to-face fights, strength outranks courage on the Homeric scale of values. Yet admiration for prowess is tempered by disapproval of going to physical and emotional extremes. A man should fight 'insofar as he has the power; he cannot fight beyond his power, even if he wanted to' (XIII.786–7; cf. VIII.294).[133] A man seeking glory so fanatically that he transcends his limitations and discards the normal etiquette of combat may be awe-inspiring, but is also mad.

Victory display: mutilating, vaunting and taking spoils

Relief at having survived combat and pride at having defeated the enemy are bound to inspire some form of victory celebration. The fact that in modern warfare there are few identifiable personal victories, and that any celebrations must wait until after battle, does not stop soldiers from indulging in private shows of triumph. The Falklands War again offers some good examples. By and large acceptable even to civilian sensibilities is Ken Lukowiak's handling of five captured Argentinian conscripts and one officer detailed to him.

> I was loving this. I marched them out of the shed and towards the shop. On the way we passed a row of their dead comrades. I asked the officer if he was having a nice day. He said he wasn't. Along the way I composed a song. It sums up very well how I felt walking around with six men on the end of my machine gun: 'I've got myself six pris-o-ners/ and all of them are mine./ You see I have a ma-chine-gun/ it's that that makes them mine./ I love to walk around with them/ so everyone can see/ that Kenny's got six prisoners/ and they're not getting free.' ... I ensured that I had my photograph taken with a prisoner. Whenever I show it to anyone I always say, 'That's me with one of my prisoners.' They're nearly always impressed.

The taking of trophy photographs appears to have been a prominent form of triumphal behaviour, ranging from inoffensive pictures of smiling British soldiers with the flag ('There's always a clump of rocks. There's always a group of men...holding guns. There's nearly always a Union Jack... There are never any dead men'), to shocking images of dead and severely mutilated Argentinians, taken privately by soldiers or taken officially by the battalion photographer and sold to the men. Some were kept in photo-albums; some were displayed on the wall of the corporals' mess at the military base in Aldershot. Victory inspired some very black humour: a picture of a headless Argentinian corpse lying shoulder to shoulder with a body without legs was captioned 'Heads I win, Tails you lose', and there were 'many soldiers lying next to the corpses while their friends took happy snaps of them.'

> One soldier picked up a dead Argentine, supported the corpse's weight underneath his arm, put a cigarette in the dead man's mouth, then one

in his own. He then held a lighter under the corpse's cigarette and his friend took a photograph. They both laughed. I also laughed. This was foolish – smoking can kill.

Even though Lukowiak is well aware of the disgust civilians might feel at such behaviour, and is inclined to distance himself from the worst excesses, he refuses to condemn any of his comrades' little triumphal displays: 'we were putting our lives on the line and by our reckoning that gave us a right to say and think as we pleased.'[134]

While modern combat only allows joking and showing off at the expense of random victims to celebrate a collective victory, face-to-face fighting allows personal triumphs over specific opponents. Moreover, cultures which value individual achievement in battle tend to require some tangible proof of victory. Severed heads or limbs are amongst the most widespread type of personal trophy. The headhunting of medieval *samurai* is unusual only in the importance attached to identifying the victims. 'A head without a name' is of little use to the *samurai*; the rule is that, if circumstances permit, 'when taking the head of an opponent you must give your name first and then let your victim give his.' If this is not feasible, every effort must be made to identify the man by his belongings, or by showing his head to witnesses. Whenever possible, the victory is announced while battle still rages, especially if there is any risk that others might claim credit; thus, 'to certify his single-handed victory over Moritoshi, [Noritsuna] stuck the head on the point of his sword, held it high, and declared firmly: "The head of Etchû no Zenji Moritoshi, the most famous devil-warrior of the Heike, was this day taken by Inomata no Koheiroku Noritsuna!" '[135]

Homeric triumphal behaviour sometimes reminds one of modern British, sometimes of medieval Japanese, practices, but the essentials of its etiquette are all its own. The poet's extended descriptions of gruesome wounds and spectacular deaths put one in mind of the photographic records kept by Falklands veterans, and both must surely be attributed not only to appalled fascination with death and mutilation, but also to a certain pride in the ability to inflict horrific injuries upon the enemy. Modern soldiers do not, of course, take photos of mutilated *comrades*, and it is no coincidence that in Homer it is almost always Trojans rather than Greeks whose injuries are described in detail.[136] The heroes indulge in some black humour at the expense of the enemy dead, too. One man, dragging away a Trojan ally's body, pretends to be inviting the corpse to come with him to his ship in order to arrange an alliance with the Greeks instead (XIII.377–84), while another man jokes that his victim can use the spear which killed him as a staff on his way to Hades (XIV.456–7). The dramatic death-dive of Kebriones – 'like a diver', according to the poet – is greeted by Patroklos with an involved joke likening him to an acrobat ('What a very agile man! How easily does he turn somersaults!') and sarcastically suggesting that such acrobatic skills might have made him a good living diving for sea-squirts in bad weather – presumably a particularly hard and lowly occupation.[137]

One could point to parallels with *samurai* customs as well: the heroes boast of killings, there are a few instances of decapitation, and in a unique instance a warrior actually raises a severed head on the point of his spear and accompanies this gesture with a vaunting speech.

The similarities, however, are superficial. When Peneleos cuts off Ilioneus's head and lifts it, 'looking like a poppy', by the spear lodged in its eyesocket, he is neither taking a trophy nor claiming credit for the kill. Rather than showing off to his comrades, 'he displayed it to the Trojans,' thereby causing a general panic among them. In his speech, moreover, he does not name himself, but merely announces that this killing constitutes revenge for the death of a Greek warrior who had fallen moments earlier (XIV.496–507). Compare the decapitation of Imbrios by Aias, son of Oileus, which explicitly is also an act of immediate revenge for the death of a Greek, and the cutting off of the head and arms of Hippolokhos by Agamemnon in revenge for offences against the Greeks by the victim's father. In each case, the act of vengeance is made deliberately conspicuous to the enemy: Hippolokhos's trunk is sent rolling through the crowd, 'like a log', while Imbrios's head is sent flying through the crowd 'like a ball', landing at the feet of Hektor (XI.138–47; XIII.202–5). Akhilleus's attempts to mutilate Hektor's body in revenge for Patroklos, too, are carried out in full view of the enemy. Retaliation by means of decapitation and mutilation is something of a *collective* responsibility. When Teukros kills Imbrios, it is Aias who takes it upon himself to exact vengeance, and when Patroklos kills Sarpedon, he asks the Aiantes to help him go further: 'There lies the first man to breach the Greek wall – Sarpedon. If only we could capture and mutilate him!' (XVI.555–61). The most strikingly executed collective act of vengeance is when each of the Greeks in turn steps up to Hektor's body to stab it, with the typically sarcastic comment that he is now 'much softer to the touch' than he was when burning the Greek ships (XXII.369–75). Mutilation of the dead, which is in any case rare in Homer, is never a show of personal success in a game of rivalry with one's comrades, and certainly not an act of random brutality, but is always motivated by a desire for revenge, and carried out to demoralise and frighten the enemy.[138]

An alternative to mutilation is simply to speak of revenge in a vaunting speech. At least one in three such speeches expressly mentions this motive. A Trojan shouts, 'Asios at least certainly does not lie unavenged!', and a very successful Greek shouts back, 'Deiphobos, may we suppose that killing *three* compensates at all for the death of one?' (XIII.414, 446–7). Even the less successful may express satisfaction at obtaining partial revenge: 'At least I have slightly relieved my heart of grief at the death of Patroklos, although the man I have killed is worse than he' (XVII.538–9).[139]

Triumphant speeches in general occur more often than the pre-combat exchanges discussed earlier, and a larger proportion of them mentions revenge, which may indicate an awareness that there is less risk of being proved wrong in boasting of one's prowess and of obtaining vengeance when the fight has already been won. Note that two out of three men who promise revenge before combat are in fact killed.[140] Apart from cracking sarcastic jokes at the expense of the dead, the victors also taunt them with having had misguided confidence in their own prowess ('I suppose you thought that you would destroy our city...you fool!' XVI.830–3), and with the fate of their corpses ('Carrion-eating birds will tug at your body and cover it with jostling wings – but *I*, when I die, will be given a proper burial' XI.452–5). Enemies who escape with their lives have insults flung at them, 'dog' being a favourite term of abuse. Words designed to humiliate the opponent are now notably more prominent than they had been prior to combat: since there is no longer a risk of stinging the opponent into action, the victorious warrior can give free rein to humiliating expressions of his own superiority.[141]

Boasts of prowess feature as before. Hektor brags to the dying Patroklos that 'Hektor's fast horses' will protect the Trojans; Pandaros boasts of the deadliness of his archery, and Poulydamas exclaims, 'I certainly do not think that this spear leapt in vain from the strong hand of the son of great Panthoos [i.e. Poulydamas], but some Greek is taking it away – in his flesh!'[142] Intimidation, too, continues to play its part. Those who escape death are told that they will not be so lucky next time, or, remarkably, that a spear-cast would have been fatal if only it had hit its target (XVI.617–18) – suggesting that force matters more than accuracy of aim. Several warriors turn from their immediate victims to a wider audience, threatening to 'kill others' or 'destroy everyone'.[143]

Vaunting words are acceptable to Homeric etiquette only when backed up by warlike deeds. When Meriones boasts to Aineias that he could kill him, but does not actually make the slightest attempt to do so, Patroklos rebukes him for talking instead of fighting (XVI.619–31). This attitude is mirrored by that of the British soldier who has few qualms about his comrades' humiliating the enemy dead, but resents triumphalism in the media, rejecting the *Sun* newspaper's notorious headline on the sinking of the *Belgrano*, 'GOTCHA', on the grounds that those who have not risked their own lives have no right to brag in this way.[144] Since the right to boast is dependent on personal achievement, and 'shouting loudly' in triumph is bound to be noticed by other warriors, it clearly serves, up to a point at least, the same purpose as the vaunting of the *samurai*: to draw attention to oneself and gain credit for one's successes. The contents of vaunting speeches, however, suggest that this is not its main purpose.

As is the case with pre-combat speeches, and with gestures of mutilation, words spoken in triumph are almost always addressed to the enemy – normally to the victim in person, sometimes to the enemy at large – rather than to one's comrades. Only Pandaros addresses his Trojan friends, and even then his boast is an oblique one, disguised as an exhortation to the troops. Only Hektor and Poulydamas, as cited, state their names in making their boasts. When there is any response to vaunting it is always from the enemy, who react with 'sorrow' or 'fear' to the death and humiliation of their man.[145] We must assume that this is precisely the reaction which a show of triumph, whether in words or in deeds, is meant to evoke, and hence that, as well as helping to vent feelings of relief and a sense of superiority and serving to draw attention, its chief function is once again to hurt and frighten the enemy.

By far the most common course of action after victory is to try to rob one's victim of armour and weapons, and sometimes to capture his horses. Such attempts at despoliation are made after almost one in four killings,[146] and perhaps are taken for granted on other occasions. On the other hand, we should not assume that it is universal practice. As has been repeatedly pointed out, much of the time Homeric heroes come no closer to the enemy than just within throwing or shooting range, whereas plundering corpses, of course, requires one to venture much further forward. It is, in fact, a matter of pride for Idomeneus that he has accumulated many spoils 'taken from those killed; for it is not my style to fight in a position far from hostile men' (XIII.262–3). The poet amply illustrates the serious risks involved: four men are wounded and five men killed in the attempt to take spoils; seven men are forced to give up and retreat empty-handed under heavy fire. Several of those who do succeed are made to fight for their lives.[147] There are two strategies to minimize the risk: sometimes there is a quick dash forward to snatch a piece of armour from a body where it has fallen, but normally the corpse is first dragged out of the danger zone and then despoiled at leisure.[148] Plundering corpses is of course much less dangerous during pursuit, when the fleeing enemy is unlikely to try to prevent it, and it is an indication of the plausibility of Homer's account that all 25 instances of despoilation during pursuit are successful, whereas during steady battle no less than 13 of 34 attempts by individuals fail.

The victorious warrior often strikes what might seem a triumphal pose, putting his foot on a victim's chest or dragging along a corpse by the heels. These gestures, however, are not merely symbolic, but arise from the need to strip corpses quickly. The foot on the chest helps pull one's spear from the body, and the most effective way of moving a body single-handedly is to drag it by the heels. It may be humiliating, but in a dangerous situation even a dead man's friends will use this technique to bring his body over to their side.[149]

Even if no special display surrounds despoilation, the act of plundering in the midst of battle does involve conspicuous risk-taking and spoils thus acquired are proof of bravery, as Idomeneus's pride in his collection bears witness. Yet their trophy-value is much diminished by the fact that most spoils fall into the 'wrong' hands. During battle it is by no means uncommon for one man to grab and plunder another man's victim, without any sign of resistance or resentment on the part of the killer.[150] Moreover, since almost 40% of attempts at despoilation during battle fail, and since presumably – given the common Homeric strategy of fighting from a distance – in many cases no immediate attempt at despoilation is made at all, the majority of the slain lie untouched until their army is routed and some enemy happens upon them during pursuit. Hence, as we saw earlier, leaders worry that their men might not throw themselves wholeheartedly into pursuit, but hang back to gather up as many abandoned spoils as they can. That warriors might do this, and that they may be ordered to give pursuit first and come back later to collect spoils, indicates, as was pointed out, that it does not necessarily matter much to Homeric heroes whether they take spoils from their own victims or from others'. Indeed, some men go out after dark to scavenge for spoils on the deserted battlefield.[151]

Two reasons for such comparative lack of discrimination in seizing spoils suggest themselves. The first is that spoils may be seen as collective no less than individual trophies. Hence the willingness of large numbers of warriors to assist a comrade in despoiling his victim;[152] hence also the freedom of warriors to plunder those whom they have not themselves killed. The second reason is that spoils are sought at least as much for their material and utilitarian value as for their symbolic significance as trophies. Twice in the *Iliad* captured arms and armour are dedicated to the gods and thus given symbolic significance, but normally spoils are sold, or given away, or kept for future use. Thus Idomeneus's supply of captured weapons helps to arm his retainer Meriones, and Nestor tells the story of how once Lykoorgos, having killed Areithoos, the Mace-man, took the man's armour 'and afterwards wore it himself in battle. But when Lykoorgos grew old at home, he gave it to his retainer Ereuthalion to wear.'[153] The more spoils are valued for their material worth, of course, the less it matters from whom one takes them. Despoliation, then, is at times motivated by a desire to obtain proof of prowess, individual or collective, but more often serves no purpose but the acquisition of equipment and the wealth it represents.[154]

There is thus more of an element of display in triumphal mutilation, vaunting and despoliation than there is elsewhere in Homeric battlefield behaviour, and the heroes clearly engage in private display to a greater extent than Classical Greek hoplites or modern soldiers do. Yet from a comparative point of view it is equally worth stressing how many opportunities for display are missed – with even potential trophies being treated as commodities rather than tokens of victory – and how few are the signs of ritualization. Even more remarkable is the extent to which display by individuals celebrates the success of the group. Occasional boasting references to the prowess of the Greeks or the Trojans at large, frequent *joint* efforts to despoil or mutilate an opponent, and the universal direction of such display as we do meet at the enemy rather than at comrades, all suggest that collective glory ranks no lower than personal fame. Appropriately, the *Iliad*'s final battle ends with a double *collective* celebration of success, as the entire Greek army joins Akhilleus in mutilating Hektor and in singing a *paian*, a song of victory, as they leave the field (XXII.391–4).

To sum up some of the main features of Homeric combat etiquette: the image of the warrior in action is of one whose main quality is his strength, rather than his skill or courage, and who applies this strength efficiently, even opportunistically, with little show or ritual, with the minimum of risk to himself, but with devastating effect on the enemy. Hence, on the one hand, even the occasional berserker is notably restrained, while on the other hand chivalry is banned from battle and confined to duels for show, since in Homeric warfare the ultimate aim is to kill and destroy, not merely to prove one's superiority.

Our earlier conclusion that, despite its thematic prominence in the *Iliad*, the desire for personal glory is by no means the most pervasive of combat drives, is borne out by our survey of combat etiquette. However prominent a hero may be in the narrative, he is only one of a crowd of *promakhoi* in action, and his deeds do not automatically stand out for all to see. Although the fighting is less 'impersonal' than modern infantry combat, the poetic convention which has the warriors know the enemy by name is misleading: the rarity of self-identification in challenge, boast or vaunt, the near-absence of identifying features of equipment, and the prevalence of brief and often long-range hit-and-run attacks, mean that in a real-life counterpart to Homeric warfare victors would normally remain anonymous not only to the enemy, but also to all but their closest companions. In these circumstances, any attempt to stand out as an individual would require much display and self-advertisement, yet we have found that, by comparison with warriors of other cultures, Homeric heroes in action rarely seek the publicity without which there can be no personal glory.

How, then, to account for the idea, voiced so clearly by Akhilleus, Sarpedon and Hektor, that glory is a hero's ultimate goal in battle? At one level, it could be seen as a convention of the genre: the poet deals with legendary warriors whose superhuman strength enables them to perform feats that stand out without any need for display and thus enables them to covet a glory to which no mere mortal could aspire. But at the level of historical experience of battle, too, personal glory could play its part despite a relative lack of opportunities to excel, for two groups of men do stand out from the rest.

The first and largest group is that of the dead. It must be remembered that the heroes are, if anything, more concerned with glory in death than glory in life. Although Akhilleus does demand immediate respect for his prowess, his chief ambition is to obtain 'imperishable' posthumous fame in exchange for his life. This is a kind of glory lesser men, too, may attain. Even if a man's performance in battle goes unnoticed otherwise, his death in combat is in itself proof of bravery and lifts his reputation above that of surviving comrades.

The second group is that of warriors notable not so much for their achievement as for their equipment: the leaders and wealthy men who are mounted on, or followed by, their chariots. One of the reasons for the use of chariots, in fact, may be the desire of these men to set themselves apart from the masses – a desire also reflected in their inclination to seek out enemies of their own social status. The Homeric élite liked to claim that victory and defeat depended on them, and that the masses were cowardly and ineffective in combat. Homer's own account of battle shows this to be false,[155] but by virtue of their more conspicuous presence leaders and princes could plausibly lay claim to greater glory and bolster the ideology of their own superiority, while their avoidance of direct confrontations with commoners prevented this alleged superiority from being challenged.

The pursuit of glory in Homer is but one combat drive among many, and its effect on combat etiquette is limited. It inspires a greater willingness to die, but contrary to common preconceptions rarely leads to reckless, showy, selfish attempts to shine. It makes the élite seek somehow to distinguish itself from its subjects, but otherwise does not inspire the widespread internal rivalry between warriors that one might have imagined.

5. Conclusion: a Greek way of war

Homeric warrior mentality is neither particularly heroic nor particularly primitive.

As for heroism, its standards vary from culture to culture. As Richard Holmes points out, whereas 'in the Japanese army, heroism was commonplace and defence to the last man routine,' a Western soldier tends to be less tenacious. 'He will fight on until he considers that the terms of his contract have been satisfied and he has "done his bit".' Thus 'Lieutenant-Colonel Lord Farnham surrendered…with 11 officers, 241 men and 41 machine guns and mortars, after requesting, and receiving, a paper stating that he had put up a good fight: honour was satisfied.' At another time, the German general Sattler announced that 'he would not surrender unless tanks were deployed against him. They duly appeared and fired a few rounds: Sattler and his men marched out into captivity.' This was in 1944. In the same year, 35 Japanese, most of them wounded, surrendered on Kwajalein Atoll – the remainder of the garrison, 5000 men strong, had fought to the death. Kamikaze missions were to start later that year.[156] Homeric attitudes to heroism are firmly in the modern Western mode of 'commonsense' self-preservation as opposed to 'fanatic' self-sacrifice.

As for the supposed primitive features of Homeric motivation in combat, a proper appreciation of the vital role of solidarity and mutual support between comrades as a driving force in Homeric battles, and a more balanced perspective on the roles of patriotism and personal glory – the former considerably more significant, the latter far less central, than generally believed – take the heroes of the *Iliad* well away from the stereotypical noble savage and much closer to the Classical Greek hoplite and the modern Western soldier. A close look at the heroes' behaviour in battle confirms this reassessment, revealing as it does a largely plain, pragmatic, opportunistic, and in that sense 'modern', style of fighting.

The mentality of the Homeric warrior is not, of course, identical to that of his ancient or modern successors. For example, since the Classical Greek army comes to rely on hand-to-hand combat in dense formation, opportunities to stand out are still further reduced and choosing one's opponents becomes impossible. The always shaky foundations of the ideology of aristocratic superiority are thus increasingly exposed. The need to maintain the integrity of the Classical formation also places greater demands on courage and self-control: soldiers can no longer afford to yield to fear or to be carried away by fits of anger, and there is little scope for personally avenging one's friends or enriching oneself. It is not to be denied that these are important changes, yet conventional contrasts between Homeric and hoplite mentality have been badly overstated. Scholars have too often been content with an impressionistic image of the Homeric warrior, derived from a few memorable but quite atypical episodes such as Hektor's 'chivalry' in single combat or his 'berserk' charges in pitched battle. Perhaps inevitably, they have taken as the other term of the comparison, not the average Greek soldier, but the ideal Spartan hoplite – fearless, utterly disciplined, and no more typical than Hektor – and thereby artificially widened still further the gap between Homeric and Classical battlefield mentality. Compare the Homeric *norm* with the Classical *norm*, however, and one will find that the differences, while notable, are essentially differences of degree.

Classical hoplites famously regarded their own style of fighting as something peculiarly Greek, something that 'barbarians' were incapable of imitating or even understanding. Somehow it appears to have escaped notice that such military self-consciousness is present in the *Iliad*, too, which is all the more remarkable since Homer is otherwise well known for failing to make clear distinctions between the Greeks and their barbarian enemies.[157] A couple of passages encountered earlier mention the Greeks' silent obedience to their commanders during the advance into battle. Each time, an explicit contrast is drawn: the advancing Trojans produce a loud incoherent noise, like the crying of a flock of birds or the bleating of a flock of sheep (III.2–8; IV.428–38). Still more striking are the numerous passages, also discussed above, which stress the importance of looking out for one's comrades and the strength to be gained from mutual support. In every single case, it is Greek warriors who recommend such behaviour and put it into practice, and again the contrast with the Trojans is spelled out. At the start of the first battle, the advancing Greeks are not only silent, but also 'eager in their hearts to protect one another' (III.9). Accordingly, in the most fiercely fought of all fights, the struggle over the body of Patroklos, many Trojans fell, but of the Greeks 'far fewer died' for, unlike the Trojans, 'they always remembered to protect one another from the sheer slaughter (XVII.364–5).[158] The fact that the Greeks are not always silent, nor always obedient, and that Trojans tend to help one another, too, does nothing to diminish the significance of the contrast. Objectively, there may be less to choose between Homer's Greeks and Trojans than between fifth-century Greeks and Persians, but the point is that nevertheless the poet already perceives a marked difference and proclaims the superiority of Greek discipline and solidarity – the very qualities which for Classical hoplites defined the Greek way of war and made it supreme.

Notes

1 For the motivation of the 'primitive' warrior, see Turney-High 1971, esp. pp. 145–9; for that of the modern soldier, see Holmes 1985, esp. p. 137 (imaginary newspaper headline from Caputo's *A Rumour of War*).

2 Detienne 1968, pp. 121, 124. More on glory and egotism: below, pp. 23–5. More on *furor*: below, pp. 44–9.

3 Lukowiak 1993, p. 56.

4 Marshall 1945, p. 66, relating an incident from the capture of Kwajalein Atoll (1944). Compare Holmes 1985, pp. 66–7, 149–50, and ill. 7 (photo of Goose Green), on 'the empty battlefield'; Keegan 1976, p. 242.

5 Some of this is controversial. I have defended the above reconstruction of mass combat in open formation at length elsewhere (Van Wees 1988, pp. 1–14; 1994, pp. 1–9) against the view of Latacz (1977) and Pritchett (1985, pp. 7–33) that mass combat *in close formation* predominates, as well as against the traditional view (still represented by e.g. Murray 1993, p. 52; Ducrey 1985, p. 43) that *a few 'champions'* fighting in open formation bear the brunt of battle in Homer.

6 Manoeuvres: XII.60–107; XIV.370–84; XV.294–305. The comparison

with Papua New Guinea warfare is developed in Van Wees 1994, pp. 1 and 8.

7 Van Wees 1992, p. 48; cf. pp. 42–4 (relationships) and 269–71 (numbers); 1995a, pp. 166–74.

8 For these (problematic) aspects of military organization in the *Iliad*: Van Wees 1986 and below, pp. 27–8.

9 Marsh et al. 1978, pp. 68–70 (hooligans); Meggitt 1977, pp. 67–9 (New Guinea).

10 While there is no disagreement on the broad outlines of Homeric equipment, it has often been argued that there are inconsistencies, and that the overall picture, especially of the use of chariots, is implausible and therefore unrealistic. I have argued that Homer's ideas on the panoply and the chariot are in fact consistent and largely plausible, even if they do contain an element of fantasy: Van Wees 1994, pp. 9–14, 131–55.

11 Comments recorded in *The Guardian*, 19 January 1991. Cf. the evidence assembled by Holmes 1985, pp. 271–2, to demonstrate 'an unfashionable and surprising fact: some men actually enjoy war.' See also Buford 1991, pp. 194–5, 206–7. It may need stressing that it surely *is* the thrill of danger, rather than bloodlust or the like, that can make combat enjoyable.

12 The title of a brief account of Chimbu warfare by L.G. Vial, cited in Brown 1973, pp. 58–9.

13 Statistics and other evidence on 'involuntary defecation' (and 'involuntary urination': 21% in the same division): Holmes 1985, pp. 205–6; Hanson 1989, p. 101. Psychiatric casualties, in some instances as much as 50–60% of the total: Holmes 1985, pp. 254–65; Keegan 1976, pp. 326–9.

14 Vermeule 1979, pp. 83–4, cites a number of different passages, none of which seem to me to provide evidence for 'pleasure' derived from war. On the rarity of such evidence in Homer, see Leaf 1900, *ad* IV.222 (and XIII.82, where he argues that *kharmê*/χάρμη, a word for battle, does *not* mean 'battle-joy' – a view since supported in detail by Latacz 1966, pp. 20–38, 125–7). Note that even the restless fighter is only keen to go *raiding* on his own account; he is not enthusiastic about joining a public war against Troy (14.237–9); Odysseus's own reluctance to go to Troy was legendary (24.115–19): Van Wees 1992, pp. 174, 207–8.

15 The point is made by Silk 1987, pp. 73–4. For 'glory-bringing', see also below, pp. 23–5.

16 Ill-sounding, used 5 times: e.g. II.686. Dreadful din, used 11 times: e.g. IV.15. Pain, exhaustion, sweat and dust, see e.g. II.386–90; V.502–5; VI.84–5; XI.811–13; XIII.85, 711; XVI.106–11; XVII.385–8; XXI.50–2; and nn. 18 and 21 below. Traumatic noise of modern battle: Keegan 1976, pp. 141–2; Holmes 1985, pp. 161–7, 401; Hanson 1989, pp. 152–3; Lukowiak 1993, p. 142 ('More than anything, it is noises that take me back to the battlefields of the Falklands... Sometimes, just for a second or two, I wish I was deaf').

17 Cf. Leaf 1900, pp. 317–18: 'This...can only belong to the decadence of the "great manner".' Food and drink are abundantly available in the Greek army, and apparently in Troy, too (VII.465–77; VIII.545–65); there is no sign of deprivation. Cf. Shay 1994, pp. 121–4 ('What Homer left out').

18 Sarpedon: V.694–8; Hektor: XI.355–9; XIV.409–39; XV.10–11, 240–2;

Agamemnon: XI.267–72. Cf. Diomedes: V.794–8; XI.398–400.

19 Glaukos: XVI.513–31; cf. XII.387–91. Diomedes (V.98–143), Aineias (V.302–46, 445–8, 512–18), and Hektor (XV.59–61, 220–70), too, require divine healing before returning to battle. Menelaos, who is slightly grazed by an arrow, is the only warrior in the *Iliad* to fight on after receiving merely *human* medical attention (IV.139–40, 190–220). Walking wounded withdrawing: XI.251–79 (Agamemnon stabbed in lower arm), 375–400 (Diomedes shot through foot), 434–88 (Odysseus stabbed in flank), 504–20, 581–95 and 809–48 (Makhaon and Eurypylos both shot in thigh); XIII.527–39 (Deiphobos stabbed in arm), 593–600 (Helenos hit in hand and bandaged; his subsequent withdrawal is initially taken for granted, but explicit at 758–83); XVII.601–4 (Leitos stabbed in wrist). Cf. Van Erp 1985, p. 8; Marg 1976, p. 14; Seymour 1907, pp. 621–2.

20 See Van Wees 1988, pp. 12–13, with further references.

21 Drying and washing: V.794–8; X.572–7; XI.619–22 (cf. XIV.5–7); XXI.560–1; and the Trojans collectively at XXII.1–3 (cf. XXI.541–2) – surprisingly, only the Trojans are also said to be parched with *thirst*.

22 On annihilation as the ultimate goal of Homeric war: Van Wees 1992, pp. 183–99.

23 Shudder: XV.436; XVI.119 (Aias); V.596; XI.345 (Diomedes); IV.148; XI.254 (Agamemnon); also: IV.150 (Menelaos); XII.331 (Menestheus); XV.466 (Teukros). Extreme symptoms:VII.215–16; XVII.732–4; cf. VIII.77; XV.280; Monsacré 1984, pp. 57–8. It may be noted that the vignette of the coward portrays a fearful man lying in ambush rather than facing a pitched battle. This is appropriate not only because fear is at its worst whilst *waiting* to go into action (Holmes 1985, pp. 138–41), but also because as a member of a select group of ambushers one would not have the option of hanging back from the fight, as one would have in full-scale battle.

24 XIII.485–6 ('If only we were of the same age...'); XVII.102–3 ('If only I could persuade Aias' to support me against Hektor, cf. 90–101); XVII.561–2 ('If only Athena gave me strength...'); XX.100–1 ('If only a god would put the issue of battle in an equal balance...', cf. 86–100).

At V.223–5 and 231–2, Aineias and Pandaros speak openly of the need for a quick retreat, should their joint attack against Diomedes fail; at XI.354–60, Hektor runs far away from Diomedes, then jumps on to his chariot and drives off to an even safer distance; Hektor and two friends are also afraid and withdraw when they see a single opponent joined by two of *his* friends (XVII.530–5). Also: XI.542–3; XIV.488; XVII.574–9. Note the habit of charioteers of retreating rather than defending their fallen partners: e.g. XX.487–9; Van Wees 1994, p. 10 n. 32. When men are *criticized* for retreating, it is because they have failed to stand up to a *weaker* man (XVII.582–90), or because they have some special responsibility to fight (e.g. III.30–57).

25 On the alleged demands of the heroic code: e.g. Mueller 1984, p. 61 (though contrast pp. 79–80); Finley 1977, p. 114 ('There were moments when even the greatest of the heroes knew fear, but then it was enough to cry "Coward, woman!" to bring him back to his senses') and pp. 115–17 (on Hektor's attempt to face Akhilleus as the only proper 'heroic' course of

action). Others have noted that showing fear and retreating when outnumbered *is* permissible in Homer: Hainsworth 1993, *ad* XI.420–7 and 473–84 ('It is unusual that Odysseus stands his ground'); Vivante 1991, p. 87; Renehan 1987, p. 111; Monsacré 1984, pp. 57–8; Starr 1979, pp. 97–9. Further instances of unusually brave resistance: Diomedes fighting Aineias and Pandaros against the advice of Sthenelos (V.241 ff.); Agenor standing up to Akhilleus (on the notable grounds that he would have little chance of escape even if he did try to run away, XXI.551–70); and Aias facing the Trojans at large, on several occasions (see pp. 45–6, below).

26 See e.g. Vivante 1991, pp. 90–2; Renehan 1987; Vernant 1981; Griffin 1980, esp. pp. 90–5, 140–3, 177 ('We see both the terrible and unalterable laws of life and death and also the greatness which man can achieve in facing them'); Marg 1976, pp. 14–19. For Akhilleus, esp. IX.410–16; XVIII.94–8; XXII.358–66; cf. Eukhenor: XIII.663–70.

27 Kapauku: Meggitt 1977, p. 65; modern military fatalism: Holmes 1985, pp. 240–1.

28 Crying: e.g. VIII.245; IX.13–16; XIII.88–9; Monsacré 1984, pp. 137–42. Pleas for mercy: pp. 26–7 below.

29 Compare Agamemnon's criticism of Kalkhas (I.68–108) and the suitors' rejection of Halitherses (2.178–82). Trojans misreading the signs: XII.256–7 (correctly explained by Poulydamas, 200–29, and completely rejected by Hektor, as cited); XV.377–80. Other signs during battle, or more generally influencing the course of war: II.299–332; IV.75–7, 381; VIII.75–7, 170–6, 245–52; IX.236–9; X.5–8; XIII.242–4; XVII.547–50 (cf. XI.27–8). Also XI.53–5; XVI.459–60 (showers of blood to mark impending deaths).

30 Lukowiak 1993, p. 174; Holmes 1985, pp. 241–2.

31 Lukowiak 1993, pp. 40–1; another example: p. 105. Holmes 1985, pp. 238–9, confirms that 'there was an undercurrent of superstition' in the Falklands War, citing the fact that the killing of a whale by the *Canberra* 'was regarded as a bad omen'.

32 The absence from Homer of a pre-battle *sphagia* is noted by Singor 1988, p. 143, who believes that Homer here offers a highly secularized image not corresponding to contemporary Greek practice. For Classical Greek attitudes, see Parker 1989, pp. 155–60 (Sparta); Powell 1988, pp. 383–413 (Athens); Pritchett 1971, pp. 109–15.

33 *The Guardian*, 14 July 1994. Compare e.g. Kiefer 1972, pp. 77–9, on war magic (and divination) as practised by the Philippine Tausug, and Goodwin 1971, pp. 245–7, on Western Apache war charms. Lucky charms: Holmes 1985, pp. 238–40.

34 *Pace* Emily Vermeule: see n. 14.

35 Holmes 1985, p. 340; also pp. 331–9.

36 Ardant du Picq 1921, pp. 51 and 115 (emphasis added).

37 Holmes 1985, pp. 274–85 (covering First and Second World Wars, Vietnam War, Six Day War, and Falklands War); quotations from pp. 276–7, 275, 276, 275 and 277.

38 Hainsworth 1993, *ad* XI.242–3 ('The heroes of course fight primarily for themselves'); Kullmann 1992, pp. 268–9; Starr 1979, p. 100; Finley 1977,

63

pp. 113–20; Lohmann 1970, p. 119 n. 44 (who argues that Hektor's appeals to fight for the fatherland [see below] are interpolations). More balanced discussions of patriotism in Homer: Raaflaub 1993, pp. 41–2, 57–8; Edwards 1987, p. 153; Greenhalgh 1972.

39 *Patrê* in the sense of 'fatherland' is used 11x in the *Iliad*, 6x in the *Odyssey*; *patris* (*gaia, aia, aroura*) is used 36x in the *Iliad*, 93x in the *Odyssey*. Examples of usage in the *Iliad* may suffice: return to fatherland: II.140, 158, 174, 454; IV.172, 180; V.213, 687; VII.335, 460; IX.27, 47, 414, 428, 691; XI.14; XII.16; XV.499, 505, 706; XVI.832; XVIII.101; XXIII.145, 150; XXIV.557; cf. XXIV.766. Exiles banned: XIII.696; XV.335; XXIV.480. Fighting and dying far from fatherland: II.162, 178; XI.817; XIII.645; XV. 740; XVI.461, 539; XVIII.99; XXIV.86, 541; cf. I.30. Hektor: VIII.359; XXII.404; cf. III.244. Note also 10.416–17: Odysseus's companions greet him with such joy as if they had returned 'to their fatherland and the very city of rugged Ithaka, where they had been born and raised'.

40 Collective defence of women, children, etc.: V.482–6; VIII.55–7; XXI.586–8; cf. IX.327; XVIII.265. At XVII.223–4, the *allies* are encouraged to protect the wives and children of the Trojans, and at X.420–2 we are told that they are less keen to do so than the Trojans themselves are. At XV.497–9, individual men are reassured that their deaths will contribute to the collective effort that will at least ensure the safety of their own families and property. Although the families and property of the Greeks are not in direct danger, their deaths or prolonged absence put them at risk, and they are at one point reminded of this (XV.663–6).

41 Cf. Iphidamas who dies 'bringing help to the townsfolk' (XI.242), and Sarpedon, an ally and thus not strictly acting from patriotic motives, who is much lamented because 'he had been a bulwark of their city, even though he was a foreigner' (XVI.548–50). In Greece, too, the 'best men' are said to 'protect the towns' (IX.396); Meleagros, for instance, 'wards off the day of evil' from the Aitolians, who themselves collectively defend their city of Kalydon (IX.531, 597). See further on this theme Scully 1990. Note also that, during the Trojan War, all Greeks are constantly encouraged to 'protect the ships' from being burnt by the Trojans (XII.154–6, and *passim*), and although this comes close to self-defence, it is still a collective and not wholly selfish effort.

42 V.663–9, 692–8 (Sarpedon); VIII.330–4 (Teukros); XI.396–8 (Diomedes), 487–8 (Odysseus), 508–18 (Makhaon), 809–48 (Eurypylos); XIII.210–15 (anon.), 533–9 (Deiphobos), 596–600 (Helenos); XIV.424–37 and XV.9–10, 241 (Hektor). Cf. also the reaction to Menelaos' wounding during a truce: all who see it 'groan', and he receives attention from a specialist physician (IV.153–4, 190–219).

43 XI.592–4; XIII.488 (calls for help from Eurypylos on behalf of Aias, XI.584–95, and from Idomeneus, XIII.477–88). Also: XI.461–86 (Odysseus, shouting loudly three times, 'as wide as his head would gape'); XII. 333–72 (Menestheus on behalf of his *hetairoi*); XIII.491–5 (Aineias); XVII.245–61 (Menelaos), 507–31 (Automedon). Only Koon calls in vain: XI.258.

44 XVII.608–19; in the sequel, Meriones, Koiranos's partner on the chariot, forgoes his own chance of escape by chariot and lets Idomeneus, his

senior in age and rank, use it (620–5); the right interpretation of the sequence is given by Willcock 1987, pp. 186–9. Note also Antilokhos's initiative in helping Menelaos, 'for he was very afraid that something might happen to him' (V.565–72). Further: V.467–9; VIII.91–115; XI.575–80; XV.540–5; XVI.319–23; XVII.605–8 (implicit); XXII.231–42 (pretend).

45 Ten instances of a one-to-one confrontation: V.297–302 (charioteer defended by fighting partner); XI.248–60 and 428–9 (both men defended by brothers); XIII.181–3 (brother-in-law), 188–94, 384–5, 417–23; XIV.476–7 (brother); XV.524–9; XVI.319–21 (brother). Individuals' failure to defend victim noted: V.20–1 and VIII.124–6, 316–19 (three charioteers/fighting partners, see n. 24 above); also VI.12–18 ('friends').

The *Iliad*'s very first sequence of fighting offers a small-scale example of a corpse-fight escalating: A is hit, B attempts to drag the body away, C kills B, and 'over him developed a hard fight between Trojans and Greeks; they rushed at one another like wolves' (IV.457–72). The culmination of this pattern is of course the long struggle over Patroklos's body, itself incorporating a few minor corpse-fights: XVII.1–XVIII.233. In between, we find another eleven such fights: IV.532–8 (over Peiroos); V.617–26 (Amphios); XIII.462–99 (Alkathoos, Hektor's brother in law), 506–11 (Oinomaos), 516–40 (Askalaphos), 549–55 (Thoon, who, dying, stretches out his hands to his comrades, who respond with an energetic defence); XIV.442–50 (Satnios); XV.422–8, 545–59 and 583–90 (Kaletor, Dolops and Melanippos, Hektor's cousins); XVI.490–683 (Sarpedon), 737–83 (Kebriones). Group failure to defend victim noted: XI.120–1; XV.650–2; XVI.290–2. Sometimes comrades carry the dead to safety without meeting resistance: V.663–9; XIII.653–9.

46 In addition to the two examples cited, there is one further instance of (intended) revenge by a brother: XX.419–23 (for Polydoros). I count six instances of revenge killings for a man described as a *hetairos* of the avenger: IV.494–500 (Leukos); V.533–42 (Deikoon); XV.436–47, 458–60 (Lykophron), 518–23 (Otos); XVII.344–9 (Leiokritos), 587–92 (revenge intended for Podes). One man is avenged by a fellow-exile living in the same household (Epeigeus, XVI.581–7); one charioteer is avenged by his fighting partner (Arkheptolemos, VIII.316–19), and one fighter by his charioteer (XVII.536–9). Three times revenge is taken (or attempted) by the leader of a contingent for a compatriot: V.561–4 (Krethon and Orsilokhos, who are from Pherai [542–9] which is part of Lakedaimon [21.13–16 with 3.488–9 = 15.186–7], ruled by their avenger Menelaos [cf. IX.149–53 = 290–5]); XIV.486–505 (Promakhos, a Boiotian [476]); XVII.350–4 (Apisaon, a Paionian). One man is avenged by his guestfriend (*xeinos*): XIII.660–2 (Harpalion); and there is one example of someone avenged by the man who happens to be nearest: XIV.458–68 (Prothoenor). Lastly and perhaps most significantly, there are four instances of revenge taken by men who have no special connection with the victim: V.610–17 (Menesthes and Ankhialos avenged by Aias), 668–78 (Tlepolemos by Odysseus); XIII.402–16 (Asios by Deiphobos: 'Now Asios certainly does not lie unavenged... I have given him an escort' to Hades), 581–96 (Deipyros by Menelaos).

To this total of 21 explicit revenge killings one should perhaps add another

7 where revenge as a motive may be implicit: IV.491–2 (Antiphos for Simoeisios), 527–31 (Thoas for Diores); XI.369–78, 581–4 (Paris for Agastrophos and Apisaon); XIII.560–75, 643–55 (Meriones for unsuccessful attacks on Antilokhos and Menelaos); XVI.603–9 (Aineias for Laogonos).

47 VI.6 (Aias); VIII.182 (Teukros); XI.797–803 and XVI.39–45 (Patroklos); XVIII.129, 200–1 (Akhilleus). Menelaos's failure 'to defend his comrades', the Pylians (whose own leader is absent) is noted: XVII.702–4.

48 Appeals to Akhilleus: IX.247–51, 300–3, 515–18, 630–2; XVI.31–2 ('How will someone of a later generation derive benefit from you [σευ ὀνήσεται], if you do not ward off ugly disaster from the Greeks?'); cf. Nestor's comment, after relating what he himself in his youth did for his fellow-countrymen: 'but Akhilleus benefits from his prowess all by himself' (XI.762–3). On Hektor, see also XVI.538–40, where he is accused of failing to protect his allies; his brothers, too, are reminded that they should try to protect their men from the enemy (V.462–6). Diomedes is also presented as a protector of the Greeks (XVI.75; cf. esp. XI.310–19, 326–7).

49 e.g. V.95–105 (Pandaros), 165–76 (Aineias), 679–91 and XI.343–4, 521–39 (Hektor); XVI.419–26 (Sarpedon). Cf. the mass retreat covered by an élite force organized by Thoas (XV.281–305).

50 Important exceptions are Cairns 1993, pp. 83–7; Starr 1979, pp. 100–1; cf. Van Wees 1988, pp. 6–7. The details of Nestor's advice are debated: see Van Wees 1986, pp. 298–9; 1994, pp. 12–13. Less emphatic instances of mutual defence: IV.534–5; XI.171 (Trojans 'waited for one another', despite panic).

51 Quotations: Holmes 1985, pp. 291, 300; Shay 1994, pp. 40, 49, 74, 69. Cf. Hanson 1989, pp. 118–19.

52 Groan: see n.42. Pity: V.561, 610; XVII.346, 352. Sorrow: e.g. XIII.403, 581; XIV.458, 475, 486; XVI.581. 'Stirred': e.g. XIV.459, 487. Shudder: XV.436. Anger: e.g. IV.494; XIII.660; XVI.585.

53 The other heavy hint is given at XXIV.130–1, when Thetis tells Akhilleus that he should stop mourning, but eat and sleep, adding 'and it is good to mingle in love, γυναικὶ περ'. The last two words mean 'with a *woman*' (emphatically), 'with a woman, at any rate' – as opposed to 'with a man'. Rather than take this to mean that Akhilleus will have to make do with a woman now that his male sexual partner is dead, I would prefer to take it as a general, and gratuitously emphatic, statement of preference which the poet puts into Thetis's mouth. The relevance of these problems to the issue of combat-motivation was brought to my attention by Daniel Ogden, who discusses them further elsewhere in this volume. See also Clarke 1978, esp. p. 396 n. 38; Mauritsch 1992, pp. 111–22. Homer might have approved of Holmes's censorious comment, 'There is much more to love in wartime than the scramble for sex' (1985, p. 108; cf. Shay 1994, p. 43).

54 Military service as a favour to Agamemnon: I.152–60; to Hektor: V.211; also 5.306–7 (cf. 3.162–4); 13.265; Van Wees 1992, pp. 48, 119–20, 174. Favour/gratitude in return for outstanding contribution to battle: Pandaros may expect '*kharis* from all the Trojans…and from prince Paris most of all' for killing Menelaos (IV.95–6). Complaints about lack of 'gratitude for always

fighting the enemy ceaselessly': IX.315–27 (fair share of booty not awarded); XVII.144–55 (no defence of fallen comrade); in the first case, the disappointed party withdraws from war, while in the second case withdrawal is merely threatened. See MacLachlan 1993, pp. 13–22.

55 Homeric ethics of honour and respect are discussed at length in Van Wees 1992, pp. 69–77, 109–38. Apart from Aineias and Akhilleus, we hear of Meleagros's refusal to fight (IX.524–99), and of the Greeks' general anger at Agamemnon's 'badness' which makes them inclined to shirk (XIII.107–10; XIV.49–51, 131–2). Both Akhilleus and Thersites regard withholding services as the proper 'manly' response to a lack of respect (I.229–32; II.235–42). The fact that Hektor assumes that Paris has left battle out of anger (which Paris in fact denies, VI.326, 335–6) confirms that this is a common phenomenon (Willcock 1957, p. 24; Collins 1988, pp. 30–5).

56 As in, for example, the *Battle of Maldon*, 202 ff. (cf. Frank 1991 and Bradley 1982, p. 519, for the view that the retainers here express an essentially eleventh-century ideal of loyalty to the feudal lord, rather than some ancient 'Germanic' code of honour). This may be used as further evidence, if any were needed, against the notion that Homeric society has a feudal basis.

57 Marshall 1945, pp. 38 and 40–1.

58 Holmes 1985, pp.141–2.

59 'Be men' (ἀνέρες ἔστε), also: VI.112; VIII.174; XI.287; XV.487, 661–2, 734; XVI.270; XVII.185. Compared to 'women or little boys': II.289; VII.235–6; XI.389; to women: II.235; VIII.163; XX.252–5; to little boys: II.337–8; XX.244–5.

60 Boasts, see also: V.473–6; VIII.229–35; XIII.219–20; XVI.200–1; XX.83–5; and cf. the demand to fulfil promises made: II.286–8, 339–43; IV.266–7. Previous performance, also: V.472, 788–91; XIII.95–122; XVI.556–7. Looks, also: III.39–45 (cf. XIII.769); V.784–92; VIII.228; XVII.142–3.

61 Diomedes is compared to his father at IV.370–400 and V.799–813; old Nestor is held up (by himself) as an example to the Greeks at large at VII.132–60; cf. XI.668–764; Hektor is twice accused of being inferior to a Greek opponent: XVII.166–8 (Aias) and 586–8 (Menelaos); cf. Diomedes's worries at VIII.145–50. Flight and defeat may also be described as shameful without reference to a definite standard: II.297–8; IV.242; XI.313–15; XV.502; XVI.422; XVII.336–7, 414–17, 556–7; so too, Agamemnon feels shame at the prospect of the whole expedition failing: II.284–8; IV.171–82.

62 Holmes 1985, pp. 140–1.

63 That the whole community forms an audience for performance in combat is also indicated by the exhortation to 'put in your heart shame before *other people*' (XV.661–2), as opposed to 'one another' (V.530 = XV.562). 'Hanging one's head' is implied in one of the words for 'disgrace', κατηφείη (III.51; XVI.498; XVII.557), 'sinking into the ground' in the wish 'may the earth gape for me/us', IV.182; VIII.150; XVII.417 (cf. VI.281–2). For an analysis of Homeric shame, see Cairns 1993, pp. 48–146, esp. 68–87; Riedinger 1980.

64 Collective κῦδος: V.33; XIII.303; XV.491 (armies in general). XIII.676; XIV.358; XV.595, 602; XX.42; XXII.217, 393 (Greeks). XI.79; XIV.73;

XVII.419, 453 (Trojans, see also next note).

65 XII.255; XV.327; XVI.730. The destruction of the Greek ships, which is clearly (and sometimes explicitly) a collective achievement, is said to bring *kudos* to Hektor personally: VIII.170–83; XIV.364–5; XV.596–8; XVIII.293–4 (at VIII.215–17 with 234–5, the glory of the capture of the ships is credited to 'the one Hektor' as a rhetorical ploy to shame the Greeks into putting up a fight). The glory to be won by Patroklos, too, is at least partly dependent on the performance of the troops led by him (XVI.84, 88, 241 – note the references to the quality of his followers: XVI.271–2 = XVII.164–5). It appears, in any case, that in some contexts the name of a leader is used to indicate him and his followers simultaneously: Van Wees 1986, pp. 288–90.

66 Lukowiak 1993, pp. 110–12; on regimental pride, see Holmes 1985, pp. 307–15; Keegan 1976, pp. 184–5.

67 Fame/glory and single combat: III.373; VII.89–91, 100, 205; breaching a wall: XII.174, 407, 437. Other feats also bring fame because they are highly 'visible': shooting of Menelaos during truce (IV.95, 197, 207); spying expedition at night (X.307, 212–13, 281–2). *Aristeiai* of Diomedes: V.1–3; of Teukros: VIII.281–5; of Hektor: XI.299–300; XV.612, 644; XVII.566; of Akhilleus: XX.502; XXI.543, 570; XXII.18; more below, pp. 46–7 and n. 123. Defeat of prominent enemies: Aineias (and Pandaros, including the capture of Aineias's immortal horses): V.225, 260, 273; Diomedes: VIII.141; Hektor: IX.303; XXII.57, 207; also Patroklos (including the capture of his/Akhilleus's armour): XVII.9–17, 130–1, 231–2; XVIII.165, 456; XIX.204, 414 (and failing to protect his corpse will mean the end of the 'good reputation' of the Greeks, XVII.415). Two somewhat unusual cases are XXI.596, where the death of Agenor, a rather less well known warrior, is said to bring Akhilleus glory, and XXII.110, 304–5, where Hektor imagines that merely trying and failing to stand up to Akhilleus might enhance his reputation (posthumously); in both cases the fight is fought in near-isolation from the rest of the army, and therefore not unlike a formal duel. The remaining references to fame do not specify the achievement that brought it, or is to bring it: V.171–3; VI.444–6; XII.318; XVII.143.

68 Further discussion of the role of fame in Homeric warfare below , pp. 57–8.

69 So too the duel between Hektor and Aias will reflect not only on the champions, but on the *armies*: VII.73, 159, 214–15, 226–7; see Van Wees 1992, p. 202. Odysseus (IX.673; X.544) and Nestor (X.87; XI.511; XIV.42) are called 'glory of the Greeks', though presumably not primarily for their *warlike* qualities.

70 XXII.99–110. For this interpretation of Hektor as remaining in character as the great defender of Troy until the very end, see Cairns 1993, pp. 81–2 ('his [shame] is not directed at the implication of cowardice, but at the charge that he has failed in his duty to protect Troy and its people', p. 81); Van Wees 1988, p. 20; De Jong 1987, p. 78; Fenik 1978, pp. 69–90; *contra* Finley 1977, pp. 116–17; Redfield 1975, p. 154.

71 Lukowiak 1993, pp. 76–7; Holmes 1985, pp. 353–5; Keegan 1976, pp. 180–1.

72 See van Wees 1992, pp. 299–310 (distribution of booty), 87 (quarrels over booty).

73 So Finley 1977, p. 119, who calls collecting spoils 'worse than absurd' since it is liable to 'jeopardize the whole expedition'. He wrongly assumes, however, that these spoils *are* taken as personal trophies (as does Hainsworth 1993, *ad* X.343), and sees in the custom evidence of heroic selfishness in the pursuit of *glory*. For detailed discussion of despoliation, see below, pp. 54–6.

74 Gould 1973, p. 94. Appeals to pity: XXI.74–9 (in special circumstances: a prior relationship exists between the two parties); XX.465 (suggested by the poet; no direct speech which might have mentioned ransom, too). Offers of ransom: VI.46–50; X.378–81; XI.131–5; XXI.80.

75 Recent attempts to explain away αἴσιμα are subtle but not ultimately convincing, since they are inspired by a desire to dissociate the poet from what is perceived as barbarity (Kirk 1990, *ad* VI.61–2; Goldhill 1990, pp. 373–6; Yamagata 1990, pp. 420–30; Fenik 1986, pp. 22–7). Without wishing to deny the poet's generally humane outlook, it seems to me quite clear that his attitude to violence differs markedly from our own. For the Tros-passage, see Edwards 1991, *ad* XX.467–8. Ransoming as common practice 'outside' the *Iliad*: e.g. II.229–31; VI.425–8; XI.101–6; XXII.48–51.

76 The twin obligation to fight and encourage others to fight is cited frequently (e.g. V.482–6; XII.367; XIII.55–6; XVI.501, 525–6; XVII.559) and presumably extends to everyone. Most men , of course, do no more than exhort those within earshot; the more active leaders wander up and down the army, haranguing everyone (e.g. V.495–6; VI.104–5; XI.64–5, 212–13 [Hektor]; XII.265–8; XV.685–8 [Aias]); Agamemnon finds a central spot to make himself conspicuous when shouting his encouragement (VIII.218–26). Donlan 1979, p. 52, notes the high success rate of attempts to exercise leadership, even by men of inferior status.

77 Fame and riches: (1) Athena promises Pandaros *kudos* (IV.94–5; cf. 197, 207) and *gifts* from Paris (IV.95–9); (2) Agamemnon promises Teukros *a special share of booty*, and *fame for his father* (VIII.281–91); (3) Hektor promises anyone who succeeds in dragging Patroklos's corpse into Trojan lines a piece of Patroklos's *armour*, and *fame* (XVII.229–32). Elsewhere, promises of fame (X.212–13, 281–2, 307) and material rewards (X.213–17, 303–32, 392–404) are held out to volunteers for a spying expedition. Nowag 1983, pp. 26–36, sees booty as a driving force throughout, but cites passages which at best refer only obliquely and secondarily to booty (II.297–8, 354–6): see Van Wees 1992, pp. 189, 250. Appeals to shame: above, esp. nn. 59–61; to solidarity: e.g. V.463–70; VIII.282; XIII.47; XVI.538–47; XVII.79–81, 149–53.

78 VI.516; XIV.216; XXII.127–8; 19.179; Vermeule 1979, p. 103 (cf. 100). 'Impersonalization': n. 4 above.

79 Pospisil 1963, p. 59.

80 Keegan 1976, p. 178, citing an episode from the Battle of Waterloo (1815).

81 Lukowiak 1993, pp. 48–9.

82 Quotations are from *Heike Monogatari* (*The Tale of the Heike*, translation Kitagawa and Tsuchida 1975), IV.12; IX.2; IX.10 [*bis*]; XI.10; IX.4; VII.8;

IX.16, respectively. *Heike Monogatari* is set in the late twelfth century, its narrative concentrating on historical events between AD 1167 and 1185; the *Tale*, and others like it, were passed down by oral tradition, sung by monks to the accompaniment of the *biwa* (a string instrument), until, and indeed after, they were written down no later than the second half of the fourteenth century, from which date several written versions survive.

83 Letoublon 1983, pp. 33–4, 41–2 ('Le héros...doit...se choisir des adversaires à sa mésure'), 48 ('Un combattant, se choisissant un adversaire prestigieux, veut prouver sa supériorité'). Letoublon evidently sees the status of the combatants in terms of their personal merit as warriors rather than in terms of social hierarchy. She further suggests that mutual identification is also intended to ensure that one does not attack gods in disguise or unrecognized guest-friends (pp. 35–6). Also Parks 1990, pp. 50, 105–6; see n. 110 below.

84 The heroes regularly address one another by name or by patronymic; they also refer by name to the cannon-fodder characters who are introduced only to be slaughtered (e.g. Promakhos, XIV.480–5; Ilioneus, XIV.501–2), and may know quite a lot about them, as in the case of Othryoneus (XIII.374–82). At one point Aias even makes a sarcastic joke of pretending to be guessing the identity of his victim, '*well knowing who he was*' (XIV.469–75). Apart from the two exceptions who are *asked* to identify themselves (see below), there are only three further occasions in the *Iliad* when a man refers to his ancestors in addressing an opponent: Tlepolemos boasts of his father's prowess to Sarpedon, who knows all about it (V.632–51); Aineias boasts of his divine descent to Akhilleus (XX.206–41), although he knows that Akhilleus is aware of it (XX.203–5); and Idomeneus recites his genealogy – without mentioning his own name – as part of a challenge to Deiphobos (XIII.449–53). Only this last instance comes at all close to a *samurai*-style statement of identity, but can equally be regarded as a boast. On these genealogies, and on pre-combat speeches in general, see below, pp. 40–3.

85 For instance: 'That day Naozane wore armour laced with red leather over a dark blue battle robe. Around his neck he wore a red scarf. He rode a peerless chestnut steed called Gonda. His son, Naoie, wore armour laced with blue and white straw-rope-patterned leather over a battle robe decorated with water plantains and rode a cream-coloured horse called Seiro. Naozane's standard bearer wore armour laced with yellow leather over a blue battle robe and rode a white horse with yellow splotches.' (*Heike Monogatari* IX.10). Cf. Hainsworth 1993, *ad* XI.15–46, for examples from other heroic traditions; compare also the heroic traditions in which the individuality of pieces of arms and armour is such that they may bear 'personal' names, like Hrothgar's sword Hrunting (*Beowulf* 1455 ff.).

86 Golden armour: II.872; VI.234–6; VIII.192–3. Double crest: e.g. XI.41–2; quadruple crest: XII.384; XXII.314–16. Sizes of shields: XIV.371–7 (generally); VI.117–18 (Hektor); VII.219–23, 245–6 and e.g. XI.485 (Aias); XV.645–6 (Periphetes). For further discussion, see Van Wees 1994, pp. 131–7; 1992, pp. 17–21, where it is argued in particular that the largest shields are not intrusive Mycenaean relics, but fantastically large versions of

contemporary round shields.

87 Meggitt 1977, p. 20.

88 *Heike monogatari* (translation Kitagawa and Tsuchida 1975) IV.11 (Battle at Uji Bridge, 1180 CE) and IX.4 (Battle at Awazu, 1184 CE).

89 *Battle of Maldon* 84–95. Bradley 1982, p. 519, stresses that 'pride' (*ofermode*) here does not have negative (Christian) overtones; Parks 1990, p. 31, however, does see an element of criticism.

90 *Sir Gawain and the Green Knight* IV.91–2 (translation Stone 1974). Duby 1990 argues that the 'slow flowering of courage' was a 'twelfth-century novelty' (p. 17), and that the ideal of individual prowess as displayed by Gawain was inspired by the rise of the tournament (pp. 84–97), which cast its 'resplendent mantle' over battle, too (p. 126). Cf. Contamine 1984, pp. 250–9, on the medieval 'history of courage'.

91 Chivalrous single combat: Parks 1990, esp. pp. 31, 46; Singor 1988, pp. 120–3; Krischer 1988, pp. 15–19; Ducrey 1985, p. 43 ('un combat rituel, défini par des règles contraignantes'); Mueller 1984, p. 78; Letoublon 1983, pp. 27–31, 48; and e.g. Seymour 1907, pp. 578–81. Kirk 1968, p. 101, and Kromayer 1928, p. 20, see single combat ('exotic and formalized military behaviour'; 'gemessenes, fast zeremoniöses Streiten…nach Rittersitte') as an intrusive Mycenaean element untypical of the overall picture.

Berserkers are seen as typical by Vidal-Naquet 1975, p. 23; Vernant 1988, pp. 235–7; a substantial but rather less prominent role is accorded to them by Shay 1994, pp. 77–99; Bremmer 1983, pp. 58–9; Griffin 1980, p. 35 ('This fighting madness is no mere figure of speech'), but cf. 39 and 92 ('We are not dealing with berserkers in Homer'); Daraki 1980 (one of two types of warrior); Lincoln 1975, esp. p. 101 ('A wild, uncontrolled rage which is possessed by certain highly gifted warriors'); Redfield 1975, pp. 201–2. By contrast, Singor 1988, pp. 132–3, and Marg 1976, p. 7, argue that the berserker is an intrusive element from an 'older phase', while Nilsson 1951, p. 358, sees Hektor as the only exception to the rule that 'für die Berserkerwut…der Homerische Mensch etwas zu zart geschaffen [ist]'; cf. Hainsworth 1993, *ad* IX.239.

92 The pattern has often been observed, but generally dismissed as an exception to the rule that 'duelling' prevails (see nn. 91, 94). Walter Marg is probably the only scholar to have noted that despite the disproportionate amount of space taken up by each duel, the one-sided assault is far more common: 'Hier ist eigentlich kein Kampf…dargestellt, sondern ein Schiessen und Erlegen. Die Szenen sind so gedacht, dass der Angegriffene den Angriff entweder nicht merkt, oder zu keiner Gegenwehr kommt… Man könnte eher von "Toden" als von Kämpfen sprechen' (1942, p. 170); 'es sind das alles ja keine eigentlichen Kämpfe und Proben kämpferischen Muten und Könnens', but 'Situationen…wo nur ein Angreifer da ist, der Andere zu keiner Gegenwehr kommt' (1976, pp. 10–11). See also Van Wees 1988, p. 5.

93 Archers relying on surprise: VIII.266–79 (Teukros, claiming 10 victims); XI.369–79 (Paris). Killed while despoiling corpse: e.g. IV.467–9; XV.524–9; XVII.288–94; see further below. Killed while dismounting: XI.423. Attacked by third party: XV.539–41; XVI.319–25; cf. XI.251–2 (surprise attack from flank). Slaughtered while in shock: XIII.434–44; XVI.401–10; XVI.806–21.

94 Quotations from Mueller 1984, pp. 77–80; similarly Parks 1990, p. 31; Edwards 1985, p. 34: 'The *Iliad* regards cunning and trickery as a last resort for those whose strength is unequal to open confrontation'; and Griffin 1980, p. 91. Despite Anthony Edwards's subtle attempt to make a distinction between *Iliad* and *Odyssey* in this respect, it seems to me clear that the *Iliad* no more than the *Odyssey* rejects the use of ambushes in warfare. Edwards admits (1985, p. 34) that Idomeneus singles out the fearless ambusher as the epitome of the brave man (XIII.276–87; see also n. 23 above), and that the ambushers on the Shield of Akhilleus have the support of Athena and Ares (XVIII.516). Against this stand only (p. 26) Diomedes's criticism of Paris for the use of the bow (*not* for his shooting from ambush, XI.385), and the utter defeat of groups of ambushers by Tydeus and Bellerophon (IV.391–8; VI.187–90). If the latter implies criticism, it is surely because these ambushes are used, not in war, but against 'innocent' victims. The very limited evidence for 'chivalry' in Homer is discussed below.

95 No response after avoiding enemy spear, even though a comrade is killed as a result: XIII.183–7, 402–12; XIV.459–75, 488; XV.520–4; XVII.304–11. No response to failed attack without unintended victim: XIII.156–64, 502–5; XVI.608–26. The last example is particularly interesting since the incident leads to a slanging match between attacker and intended victim, but does not result in retaliation even when the 'victim' is rebuked for talking back instead of fighting back. Running away from a single (strong) enemy: see pp. 8–9 (with n. 24) above, and also IV.495–500; XVII.574–81; XX.487–9. For failure to take up a verbal challenge, see the discussion of 'face-to-face' combat below.

96 XI.434–46; XIII.561–6, 643–51; XVI.806–15; XVII.43–50. Cf. XI.251–60 (after wounding Agamemnon, Koon immediately attempts to retreat while dragging away the body of his dead brother). The poet finds it noteworthy that Dolops after an unsuccessful blow does *not* retreat: 'he still hoped for victory' (XV.535–9).

97 So Mueller 1984, pp. 80–1; his total of 'specified encounters', however, is 140 rather than 170, and I have subtracted from his figures (of 20 and 8) the two formal duels that take place outside battle. See n. 104 below. My figure of 170 is comprised of all the actions about which we are told at least the nature of the blow or the weapon used, and includes a few confrontations in which it does not ultimately come to blows. The remaining 130 are cases in which we are told only the names or numbers of those killed. The figures given by Armstrong 1969, p. 30 (264 wounded or killed) are too low: he does not count all the unnamed victims, or the encounters that do not lead to wounding or killing. The figures given by Seymour 1907, pp. 617–18 (306 killed) are puzzlingly high.

98 Tedium: Edwards 1987, pp. 78–81. Death: Griffin 1980, pp. 90–5, 143 (Renehan 1987, pp. 108–11, argues persuasively against Griffin on this point). See also Mueller 1984, pp. 81–2; Schein 1984, pp. 76–7.

99 Entrails spilling out: IV.525–6 = XXI.180–1 (χύντο χαμαὶ χολάδες, as cited; trsl. Stanford/Hammond); through corslet: XIII.508; XIV.517; XVII.314–15; XX.413–20 (cf. Van Wees 1994, pp. 135–6, against the view

that in these passages the corslet is intrusive). Skull split: XII.384–6; XVI.411–13; XVI.578–9. Blood spurting: XVI.345–50; brains slithering: XVII.297–8; XX.387; eyes popping out: XIII.616–18; XIV.493–5; XVI.740–2. Falling like a diver: XII.385; XVI.742 (cf. XII.394–6; XVI.404–10); landing upside-down: V.585–8. Akhilleus: XX.413–20, 472–4, 481–3; Aias: XIV.465–8.

100 Marg 1976, pp. 10–11, 15; 1942, p. 175, is clearly wrong to assume that Homer's descriptions of wounds are always realistic and that even the most grisly injury is described with the clinical precision and detachment of the professional soldier or hunter. Discussion and further examples in Friedrich 1956, esp. 11–29 ('fantasies') and 43–51 ('fake realism'), followed by e.g. Mueller 1984, pp. 83–9, and Edwards 1987, p. 156. The latter are concerned to dissociate the poet from any 'delight in gore': Edwards rather vaguely attributes it to 'the poet's desire to parallel the vividness of other physical descriptions' (ibid.), while Mueller suggests that such graphic descriptions are implicitly critical of the 'increasing brutality' of war (p. 86). To my mind, the fact that Homer attributes at least one horrific head-injury to 'the huge spear and powerful hand' of a hero (XVII.296) suggests admiration for the physical prowess that can do such damage. This would appear to find support in Mueller's own important observation that almost all those who suffer particularly nasty injuries are Trojans. Homer betrays his pro-Greek bias by not describing the wounds of the Greeks in such shocking detail (p. 85), just as he betrays it by having far more Trojans than Greeks killed although the Trojans are supposed to be winning (pp. 82, 89, 99; a ratio of *c*. 170:50 on his count, 221:52 on mine). See also below, pp. 51–2 and n. 136.

101 Homer's lack of interest in fighting skill has been noted by e.g. Mueller 1984, pp. 77–8; Kirk 1978, p. 28; Marg 1976, p. 13. The one passage which alludes to skill, featured in a formal duel, is discussed below. Contrast for example the emphasis in *Heike monogatari* on the skills of swordsmanship ('He wielded the sword like a spider's legs', etc., as cited above), on exceptional feats of archery (e.g. ibid. XI.8), and even on feats of self-defence, such as that of Arrow-Cutter Tajima, who got his name because he 'ducked to avoid the arrows that came high, leaped over those that came low, and split with his halberd those that came straight toward him' (IV.11).

102 So Lukowiak 1993, p. 58, on a British sniper exposing himself to enemy fire. More below, pp. 47–50.

103 There are 28 duels in a total of 170 confrontations described; if one were to include also the 130 killings merely referred to, the proportion of 'duels' would be less than 1 in 10. The duels (including 10 preceded by challenges or exchanges of words, printed in italics) are: (i) standing ground while enemy approaches: V.297–329; VIII.320–34; XI.94–8, 343–60, *428–58*; XIII.384–93, 550–66, *581–97*; XVI.313–16, 593–600; *XVII.3–69*; 492–542; XX.382–93; *XXI.544–98*; (ii) adversaries seeking out one another: V.12–26, *240–96, 628–69*, 841–67; VIII.87–126; XI.231–40; XIII.601–42; XVI.335–41, 426–507, 731–63; *XX.158–352, 419–54*; XXI. *139–204*; *XXII.248–369*. In addition, there are 4 challenges/verbal exchanges which do not lead to a fight: III.19–20; VI.119–236; XIII.445–59, 809–37.

104 13 duels consist of a single blow or cast. Of the longer engagements, 9 duels take 2 blows, 4 take 3, and 2 take 4. Cf. n. 97 above.

105 This trial by combat is fought between Menelaos and Paris in order to settle the dispute between them and end the war. It is preceded by formalities which do not, and could not, feature in pitched battle: animals are sacrificed, oaths are sworn, the arena measured out, and lots drawn to determine who is to cast his spear first (III.264–96, 314–25). To my knowledge, no one has suggested that the kind of restraint practised here indicates a more generally prevalent code of chivalry: see e.g. Van Wees 1992, pp. 190–9; Singor 1988, pp. 120–3; Kirk 1978; Bergold 1977, pp. 98–101; Fernandez Nieto 1975, pp. 37–69; Armstrong 1950, pp. 73–8.

106 Mueller 1984, p. 78; cf. nn. 91, 94 above.

107 The number 14 does not include the exchange preceding the formal duel between Hektor and Aias, but does include two references to a challenge (III.19–20) and a threat (XIII.582) uttered before battle which do not give us the actual speech.

108 The remaining seven threats are: V.278–9, 646; XI.431–3; XIII.453–4, 812–20; XVII.17; XXII.268–72 (add the reference to threatening at XIII.582; only the reference to Paris challenging 'all the best men' [III.19–20] does not explicitly refer to threats uttered). There are 7 counter-threats: XVII.30–2, as cited, and also: V.287–9, 652–4; XI.442–5; XIII.825–32; XVII.34–42; XXII.285–8 (in addition, Agenor is said to answer 'threateningly' [XXI.161] although his actual words contain no explicit threat; in two instances there is no reply at all). Apart from the two instances cited of warriors who respond with a claim that they will not be intimidated, similar sentiments are uttered at XIII.810–11; XX.211–12, 244–58; XXII.281–2.

109 As convincingly analyzed by Adkins 1975, pp. 241–7, against older views which treated these episodes as irrelevant interpolations by inferior poets. Cf. Lang 1994, pp. 1–6, for literary variations in the contents of genealogical boasts.

110 The issue of divine support is implicitly at stake in the confrontation between Sarpedon and Tlepolemos, who are, as the poet points out, respectively a son and grandson of Zeus (V.631), and whose degrees of closeness to Zeus are reflected in the outcome of the fight: the grandson inflicts a wound on the son, but the son then kills the grandson (655–62). Tlepolemos vainly tries to compensate for his greater distance from Zeus by boasting that his father Herakles was a far more powerful son of Zeus than Sarpedon is (635–42). Sarpedon confidently ignores this. In a later battle, Idomeneus challenges Deiphobos to a fight, 'so that you may know what kind of descendant of Zeus I am', and recites his genealogy to show that he is in fact the god's great-grandson (XIII.449–53). Deiphobos duly retreats. Only Glaukos does not trace his descent explicitly to Zeus, but, as pointed out earlier, in his case there is a special reason for introducing his ancestors: the plot requires that he be recognized by Diomedes as a hereditary guest-friend (VI.150–236). This is a unique incident, and hardly, as Letoublon suggests, a regular motivation for reciting genealogies (see n. 83 above). Parks's recent and otherwise interesting analysis of 'verbal duelling' as a literary genre includes the unconvincing

suggestion that reciting genealogies springs from an evolutionary imperative to ensure the survival of one's 'bloodline' (1990, pp. 108–9).

111 For genuine, as opposed to rhetorical, challenges, and for insults uttered *after* combat, see below. The use of complimentary epithets (e.g. V.277; XVII.12; XXI.153) is noted by Parks 1990, pp. 105–6, who explains that it 'ennobles the enterprise and magnifies the stakes'. Some respect for the enemy is implied, and one might perhaps regard this as an element of 'chivalry' (Dorjahn 1946, p. 12). The idea that the speeches aim to humiliate and provoke is found in Vermeule 1979, p. 99, and Murray 1934, p. 150 ('A happily directed insult might make him start, lift his head too high, or expose a piece of his flank. Then you speared him').

112 Willcock 1976, *ad* VI.150–211 and XX.200–258; Glück 1964, p. 28 ('they concealed their apprehensions by flinging lusty abuse, scorn and curses at each other').

113 Shaking spears: III.18–19, 345; V.561–3; XIII.583; XXII.133. Long strides: III.22; XIII.809. Shouting piercingly at the enemy: V.302; VIII.321; XVI.785; XX.285, 382, 443. Other threatening shouts: V.591; XI.168, 344; XVI.428–30; XVII.88. Note especially the terrifying shouts of Poseidon (XIV.147), Apollo (XV.321), and Akhilleus (XVIII.217–31). Collective shouts are raised when the mass advances: IV.433–8; XII.124–5, 251–2; XV.312–13, 353–5; XVI.267. See Singor 1988, pp. 149–50; Seymour 1907, pp. 573–4.

114 Marshall 1945, pp. 12 and 32.

115 Ward Parks makes a useful distinction between the elements of a warrior's pre-combat speech aimed at establishing 'a position of superiority to his foe', which he calls the 'eristic impulse', and the element of 'establishing the terms and meaning of the contest', dubbed the 'contractual impulse' (1990, pp. 43–4; cf. 50, 56, 181). To my mind, however, Parks overstates the prominence of 'contractual' elements: most of these speeches are predominantly 'eristic'. Cf. Vermeule 1979, pp. 99–100.

116 See Van Wees 1992, pp. 200–2; Kirk 1978, esp. p. 40.

117 No sooner does he enter battle than he retreats again: he casts his spear, but it breaks and he leaves to get a new one (159–68). Later, we meet him again when he suddenly leaps forward and wounds a Trojan who is trying to despoil a corpse. Meriones runs up to retrieve his spear, but then immediately retreats 'into the crowd of his companions' (528–33). Still later, he seizes a chance to kill a man attempting to retreat to safety: he again runs up to retrieve his spear and we are left to infer that he retreats once more (567–75). Finally, he spots a second Trojan trying to leave the field, and shoots him with an arrow (650–2).

118 Although Odysseus, and later Aias, are said to be 'alone', the text implies that they are accompanied by a substantial number of men (XI.336–7, 540–2; see Van Wees 1986, p. 289). Presumably these are bands of anonymous personal followers. Aias, at least, is normally accompanied by his followers: XIII.709–18.

119 One further example of prolonged individual defensive action: before the Greek walls, Leonteus kills one man with a spear, then draws his sword and leaps forward to slaughter another four men 'one after another'

(ἐπασσυτέρους, XII.188–94). At this point, he and his partner Polypoites (who has killed 3 men, 182–7) stop to plunder the corpses (195).

120 So too, the onset of the charges of Diomedes and Patroklos is accompanied by lists of killings by other leaders, to indicate that they do not attack alone (V.59–83; XVI.306–56). It is said explicitly that 'the other Greeks' follow Agamemnon as he attacks (XI.148–9), and the Trojans, too, follow Hektor when he charges forward (e.g. XI.284–98; XIII.136–58; XV.592–5). Cf. Van Wees 1988, pp. 15–17.

121 Diomedes: kills 2 men while battle is still level (V.9–29), then, when the Trojans start running (37–84), he wreaks havoc everywhere (85–94) and kills 4 pairs of men in quick succession (144–65; at least one of the pairs shares a chariot, and probably so do the others: their having mounted confirms that they are in flight [Willcock 1976, *ad* V.144–65, and p. 280; cf. 1987, p. 186; 1993, pp. 143–4]). He meets resistance only from Pandaros, whom he kills as well, and Aineias, but he does sustain an arrow wound (95–135, 166–330).

Agamemnon: kills his first victims when the Trojans are already fleeing (XI.90–1). He meets no resistance from 3 pairs of men (all mounted on their chariots, 91–148), and proceeds to slaughter many anonymous Trojans in 'constant' pursuit (148–54). After the Trojans rally, he kills only two more men and is wounded in the process (216–63), though he does continue to fight energetically for a while (264–5).

Patroklos: there is incipient panic amongst the Trojans at his first appearance (XVI.276–83), but no outright panic until he has killed his first 2 victims (356–7). Subsequently, he kills 12 men in pursuit (394–418; the last 9 of these explicitly 'one after another'). He meets resistance only from Sarpedon and his charioteer, both of whom he kills as well (419–86). When the Trojans rally, Patroklos kills one man only (581–92), but as soon as they are put to flight again he slaughters 9 (692–8). After this, the fight appears to draw level again, but Patroklos, apart from killing Kebriones, still accomplishes the extraordinary feat of charging at the Trojans three times, killing 9 men on each occasion (784–5).

Akhilleus: fights Aineias, and then kills his first two victims, while the battle is still level (XX.382–400), but his third victim is already running away (401–6) and the battle clearly turns into a rout from this point onwards. He kills another 21 named men after this, and slaughters an anonymous multitude, meeting resistance only from Hektor (twice), Asteropaios, and Agenor.

One may add to this list a very brief *aristeia* by Aias whose appearance makes the Trojans scatter: he kills 5 men in pursuit (XI.485–97). Hektor kills 9 men, plus a nameless multitude, in pursuit at XI.299–309. Whether the 7 Lykians killed by Odysseus are fleeing or resisting is not clear (V.669–78). Compare Krischer 1971, pp. 13–89, for an analysis of *aristeiai*; to my mind, he too arbitrarily imposes formal patterns upon them, and overstates their importance as part of the battle narrative (esp. p. 85).

122 Diomedes: V.164–5; Agamemnon: XI.100, 110; Patroklos: XVI.663–5; Akhilleus: XXI.183. Akhilleus also takes a break when 'he had tired his hands with killing' (XXI.26), but soon resumes pursuit (33).

123 Diomedes is given *menos* by Athena 'so that he might become

conspicuous above all Greeks and acquire a fine reputation' (*kleos*, V.1–3). Patroklos is to gain *kudos* for Akhilleus – and presumably for himself (XVI.84, 88). For the *kudos* of Hektor and Akhilleus, see n. 67 above.

124 Diomedes: V.123–35, 406–15, 432–44; cf. V.185; VIII.111; XVI.75; also Silk 1987, p. 72. Patroklos: XVI.83–96, 684–7 ('an act of great folly'), 698–711; cf. XVI.245. Hektor's *lyssa*: also IX.239, 305; his 'madness' also VIII.355; XV.605; XXI.5.

125 XII.196–252; XVIII.243–313; XXII.99–107. Redfield 1975, esp. pp. 146–59, offers a not dissimilar view of Hektor's motivation. Maria Daraki, 1980, pp. 1–24, points out that warriors attacking fiercely are often described as 'like a *daimon*' or 'like Ares', and attractively suggests (pp. 11–13, 20–1) that this too is an implicit criticism, since Ares is associated with a 'crazed' style of fighting, and is unduly keen on fighting (V.717, 831, 890–1; cf. XV.128, 606). Cf. Bremmer 1983, p. 59; Janko 1992, *ad* XV.605–9 and XVI.784–6.

126 So Redfield 1975, pp. 201–2; even Griffin 1980, p. 35, exaggerates the Homeric picture by claiming that 'his face is distorted by madness, he utters a terrifying shriek', although he rightly goes on to stress that heroic fury in Homer does not begin to approach the level of Cú Chulainn's rage: see n. 131 below. Further flashing eyes: XII.466; XIX.365–6.

127 Quotations from Shay 1994, pp. 78, 84, 90 (expletives deleted), 97, 90; on the attraction of berserkers to other soldiers, ibid., pp. 90–1. Shay's discussion draws explicit Homeric parallels.

128 Marsh et al. 1978, pp. 70–2. See also e.g. Murphy et al. 1990, p. 139 (cf. 134–5).

129 See above p. 8, and n. 23.

130 XVIII.188 (part of a lengthy discussion, XVIII.126–201, reminiscent of the one about the importance of taking food before battle; see above, pp. 6–7 and n. 17), and Shay 1994, pp. 97 and 219–20 n. 16.

131 XX.372; V.135–6. As Jasper Griffin puts it: the hero's fury merely 'carries his normal heroism to a special level and intensity' (1980, p. 39). Note also the comments of Singor 1988, pp. 132–3. Daraki's contentions that fighting 'like a *daimon*' is the polar opposite of fighting with *menos*, and that the use of 'natural' weapons such as stones is typical of the 'mad' warrior (1980, pp. 1–2, 6, 21) seem to me untenable.

132 See Van Wees 1994, p. 137, for the compatibility of Homeric armour with Homeric tactics.

133 For other passages suggesting 'apprehension or rebuke of the excessive in heroic self-will and martial spirit', see Griffin 1987, pp. 89–90.

134 Lukowiak 1993, pp. 83–5 (prisoners), 145–7 (photos with Union Jack), 99–101, 147–8 (pictures of mutilated dead; black humour), 101, 127 (no condemnation).

135 *Heike monogatari* IX.13 (quoted); also IX.4 and 14; cf. e.g. IX.16 (for identification of heads), and IV.13; X.1 (for display of enemy heads, accompanied by 'exultant shouts', after return from war). Note that modern Western soldiers cannot always resist the temptation of taking physical trophies: according to newspaper and television reports at least one British soldier in the Falklands War was found to have cut off and kept the ears of enemy dead.

136 See above, p. 39, and esp. n. 100.

137 XVI.740–50, as explained by Janko 1992, *ad* XVI.740–4, 745–50, 747–8.

138 Revenge: see also XVI.545–7; XVIII.91–3; XXII.271–2. Apart from the three instances cited, there is only one further case of decapitation. Agamemnon cuts off the head of Koon (XI.259–61): no explicit reason is given here, but the fact that Koon had succeeded in wounding Agamemnon may supply one. Elsewhere, there are a few threats of decapitation which are not carried out: XVII.34–40; XVIII.176–7; XVIII.334–5. *Killing* men by cutting off their heads (e.g. XVI.330–41 [*bis*]) is of course a very different matter from mutilating the dead, and is not relevant to the present discussion (as Segal 1971, esp. p. 20, failed to realize). When this distinction is made, it becomes very hard to uphold the view that the fighting in the *Iliad* is marked by a rising tide of brutality (Segal 1971, esp. p. 18), since all four actual post-mortem decapitations take place in the early part of the main battle (Books XI–XIV). Furthermore, given that in each case revenge is the specific motive for mutilation, one cannot accuse the heroes of mindless savagery, and one need not worry about dissociating the poet himself from such behaviour (Segal 1971, esp. pp. 10–14). Revenge is eminently respectable by Homeric standards, and although it is possible to go too far (as Akhilleus ultimately does in his treatment of Hektor), there is nothing to suggest that simple decapitation and mutilation are disapproved of by the poet (Van Wees 1992, pp.129–30; Bassett 1938, pp. 203–7; Sandstrom 1924, pp. 12–23). Finally, I can see no reason to look for some 'primitive' and 'ritual' origin for the Greeks' stabbing of Hektor (e.g. Richardson 1993, *ad* XXII.370–1; Devereux 1979, pp. 14–15): it makes perfectly good sense on Homer's own terms as a conspicuous and collective act of vengeance.

139 Also XIV.470–4 (Aias), 482–5 (Akamas), 501–5 (Peneleos, paraphrased above); XXI.133–5 and XXII.331–5 (Akhilleus). This is a total of 8 references to revenge in 24 vaunting speeches (only 20 of which do in fact offer scope for comments on revenge, since the other 4 are addressed to enemies who have survived the attack). The Greeks' sarcastic comment about Hektor (XXII.373–4), too, is surely an indirect reference to revenge for the burning of the ships. Vaunting speeches: V.101–6, 283–5; VIII.160–7; XI.361–8, 379–83, 449–56; XIII.373–83, 413–17, 445–55, 619–40; XIV.453–8, 469–75, 478–86, 500–6; XVI.616–18, 744–51, 829–42; XVII.537–40; XX.388–93, 448–55; XXI.121–36, 183–200; XXII.344–67, 372–5.

140 Failure to obtain revenge after boast: XI.431–3; XVII.34–40 (see p. 42 above). Revenge is mentioned in 3 out of 14 pre-combat speeches; for its frequency in post-combat speeches, see previous note). The length of speeches made after combat is similar to that of speeches made before; with two exceptions (of 16 and 20 lines), no speech is longer than 14 lines, and some are as short as 2 lines. Again their length is not necessarily unrealistic, though their literary style, of course, is.

141 See above, p. 42, on the limited role of humiliation and provocation prior to combat. For misguided confidence, see also XIII.374–6; XVI.837–42; XXI.184–99; XXII.331–3. For non-burial of corpse: XVI.836; XXI.122–7; XXII.335–6 (also XX.389–92, where the emphasis is on death 'far from

home'). For insults: XI.362; XX.449; XXII.345 ('dog'); XVI.617 ('dancer'); VIII.163–4 ('woman' and 'doll'); XIII.621–39 ('aggressors'); XIV.479 ('boasters').

142 Hektor: XVI.833–6; Pandaros: V.102–5; Poulydamas: XIV.454–6; cf. V.283–5; XI.380–3.

143 VIII.166; XI.362–7=XX.449–54; XIII.620, 630; XIV.480–1; XXII.128–9.

144 Lukowiak 1993, p. 127. Patroklos's rebuke is thus neither 'comical' nor inconsistent with his own vaunting, later on (as e.g. Janko 1992, *ad* XVI.627–32, suggests): his own boast is spoken over a man he himself has killed.

145 Pandaros: V.102 ('Forwards, Trojans!'). Sorrow: XIII.417; XIV.458, 486 (of the Greeks); XIV.475 (of the Trojans). Fear: XIV.506–7 (Trojans).

146 I count 66 attempts at despoliation (including 7 collective attempts) for a total of 274 men killed. This does not include a further 41 uses of the verb (ἐξ)εναρίζω, which, despite its etymological connection with 'taking spoils' appears to mean simply 'kill'.

147 Wounded but successful: XI.246–61, 368–400, 580–5; wounded and unsuccessful: XIII.527–30; killed IV.465–7, 491–3; XIV.477; XVI.577–80; XVII.289–90; repelled: IV.532–5; V.621–4; XIII.182–3, 188–94, 509–11; XV.582–91; XVII.60–105; made to fight: XIII.550–3; XV.524–41.

148 Snatching: XIII.189–90, 527. Dragging: IV.465–7, 492, 506; V.573; XIII.383–5; XIV.477; XVII.289.

149 Foot on chest to pull out spear: V.620; VI.65; XVI.503, 863; to pull off armour: XIII.618. Dragging corpse by the foot: XIII.383–5; XIV.477; XVII.289 (cf. XXI.120; all by enemies); XI.258 (by victim's brother); XVIII.537 (by *Kêr*); X.490 (to clear space); XVI.763; XVIII.155 (in attempt to snatch corpse from enemy hands). Hainsworth 1993, *ad* X.490 regards it as 'more natural, as well as more dignified, to draw the corpses aside by lifting them under the arms', but of course this would require the use of both hands, and would force the warrior to dispose of his shield and thereby expose himself to attack.

150 IV.463–6 (Antilokhos kills; Elephenor attempts despoliation), 491–3 (Aias; Leukos); XIV.476–7 (Aias; Promakhos); XVI.570–8 (Patroklos; Epeigeus); XVII.288–95 (Hektor; Hippothoos). Note also the *joint* despoliation of victims by the Aiantes (XIII.197–202) and by Meges and Menelaos (XV.540–5).

151 Hanging back to collect spoils: VI.68–71; XV.347–9; see above p. 26. Scavenging: X.387. The texts offer no support for Hainsworth's view that the order to collect spoils later refers to 'fighting men returning to the scene of their victory', and that scavenging for spoils is an 'unheroic' practice (1993, *ad* X.343).

152 See the corpse-fights discussed above, p. 16, esp. n. 45.

153 VII.136–50; Meriones takes a spear from amongst his leader's spoils although he himself also has spoils available for use: XIII.254–68, 294–7. Hektor, of course, eventually decides to wear the captured armour of Patroklos/Akhilleus: XVII.186–214. Sale of spoils is implied at VII.472–3, as Donlan has pointed out (1981, p. 113 n. 14). Suits of armour are given away as

79

prizes at Patroklos's funeral games (XXIII.798–809). Dedications of armour: VII.81–3; X.458–68 with 526–9 and 570–1.

154 Hackett 1971, p. 17, describes Homeric battles as 'recovery battles, reflecting a general shortage of heavy equipment' and sees the material need as primary and the prestige element as derivative ('the satisfaction of a basic operational requirement comes to be given a moral and even a mystical significance'). I would regard acquisitiveness, rather than absolute shortage, as the main drive, and treat the prestige element as a secondary, but not necessarily derivative, motive.

155 As demonstrated by Latacz 1977; Van Wees 1988, pp. 15–22, and 1995b, pp. 165–70.

156 Holmes 1985, pp. 323–4; for kamikazes, see e.g. Hoyt 1983.

157 As is well shown by Taplin 1992, pp. 110–15, who does not acknowledge, however, that battlefield mentality is an exception to this rule.

158 Obedience: see pp. 27–8; mutual support: see pp. 16–21. Taplin (1992, p. 113) argues that the Trojans, too, advance silently on one occasion (XIII.39–44), apparently taking ἄβρομος here to mean 'without shouting', although the context and a number of scholia (including Aristarkhos; see Janko 1992, *ad* XIII.41–2) suggest that 'shouting *together*' is a more plausible interpretation.

Bibliography

Adkins, Arthur W.H.
   1975   'Art, Beliefs and Values in the Later Books of the *Iliad*', *CPh* 70, 239–54.
Ardant du Picq, C.-J.-J.-J.
   1921/1868[1]   *Battle Studies. Ancient and Modern Battle* (trsl. J.N. Greely, R.C. Cotton) (New York).
Armstrong, A. MacC.
   1950   'Trial by Combat among the Greeks', *G&R* 19, 73–9.
Armstrong, C.B.
   1969   'The Casualty Lists in the Trojan War', *G&R*, 30–1.
Bassett, Samuel Eliot
   1938   *The Poetry of Homer* (Berkeley).
Bergold, Wolfgang
   1977   *Der Zweikampf des Paris und Menelaos* (Bonn).
Bradley, S.A.J. (ed.)
   1982   *Anglo-Saxon Poetry* (Everyman).
Bremmer, Jan
   1983   *The Early Greek Concept of the Soul* (Princeton).
Brown, Paula
   1973   *The Chimbu* (London).
Buford, Bill

1991   *Among the Thugs* (London).
Cairns, Douglas
1993   *Aidos. The Psychology and Ethics of Honour and Shame in Ancient Greek Literature* (Oxford).
Clarke, W.M.
1978   'Achilles and Patroklos in Love', *Hermes* 106, 381–96.
Collins, Leslie
1988   *Studies in Characterization in the Iliad* (Frankfurt am Main).
Contamine, Philippe
1984/1980[1]   *War in the Middle Ages* (trsl. M. Jones) (Oxford).
Daraki, Maria
1980   'Le héros à *menos* et le héros *daimoni isos*. Une polarité homerique', *ASNP* 10, 1–24
Detienne, Marcel
1968   'La phalange: problèmes et controverses', *Problèmes de la guerre en Grèce ancienne*, ed. J.P. Vernant (Paris), 119–42.
Devereux, George
1978–79   'Achilles' "Suicide" in the *Iliad*', *Helios* 6, 3–15.
Donlan, Walter
1981   'Scale, Value and Function in the Homeric Economy', *AJAH* 6, 101–17.
Dorjahn, Alfred P.
1946   'Homeric foemen', *The Classical Weekly* 40, 10–12.
Duby, Georges
1990/1973[1]   *The Legend of Bouvines. War, Religion and Cult in the Middle Ages* (trsl. C. Tihanyi) (Cambridge).
Ducrey, Pierre
1985   *Guerre et guerriers dans la Grèce antique* (Fribourg).
Edwards, Anthony T.
1985   *Achilles in the Odyssey. Ideologies of Heroism in the Homeric Epic* [Beiträge zur klassischen Philologie 171].
Edwards, Mark W.
1987   *Homer, Poet of the Iliad* (Baltimore/London).
1991   *The Iliad: A Commentary. Books XVII–XX* (Cambridge).
Fenik, Bernard (ed.)
1978   *Homer. Tradition and Invention* (Leiden).
Fenik, Bernard
1986)   *Homer and the Nibelungenlied. Comparative Studies in Epic Style* (Cambridge, Mass./London).
Fernandez Nieto, F.J.
1975   *Los Acuerdos Belicos en la Antigua Grecia (época arcaica y clásica). I.Texto* (Santiago de Compostella).
Finley, M.I.
1977/1954[1]   *The World of Odysseus. Second revised edition* (London).
Frank, Roberta
1991   'The Ideal of Men Dying with their Lord in *The Battle of Maldon:*

Anachronism or Nouvelle Vague', *People and Places in Northern Europe 500–1600. Essays in Honour of P.H. Sawyer*, eds I. Wood, N. Lund (Woodbridge), 95–106.

Friedrich, Wolf-Hartmut
1956   *Verwundung und Tod in der Ilias. Homerische Darstellungsweisen* (Göttingen).

Glück, J.J.
1964   'Reviling and Monomachy as Battle-preludes in Ancient Warfare', *Acta Classica* (S.A.) 7, 25–31.

Goldhill, Simon
1990   'Supplication and Authorial Comment in the *Iliad: Iliad* Z 61–2', *Hermes* 118, 373–6.

Goodwin, Grenville
1971   *Western Apache Raiding and Warfare. From the notes of Grenville Goodwin*, ed. K.H. Basso (Tucson).

Gould, John
1973   '*Hiketeia*', *JHS* 93, 74–103.

Greenhalgh, P.A.L.
1972   'Patriotism in the Homeric World', *Historia* 21, 528–37.

Griffin, Jasper
1980   *Homer on Life and Death* (Oxford).
1987   'Homer and Excess', *Homer: Beyond Oral Poetry. Recent Trends in Homeric Interpretation*, eds J.M. Bremer et al. (Amsterdam), 85–104.

Hackett, General Sir John
1971   'Reflections upon Epic Warfare' *Proceedings of the Classical Association* 68, 13–32.

Hainsworth, J.
1993   *The Iliad: A Commentary. Books IX–XII* (Cambridge).

Hanson, Victor Davis
1989   *The Western Way of War. Infantry Battle in Classical Greece* (London).

Holmes, Richard
1985   *Firing Line* (London).

Hoyt, Edwin
1983   *The Kamikazes* (n.p.).

Janko, Richard
1992   *The Iliad: A Commentary. Books XIII–XVI* (Cambridge).

Jong, I.J.F. de
1987   'The Voice of Anonymity: *Tis*-speeches in the *Iliad*', *Eranos* 85, 69–84.

Keegan, John
1976   *The Face of Battle* (New York).

Kiefer, Thomas M.
1972   *The Tausug. Violence and Law in a Philippine Moslem Society* (New York).

Kirk, G.S.
1968   'War and the Warrior in the Homeric Poems', *Problèmes de la guerre en Grèce ancienne*, ed. J.-P. Vernant (Paris), 93–119.

1978 'The Formal Duels in Books 3 and 7 of the *Iliad*', *Homer. Tradition and Invention*, ed. B. Fenik (Leiden), 18–40.
1990 *The Iliad : A Commentary. Books V–VIII* (Cambridge).

Krischer, Tilman
1971 *Formale Konventionen der homerischen Epik* [Zetemata 56] (München), 13–89.
1988 'Dynamische Aspekte der griechischen Kultur', *Wiener Studien* 101, 7–40.

Kromayer, Johannes; Veith, G.
1928 *Heerwesen und Kriegführung der Griechen und Römer* (Munich).

Kullmann, Wolfgang
1992 *Homerische Motive. Beiträge zur Entstehung, Eigenart und Wirkung von Ilias und Odyssee*, ed. R.J. Müller (Stuttgart).

Lang, Mabel L.
1994 'Lineage-boasting and the road not taken', *CQ* 44, 1–6.

Latacz, Joachim
1966 *Zum Wortfeld 'Freude' in der Sprache Homers* (Heidelberg).
1977 *Kampfparänese, Kampfdarstellung und Kampfwirklichkeit in der Ilias, bei Kallinos und Tyrtaios* [Zetemata 66] (Munich).

Leaf, Walter
1900 *The Iliad. Second edition* (London).

Letoublon, Françoise
1983 'Défi et combat dans l'*Iliade*', *REG* 96, 27–48.

Lincoln, Bruce
1975 'Homeric λύσσα: "Wolfish Rage" ', *Indogermanische Forschungen* 80, 98–105.

Lohmann, Dieter
1970 *Die Komposition der Reden in der Ilias* (Berlin).

Lukowiak, Ken
1993 *A Soldier's Song* (London).

MacLachlan, Bonnie
1993 *The Age of Grace. Charis in Early Greek Poetry* (Princeton).

Marg, Walter
1942 'Kampf und Tod in der *Ilias*', *Die Antike* 18, 167–79.
1976 'Kampf und Tod in der *Ilias*', *Würzburger Jahrbücher für die Altertumswissenschaft* 2, 7–19.

Marsh, P., Rosser, E., Harré, R.
1978 *The Rules of Disorder* (London).

Marshall, S.L.A.
1945 *Island Victory. The Battle of Kwajalein Atoll. From Official Interviews With All The Men Who Fought* (Washington).

Mauritsch, Peter
1992 *Sexualität im frühen Griechenland. Untersuchungen zu Norm und Abweichung in den homerischen Epen* (Vienna).

Meggitt, Mervyn J.
1977 *Blood is their Argument. Warfare among the Mae Enga Tribesmen of the New Guinea Highlands* (Palo Alto).

Monsacré, Hélène
  1984   *Les larmes d'Achille. Le héros, la femme et la souffrance dans la poésie d'Homère* (Paris).
Mueller, Martin
  1984   *The Iliad* (London).
Murphy, P., Williams, J., Dunning, E.
  1990   *Football on Trial. Spectator Violence and Development in the Football World* (London).
Murray, Gilbert
  1934/1907[1]   *The Rise of the Greek Epic*[4] (Oxford).
Murray, Oswyn
  1993/1980[1]   *Early Greece*[2] (Fontana).
Nilsson, M.P.
  1951   'Götter und Psychologie bei Homer', *Opuscula Selecta, Vol. I* (Lund), 355–91 (From *Archiv für Religionswissenschaft* 22 [1924], 363–90).
Nowag, Werner
  1983   *Raub und Beute in der archaischen Zeit der Griechen* (Frankfurt).
Parker, Robert
  1989   'Spartan Religion', *Classical Sparta: Techniques Behind Her Success*, ed. A. Powell (London), 142–72.
Parks, Ward
  1990   *Verbal Duelling in Heroic Narrative. The Homeric and Old English Traditions* (Princeton).
Pospisil, Leopold
  1963   *The Kapauku Papuans of West New Guinea* (New York).
Powell, Anton
  1988   *Athens and Sparta. Constructing Political and Social History from 478 BC* (London).
Pritchett, W. Kendrick
  1971   *The Greek State at War. Vol. I* (Ancient Greek Military Practices) (Berkeley).
  1985   *The Greek State at War. Vol. IV* (Princeton).
Raaflaub, Kurt A.
  1993   'Homer to Solon: The Rise of the Polis. The Written Sources', *The Ancient Greek City-State*, ed. M.H. Hansen (Historisk-filosofiske Meddelelser 67) (Copenhagen), 41–105.
Redfield, James M.
  1975   *Nature and Culture in the Iliad: The Tragedy of Hektor* (Chicago).
Renehan, R.
  1987   'The *Heldentod* in Homer: One Heroic Ideal', *CPh* 82, 99–116.
Richardson, N.
  1993   *The Iliad: A Commentary. Books XXI–XXIV* (Cambridge).
Riedinger, Jean-Claude
  1980   'Les deux *aidos* chez Homère', *Revue de Philologie* 54, 62–79.
Sandstrom, Oscar
  1924   *A Study of the Ethical Principles and Practices of Homeric Warfare* (Philadelphia).

Schein, Seth L.
    1984   *The Mortal Hero. An Introduction to Homer's Iliad* (Berkeley).
Scully, Stephen
    1990   *Homer and the Sacred City* (Ithaca/London).
Segal, Charles
    1971   *The Theme of the Mutilation of the Corpse in the Iliad* (Mnemosyne Supplement 17) (Leiden).
Seymour, Thomas Day
    1907   *Life in the Homeric Age* (New York).
Shay, Jonathan
    1994   *Achilles in Vietnam. Combat Trauma and the Undoing of Character* (New York).
Silk, Michael S.
    1987   *Homer: The Iliad* (Cambridge).
Singor, H.W.
    1988   *Oorsprong en betekenis van de hoplietenphalanx in het archaische Griekenland* [Ph.D. dissertation] (Leiden).
Starr, Chester G.
    1979   'Homeric Cowards and Heroes', *Essays on Ancient History. A Selection of Articles and Reviews* (by C.G. Starr), eds A. Ferrill, T. Kelly (Leiden), 97–102 (from: *The Classical Tradition: Studies in Honor of Harry Caplan*, ed. L. Wallach [Ithaca 1966], 58–63).
Taplin, Oliver
    1992   *Homeric Soundings. The Shaping of the Iliad* (Oxford).
Turney-High, Harry Holbert
    1971/1949[1] *Primitive Warfare. Its Practice and Concepts. Second edition* (Columbia, S.C.).
Van Erp-Taalman Kip, A.M.
    1985   'De Held', *Lampas* 18, 4–19.
Van Wees, Hans
    1986   'Leaders of Men? Military Organisation in the *Iliad*', *CQ* 36, 285–303.
    1988   'Kings in Combat. Battles and Heroes in the *Iliad*', *CQ* 38, 1–24.
    1992   *Status Warriors. War, Violence and Society in Homer and History* (Amsterdam).
    1994   'The Homeric Way of War. The *Iliad* and the Hoplite Phalanx (I) and (II)', *G&R* 41, 1–18 and 131–55.
    1995a   'Princes at Dinner. Social Event and Social Structure in Homer', *Homeric Questions*, ed. J.P. Crielaard (Amsterdam), 147–82.
    1995b   'Politics and the Battlefield. Ideology in Greek Warfare', *The Greek World*, ed. A. Powell (London), 153–178.
Vermeule, Emily
    1979   *Aspects of Death in Early Greek Art and Poetry* (Berkeley).
Vernant, Jean-Pierre
    1981   'Death with Two Faces', *Mortality and Immortality. The Anthropology and Archaeology of Death*, eds S.C. Humphreys, H. King (London), 285–91.
    1988   'Artémis et les pratiques guerrières', *REG* 101, 221–39.

Vidal-Naquet, Pierre
  1975   'L'*Iliade* sans travesti' (Preface to Gallimard edition of Paul Mazon's translation of the *Iliad*) (Paris), 5–32.
Vivante, Paolo
  1991   *The Iliad. Action as Poetry* (Boston).
Willcock, M.M.
  1956/7 'B356, Z326 and A404', *PCPhS* 4, 23–6.
  1976   *A Companion to the Iliad. Based on the Translation by Richard Lattimore* (Chicago/London).
  1987   'The Final Scenes of *Iliad* XVII', *Homer: Beyond Oral Poetry. Recent Trends in Homeric Interpretation*, eds J.M. Bremer et al. (Amsterdam), 185–194.
  1993   'The Fighting in the *Iliad*', *Spondes ston Omiro* (Proceedings of the Sixth Conference on the *Odyssey*, Ithaki 1990) (Ithaki), 141–7.
Yamagata, Naoko
  1990   'Aisima Pareipon. A Moral Judgement by the Poet?', *La Parola del Passato* 45, 420–30.

2

HOPLITE WARFARE IN ANCIENT GREECE

Stephen Mitchell

The choice of 'Battle in Antiquity' as a topic for a volume of studies is a tribute to the influence of a single book. John Keegan's *The Face of Battle* is one of those rare studies that genuinely revitalizes a well-worn subject. It also does something more than that, for it teaches us something important about ourselves. His subject is warfare, regrettably a universal human experience, and more specifically battle, the essential experience of war, containing the moments when the will, the motivation, and the psychological reserves of the combatant were tested to their fullest extent – the moments when a man played for his life. Keegan's emphasis on the battlefield as the focal point of warfare explains its persuasive impact and the influence that it has had on other scholars and lay readers, an influence which has been particularly felt by students of archaic and classical Greece. As will be clear from what follows in this essay, the warfare of the classical Greek states was concentrated in the experience of battle to a much greater extent than in most other ancient or modern societies. Military confrontations up till the time of the Peloponnesian War were resolved not by extended campaigns, but by single battles. Furthermore Keegan's disciple, Victor Hanson, through a group of deservedly influential publications, has not only applied Keegan's line of enquiry and method of analysis to the abundant evidence for Greek hoplite battles, but also suggested that modern European conceptions of battle and warfare, in his phrase 'the western way of war', should be traced back to this Greek archetype.[1] If battle is the heart of war, and if hoplite battle is the quintessence of this experience, then hoplite warfare is of much more than antiquarian or academic importance.

The primary evidence for ancient Greek warfare is both familiar and well-studied. While Daniel Ogden's contribution to this volume attempts to demonstrate that the relationship between homosexuality and Greek military organization and practices has been unduly neglected, at least by military historians, other aspects of Greek, and especially hoplite warfare have received abundant attention in recent years. Hans van Wees' recent study, *Status Warriors*, not only assembles the evidence for Homeric warfare more accessibly than ever before, but also provides a lucid and compelling account of warrior motivation within the wider context of Homeric society.[2] Snodgrass's archaeological appraisal of the evidence for early Greek armour and weapons has encouraged a series of important studies, some concerned with the date when hoplite warfare and military organization first developed, others exploring their social and political consequences for the internal organization of Greek states.[3] A mass of evidence for Greek military practices has been assembled in W.K. Pritchett's series of volumes on *The Greek State at War*.[4] The conduct of war on the ancient battlefield is specifically addressed in the splendid and highly focussed series of studies of hoplite battle recently edited by Victor Hanson. In contrast, the essays collected in the two volumes on Greek and Roman war and society, edited by Graham Shipley and J.W. Rich, have been written to a more permissive brief, and range widely over the relationships between warfare, society and economic behaviour in the ancient world.[5] At all events, the material for the study of ancient Greek warfare is accessible for study and reflection as never before. Nonspecialists as well as experts should be encouraged to try their hand at making sense of the material.

Why should the Greek style of battle have something to teach us? The answer lies not only in the details of how men organized and fought their combats, but also in the way in which Greek writers commemorated wars in their literature. The prose and verse writings of the ancient Greeks concentrated on three subject areas more than any others: on the worship of the gods, on the moral duties of men, and on warfare. The greatest poem of antiquity, Homer's *Iliad*, unfurls a view of human behaviour against a backdrop of war and battle, a context whose urgency sharpened moral choices. Historians from the fifth century BC to the present day have made the same judgement as Homer about the importance of war. War has always provided the main raw material for historical study, and this tradition stems directly from the twin founders of the western historiographical tradition, Herodotus and Thucydides, who together dictated the essential rules of historical writing that have remained in force ever since. History can and should be prepared to embrace every variety of human experience in the past, but its overriding goal – in these two cases and in countless others – was to uncover the truth about a great war. Thucydides in a famous remark observed that war is a violent instructor, *biaios didaskalos*. His history of the Greek world at the end of the fifth century BC, and of classical Athens at the apogee of its civilization, is the fullest and most precise demonstration of the fact that only under wartime conditions are political and social behaviour revealed in their truest form, only then is man truest to his nature.[6] That is why warfare is the central theme of historical enquiry.

What was a hoplite? Or rather, what were hoplites? For, as we shall see, a single hoplite would not have made much sense. Hoplites were the standard infantry soldiers of Greek states from the 7th to the 4th century BC, the period of classical Greek civilization. They took their name from their most conspicuous piece of defensive armour, a concave, usually circular shield, up to 3 feet across, made of bronze, wood, and leather, whose lip could be rested on the warrior's left shoulder and which was carried by a leather strap at the elbow and by a grip at the rim for the left hand.[7] The remainder of a hoplite's protective armour was equally characteristic: a bronze breast-plate or *thorax*, bronze greaves to protect the shins, and an enveloping bronze helmet.[8] The infantryman was accordingly almost completely encased in metal armour. The vulnerable points were a possible gap between the helmet and the breast-plate, and the area around the groin and the thighs, where the fighter had to rely largely on his shield for protection. Both the pictorial and the literary evidence suggest that the two main types of offense against a hoplite were an overarm spear thrust towards the neck area, and an underarm thrust towards the groin.[9]

This equipment, and above all the helmet, reveals much about the nature of hoplite warfare and the social conditions which produced it. The most widely favoured helmet was the so-called Corinthian type. This encased the entire head and neck, save only narrow slits for the eyes and a breathing space for the mouth. A glance is enough to show that this was designed with a single and overriding aim in view, maximum protection. The wearer could see nothing except what was directly in front of him. Even if he wore a leather or cloth head-piece as padding, the discomfort, and especially the heat, would have been extreme.[10] No one would have worn such a thing into battle unless his life depended on it. The manufacture and production of such helmets were equally remarkable. They, like the other elements of the hoplite panoply, required large quantities of expensive bronze, an alloy of copper and tin, neither of which was ever mined in classical Greece in any significant quantity, but which had to be imported, chiefly from the Balkans, from Asia Minor, and from Cyprus. Obtaining the raw material for this armour was a major trouble and expense.[11]

Furthermore, the helmet, which was cast from a single sheet of hand-beaten bronze, demanded outstandingly skilled workmanship. No wonder that the smith was the aristocrat of ancient Greek craftsmen and the only one to be privileged with his own Olympian deity, Hephaistos. The skill of the archaic Greek smith was deservedly celebrated in Homer's lengthy description in *Iliad* XVIII of how Hephaistos forged a new suit of armour for Achilles.

Although helmets themselves were designed entirely for the protection of the wearer, one feature had a different purpose, the crest, the outward symbol of pride and aggression, designed perhaps not so much to inspire fear in the foe as to to bolster the morale and self-esteem of the warrior himself.[12] Soldiers charged into battle like cocks, with combs raised and bristling. Homer's famous vignette in *Iliad* VI, where Hector's infant son flinches from his father into the arms of his nurse, until Hector removes his helmet, transfers the psychological impact of the bristling plume from the battle field to a touching, domestic setting. We would expect any infant today to recoil from the unrecognisable sight of his father in full camouflage gear.[13]

In contrast to the defensive armour, a hoplite's specifically offensive weaponry was less imposing or expensive. A warrior usually carried two spears, used for thrusting rather than for throwing, one held in reserve for use when the first broke, as it often did at the initial collision of the two armies. Spears also often had a pike fixed to the butt end, to be used either if the point had broken, or for thrusting down on a fallen enemy. Swords were an option, commonly but not always carried, and used for close-quarters work. Other weapons were rare and, as will be seen, a hoplite battle allowed little use for them.[14]

The nature of the equipment naturally reflected the type of battle which hoplites fought. Some commentators have been tempted to reverse the proposition and state that the type of battle itself was dictated by the armour available to a hoplite, but this is a misconception which has been corrected by several recent studies of the evidence for early Greek warfare.[15] Massed-rank battle, the essence of hoplite warfare, certainly pre-dated the introduction of hoplite equipment in the Greek communities. Homer's conception of battle in the *Iliad*, although he often concentrates on individual combats, presupposes and often actually describes the presence of massed-rank formations.[16] One can compare the way in which archetypical, physical-contact team sports, such as American Football or Rugby, are represented so as to highlight individual achievements, the touchdowns and the tries, thus profoundly misrepresenting the nature of the contest as a whole.

Geometric vase-painting, clearly pre-dating the earliest discovery of hoplite armour from a grave in the Argolid of *c.* 720 BC, shows lines of helmeted, spear-carrying men, as well as individual warriors.[17] Furthermore the introduction of the separate elements of a hoplite's equipment was certainly a piece-meal process which lasted between two and three generations, between *c.* 720 and 650 BC.[18]

There is no evidence that a blue-print for hoplite equipment was sketched out on the drawing board of some archaic Greek weapons designer and then issued to a citizen army. On the contrary, individuals were expected to obtain and pay for their own armour; hence the hoplite was always one of the richer members of a Greek community. A system which relied on the individual to procure his own weapons was not likely in the first instance to lead to standardized equipment. Hoplite weapons were introduced as and when they became available and affordable; these conditions of course varied from individual to individual and from city to city. Systematic and full hoplite equipment could not be taken for granted until the second half of the seventh century BC, and even thereafter poorer states may have had to make do with less than their more successful competitors.[19]

The gradual introduction of hoplite equipment implies that the style of battle for which it was designed was essentially laid down at an earlier date. The Greeks had evolved a style of massed infantry warfare before these new technological innovations. Hoplite armour, therefore, and the technology of Greek warfare can illustrate much about the Greek battle, but they do not explain its basic characteristics or the ultimate reasons why Greek warfare took the form which it did. These are nowhere better summed up than in the description which Herodotus put in the mouth of Mardonius, who had already experienced Greek ways of fighting, when he advised Xerxes about the enemy he was due to face on the eve of the great invasion of Greece in 480 BC:

> From what I hear, the Greeks are pugnacious enough and start fights on the spur of the moment without sense or judgement to justify them. When they declare war on each other, they go off together to the smoothest and levellest piece of ground they can find, and have their battle on it – with the result that even the victors never get off without heavy losses, and as for the losers – well they're wiped out. Now surely, as they all talk the same language, they ought to be able to find a better way of settling their differences: by negotiation, for instance, or an interchange of views – indeed by anything rather than fighting. Or if it really is impossible to avoid coming to blows, they might at least employ the elements of strategy and look for a strong position to fight from.[20]

Not everything here is indisputable – the battle losses, for instance, are exaggerated – but two points made by Mardonius are highly germane: hoplite battles took place on specially chosen, almost predetermined areas of level ground; they also involved no ingenious strategy or attempts to fight from strategic strong points. They were, in other words, and as far as is possible in war, a straight and honest contest between the two sides. Although the contestants in hoplite battles naturally looked for ways of taking the enemy by surprise, and sometimes even managed to do so, the nature of the battles themselves minimized the impact of unexpected or unorthodox strategic initiatives.

There is another point to be picked up from this passage, namely the hint that as all Greeks spoke the same language, they might have found ways of resolving their differences through negotiation. In fact, it seems that precisely because the Greeks shared a common culture, they evolved a style of warfare which had its own common language and its own rules of combat. War was, in a sense, a means of settling diplomatic differences in a way which both sides understood. Greek fought against Greek, on a level. This is reflected not only in literature but also in pictorial representations. When sculptors or vase painters depicted men in battle they showed them, almost heraldically, as opposed equals, man against man. There is a fundamental contrast between this and the depictions of Near Eastern or Roman warfare, where the victors are commonly represented as larger than life, triumphing over cowering or humiliated foes.[21]

During most of the archaic and classical periods it is appropriate to describe military conflict between Greek states as limited warfare. On the one hand its essence was the hoplite battle itself, without (at least until the end of the fifth century BC) any significant extension into the total war of sieges, naval assaults, night raids, ambushes, and so forth; on the other hand, the battles themselves were conducted according to well-defined rules of conflict. These emerge clearly from many descriptions. I pick as one example the detailed account of an encounter between the Athenians and the Syracusans in Sicily. Thucydides' careful description was probably intended to stand not merely as a record of this single encounter but of the hoplite battle in general during this phase of the Peloponnesian War. Soon after their arrival in Sicily in 415 BC the Athenians skilfully managed to engineer themselves a position where they could confront the Syracusans on flat ground, protected from flank attacks on either side. They lined up, eight rows deep, with their Argive and Mantinean allies on the right, themselves in the centre, and their other, less dependable allies on the left. Half the forces were held in reserve in a hollow square formation, also eight rows deep, which enclosed the non-combatant camp-followers and baggage train. Their opponents, the Syracusans and their other Sicilian allies, opposed them with a line sixteen ranks deep.[22]

The Athenians were in a position to attack first and were addressed by their general Nicias. His words of encouragement reminded them that they were excellent troops facing a mixed bunch of opponents. They should fight all the more determinedly because they were far from home and there was no friendly territory to escape to in case of defeat. This ominously foreshadowed the eventual Athenian disaster in Sicily, when the disastrous overland retreat from Syracuse ended in a wholesale massacre of the Athenian forces in the battle of the river Assinaros, when they were exposed to the enemy with literally no place to hide. The Syracusans, Nicias observed, would doubtless be telling their troops exactly the opposite, namely that they were fighting to preserve their own country.[23]

The Athenians, we are told, attacked swiftly, almost but not quite catching the Syracusans off guard. In fact the form of battle hardly allowed for real surprise. The first engagement was an onslaught by stone-throwers, slingers, and archers, with the advantage going first one way then the other. Then the soothsayers came forward and conducted the usual blood sacrifice, the *sphagia*, an animal swiftly and dramatically killed in such a way that the omens of battle could be read from the way the beast fell and from the flow of blood from its severed neck. The religious origins of this action probably lie in a scapegoat ritual, with the slaughtered animal designed to avert slaughter of the warriors, but the essential point surely lay in the drama and tension of the moment, as the priests did their bloody business and captured the full concentration and the rising adrenalin flow of the warriors. Immediately afterwards the trumpets sounded and the two sides charged.[24] Thucydides rather coldly analyses the motivation of the hoplites on either side. The Syracusans fought collectively for their country, and each man for his life and future liberty; the Athenians fought to conquer another city, and to save their own from suffering by a defeat; Athens' Argive allies fought in the hope that as a reward for helping the Athenians they would return safely to their own country; Athens' other subjects fought for their own lives, and in the vague hope that victory, which enabled the Athenians to extend their empire, might lead them to be less oppressively governed in the future. It is important to notice that the types of motivation given here, and in the

descriptions of other hoplite battles, were in the first instance collective
and political. Men fought explicitly to further their country's interests,
whether offensive or defensive, but they did so with added urgency,
for their lives individually were at stake.[25]

The clash involved fierce, close-quarters fighting until the Argives
pushed forward on the right and the Athenians overwhelmed the
Syracusan centre. A thunderstorm which broke over the battlefield
had unnerved the less experienced Syracusans and tipped the scales
against them. The Sicilians took flight, but the Athenians only pursued
as far as it was safe to do so in compact bodies, in fear of the Syracusan
cavalry, before they returned to their lines and erected a victory
trophy. The following day the Syracusans removed their 260 dead
under an armistice; the Athenians had already cremated the fifty men
who had fallen on their side.[26]

Although this battle took place in the context of a life-and-death
struggle, leading eventually to the greatest disaster ever to befall the
Athenians, it is critical to appreciate how strictly the rules of battle were
observed. Level ground, ritual preparation, a short, sharp encounter
involving significant losses on the two sides but certainly not the
annihilation suggested by Mardonius's description to Xerxes, flight
but no pursuit, the setting-up of a symbolic victory trophy, and a truce
for the collection of the dead. The analogy, which has often been
made, between such battles and the contact team sports of the modern
age is remarkably telling. Indeed the peaceful sporting competition of
Greek festivals such as the Olympic Games explicitly prepared competitors for the bloody sport of Greek battle.[27]

In an important passage of his *Histories* Polybius drew attention to
the significant differences between warfare in the second century BC
and the former practices of the Greeks, who

> so far from using a fraudulent policy towards their adversaries, were
> scrupulous even as to using it to conquer their enemies; because they
> did not regard a success as either glorious or secure, which was not
> obtained by such a victory on the open field and served to break the
> confidence of their enemies. They therefore came to a mutual under-
> standing not to use hidden weapons against each other, not such as
> could be projected from a distance, and held the opinion that the only
> genuine decision was that arrived at by a battle fought at close quarters,
> foot to foot with the enemy. It was for this reason that it was also their
> custom mutually to proclaim their wars, and give notice of battles,
> naming the time and place at which they meant to be in order of battle.
> But nowadays people say that it is a mark of an inferior general to
> perform any operation of war openly.[28]

A story told by Herodotus illustrates clearly how Greek warfare might be confined, almost ritualized, so that a major inter-state conflict was to be resolved in a limited fight between representatives of the warring parties. Sparta and Argos prepared to do battle over the disputed territory of Thyreai, and the contestants agreed that a battle should be staged between 300 warriors on each side. The remainder of the forces were to withdraw, thus avoiding the temptation to join in. At the end of the day two Argives and one Spartan remained alive on the battlefield. The former assumed victory and left for Argos, but the Spartan remained behind to strip the dead of their arms before returning home. The following day a further dispute arose between the two sides as to who was victorious, which led to battle being rejoined, heavy losses, and a Spartan victory. The unfolding of the story eloquently makes the point, that placing artificial limits to a war was easier in theory than in practice. The analogy between hoplite battles and sporting contests can easily be overstressed.[29]

The battle between the Athenians and the Syracusans in 415 BC, as always in hoplite warfare, had been a confused affair of shoving and thrusting, with total reliance on the collective effort, courage, and discipline of the troops, leaving no room for individual heroics of any kind. Men had little idea of what was going on, amid the dust and clamour; if he fell or slipped out of the protective line of his own side, a hoplite was as much at risk of being trampled or crushed by his fellows as by the enemy.[30] Shortly afterwards in the campaign at Syracuse the Athenians attempted a virtually unheard-of tactic in Greek warfare, a night attack on the enemy positions. Commenting on the total confusion which this produced, Thucydides observed that even in day time combatants had scarcely any idea of what was going on in a battle except for the small part which they were themselves engaged in.[31]

Why did hoplite battles take this form? To answer the question we must consider what the Greeks fought about. In almost every case where we have any reliable information, we know that the Greeks fought one another about territory.[32] Until the latter part of the fifth century BC, when the great struggle between Athens and Sparta rewrote the rules not only of Greek warfare but of Greek political life as a whole, almost all Greek wars were fought about areas of agricultural land which lay between the two contending states, as between Chalcis and Eretria over the Lelantine plain or between Sparta and Argos over the plain of Hysiai or the Thyreatis. In other words they tended to be border wars.[33] If land was at stake it was illogical to decide its fate with ambushes in mountain passes or by other devious tactics.

Furthermore, except at Sparta where the presence of the helot labour force enabled the élite body of Spartiatai to concentrate on military training, the contestants themselves were not a specialist warrior class but precisely the owners of this land, the peasant farmers who constituted overwhelmingly the most important part of the population of any Greek city. Their fierce attachment to their family plots of land, the basis both of their livelihood and of their citizen status, was the factor which determined their part in the hoplite battle.[34] The point has been well made that the physical as well as the mental qualities of a farmer were the ones that made for the best hoplite. Hesiod's description of a good ploughman in his *Works and Days*, a vigorous, well-fed fellow of forty years, who could drive a straight furrow and was not to be distracted by his companions like his younger fellows, evokes the hoplite as well as the farm labourer.[35] Soldiers were not always, or typically, young men, but men in the prime of life, even approaching old age, like Socrates, the sturdy tent companion of the young Alcibiades when Athenian hoplites met their greatest test at the battle of Delium against the Thebans in 424 BC, or the old man of the Spartan poet Tyrtaeus' description: 'It is shameful when an old soldier lies fallen in the front rank before the young men; his head is white already and his beard is grey as he breathes out his great heart in the dust, holding his bloody genitals in his dear hands.'[36]

The description of hoplite armour has already shown that the main emphasis in the conflict was on defence and protection. Methods of attack were crude and unsophisticated, relying, quite literally, on the weight of numbers and, of course, on disciplined courage. The emphasis on defence is also clear in the wider context of Greek warfare. Hoplite armour was heavy and cumbersome; Greek means of transport were primitive and slow. Although a warrior was in most cases accompanied to the battlefield by non-combatant helpers, slaves or dependants to carry his armour and provisions, it was deeply impractical to travel far to a battle. Long distance expeditions were impossible without very elaborate organization.[37] When the rules of hoplite battle became increasingly outmoded during the Peloponnesian war of 431–404 BC and Greece flared up for the first time into total warfare, fighting abroad was rarely, if ever, conducted by regular hoplites. Athens relied on her navy for the most part, but we should also note that the plans of her innovative general Demosthenes for land campaigning in northern Greece relied on the ingenious and, as it eventually turned out, over-elaborate utilization of light-armed troops supplied by her allies.[38] When Demosthenes' counterpart Brasidas led the

Spartans out of their laager in the dark days after their defeat at Pylos and took an expedition against the Athenian colonies of the Chalcidice and against Amphipolis, his force was made up of helots who had been promised their freedom, former slaves, not the regular Spartan phalanx.[39]

Not only were such expeditions hard to mount, but they placed the advantage in battle firmly with the defending force, which had no need to expend resources and critical physical energy in getting to a distant battlefield, but could concentrate on the simple matter of defending their own land, on a site of their own choosing. They also could draw on superior psychological motivation. Defending one's own territory was at the heart of Greek warfare. This was universally recognised as the strongest incentive to fight. At the battle of Mantinea in 418 BC, the greatest hoplite battle known to Thucydides and the one most fully described in any ancient source, the critical positions at the right of the formations, where the line was most likely to disintegrate, were taken not by the main contestants, Argos and Sparta, but on the Argive side by the men of Mantinea, defending their own territory, and on the Spartan side by the Tegeans, who stood to gain part of this territory if they were victorious. When the dead were retrieved under the usual armistice it was clear that the majority of the defeated Argives had got away while many of the Mantineans, fighting for their own country, their *patris*, were dead on the battlefield. The ones with most to lose could be expected to fight most doggedly.[40]

The psychology of battle is revealed even more clearly by another example. When the Spartan king Archidamus led his troops into Attica at the outbreak of the Peloponnesian war, he advanced to the plain of Acharnae, in full view of the city walls, and ravaged it in the confident expectation that the Athenians would give battle. He could not believe that the enemy would stand idly by while their fields and farms were occupied. In the city Pericles was barely able to hold his hoplites back, above all the Acharnians themselves who were the backbone of the city's hoplite force, from abandoning the long-agreed strategy of remaining within the city walls and allowing the territory of Attica to be plundered.[41]

Logistics and motivation, therefore, ensured that hoplite warfare rarely allowed long-distance expeditions and heavily favoured defending forces. This had a critical long-term effect on the history of classical Greece. It ensured to a large extent the territorial integrity of the Greek city states. Although the Greek cities were constantly feuding (although less often actually at war with one another), it was very unusual for one to be able to assert lasting domination over another, to the extent of occupying its territory and subordinating its population to any significant degree. Where a major settlement managed to assert permanent domination over a weaker neighbour, as Argos did over the old Mycenaean stronghold of Mycenae or Athens over Eleusis, the territorial gain belongs to the period before the development of hoplite warfare. The point is most tellingly illustrated by the experience of Sparta, which conquered its western neighbour Messenia in the 8th century BC, at a period before hoplite battle had been introduced to the Greek world. In order to cling on to this territorial gain for the next three centuries Sparta was obliged to adopt an extraordinary form of military and political organization, involving the enslavement of the conquered Messenians and the militarization of her own citizens, whose overriding purpose was to maintain secure control over her new land. Sparta, therefore, of all the Greek states had the most fearsome military reputation, based on a large army, which was virtually professionally trained and organized. Yet the limits of even Sparta's power were almost as tightly confined as those of her weaker neighbours. For when around the middle of the sixth century BC the Spartans attempted to conquer and annex the territory of their far less powerful northern neighbours, the Tegeans, the attempt ended in disaster. The Delphic oracle had predicted that if Sparta attacked Tegea men would dance in chains on the plain (about which the battle had, of course, been fought). The chains were worn by Spartan captives not by enslaved Tegeans, and Sparta never again attempted to occupy the territory of one of her neighbours.[42]

In trying to understand ancient Greek warfare it has been hard to resist the comparison between the hoplite battle and modern team sports, but it is important to appreciate that this approach only takes us a small part of the way to understanding the motivation of hoplite warriors fighting for their cities. A fuller understanding of Greek battle involves a closer look at the Greek state and at Greek culture as a whole. Hoplite warfare indeed played a critical part in creating the political framework within which the Greeks lived their lives.

Greek warriors fought for their cities in defence of their most valuable resource, their land. They could only do so if they banded together and fought not for themselves but for the community. The ideal they shared to achieve this was patriotism, love of and commitment to their native city. This is abundantly clear from the earliest Greek poet whose works refer unequivocally to hoplite fighting, the

Spartan Tyrtaeus, writing in the second half of the seventh century BC. The surviving fragments of his verse are concerned with the suffering and sacrifice of war, with the courage demanded of a warrior, and with the need to stand together for the common good:

> You know the destructive work of Ares, god of sorrow, you have experienced all the fury of painful war. Young men, you have belonged both to the pursued and to the pursuers, and have had your fill of both. Those who dare, standing by one another, to join in the hand-to-hand fighting in the front line lose fewer men and protect the people behind. When men flinch, the courage of all perishes.[43]

Courage in the common cause was the essence of success:

> This is courage, this is the finest possession of men, the noblest prize that a young man can win. This is the common good for the city and for all the people, when a man stands firm and remains unmoved in the front rank and forgets all thought of disgraceful flight, steeling his spirit and heart to endure, and with words encourages the man standing beside him. This is the man good in war.[44]

It is important to appreciate that these lines were written by a man who was not only a poet but a general, who had led Spartan troops during the immense struggle of the enslaved Messenians to free themselves in the mid 7th century BC.[45] Moreover, two items of antiquarian information, preserved by later authors, indicate the probable context in which the poems were performed, precisely on the eve of battle in the army's encampment, in front of the tent of the king and commander-in-chief of the Spartan army. This was evidently the occasion for which the lines had been composed, and their performance became a Spartan martial tradition.[46] The emphasis was not only on solidarity, for tactical reasons, but explicitly on patriotism, fighting not for oneself but for one's country. Since the warrior fought for the common good, his death earned himself honour from the whole city:

> Young and old alike weep for him, and the whole city is filled with sad longing, and a tomb, his children famed among men, his childrens' children and his family survive him. Never does his noble fame or his name perish. But though he is under the earth he becomes immortal, whoever excelling, standing firm, and fighting for his land and children is killed by mighty Ares.[47]

There were no medals for the Greek soldier, only this consolation of posthumous fame, the same consolation as Pericles offered the dead in his famous funeral speech delivered in Athens at the end of the first year of the Peloponnesian War. For the patriotic motivation of the soldier revealed by Tyrtaeus, when hoplite warfare had been recently introduced to Greece, remained the same until the end of the fifth century BC.

The spirit of Tyrtaeus's lines was echoed by virtually every Greek commander, addressing his men before battle. There is no clearer instance than the speech of Pagondas, the Theban general, to his Boeotian troops facing the Athenians at the battle of Delium in 424. Men should fight for their city to protect their land:

> When one is being attacked and has to think about the safety of one's country, one cannot go in for calculations about what is prudent... It is your tradition to fight against a foreign army of invasion, whether it is in your country or anywhere near it. Much more should we do so in the case of the Athenians, who share a common frontier with us. In all relations with one's neighbours freedom is the result of being able to hold one's own... We should realize that while others fight battles with their neighbours for one frontier or another, in our case, if we are conquered there will be no more frontier disputes, because there will be only one frontier for the whole country. They will just come and take what we have by force... We always make it a point of honour to fight for the freedom of our country and never unjustly to enslave the country of others, and from us they will not get away without having to fight for it.[48]

Defence of a city's land here is linked to the wider theme of defence of a city's freedom. Success was only possible if men suppressed the mutual rivalries and jealousies, which were endemic in Greek society, and functioned as a community. It happens that the works of the two poets at the beginning of Greek literature, Homer and Hesiod, emphasize the world of the individual acting for himself. In the *Iliad* Achilles in his tent, refusing to join battle on the Greek side because he has been insulted by his commander; in the *Works and Days* the self-sufficient Boeotian peasant, defending the interests of his household at all costs, and avoiding all contact with the wealthy class of the city, whose only purpose was to exploit him.[49] It is hard to imagine Hesiod's peasant being prepared to join with them and fight for his city, but that is what he was to do all over Greece within a generation or two of Hesiod's time. When hostilities threatened from outside the community, local jealousies and mistrust were suppressed by the necessity of defending one's land and one's freedom by collective action.

This was the period when the small village communities of Greece were growing up to form fledgling cities, the forerunners of the classical Greek states. Villages banded together for mutual support; they built walls to protect themselves. The inter-communal violence of a previous generation, cattle-raiding and piracy, gave way imperceptibly to organized warfare.[50] Individuals no longer fought for themselves but for the community which embodied their interests. Here lies the birth of patriotism which was the central motivation for hoplite warfare. No human experience unites a community more closely than sharing the risk of war. The hoplite battles of early Greece may have played a larger part than any other single factor in shaping its city states, providing them with their sense of nationhood and common identity.

Before the middle of the fifth century BC and the hegemonic clash between Athens and Sparta the wars of archaic and classical Greece were not imperialistic but ultimately defensive. They served to maintain the status quo of communities, just as good farming practice and hard work enabled individuals to maintain the status quo of their households. The moral world of early Greece helped to reinforce Greek attitudes to warfare. The peasant sense of limited good told them that anything to be gained from war could only be at the expense of someone else, and that gains today might be offset by losses in the future. Greek religious morality drummed home the message that a man or a state which aspired too high or took too much would be punished by the gods. It was not only the Greek way of life but the Greek way of thinking which put a brake on military ambitions; and it is no surprise that the Greek states evolved the strict rules of combat which constrained and even ritualized their battles. Max Weber characterized the ancient Greeks as a *kriegerisches Volk*, a warlike people. This judgement is misleading.[51] Certainly the Greek cities were well prepared for the wars which they were constantly fighting, but as long as the pattern of the hoplite battle remained intact, the potential gains from warfare remained strictly limited. War was kept in its place; it was a necessary institution if a community was to defend its land and its freedom, but it served no other important purpose and did not spill over to dictate other aspects of Greek life. The hoplite battle remained the way in which modest agricultural communities worked out their rivalries and settled their border disputes.

It was not until the emergence of great power rivalry and the imperialist aspirations of Athens during the fifth century BC that warfare began to break out from these traditional bounds, a process which the contemporary Thucydides observed and analysed with a chilling and timeless clarity. His history charted the birth and development of a new kind of warfare, without limits and without rules, the warfare we know from the Somme and from Stalingrad, from Vietnam and from Bosnia. Victor Hanson has argued that the concepts which underlie all modern European war can be traced back in origin to the hoplite battlefields of Greece. This ambitious claim seems to be one of the few misjudgements of a splendid study. The Greeks of the archaic and classical period kept war in its place; the culture of their classical cities owed not a little to this. The contemporary world has sadly learnt most of its lessons not from the frontier struggles and territorial defence of archaic Greek states but from the implacable rivalries of the great powers Athens and Sparta during the Peloponnesian war, which announced the end of the age of the hoplite battle and the beginning of a new phase in European warfare.

Notes

I am grateful to Anton Powell for his comments on a draft of this paper.

1 V.D. Hanson, *The Western Way of War: Infantry Battle in Classical Greece* (New York, 1989). The study was directly inspired by John Keegan, *The Face of Battle*. Hanson's important edited volume, *Hoplites. The Classical Greek Battle Experience* (henceforward *Hoplites*) (London, 1991), is dedicated to Keegan 'for *The Face of Battle*', and the debt is made clear in the preface p. xvi.

2 H. van Wees, *Status Warriors. War, Violence and Society in Homer and History*. Dutch Monographs on Ancient History and Archaeology 9 (Amsterdam, 1992).

3 A.M. Snodgrass, *Early Greek Armour and Weapons* (Edinburgh, 1964); see also *Arms and Armour of the Greeks* (London, 1967). See the consequent studies of Snodgrass himself, 'The Hoplite Reform and History', *JHS* 85 (1965), 110–22; P. Cartledge, 'Hoplites and Heroes', *JHS* 97 (1977), 11–23; J. Salmon, 'Political Hoplites', *JHS* 97 (1977), 87–122; A. J. Holladay, 'Hoplites and Heresies', *JHS* 102 (1982), 94–104; P. Krentz, 'The Nature of the Hoplite Battle', *Classical Antiquity* 4 (1985), 50–61.

4 W.K. Pritchett, *Ancient Greek Military Practices* (later retitled as *The Greek State at War*) I (Berkeley, 1971), *The Greek State at War* II (1974), III (1979), IV (1985), V (1991) (henceforward Pritchett I–V).

5 *Hoplites*, with contributions by Hanson himself, J.K. Anderson, Pamela Vaughn, J. Lazenby, P. Krentz, Everett Wheeler, Josiah Ober, Michael Jameson, and A.H. Jackson. G. Shipley and J.W. Rich, *War and Society in the Greek World* and *War and Society in the Roman World* (both 1993).

6 For war as central to the agenda of Homer and the historians, see W.R. Connor, 'Early Greek Warfare as Symbolic Expression', *Past and Present* 119 (1988) (henceforward Connor), 3–29 at 4–7, citing E.A. Havelock, 'War as a Way of Life in Classical Greece', in E. Gareau (ed.), *Classical Views and the Modern World* (Ottawa, 1972), 19–78. For Thucydides see P.A. Brunt, 'Introduction to Thucydides', *Studies in Greek History and Thought* (Oxford, 1993),

137–80, at 156–9.

7 Hanson, *Hoplites*, 68–71 (queried by J. Lazenby, *JHS* 112 (1992), 204); J.K. Anderson, *Hoplites*, 15–37.

8 Snodgrass, *JHS* 85 (1965), 110–13; *Arms and Armour of the Greeks*, 49–57; Cartledge, *JHS* 97 (1977), 12–15.

9 Lazenby, *Hoplites*, 92–3.

10 Snodgrass, *Early Greek Armour and Weapons*, 20–31.

11 Snodgrass, *Early Greek Armour and Weapons*, 189–212 on the varied origins of the material and technology needed to make hoplite armour; *Arms and Armour of the Greeks*, 51 on the skill needed for forging helmets.

12 A.H. Jackson, *Hoplites*, 235. Note the use of the cock with raised comb as a shield emblem, depicted on the Corinthian aryballos illustrated by Salmon, *JHS* 97 (1977), 88 fig. 3.

13 *Iliad* VI, 466–70.

14 Spears: Anderson, *Hoplites*, 18–24; spear-butts: Hanson, *Hoplites*, 71–74.

15 Hanson, *Hoplites*, 74–78.

16 Pritchett IV, 7–33; H. van Wees, 'The Homeric Way of War: the Iliad and the Hoplite Phalanx I', *Greece and Rome* 41 (1994), 1–18 .

17 H.L. Lorimer, 'The Hoplite Phalanx', *ABSA* 42 (1947), 76–138.

18 Snodgrass, *Early Greek Armour and Weapons*, 189–204; *JHS* 85 (1965), 110–22; Hanson, *Hoplites*, 65; *contra* Cartledge, *JHS* 97 (1977), 18–24.

19 Cartledge, *JHS* 97 (1977), 18; Salmon, *JHS* 97 (1977), 85–92. There is sporadic evidence that states helped to provide armour or weapons, and this may have been regular at Sparta, but this was not generally the case. See Pritchett I, 3–4 n. 3; Cartledge, *JHS* 97 (1977), 27.

20 Herodotus VII. 9 (Penguin translation). For casualty figures see P. Krentz, *GRBS* 26 (1985), 13–21. According to his statistics the losers of hoplite conflicts might have had battle losses of between 5 and 25 % (average 14 %); the figures for the winners are between 2 and 10 % (average 5%). Such casualty rates would have been seriously damaging if hoplite battles were a regular, even an annual occurrence, but Connor 3–8 and 21–2 rightly contests the widely held view that the Greek states engaged in 'continuous warfare'.

21 For the 'rules of war' (*ta nomima*) see Connor, 19–24. The contrast between Greek and Roman and oriental depictions of warfare has been stressed by P. Zanker in a recent unpublished lecture, 'Der Feind im Kopf: Krieg und Barbaren in der Kunst der Kaiserzeit'.

22 Thucydides VI. 66–67. M.H. Hansen, 'The Battle Exhortation in Ancient Historiography. Fact or Fiction', *Historia* 42 (1993), 161–80, sums up his article with the reasonable point that 'the battle exhortation takes the form of a full speech in historiography and newsletters, but wherever more reliable information is available, it takes the form either of a few apophthegms that could be shouted by the general as he traversed the line or of a speech made to the officers only who passed it on to the soldiers.' On the other hand there is no evidence that the relatively elaborate speeches recorded by historians misrepresented the substance of the message that generals addressed to their troops.

23 Thucydides VI. 68, anticipating the disaster described in VII. 72–87.

24 Thucydides VI. 69. For the *sphagia* see Pritchett I, 109–15 with earlier bibliography; Connor, 13; and especially Jameson, *Hoplites*, 197–227.

25 Thucydides VI. 69. 3.

26 Thucydides VI. 70–1.

27 Trophies: Pritchett II, 246–75; collection of the dead: Pritchett II, 156–76, esp. 173–6.

28 Polybius XIII. 3. 2–6 trans. Shuckburgh. Cited by Connor, 19 who refers also to Strabo X. 1. 12, 448, the ban on missiles in the Lelantine War.

29 Herodotus I. 82. The ritualization of Greek warfare is usefully highlighted, but perhaps overstated by Connor, 22–24.

30 Pritchett IV, 1–93, 'The Pitched Battle', esp. 54–73.

31 Thucydides VII. 44. 1–2.

32 G.EM. de Ste Croix, *The Origins of the Peloponnesian War* (London 1972), 218–20.

33 Even in the context of the Peloponnesian War this was often a paramount consideration, as is shown, for example, by the speech of the Boeotian Pagondas during the Delium campaign, Thucydides IV. 92, cited below on p. 100.

34 V.D. Hanson, *Warfare and Agriculture in Classical Greece* (1983). L. Foxhall, 'Fighting and Farming in Ancient Greece', in J. Rich and G. Shipley (eds), *War and Society in the Greek World* (London, 1993), 134–45 argues that the private concerns of farmers for the security of their scattered land holdings undermined their commitment to the collective security of the polis. This seems incoherent, since they will have known that the defence of their land was only possible through collective action.

35 Hesiod, *Works and Days*, 441–7.

36 Alcibiades and Socrates: see Daniel Ogden in this volume; Tyrtaeus fr. 10, 19–25 (West).

37 J. Ober, *Hoplites*, 173–96, esp. 174–9; J.K. Anderson, *Military Theory and Practice in the Age of Xenophon* (Berkeley, 1970), 43–66.

38 Thucydides III. 94–95; IV. 76–77; and the whole account of the campaign in North West Greece.

39 Thucydides IV. 80–81 shows that Brasidas had only 700 hoplites; the bulk of his force was made up from helots who had been promised their freedom and mercenaries, although other Peloponnesian states (IV. 70) and the Boeotians (IV. 72) helped him with hoplites when their own immediate territorial interests were at stake .

40 Thucydides V. 66–73.

41 Thucydides II. 20–2.

42 Herodotus I. 66. For Spartan military organization see J. F. Lazenby, *The Spartan Army* (Warminster, 1985).

43 Tyrtaeus fr. 11, 7–14 (West). For these passages see especially O. Murray, *Early Greece* (London, 1980), 128–31.

44 Tyrtaeus fr. 12, 13–20 (West).

45 Strabo VIII. 4. 10, 362; E. Schwartz, 'Tyrtaeos', *Hermes* 34 (1899), 428–68.

46 E.L. Bowie, 'Miles Ludens? The Problem of Martial Exhortation in Early Greek Elegy', in O. Murray (ed.), *Sympotika. A Symposium on the* Symposion (Oxford, 1990), 220–9.

47 Tyrtaeus fr. 12, 27–34 (West).

48 Thucydides IV. 92.

49 P. Millet, 'The World of Hesiod', *PCPhS.* 30 (1984), 84–115.

50 Y. Garlan, *War in Ancient Society* (London, 1966). T.R. Rihll, 'War, slavery and settlement in early Greece' in Shipley and Rich, *War and Society in the Greek World* (1993), 77–107.

51 See Connor, 3–8, and, from a different perspective, R. Sallares, *The Ecology of the Ancient Greek World* (London, 1991), 160–63.

3

HOMOSEXUALITY AND WARFARE
IN ANCIENT GREECE

Daniel Ogden[1]

The Ministry of Defence sacks up to one hundred men and women
each year from British armed forces for homosexuality, which is
deemed 'incompatible with military service'. The cost to the taxpayer,
both in terms of the loss of experienced personnel and in terms of the
detailed investigations into and surveillance of the private lives of
suspected individuals, is estimated to be between ten and twenty million pounds a year (see the article by Edmund Hall in *The Independent*,
Saturday 11 March, 1995, p. 15, and his forthcoming *We Can't Even
March Straight* [London, 1995]). The Ministry's attitude would have
astounded the folk of the many historical societies that have considered the army the social home of homosexuality, and developed ideologies that associated it with the structuring of the fighting force and
the promotion of valour: the Celts,[2] the Vikings, the Templars,[3] the
Zulus,[4] the Hitler Youth[5] and the pirates of the Spanish Main[6] are
among the more obvious examples of such societies. And indeed such
customs and beliefs can still be found in a number of societies in Papua
New Guinea (see appendix). We shall see that at least some of the
Greeks also entertained similar ideas.[7] It is the purpose of this paper to
assess the character, extent and role of homosexuality in Greek armies,
to examine the ways in which the Greeks conceptualised homosexuality in the context of battle, and to consider how conducive was homosexuality, as constructed by the Greeks, to the making of efficient
warfare.[8]

Warfare, pederasty and the other Greek homosexuality
In his famous *History of Education in Antiquity*, first published in French
in 1948, Marrou attempted to explain Greek homosexuality as deriv-
ing from 'the comradeship of warriors', and built up his case with
series of historical and ethnographic parallels from societies similar to

those listed above.[9] More recent scholars tend to refer fleetingly to Marrou's idea, and dismiss it.[10] Two reasons might be advanced for this dismissal – one proper, the other improper.

The proper reason is that it is now recognised as at best naïve and at worst dangerous to seek the 'cause' of homosexuality in any context, whether historical, sociological, psychological or biological, since attempts to do so almost inevitably present it as an *aberration* from or *failure* of heterosexuality (which is taken as a given and without cause). Such attempts therefore, whether intentionally or otherwise, licence the marginalisation and oppression of homosexuality. For this and other reasons recent writing on Greek homosexuality does not seek its *cause*, but seeks rather to elucidate the ways in which the Greeks *constructed* it, that is, to understand the modes and contexts of its practice and the meanings attributed to them.[11] Indeed Halperin considers the concept of 'homosexuality' itself as a construct of the last century and not an appropriate tool for the investigation of any part of ancient Greek sexuality.[12]

The second, and improper, reason for the relative lack of attention given to Marrou's thesis is that it apparently requires the widespread existence of a mode of homosexuality among the Greeks that is almost totally excluded from the currently received model of Greek homosexuality: the received model is pederasty,[13] and the excluded mode is sex between two adult males. The received model, largely constructed from Athenian evidence (some of which we shall see later) might be summarised as follows:

> Sex between males in Greece almost always consisted of an *erastēs* (lover), a young man, ideally a bachelor, courting a beardless adolescent boy, the *erōmenos* (beloved)[14] between the ages of 12 and 18,[15] and, if successful, consummating his desire by sodomy.[16] As the boy turned to manhood in the period between the ages of 18 and 20 (the period of life associated with the *ephēbeia*), he would himself cease to be a passive partner, and himself in turn pursue other boys, and then later on, by around the age of thirty, give up homosexuality altogether in favour of marriage.[17] The *erastēs'* role was one of dominance, the *erōmenos'* one of subjection (see below for further discussion of this particular point). As a result, the pursued boy was in a morally precarious situation, but he retained his honour so long as he was extremely discriminating in his acceptance of a lover, took extravagant gifts for his favours,[18] but money on no account, and did not enjoy being sodomised. The lover would use his dominant position to give the boy valuable help – material or ethical – in becoming a full adult member of the community (this particular aspect of Greek pederasty encourages many scholars to derive it from an 'initiation rite').[19] It is the educative aspects of pederasty that led Plato to

dwell so much upon it in the *Symposium*. In the Greeks' view, only an extremely deviant grown man would put himself in the role of the *erōmenos*, and those who did, whether as prostitutes, as Timarchus was alleged to have been,[20] or as men who simply enjoyed and actually sought to be sodomised, '*kinaidoi*',[21] were conceptualised as effeminate and utterly reviled; and at Athens the former group was deprived of citizenship.

It can be seen at once that this model militates against the acceptance of widespread and institutionalised homosexuality in Greek armies, since Greek armies were normally made up entirely of grown men (aged 20+; indeed fitness to be taken into the army might be said to have been the basic criterion of manhood); all soldiers therefore ought to have been either only heterosexually interested (if over 30) or (if under 30) potential *erastai*, and there ought not to have been any *erōmenoi* available,[22] apart, I suppose, from the few that dared risk the 'life of the *kinaidos*'.[23]

Inadequacies of the pederasty model

Nonetheless Greek homosexuality in a military context is worth pursuing, in defiance of the pederasty model, not only because comparative evidence from other societies obliges us to suspect its existence, but because there is firm evidence that there was indeed institutionalised military homosexuality in some Greek states at least (as we shall see later on). And, furthermore, there is reason for doubting the integrity of the pederasty model in itself, particularly in regard to its hierarchical differentiations and age-boundaries.

Firstly, much iconographical evidence has been collated recently for homosexual relationships between adolescent age-peers (and indeed the vases of one, admittedly idiosyncratic, painter, the 'Affecter', actually portray bearded *erōmenoi*).[24] Some scholars do grudgingly concede the possibility of the existence of adolescent peer homosexuality within the Spartan schooling system.[25] On the basis of what criteria were the roles of *erastēs* and *erōmenos* assigned within such relationships? Perhaps such roles simply were not assigned. Adolescent relationships disturb the pederasty model's requirement of hierarchical differentiation between the members of the couple, but not necessarily its age-boundaries, if we assume that such couples belonged to the transitional phase of 18–20 years.

But there is nonetheless plenty to indicate the inadequacy of the model's age-boundaries. Aeschines makes it clear that grown men of any age are potentially interested *erastai*: he talks of himself (in his

early forties) as such, and mentions men older than himself still interested in boys.[26] Sophocles is known to have courted boys at 55 and 65.[27]
Lysias speaks of his love for Theodotus when aged over 50.[28]

Erastēs-erōmenos relationships that endure well past the boyhood of
the *erōmenos* are attested. Agathon is the *erōmenos* of Pausanias at 18 in
Plato's *Protagoras*,[29] and is still such in his *Symposium*, which has a
dramatic date twelve years later (416), and it is also known that
Pausanias went on to follow Agathon to Macedon at some point after
411;[30] the adult and bearded Agathon was also the *erōmenos* of
Euripides until the former was 40 and the latter 72.[31] If the historical
indications of Plato's references to the relationship between Socrates
and Alcibiades are taken literally, the two had a relationship for at least
twenty years, beginning when the *erōmenos* Alcibiades was well past 15,
and hence going on until he was well past 30.[32] Athenaeus tells that the
Stoics maintained that one should keep an *erōmenos* until he was 28.[33]
And the *relative* age relationship of the traditional model is violated by
the couple mentioned in Xenophon's *Anabasis*, where the *erastēs* is a
beardless youth, Aristippus, and his *erōmenos* bearded.[34]

Nor does marriage clearly operate as a watershed: quite apart from
all the old married *erastai* just mentioned, Xenophon in his *Symposium*
portrays a just-married *erastēs* pursuing an *erōmenos*.[35] Even granted
that Greek male sexuality was structured in a radically different fashion to our own (in that all young men – at least of certain classes – were
presumed to have and apparently did have a significant interest in
boys as well as women), it is difficult to accept that their sexuality
underwent a sea-change at a certain time of life; those socialised to
pederasty before 30 must have retained some homosexual interest
after 30. (However the Sambian material reviewed in the appendix
does provide a possible model for such a change, and one that would
accommodate our new bridegroom and his *erōmenos*.)

Therefore all members of Greek armies were potential '*erastai*', and
undoubtedly many of them were potential '*erōmenoi*' also. And in any
case, modern scholars often work with excessively rigid ideas about the
exclusivity and differentiatedness of 'active' and 'passive' sexual roles
within even truly pederastic relationships: who is to know the secrets
of the boudoir?[36] It is very hard to imagine, given this background,
that there was no significant institutionalised homosexuality in Greek
armies in the field, where women will have been hard to come by.
Evidence for hosts of female camp-followers in the trains of Greek
armies is rather scant: the big exception is Alexander's *anabasis*;[37] less
can be made, for instance, of Theopompus' description of the de-

bauched Chares taking around with him flute-girls, dancing girls and 'foot-prostitutes' (*pezai hetairai*) in 343/2.[38] Indeed the Greeks themselves clearly believed that soldiers sodomised each other on campaign. An important fragment of the Athenian comic playwright Eubulus, to which we shall return, tells of the Greek army during the siege of Troy:

> Nor did any of them see a courtesan (*hetairan*), but they kneaded (*edephon*, i.e. masturbated) themselves for ten years. Bitter was the military service they saw, who, having taken but one city, went away far wider-arsed (*eurypröktoteroi* – i.e., more thoroughly buggered) than the city which they took at that time.   Eubulus F118 K-A[39]

The pederastic model (which is, for the most part, legitimately constructed from the Greek evidence) represents an ideal of Greek homosexuality that in no way accounts for the entirety of the practice. 'Military' homosexuality has impinged relatively little on the consciousnesses of modern scholars partly because it impinged relatively little on the consciousness of the Greeks themselves; we shall investigate the reasons for this below.

Modern scholarship's tendency to identify Greek homosexuality with pederasty may, paradoxically, stem from a desire to 'neutralise' it. Pederasty may seem initially more threatening, since the phenomenon in our own culture which most closely, albeit quite misleadingly, translates it is paedophilia (a point that particularly exercises Buffière);[40] but pederasty, particularly when explained with reference to initiation, has the advantage of belonging to the distant and morally unevaluable realm of the anthropological, and so tends to remove the practices of the ancient Greeks far from the threat of the banal inter-adult homosexuality of our own culture.

Let us turn to the evidence for institutionalised homosexuality in the context of warfare in ancient Greece. I shall present the evidence out of chronological order, for the sake of greater clarity.

Classical Thebes and elsewhere
Thebes (Boeotia)
The most detailed account of institutionalised military homosexuality at Thebes in the fourth century is provided by Plutarch in a text that is worth quoting at some length, because it introduces many important ideas that we will meet in other contexts:[41]

> 18. Gorgidas first founded the Sacred Band (*hieros lochos*), as they say, from three hundred picked men [possibly in around 378].[42] The city provided them with their daily bread and gave opportunity to

111

exercise. They encamped on the Cadmeia [the acropolis]. Because of this they were called the Band from the City, for the men of those days properly used to call acropolises 'cities' (*poleis*). Some say that this unit was formed from *erastai* and *erōmenoi*. A joking remark of Pammenes is recorded:[43] he said that Homer's Nestor did not understand tactics when he bade the Greeks to be ordered by tribes and phratries, 'So that phratry may help phratries, and tribes tribes,'[44] and that instead he ought to have drawn up *erastēs* beside *erōmenos*. For tribesmen did not take much account of other tribesmen nor phratrymen of other phratrymen in times of danger, but a band that was fitted together (*synērmosmenon*) by sexual love was indissoluble and unbreakable, since they stood firm in the face of danger on account of each other, the *erastai* out of love for their *erōmenoi*, and the *erōmenoi* out of shame before their *erastai*. This is not surprising, since men feel more shame towards their partners when absent than towards other people that are actually present. So it was that an *erastēs* begged and besought the enemy that was about to slaughter him as he lay on the ground to put the sword through his breast, 'So that,' as he said, 'my *erōmenos* may not see me with a wound in my back and be ashamed of me.'[45] It is said that Iolaus participated in Heracles' labours and fought by his side (*paraspizein*) as his *erōmenos*, and Aristotle[46] says that still in his time *erōmenoi* and *erastai* exchanged their pledges at the tomb of Iolaus.[47] So it was reasonable that the band should have been called 'sacred', because Plato termed the *erastēs* a friend 'inspired by god.'[48] It is said that the band continued unbeaten until the battle at Chaeronea. And when Philip was looking over the dead after the battle, he stopped at that place at which it happened that the Three Hundred had fallen, in their armour, after having met, every one of them, the sarisas head on, all mixed up with one another. It is said that he was amazed by the sight, and, on discovering that this was the band of the *erastai* and the *erōmenoi*, wept and said 'May those that suppose that these men do or suffer something shameful perish!'[49]

19. More generally, it was not, as the poets say, the passion of Laius [for Chrysippus][50] that made a beginning of the customs concerning *erastai* for the Thebans, but the lawgivers, who wished to relax and soften their naturally undilutedly hot-tempered ways from earliest boyhood, involved the flute (*aulos*) in their work and play in a major way, bringing the instrument to a position of respect and precedence, and they reared love to be splendid in the palaestras, and thus diluted the tempers of the young men.[51] In view of this they were right to establish in their city with them the goddess that is said to have been born of Ares and Aphrodite, since, wherever a battleworthy and warlike nature is associated with one that is persuasive and graceful, all are brought to a most melodious and orderly civil life – through Harmony. Anyway Gorgidas at first divided up and distributed this Sacred Band along the front rank of the whole phalanx of the hoplites, but by doing that he did not allow the valour of the men to distinguish itself, and the band was

not able to use its power for a common end, since the power was all broken up and mixed up in a large body of inferior soldiers. But then Pelopidas, when their valour shone out at Tegyra, where they fought alone and unmixed around him, did not continue to divide them up and distribute them, but using them as a single body put them in the forefront of the most dangerous battles. For just as horses run more quickly when harnessed to a chariot than they do on their own, not because they force the air out of the way by throwing themselves at it more heavily, but because the competition and rivalry with each fires their spirit, so he thought that brave men were more helpful and eager in pursuit of a common end when inspiring in each other the desire to do glorious deeds.[52]   Plutarch *Pelopidas* 18-9

The culture described here is encapsulated in a dedicatory Boeotian epigram by Phaedimus, for a certain Melistion (written in the mid third century):

> ... Apollo...your wolf-slaying quiver is of no use to you in redirecting the arrows that Love sends against the Bachelors, whenever they defend their fatherland, made bold by the love of lads. Love has the strength of fire [?], and is the chief of the gods in helping those that fight in the forward line...   Phaedimus *Palatine Anthology* 13.22[53]

A number of observations may be made. Firstly, and most importantly, Plutarch's passage clearly attests the extreme institutionalisation of homosexual relationships between adult males in the Theban army, and the positive value attached to them. Such relationships are specifically argued to enhance the efficiency and abilities of the fighting force as a whole (marshalling by sex-partner being held superior even to the organisational advice of Nestor).[54]

Because the relationships within the army are inevitably between adults, they cannot be in the normal sense pederastic. Nonetheless, Plutarch does actually use the vocabulary of pederasty of them ('*erastai*', '*erōmenoi*' etc.), and associates them with pederasty both in his reference to education from 'earliest boyhood', possibly in his reference to the gymnasium[55] (in Athens and Sparta at any rate a locus for pederasty: see below), and in his reference to the love of Laius for Chrysippus. Pederasty is indeed attested at Thebes by other sources: Pindar speaks of pederasty there in the fifth century;[56] Xenophon says that in Boeotia men and boys form unions and live together;[57] and the love of Pammenes for Philip of Macedon, who was aged between 14 and 18 during his sojourn at Thebes,[58] would have been pederastic. Presumably then, if pederasty was to have anything at all to do with homosexuality in the Theban army, the loving partners in the army were of unequal age and initially came together when the younger was still a boy (*pais*), though he will have matured to manhood by the time of his inclusion in the army. This is consonant with Plutarch's statement elsewhere that at Thebes it was the custom of the *erastēs* to present his *erōmenos* with a suit of armour upon his official coming of age.[59] The lover therefore seems to bring the *erōmenos* into the army under his own wing. Perhaps the elder continued to sodomise the younger, and perhaps the master-pupil relationship was preserved. Such relationships could perhaps be termed 'post-pederastic'. That homosexual relations were altogether less morally circumscribed at Thebes than at Athens is the message of Plato, when he scornfully tells us that since the Boeotians have no art of speaking, they ordain that it is fine and not all disgraceful to gratify an *erastēs*, in order to save themselves the trouble of having to persuade their *erōmenoi*.[60] But we must bear in mind that Plutarch may be drawing upon Athenian sources that have to some extent recast Theban military homosexuality between men who are more or less peers into an Athenian pederastic mould; his account of the lovers' exchange of vows at the tomb of Iolaus perhaps implies that the relationship between the men was more symmetrical.

There may in fact have been a significant precursor to the Sacred Band. Diodorus mentions another élite Theban force of 300 in 424, who were known as 'charioteers and chariot-fighters' (*hēniochoi kai parabatai*).[61] Diodorus tells that they acted as the front rank the length of the army, so their role was precisely the initial one attributed to the Sacred Band by Plutarch. The names applied to this older élite force are terms from Homer, where they describe pairs that work together in chariots, the one man steering, and the other using his spear (the term I have translated as 'chariot-fighter', for want of anything better, *para[i]batēs*, literally means 'one that goes beside'). This élite band was, like the Sacred one, a band of footsoldiers, and so these terms are applied metaphorically.[62] It is difficult to resist the conclusion that the metaphor of chariot-pairs is applied to actual sexual pairs of *erastai* and *erōmenoi*. It is not clear which of the terms was supposed to describe the *erastēs* and which the *erōmenos*, or indeed whether the metaphor was pressed so far. One might think that 'chariot-driver', literally 'reins-holder', denoted the *erastēs*, since horsemanship was a fertile source of sexual metaphor for the Greeks, as for us, and as such usually described the active role.[63] Furthermore, the term 'the one that goes beside' (*parabates*) strongly resembles the technical term for the *erōmenos* of the Cretan warrior, 'the one that is stood beside' (*parastatheis*).[64] And note Plutarch's description of Iolaus, the *erōmenos*

114

of Heracles, in the passage quoted above as 'fighting beside' (*paraspizein*) his *erōmenos*. On the other hand, it seems likely that in Homer it was the *parabatēs*, the man doing the actual work of the warrior, that was, in military terms at any rate, the dominant member of the pair, since the *Iliad* gives us a pair of half-brothers, sons of Priam, acting as chariot-fighters, the legitimate brother Antiphus as *parabatēs*, and the bastard brother Isus as *hēniochos*.[65] At any rate Dover is perhaps wrong (in his attempts to date Plato's *Symposium*) to build so heavily on the assumption that 'until 378 nothing had been done to justify dissemination of a belief that any Theban or Boeotian force was deliberately organised on an erotic principle.'[66]

It is noteworthy that the Sacred Band seems, from what Plutarch says, to have lived permanently in a separate mess (akin to the Spartan *syssitia*), apart from women, in war and peace alike.

It is also noteworthy that Plutarch is a little uneasy with the material he relates here: he introduces it almost as if it is disputed matter ('but according to some accounts...'), even though the very detail into which he goes indicates strongly both that the basic facts at any rate are beyond dispute and that Plutarch himself accepts them to be true.[67] And the utterance of Philip of Macedon is doubtless included to allay any misgivings we may feel about the information provided. We shall consider a possible reason for this diffidence below.

Elis (and Megara?)
Both Xenophon (twice) and Plato mention Elis in the same breath as Boeotia, which it is taken to resemble for holding it in no way shameful to gratify an *erastēs*,[68] and Xenophon also says that it was the practice of the Eleans to place *erastai* and *erōmenoi* side by side in battle line, just like the Thebans.[69] Elsewhere Xenophon refers to Elean élite forces of 300 and 400 in the year 366; perhaps, as with the Sacred Band, it was these groups in particular that were formally organised along homosexual lines.[70] Quite compatibly with this, it is known that the Eleans held beauty competitions for boys, and that the prize was a set of arms, which the winner would immediately dedicate to the warrior-goddess Athene.[71] The bestowal of arms upon the desirable boy suggests, in the light of the Theban material, and the Cretan material (discussed below), that he is henceforth to be incorporated into the army. (Perhaps the boys' kissing competition at Megara was a similar thing.)[72]

Chalcis (Euboean and Thracian) and Pharsalus (and Thessaly in general)
There is a scrap of evidence for what appears to have been a similar

115

kind of military homosexuality in Chalcis on Euboea and Pharsalus in Thessaly – or possibly Chalcis in Thrace. The former Chalcis is separated from Boeotia only by the strait of the Euripus. Plutarch tells that during the Lelantine war the Chalcidians were aided by Cleomachus of Pharsalus, who was accompanied by his *erōmenos*. Cleomachus was much encouraged on learning that his *erōmenos* was going to watch him in battle, and on being kissed by him.[73] Cleomachus gave up his life in the battle, and his bravery led the Chalcidians to institutionalise homosexuality in their army. Plutarch goes on to say that an Aristotle[74] told that the inspired and inspiring *erastēs* was a different man, from Thracian Chalcis (the poet Dionysius identified him as Anton), and quoted this song in proof:

> O boys to whose lot has fallen good grace and good fathers, do not begrudge brave men association with your youthful beauty (*hōra*). For Love (*erōs*), who slackens limbs, thrives beside Courage in the cities of the Chalcidians.[75]

Also, one of the Greeks' many terms for sodomy was 'Chalcidise' (*chalkizein*).[76]

But if it was indeed Cleomachus of Pharsalus, he can be put in context: Plutarch also goes on to tell of another Thessalian, Theron, who, in competition over an *erōmenos* with another *erastēs*, cut off his thumb as a gesture of bravery.[77] Quite apart from the fact that a sword was evidently to hand, this passage seems to relate to homosexuality in a military context because it is situated in a discussion of military homosexuality at Thebes.

Plutarch tells that the Boeotians, Spartans and Cretans are both the most susceptible of the Greeks to (sc. homosexual) love,[78] and the most warlike, again linking homosexuality to military prowess[79] (a further thing that distinguishes these three in particular is that in them the élite of the warriors at least lived sexually segregated lives).[80] We turn now to the two states that Plutarch compares with the Boeotians in this way.

Crete

The main evidence for homosexuality in Crete consists of a fragment of Ephorus (quoted by Strabo), a text of great importance for the Greek schematisation of homosexuality as initiatory.[81] Ephorus tells how the Cretans take their *erōmenoi* by capture (*harpagē*)[82] rather than persuasion (perhaps like the Thebans, who had not the art to persuade?). The *erastēs* enlists the help of the boy's friends, and sets up an ambush in advance. If the friends think the *erastēs* is worthy, they help him catch the *erōmenos* (the Cretan term is *parastatheis*, 'stander-be-side'). The caught boy is taken to the men's house (*andreion*: akin to the Spartan *syssitia* and the Theban *Cadmeia*).[83] The *erastēs* then gives the boy presents and takes him off into the country, together with the friends that helped in the capture, where they hunt together and are feasted by him for two months (the hunt was an important locus of homosexuality).[84] The boy is then released back to the city and given statutory presents: a military cloak, an ox for sacrifice and a drinking cup. While feasting on the ox, the boy recounts his adventures, and declares whether or not he is pleased with his *erastēs*. The law allows him this privilege, we are told, in order that, if he has been taken against his will, he may be avenged on his *erastēs* and be rid of him. It is disgraceful for handsome or well-born youths to fail to acquire an *erastēs*.[85]

This is a key text for the pederasty model, but it does in fact imply that *erastēs* and *erōmenos* would normally continue their relationship together in the army. It is true that the process does initiate the boy (and his friends) into manhood, and is therefore at least in part 'pederastic': he is introduced to the man's house of his *erastēs*, given a cup to use for the drinking parties in it, and a military cloak that symbolises and surely entails his inclusion in the army.[86] But it also is clear from the fact that the boy is given the opportunity to rid himself of a bad *erastēs* after the country sojourn that the relationship between *erastēs* and *erōmenos* normally continued beyond the latter's inclusion in the army. There is no specific evidence about the usual or (if applicable) statutory age limits for *erastēs* and *erōmenos* in Crete.[87] The probability that couples did exist in the same units (which were perhaps based on *andreia*), and did fight side by side, is suggested by the information of Athenaeus that the Cretans sacrificed to Eros before going into battle;[88] the Spartans did the same (see below), and, as we saw, members of the Theban Sacred Band exchanged their vows at the tomb of Iolaus.[89] Buffière thinks that the perceived function of the kidnap rite was to inculcate (by insemination) warrior-courage into the boy (as at Sparta: see below and appendix).[90] It is interesting that although it is the implication of Ephorus and Strabo that homosexual relationships continued between adult members of the army, they fall short of making the point explicitly; we shall consider some possible reasons for this below.

Sparta

The entire Lycurgan system, and the hard physical training regime of *agōgē* in particular, in which Spartan male citizens were reared and lived (at least until 30), segregated from the womenfolk, was conceived to be a training for warfare. Consequently, homosexual practices within it were almost inevitably likewise conceived in terms of their efficacy in the creation of warriors.[91] In Plato's *Laws* the Athenian tells the Spartan that it is his gymnasia that undermined the old and natural law (of heterosexuality).[92]

Plutarch tells that when boys in their training 'herds' (*agelai*) had turned twelve, they became subject to the interest of 'respectable young men' (*erastai tōn eudokimōn*) and 'older men too' (*presbyteroi*), even more so, and particularly in the gymnasium.[93] This again indicates no upper limit on the age of potential *erastai* in Sparta. Elsewhere in the *Lycurgus* Plutarch indicates the existence of adult warrior *erōmenoi*: at 25.1 he tells that men under thirty never went to market but had their household business carried out for them by their kinsmen and their *erastai*. The simple reading of this passage suggests the existence of male adult *erōmenoi*, although it is conceivable that *erastai* only shop for those under eighteen, whilst kinsmen alone do the shopping for those between eighteen and thirty.[94] Xenophon implies that it was normal practice for Spartan loving couples to be drawn up alongside each other in the battle line, by beginning a hypothesis about Spartan *erōmenoi*, 'even when (*kan*) *not* stationed in the same line with their *erastai*...'[95] Also, Athenaeus tells that before battle the Spartans sacrificed to Eros on the ground that safety resided in the love of those drawn up alongside each other.[96] This similarly suggests that loving couples were posted side by side in the battle lines as at Thebes. A specific example of a loving couple fighting side by side in a Spartan army is to be found in Anaxibius and his *erōmenos*: Xenophon tells that when the Spartan leader Anaxibius sought death in battle, his *erōmenos* stayed with him to the end.[97] Another adult *erōmenos* may in fact be identifiable: Cleonymus, son of Sphodrias, was the *erōmenos*, after his completion of *agōgē*, of Agesilaus's son Archidamus.[98] Some scholars have speculated, also outside the pederasty model, on the existence of homosexual relationships between adolescent peers within their military or training units at Sparta, and the possible bonding or loyalty-enhancing effects of these.[99]

It seems likely that there were other ways in which the Spartans considered homosexuality to be conducive to effectiveness in battle. Bethe hypothesised that the Spartans considered that the semen injected during sodomy transmitted the *erastēs*'s military prowess to the *erōmenos*.[100] The hypothesis, based upon an interpretation of some obscure Spartan homosexual technical terms, and fleshed out with anthropological parallels from New Guinea, is an important one, and has been followed by many scholars, including Cartledge. It is discussed in detail in the appendix.

There may be a homoerotic undercurrent in a fragment of the archaic Spartan poet Tyrtaeus (F10.27–30 West) which praises the death of a beautiful young man on the battlefield, 'desirable for women, admirable for men.'[101] And similarly in the tale of Isadas, who astonished Epaminondas and his Thebans when they attacked Sparta by fighting against them in the streets, nude, oiled and beautiful.[102]

Other evidence testifies to the high value placed upon homosexual relationships at Sparta. Aelian tells that a fine *kaloskagathos* who did not act as *erastēs* to a boy was fined by the ephors.[103] Plutarch also says that *erastai* shared the standing of their *erōmenoi*, with the result that an *erastēs* was once punished for a cowardly cry his beloved had let out during a fight;[104] this demonstrates the importance attributed to the lover in the education of the boy. And *erastai* who found themselves in competition for the same boy, he tells us, worked together to educate the beloved;[105] however, this seems a highly implausible thing in agonistic Sparta[106] (we shall return to this problem below). Cartledge believes that the masculine forms of female nudes from Sparta are the product of a male homosexual aesthetic.[107]

We saw in the case of Crete that the time of the 'ritual marginalisation' of the youth in transition, his relegation to the countryside and the life of the hunter, was also an occasion for his sodomisation (perhaps partly because he had to play the extreme opposite role of a woman in order to define better his transition to manhood). Spartan youths also underwent a period of ritual marginalisation to the countryside and the life of the hunter in the *krypteia*, and perhaps homosexuality was practiced there (again it was viewed as a preparation for warfare). However, no texts explicitly attest homosexuality in the *krypteia*.[108]

Again it is interesting that the evidence does indeed imply the existence of homosexual relationships within the army, but the sources fall short of asserting this explicitly. Nonetheless, despite Cartledge's assertion that 'Pederasty never became the basis of the Spartan military organisation,'[109] the Spartans do seem to have thought that homosexuality did them some military good.

Macedon

As Plutarch's comparison of Thebes, Crete and Sparta suggested, these three states form a natural group in regard to the evidence for military homosexuality. This may be more because the three were associated together in the Greek tradition of constitutional analysis than because they did in fact have more in common with each other than with other Greek states. Whatever the case, we move on now to consider three other Greek military homosexualities for which the evidence is a little less neat, beginning with Macedon.

Theopompus humorously attests a high level of homosexual behaviour between the (necessarily) adult members of the Royal Companions:

> Some of them used to shave themselves and keep making their bodies smooth, even when they were men, and others dared to permit others to sodomise them, despite having beards. They took round with them two or three catamites (*hetaireuomenous*), while themselves providing the same services to others. Therefore, one might justly refer to them not as 'companions' (*hetairoi*), but as '[female] prostitutes' (*hetairai*), and not soldiers but common whores (*chamaitypoi*: literally 'earth-pounders'). For although they were by nature man-slayers (*androphonoi*), they behaved like man-whores (*andropornoi*).
>
> Theopompus FGH 115 F225a (= Polybius 8.9.9–12)[110]

However Theopompus delighted in ridiculing the Macedonians (notice the opportunistic wordplay here), and his assertions may not be taken at face value.

A safer example of institutionalised homosexuality in Macedon is that of the Royal Pages (*basilikoi paides*).[111] The Royal Pages were established as we know them by Philip, although a similar but perhaps less formal institution seems to have existed under earlier kings at least as far back as Archelaus.[112] These were boys, sons of the nobles and companions, who served the king at table and guarded him as he slept;[113] they were treated and beaten as slaves by the king.[114] Griffith guesses that they were aged between around 14 and 18, and that there would have been about 85 at any one time, at least under Alexander.[115] The institution certainly socialised the sons of the great to respect for the king, though it may also have had the darker function of hostageship against those in a position to threaten the king's authority.[116] It would be from amongst these that the king was likely to draw his *erōmenoi*[117] (they also assisted the king in other sexual matters: it was their job to escort his concubines to him).[118] A connection therefore between pederasty and preparation for warfare is implied by Curtius's observation that the institution was 'a kind of school for generals and commanders'.[119]

Hammond notes that all attempts on the lives of Philip and Alexander came from among the Royal Pages, or former Royal Pages.[120] We may add that all the attempts seem to have had some homosexual affair turned sour in their background: the 'school' was clearly one of intense sexual passions and jealousies.

Diodorus tells how Philip was assassinated by one of his bodyguards, Pausanias, who had been his *erōmenos*.[121] When the king turned his attention to another Pausanias, the first abused the second as an androgyne, who in grief let himself be killed in defence of Philip in a battle against the Illyrians. Attalus, friend of the dead Pausanias, in revenge got the first Pausanias drunk, and gave his inebriated body over to the pleasure of his muleteers. Pausanias appealed to Philip, who needed Attalus too badly to punish him, and so merely compensated Pausanias with promotion. Pausanias's resentment simmered until he assassinated the king.[122]

The most famous episode involving the Pages was their conspiracy against Alexander. Arrian explains that the Page Hermolaus had killed a boar on the hunt before Alexander had the chance to strike it (NB the homoerotic context of hunting), and Alexander had him whipped before the other Pages, and took his horse from him. Hermolaus then got up a conspiracy to murder Alexander among the Pages, with the prime help of his *erastēs*, another Page, Sostratus.[123] Alexander's crime was *hybris*: almost akin to a sexual humiliation.

Possibly the killers of Archelaus (*c.* 399) were drawn from a group of boys around the king that foreshadowed the Pages. Crateuas and Hellenocrates of Larissa had been the *erōmenoi* of Archelaus, but both felt themselves the victims of *hybris* rather than love because they had seen their concession of favours to Archelaus as part of a bargain upon which the king reneged: he had promised the one a daughter for bride, and the other a dispatch home.[124] He had also given a third boy Decamnichus to Euripides to be beaten, for abusing the poet's bad breath.[125] A similar thing may have occurred a few years later when Amyntas the Little was reputedly killed by Derdas (another proto-Royal Page?), since Amyntas had taunted Derdas with his youthfulness.[126]

There is clear evidence of peer-homosexuality among the Royal Pages (which Berve considers a phenomenon of military comradeship):[127] the Page Sostratus, the *erastēs* of the Page Hermolaus, is said to have been the same age as him.[128] And the Page Charicles was the *erastēs* of the Page Epimenes.[129]

Some homosexual *rite de passage* may underlie the tale that Alexander I murdered some ill-mannered Persian envoys by dressing up beardless youths as women to assassinate them.[130]

Both Philip and Alexander are known to have had a number of male partners. Philip himself had been the *erōmenos* of the Theban Pammenes whilst a hostage in his house;[131] if one *were* to suggest that Philip invented the institution of the Pages, then it was perhaps because of the Theban example that he encouraged homosexual relations between them (and cf. again Plutarch's report of Philip's approval of the homosexuality of the dead Thebans at Chaeronea). We have also seen that he loved the two Pausaniases. Justin tells that Alexander of Epirus, brother of Philip's wife Olympias, was another *erōmenos* of Philip.[132]

Alexander's homosexual preference was famous in antiquity.[133] Athenaeus (possibly quoting either Hieronymus of Rhodes or Theophrastus) tells that Philip and Olympias put the beautiful Thessalian courtesan Callixeina to live with him, fearing that he might prove to be womanish (*gynnis*),[134] and elsewhere tells that he was 'madly obsessed with boys' (*philopais ekmanōs*).[135] Alexander's most famous homosexual affair was that with Hephaestion,[136] whom he ultimately made his chiliarch. The relationship was between age-peers, for they were brought up together.[137] Aelian tells that when Alexander made his pilgrimage to Troy, he garlanded the tomb of Achilles, whilst Hephaestion garlanded that of Patroclus, allowing it to be understood that he was the *erōmenos* of Alexander, as Patroclus had been that of Achilles.[138] Alexander continued the analogy after the death of Hephaestion by an extravagant show of mourning for him, similar to that of Achilles for Patroclus.[139] Alexander gave other clear indications of his affection: he claimed to value Hephaestion as much as his own life,[140] and that Hephaestion was himself Alexander too (in response to Sigambris' mistaken identification).[141] Hammond apparently believes that a clique, in part bound together by homosexuality, formed itself around Alexander when he was himself a Page of his father, and that this clique consisted of many of the men that came to power after Alexander's accession – Hephaestion, Ptolemy, Nearchus, Erigyius, Laomedon and Harpalus.[142] Curtius refers briefly to another homosexual liaison of Alexander's with a young man (*iuvenis*) usually known as Excipinus, who had the look of Hephaestion.[143] Perhaps Alexander's most distinctive homosexual affair was with the eunuch Bagoas;[144] however, Alexander's adventures with him, despite Bagoas's appointment to a trierarchy,[145] are not really relevant to the sort of *military* homosexuality we are discussing here.[146]

Virtually all our evidence for homosexuality in the Macedonian army has focused on the Pages, veterans from the school of Pages, and the historical forerunners of the Pages. It has also focused around the person of the king. This may be simply due to the fact that our sources for obvious reasons focus on the court and its élite. But it may also be that it was particularly among the group of élite trainee warriors around the king that homosexuality was promoted as part of a military ethic. That many of the rank and file could turn to heterosexual comfort on campaign is evidenced by the existence of a host of campfollowers that attended Alexander's *anabasis*.[147]

There is little evidence for homosexuality in hellenistic armies. Launey draws attention to the (humorously alleged) slave-catamite of the soldier-master at Plautus' *Pseudolus* (though this can hardly portray military homosexuality proper), and to the graffito 'Amatokos is beautiful' (*Amatokos kalos*), inscribed by a hellenistic soldier on the Memnonion at Abydos.[148] Perhaps the decline in military homosexuality in the hellenistic period should be related to the apparent rise in the tolerance of campfollowers (see above).

Homer's Achilles and Patroclus

It was a controversy among the ancients and continues to be among modern scholars whether or not Achilles and Patroclus are sexual partners in the *Iliad*.[149] Although they are not explicitly so described, a number of the details of their representation imply that they are; and in particular, it is Achilles's love for Patroclus (and his desire to avenge his death), that finally brings him back to the battle after all else, including magnificent gifts, has failed.[150] Before proceeding further with the issue, we should bear in mind that the *Iliad* is the product of many minds, many epochs and indeed many sexualities and moralities, and the representation of the relationship between Achilles and Patroclus is bound to some extent to be a compromise between all of these. We may suggest, by way of example, two possible ways in which representation of the relationship as we have it developed:
1. An 'original' full homosexual relationship, first represented in the Mycenean age, where such things may have been a banal fact of military life, is inherited by more prudish dark age singers, who tone down the descriptions of the relationship to a point where it is at least arguably compatible with being merely strongly homosocial;[151]
2. An 'original' Mycenean homosocial relationship is recast by a dark age which assimilates the relationship to the sort of homosexual relationship with which it is now familiar.

There are of course many complex variants available between and even beyond these two models. My own view is that there is at least one homosexual strand in the representation of the relationship, and that this therefore attests homosexuality in a military context in or before the dark age.

So to the evidence: the case for the representation of the relationship between Achilles and Patroclus as homosexual has been made most emphatically by Clarke.[152] He draws attention to three passages in particular. Firstly Achilles expresses the extreme wish that all the Trojans and Greeks should perish alike, and that only he and Patroclus should be left to take the city.[153] Secondly he is shown weeping in his desire for the 'manliness and goodly might of Patroclus' (*potheōn androtēta te kai menos eu*).[154] Thirdly Achilles's mother addresses her grieving son and tries to encourage him to forget his cares by eating, sleeping and having sex with a woman;[155] the encouraging phrase she uses (*agathon de gynaiki per en philotēti misgesthai*) must be translated along the lines of: 'it is a good thing to copulate in love *even* with a woman,' or 'it is a good thing to copulate in love – at any rate with a woman'[156] (commentators tend to deny this interpretation on the basis of a bogus philological claim).[157] Either way, it is implied that Achilles has recently been copulating with a man (though clearly he also has a woman – Briseis – in his past). Further evidence for the physicality of the relationship may be drawn from the fact that Achilles lay in the arms of the dead Patroclus,[158] and indeed the *Odyssey* adds that the bones of Achilles were later buried mingled in a coffer with those of Patroclus, while those of Antilochus, his favourite after the death of Patroclus, were buried separately nearby.[159] A number of other passages also show Patroclus doing services for Achilles that are elsewhere typically done by a wife for her husband,[160] and it is particularly noteworthy that Patroclus, in sending Achilles back to war after his wrath, fulfils the same function as Meleager's wife in the tale told by Phoenix.[161] (Other myths of Achilles may associate him more indirectly with homosexuality, most notably the myth that he was brought up on Scyrus dressed as a girl, which may reflect a rite of passage towards adult manhood, but which has also been seen as a reflection of a homosexual initiation rite.)[162]

Ancient sources and modern scholars that deny the homosexuality of the relationship between Achilles and Patroclus point to the fact that it does not fit into the expected pederastic model: Patroclus is the elder – though lower born – of the two,[163] yet Achilles is clearly the dominant partner,[164] and indeed Patroclus is often referred to as the servant (*therapōn*) of Achilles.[165] Hence, for example, Xenophon's representation of the relationship as merely a strong friendship between men, and Sergent's approval of this view.[166] But of course the relationship does not even begin to fit the pederasty model proper because it is between two adult warriors. We have already seen that the pederasty model does not describe all Greek homosexuality, and is particularly problematic in the context of war. We should simply accept that the sexual relationship between Achilles and Patroclus is an unhierarchised one between men who are to all intents and purposes peers: it is 'military' homosexuality.

The Hadrianic Straton of Sardis took the relationship between Achilles and Patroclus to be the archetype of homosexual relations within Greek armies:

> You're going off as a soldier...and you're just a boy still white and soft. Think about what you're doing, and change your mind. Oh! Gods! Who inspired you to take up the spear and take a shield in your hand? Who told you to hide this head inside a helmet? Well blessed is this new Achilles, whoever he be, that's going to enjoy such a Patroclus in his tent!
>
> *Palatine Anthology* 12.217

There is possibly a further example of homosexuality between peers in Homer: Pisistratus sleeps beside Telemachus in the *Odyssey*.[167] But both are clearly adult and approximately equal in age and status: Telemachus has significantly reached adulthood in making the decision to strike out in search for his father, whilst Pisistratus is still unmarried, but already a 'leader of warriors'. And again, because these indications sit uncomfortably with the pederasty model, scholars have pointlessly disputed which of the two is the elder and the *erastēs*.[168]

At any rate it seems that the Homeric evidence probably does acknowledge military homosexuality, but is reticent about it, as we have seen other sources to be.

Athens

Military homosexuality in theory and practice

Although we have a great deal of evidence for Athenian warfare, although most of our evidence for homosexuality in general comes from Athens, and although in fact much of the evidence quoted above for military homosexuality in other places was filtered through Athens at some stage in its life, there is little that can be considered direct evidence for military homosexuality at Athens.[169] This is not to say that it did not exist, and indeed we will assemble some indications that it did. But the inexplicitness of our sources on the matter is something that will also require explanation.

To begin with, it is worth recalling the fragment of the Athenian (middle) comic playwright Eubulus (quoted above), that assumes that armies in the field turn to sodomy for sexual gratification.[170] And we perhaps see a hint of homosexual comradeship at arms in a fragment of Sophocles's *Niobe*, in which one of her sons calls out for aid to his *erastēs*, as he is being shot and is about to die.[171]

The nearest we come to the purposeful exploitation of homosexuality in a military unit among Athenian armies is an intriguing reference in Xenophon's *Anabasis*.[172] Xenophon relates how (in the campaign which took place at the beginning of the fourth century) he explained to the Odrysian Seuthes how fond of boys was his soldier, the Olynthian Episthenes,[173] who had just impulsively offered his own life in exchange for that of a beautiful boy that Seuthes was about to execute. Xenophon tells that he had himself once put together a company of soldiers solely on the criterion of beauty (*kaloi*), and that Episthenes had been a brave fighter in the midst of them. Presumably then Episthenes was himself one of the beautiful. Clearly he was inspired to bravery by his attraction to the other beautiful men around him, or perhaps to one of them in particular. At any rate, it seems that Xenophon's purpose in assembling the unit was to exploit homosexuality in the interests of warfare. It is frustrating that Xenophon does not tell us more about his reasons for and methods in assembling the unit, and why he only did it once; perhaps he had Theban practice in mind.

Military homosexuality was later to play an important role in the Socratic school of philosophy. In his *Symposium*, probably published in the late 380s or early 370s,[174] Plato hypothesises that an army composed of loving couples would be invincible:

> If therefore there could be some means for a city or army of *erastai* and *erōmenoi* to come about, there is no way in which they could inhabit their city better than by refraining from all that is shameful by competing with each other for honour. And if such men fought side by side with each other in battle, it is almost true that a few of them could beat all the men in the world. For an *erastēs* would find it less acceptable to be seen leaving his post or throwing away his arms by his *erōmenos* than by all the rest, and would choose to die many deaths before this.
>
> Plato *Symposium* 178e–179a[175]

It is difficult to believe that Plato does not have the Theban élite force in mind in writing this; he does indeed go on to mention Boeotian homosexuality a few sentences later,[176] albeit disparagingly and in a rather different context, and Xenophon does indeed make explicit mention of the Theban élite in what might be considered a parallel passage in his *Symposium*.[177] Dover, however, argues hard that Plato's *Symposium* was written *before* the formation of the Sacred Band (which he locates in 378) and therefore in ignorance of it, while Xenophon's was composed subsequently to it[178] (it should be stressed that there is no agreement in general about the priority of the two *Symposia*).[179] But we have seen that there is a strong case for believing that the Theban élite force was homoerotically organised from at least 424, so that it is quite possible that Plato did after all have Thebes in mind, whenever precisely he composed his *Symposium*, and whenever precisely the Theban élite became the 'Sacred Band.' Although he does not make it explicit, Dover's argument, if accepted, surely entails the supposition that the Sacred Band was formed *in response to* the 'hypothesis' raised by Plato's *Symposium*.[180]

Homosexuality encourages valour also in a work of Plato's which is even harder to date – the *Republic* (guesses range from the early 380s to the early 360s); here it is suggested that guardian-knights be rewarded for the display of valour by a kiss from the lads on campaign with them.[181]

Perhaps we also have an example of homosexuality operating in a more mainline (and exclusively Athenian) force. Alcibiades tells, again in Plato's *Symposium*, how he tried to become the *erōmenos* of Socrates; he denies, implausibly, that Socrates sodomised him, but even if we take Plato's Alcibiades at his word, he and Socrates clearly developed a traditional homosexual relationship in all but actual copulation.[182] Alcibiades then recounts their experiences as hoplites[183] on campaign together at Potidaea in 432 (by which time, other Platonic evidence suggests, they had already been partners for three years).[184] They were messmates (*synesitoumen*[185]), which is probably significant in itself. Alcibiades speaks of the fantastic feats of endurance he admiringly observed in Socrates there, and in particular his endurance of cold – he would walk unshod on the ice.[186] But it was the circumstances under which Alcibiades won his prize for valour that best reveal the two as loving partners on the battlefield:

> You should hear about him in battle. It is just that we pay him this due. For when it was the battle as a result of which the generals actually gave me the prize for valour, it was no other man that saved me than this one. He refused to abandon me in my wounded state, and he saved my armour as well as my person. And I, Socrates, at that point bade the generals give you the prize for valour, and I don't think you will find fault with me here or say that I'm lying. But when the generals wanted to give me the prize for valour out of consideration for my social

> standing, you yourself were more insistent than they were that I should
> take the prize rather than you.   Plato *Symposium* 220de

Alcibiades goes on to explain how he stood in wonder of Socrates also at Delium, eight years later.[187]

Socrates had clearly gone out of his way to save his *erōmenos*. The competitive attempts of the pair to have the other considered the braver seem typical of homosexual couples on the battlefield (we shall pursue this point below).

Perhaps we get a feel of the ethos of homosexual hoplite life from the austere work of Thucydides, whose mainly military narrative hardly even mentions women, with such references as there are typically being of a scathing nature.[188] While homosexual love affairs are featured, such as that of Pausanias and his *erōmenos*[189] and that of Harmodius and Aristogiton,[190] there is some reason to think that Thucydides goes out of his way to suppress heterosexual ones, at least two of which were arguably of some significance for the course of the Peloponnesian war, namely that between Pericles and Aspasia[191] and that between Alcibiades and Timaia, the wife of king Agis.[192]

Homosexuality and preparation for war: the gymnasium and ephēbeia

There is some evidence for homosexuality playing an important role in the preparatory stages for warriorhood at Athens. Admittedly, homosexuality in this context does conform much more to the pederasty model.

Firstly, an important association between homosexuality and the preparation for warfare can be found in the culture of the gymnasium, when we consider that the Athenians conceptualised it as a training ground for warfare on the one hand, and the prime site for the enjoyment of homoeroticism and the courting of boys on the other.

A number of ancient sources represent effective warfare as the goal of gymnastic exercise.[193] The Lyceum gymnasium at Athens, built by Pericles, was the place where the soldiers actually drilled before war, and where military reviews were held.[194] Plato says in the *Protagoras* that boys are sent to the gymnastic trainer so that they will not play the coward in war,[195] and in the *Republic* he overrides the distinction between athletics and the training for warfare altogether.[196] Euripides is (as often) being sophistically controversial when he denies the usefulness of athletics as a training for war.[197] (In Sparta those that had won a victor's wreath in the games were stationed in line next to the king in battle.[198]) The most sustained treatment of athletics as a preparation for warfare is that of Philostratus in his *On Gymnastics*.[199] A number of games, dances and exercises were explicitly military in nature: e.g. the *hoplitodromos*, a race in hoplite armour,[200] the Pyrrhic dance, a preparation for drilling, performed in half armour, and the *gymnopaidikē* dance, itself a preparation for the Pyrrhic.[201] Socrates claimed the best dancers made the best soldiers.[202] Delorme argues that the growth in athletics in Greece, marked by the introduction of the great Games, was occasioned by the introduction of hoplite tactics.[203] Some modern writers view Greek athletics as a displacement of warfare.[204]

The homoerotic atmosphere of the gymnasium needs little illustration.[205] It is present already in Theognis: 'Blessed is the man in love that exercises in the gymnasium (*gymnazetai*), and goes home to sleep with a pretty boy all day long.'[206] Plato in general represents the gymnasium as the home of homosexual interest.[207] In the *Euthydemus* the boy Cleinias enters followed by a host of *erastai*, including Ctesippus.[208] In the *Lysis*, Socrates takes an interest in a beautiful boy in the gymnasium.[209] In the *Charmides* Socrates looks for the most beautiful boy in the wrestling school, and sees that Charmides stands out from the rest.[210] In the *Theaetetus* nude boys are spied on in the gymnasium.[211] In the *Symposium* Plato has Alcibiades tell how he attempted (as prospective *erōmenos*) to seduce Socrates by wrestling with him.[212] In Aristophanes's *Clouds* the Better Argument drools over the boys as they do their exercises.[213] In his *Birds* Euelpides hopes to find a place where the father of an attractive boy will upbraid him for not kissing and playing with the testicles of his son as he comes home from the gymnasium.[214] In two parabases Aristophanes denies that he himself revelled around the wrestling schools trying to seduce the boys.[215] Aeschines repeatedly talks of the attraction of the gymnasium for *erastai*.[216]

In the *Laws* Plato brings these ideas together: Sparta and Crete are said to have framed their laws with regard to their military organisation; their common meals and gymnasia in particular are said to promote valour, but in the process these states have become primarily responsible for 'corrupting the pleasures of love' (i.e. instituting homosexuality).[217] And we saw above that Plutarch made the gymnasium the home of Theban military homosexuality.

Secondly, there was a more formal training institution for the Athenian army: the *ephēbeia*.[218] Again there are some reasons for supposing that ephebes were particularly associated with homosexuality.[219] There is little that can be said about the *ephēbeia* that is not disputed, but most would agree that it was, as we know it, an institution reorganised in the later classical period (on the basis of a very similar forbear),[220] in accordance with which young men, who had just been admitted to the deme at eighteen, were dispatched to patrol the borders of Attica under light arms in a lone-hunter and wolf-like fashion for two years (again, the homoeroticism of the hunt).[221] The ephebes were at an oddly transitional stage between boyhood and manhood, as their name implies, and although they were theoretically adult, could not actually exercise their full citizen rights until the period of their service was over (at which point, rather like the 'initiated' Cretan boy, they received their panoply from the state).[222] The roots of the *ephēbeia* in a Greek *rite de passage* are clear: it represents the ritual marginalisation of youths in transition, and parallels the Spartan *krypteia* (wherein the boys were again compared to wolves) and the Cretan hunting expedition[223] (and indeed Athenian ephebes were often conceptualised as hunters).[224]

It is in the mythological prototypes for Athenian ephebes that the homosexual culture of the institution is best revealed: Melanion (the 'Black Hunter') and Hippolytus. Both these characters flee to the rural margins in order to avoid sex with women. Thus Aristophanes tells of Melanion:

> I want to tell you a story which I heard once when I was a child. There once was a young man (*neos*), Melanion, who fled from marriage, and came to the wilderness, and lived in the mountains. And then, weaving nets, he hunted for hares, and he had a dog, and he wouldn't go back home again because of his hatred, so much did that man abominate women, and we, being prudent men, hate them no less than Melanion did.
> Aristophanes *Lysistrata* 781–96

And Euripides says in the *Hippolytus*:

> The son of Theseus, the child of the Amazon [says Aphrodite], Hippolytus, the pupil of holy Pittheus, alone of the citizens of this Troezenian land, says I am the worst of deities, and refuses the bed and does not touch marriage.
> Euripides *Hippolytus* 11–14.[225]

Granted, the eschewing of women is not the simple equivalent of homosexuality, but it encourages the presumption of it. The two men themselves exhibit womanish traits: Melanion is closely associated with Atalanta (whom, surprisingly, he eventually marries), and Hippolytus is very much the son of his Amazon mother. The associations, in turn, between these androgynous women, the Amazons, and ephebes have been recognised: they too live the wild lives of light-armed huntresses on the margins of civilisation, the antitheses of hoplites.[226] It has often

been noticed that the life of the lone wolf which ephebes were supposed to lead was, despite its purpose, in fact rather inappropriate
training for hoplite warfare as it developed, which depended on precise team discipline; indeed Vidal-Naquet argues that it is the significantly symbolic opposite of the hoplite's life – it is rather, as being a
kind of *rite de passage*, a mode of life symmetrically inverted from that
which it precedes and defines.[227] We shall return to this important
observation.

So why, if there was institutionalised homosexuality in the Athenian
hoplite army, are our sources so reticent about it? It is to this problem
we turn in the next section.

Sodomy on the battlefield

There have been two curious reticences in the evidence we have
reviewed. As to the first of these reticences, we have noticed that
although Athens provides us, separately, with the most information on
both homosexuality[228] and Greek warfare, both in an Athenian context
and in a wider Greek one, there is a particular dearth of information
about institutionalised homosexuality in Athenian armies. This may
simply be because there was not any, or at any rate because there was
comparatively little, but I think other answers are preferable. One
reason might be that, whatever homosexual licences were sanctioned
in Athens, homosexuality remained something that fundamentally
belonged to the 'other', with the result that the Athenians felt happier
describing the homosexual customs of others rather than their own, or
indeed tended to ascribe homosexual customs to others in preference
to themselves.[229] But such a theory perhaps sits uneasily with the heavy
discussion of homosexuality among Athenians that we do get in Plato
and other Athenian sources.

As to the second reticence, we have seen that our evidence time and
again indicates that there was institutionalised homosexuality in some
Greek armies, or at any rate some parts of them, but that it often falls
short of explicitly affirming its existence. The sources are in general
much happier discussing military homosexuality at a certain remove,
attributing their assertions to others (as does Plutarch on Thebes),[230]
or at a theoretical level (as does Plato in the *Symposium*),[231] or at what
might be called the training phases of soldiery (as do Ephorus on Crete
and Plutarch on Sparta),[232] than they are discussing it between actual
soldiers in the camp or on the battlefield.

The reason for this second reticence, I would like to suggest, is due
to a conflict between ultimately incompatible conceptual paradigms of

homosexuality (and its ethical significance) among the Greeks. The first paradigm we may call the 'education' model:[233] it is a positive one for the *erōmenos*, and it is the model that the Greeks on the whole felt most comfortable in discussing. According to this model, the *erōmenos* achieves a prize in exchange for being sodomised, or indeed simply by being sodomised: Plato has it in the *Symposium* that the *erōmenos* is educated in virtue; the Spartans had it that the *erōmenos* was imbued with valour (see appendix); the Cretans had it that the *erōmenos* was initiated into the community of men. It will be immediately clear that the mode of homosexual practice that is most easily assimilated to this model is pederasty. Hence, I think, the relative willingness of our sources to discuss pederasty (and the extent to which pederasty has come to dominate modern discussions of Greek homosexuality); in particular, as we have seen, our sources are quite content to discuss homosexuality in the context of the training of the warrior. The education model is also specifically positive for the *erastēs*, because it encourages him to be exemplary and to be the best in the eyes of his *erōmenos*.

The second paradigm may be called the 'subjection' model: this model is a distinctly opprobrious one for the *erōmenos*.[234] The important concept here appears to be that of penetration: to penetrate is to subject, and to be penetrated, to be subjected; the penetrated are to some extent assimilated to women, who can only *be* penetrated and not themselves penetrate (and whose sexual role correspondingly affirms their subject status).[235] A simple example of this way of thinking is provided by Mnesilochus in Aristophanes's *Thesmophoriazusae*: after being insulted by the pomposity of Agathon's slave, he retorts that he is ready to bugger the 'foundations' of slave and poet alike.[236] Subsequently the old man abuses Agathon himself: 'And you, you *katapugōn* ('habitual pathic' [?]), are wide-arsed – not just in words, but in submissiveness.'[237] A more complex example is provided by the punishment meted out to the adulterer, in accordance with which the cuckold, having singed off the adulterer's pubic hair (a thing women do to themselves), inserts a radish or a mullet into the anus of the adulterer (*raphanidōsis*).[238]

Therefore homosexuality on the battlefield constituted a conceptual aporia for the Greeks: the battlefield is precisely an arena of defeat and subjection. In such a context the bad, 'subjection' model of homosexuality must come into play. The Greeks, as we shall see, often conceptualised military defeat in particular in terms of being buggered; indeed vase paintings often identify penetration by penis and penetration by weapon.[239] Consequently, it was difficult for them to rationalise homo-sexuality within an army at the site of and on the point of battle. If an army was sodomising itself on the battlefield, then it was *already* defeated – or at least half of it was: buggery was for the vanquished, not the victors.

A number of passages may be quoted to illustrate the 'subjection' model of homosexuality in a military context. The most obvious passage is the fragment of Eubulus (F118 K–A) quoted above: the Greeks spent ten years defeating Troy, but, the joke is, they came back wider-arsed than the city they took – in other words, it was they themselves that were, paradoxically, the more defeated.[240]

Perhaps the most renowned example of buggery as metaphor for military defeat is the Attic red-figure 'Eurymedon vase', first published by Schauenburg in 1975 (Hamburg, Museum für Kunst und Gewerbe, inv. 1981.173).[241] The pot depicts a man, wearing only a Thracian mantle, running, erect penis guided by hand, towards the proffered bottom of a second. A four-word text stretches between the head of the pursuer and foot of the pursued, of which the meaning is not in doubt, even though the end of the third word is illegible: 'I am Eurymedon. I stand bent over.' The usual interpretation of this picture takes the running figure to be a Greek and the bending figure to be a Persian, and ascribes the text as a whole to the bending figure. Thus the image can be taken to illustrate the Greek military victory over the Persians at Eurymedon by a sexual metaphor: 'We buggered the Persians at Eurymedon.'[242]

In Aristophanes's *Frogs* Dionysus jokes that he recently served as a marine aboard (the) Cleisthenes, and sunk twelve or thirteen of the enemy's ships. The phrase that describes his service, *epebateuon Cleisthenei*, is a *double entendre* which also means 'I buggered Cleisthenes.'[243] So here again the act of sodomising is associated with victory, and by implication, the act of being sodomised with defeat.

Dover persuasively argues that the Athenian comic abusive term *kysolakōn* ('arse-Spartan', used of the laconising Cleinias) is to be explained with reference to the fact that Sparta and Athens were almost constant enemies during the period of Old Comedy.[244] Presumably then the Athenians express their wish to defeat the Spartans in using the term. Perhaps in a similar way Theopompus's assertion that the Macedonians were ever eager to be buggered, quoted above, is an example of a similar wish-subjection of a feared enemy.[245]

The importance of the differentiation for the (Athenian) Greeks between those in the army and the buggered is clearly shown by a famous passage of Aeschines, addressed against Demosthenes and in defence of Philon:

> I am amazed that you should dare to abuse Philon, especially since we are among the most respectable Athenians, who have come here to make a judgement upon what is best for the city, and who pay more attention to our lives that to our rhetoric. For which of the two do you expect that they would pray for – ten thousand hoplites like Philon, with bodies like his and as disciplined in soul as he is, or thirty thousand *kinaidoi* like you?
> Aeschines 2.150-1[246]

The *kinaidos* is an eager pathic, effeminate both because of his habitual role as the penetrated (the only role that women can take on), and because he has lost control over his desires (the state of '*akrasia*', similarly regarded as typical of women: see above). Winkler shows well that by contrast the ideal hoplite-citizen[247] is a staunch defender of household and country:[248] 'The contrast between hoplite and *kinaidos* is a contrast between manly male and womanly male.'[249]

That successful warriorhood is associated with integrity from penetration, and unwarlikeness with being penetrated, is evidenced also by the alternative surviving titles for a lost comedy of Eupolis: *Astrateutoi* and *Androgynoi*: '*Those who have not seen military service*' and '*Men-women*.'[250] At Sparta those who were classed as cowards, *tresantes*, had to shave off half their beards, and so become half man, half woman – precisely *androgynos*.[251] According to Plato in the *Timaeus* cowardly males are in fact reincarnated as women.[252]

If we turn again to the Amazons and some similar mythical warrior women, the equivalence between sexual penetration and military defeat (penetration by a weapon) becomes clear. It was told that Achilles slew the Amazon Penthesilea on the plain of Troy, and on the point of killing her, fell in love with her; indeed the incorrigible Thersites abused Achilles for his love for Penthesilea (accusing him of necrophilia?), and for this was slain himself.[253] It is clear that the moment of defeat, the moment of weapon-penetration, is equated with the moment of (at any rate desired) sexual penetration, and indeed the two are somewhat assimilated in portrayals of the scene, for example, in that by the great black-figure painter Exekias.[254] Tyrrell well makes the point that slaying an Amazon and marrying her are structurally equivalent acts.[255] (Also, Loraux has interestingly argued that the sacrifice of virgins, in which their throats are cut with a knife ['*sphagē*'], is a kind of displacement of marriage, where the 'upper neck' is penetrated in place of the 'lower neck.'[256]) Similarly there was a Spartan myth that served as an aetiology for that state's cult of Armed

134

Aphrodite: the women of Sparta took up armour in order to beat off an ambush by the Messenians, but they then met the Spartan men, who took them to be a Messenian force and attacked them in turn; they preserved themselves by baring their breasts and having sex with their menfolk in the field.[257] Military defeat is deflected at the last minute into its metaphor, sexual defeat. (These myths make it clear that in so far as it is a woman's natural role to be penetrated, so she must always be in the position of vanquished enemy towards man.)

To conclude this section: Greeks found it difficult to think about homosexuality close to the battlefield and between members of the same army because at such a point the paradigm of penetration as military defeat seemed far more relevant than any more positive paradigms of homosexuality.

Homosexuality and the efficiency of the fighting force

Having reviewed the evidence for military homosexuality, and having attempted to account for a partial dearth in evidence for something we have reason to believe did exist, we are now in a position to consider a question consonant with the main theme of this volume: Did homosexuality in Greek armies make them more cohesive, efficient fighting forces? Some scholars have argued that it did, particularly in the cases of Sparta and Crete.[258] But the evidence is far too scant for a definitive answer, and far too many other unquantifiable factors, for which we can not control, obviously contributed importantly to efficiency. But what we can do is investigate some theoretical possibilities, suggested by the Greek evidence itself, for the effects of homosexuality on Greek armies; ultimately then we are not answering the question at a truly sociological level, but merely at the level of what the Greeks themselves believed.

At a superficial level, it is clear, particularly from Plutarch's writings on Thebes and the theoretical assertions of Plato and Xenophon,[259] that the Greeks did believe, in general, that homosexual relations within or around an army improved its efficiency. Leaving aside Sparta's custom of physical valour-insemination, we learn from Plutarch's account of the Theban army that it was precisely the homosexual relationships within the Sacred Band that made it such a superlative force. In this account homosexuality is elevated to the position of tactical principle: posting lovers side by side is joked by Pammenes to be a better tactic even than Nestor's hallowed advice to marshal clan by clan and tribe by tribe; and the soundness of the tactic is vouched for by the approval of the greatest of all tacticians, Philip. And it is further argued that when pairs of lovers are concentrated together in the same unit, the effect of the whole is greater than the effect of the sum of the parts; this effect is seen in terms of an extrapolatable natural principle, comparable to a phenomenon observable in chariot teams.

Loving couples are said by Plutarch to be brave for two reasons: firstly, because they have the highest interest in protecting the body of the one they love; and secondly because they are ashamed to be disgraced by cowardliness before the one they love, and therefore compete with their fellows to appear to be the bravest (Greek agonism again).[260] It is presumably this last factor that is supposed to create the 'booster effect' of concentrating pairs of lovers together in the same unit: competition with other competitive pairs will be fiercer than that between a single loving pair and the non-paired men around them. However, it perhaps appears from Xenophon's tale of Episthenes that a man could be inspired to display bravery not just before one special partner of his own, but also before a wider range of men he found attractive, and perhaps saw as potential partners. There could also be an element of competitiveness between the two members of a loving couple: such we observe in the dispute between Socrates and Alcibiades over the prize for valour at Potidaea.

It is perhaps in Homer above all that homosexuality is seen as a positive force for an army and its prospects: the dreadful war was brought upon the Greeks in the first place by a heterosexual love, that of Paris for Helen; the Greek army is devastated by the withdrawal of its principal champion, Achilles, again for a reason that is at any rate connected with heterosexual love – his loss of the woman Briseis to Agamemnon (itself motivated in turn by Agamemnon's loss of his heterosexual love, Chryseis); the Greeks' fortunes in the battle are only restored when Achilles is inspired by his homosexual love for Patroclus to return to the fray.

But the competitiveness that homosexual love induces is a double-edged thing: it might encourage outstanding feats at an individual level, but only at the cost of group cohesion, for it is often plainly a divisive thing. Homosexual relationships are usually characterised as extremely selfish at the level of the couple: they care about each other but no-one else. The most graphic example of this is Achilles's wish (discussed above), that not only the whole Trojan army should perish, but the whole Greek one too, except for him and his love. When Alcibiades's *erastēs* Socrates was the only one of the Athenian army to come to Alcibiades's aid when he lay wounded, what was the rest of the army doing? Was Socrates breaking rank to help his *erōmenos*? (And might this have been another reason why the generals were unwilling to award the prize for valour to Socrates?) In his Theban material Plutarch apparently thinks that the strong bonding within each pair also operates across the group as a whole, but he is not persuasive: 'a band that was fitted together (*synērmosmenon*) by sexual love was indissoluble and unbreakable, since they stood firm in the face of danger on account of each other, the *erastai* out of love for their *erōmenoi*, and the *erōmenoi* out of shame before their *erastai*.' No account is given of how the 'indissoluble sexual love' between the two men in each loving pair expands to become an indissoluble bond between all the men in the army: Plutarch does not seem to think that all members of the loving couples are like Episthenes. Perhaps in a similar vein, Plutarch talks of the co-operation between competing *erastai* who find themselves in pursuit of the same boy at Sparta; but as Cartledge observes, this is hardly plausible.[261] Even more implausible is Xenophon's assertion that (chaste!) homosexual education at Sparta is so successful at inculcating the virtues of valour and loyalty that the warriors never abandon a companion on the battlefield, whether their *erastēs* or not.[262]

The most extreme example of the selfishness, at the level of the couple, of those inspired by homosexual love is their often-reported desire for self-sacrifice: Plutarch remarks that such men often seek danger beyond need.[263] Thus Achilles is told by Thetis that he will live into old age if he does not slay Hector, but will die himself if he does, but he nonetheless scorns the interest of the Greek army as a whole (that he should live to fight on), and kills Hector to avenge his partner.[264] We recall how Cleomachus of Pharsalus sacrificed himself in battle after a kiss from, and before the gaze of, his *erōmenos*. Xenophon tells that the Spartan leader Anaxibius sought to throw his life away in battle, to make up for his military negligence (this was selfish enough), and that his *erōmenos* stayed by his side to the end.[265]

The wasteful selfishness of self-sacrificing loving pairs is perhaps best illustrated by a Roman source – Virgil's tale of Nisus and Euryalus, a pair of very Greek-seeming Trojans.[266] Here was a pair of lovers that fought side by side in battle.[267] The elder of the two, Nisus, is inspired to undertake the foolhardy mission by his love for the 'boy' Euryalus.[268] Euryalus in turn insists on coming too, inspired by his love for Nisus.[269] When Euryalus is caught by the Rutulians, Nisus compromises his mission by leaping out of hiding and offering his own life in Euryalus's place.[270] Both, of course, are slaughtered. (An indication of Virgil's disapproval of the effect of love on these soldiers may be found in the preceding episode in Book 5,[271] where Nisus is inspired by his love of Euryalus to cheat and trip up Salius in a race so that the boy can win.)[272]

Some further Greek examples away from the battlefield itself are nonetheless relevant. Neanthes of Cyzicus tells that when Cratinus, a beautiful youth, offered himself for sacrifice, his *erastēs* Aristodemus killed himself too.[273] Likewise Cleomenes's *erōmenos* Panteus committed suicide over his body.[274] Again, we remember that Episthenes was prepared to throw his own life away for the sake of a boy he had no more than clapped eyes upon. Aristogiton was prepared to throw his own life away on a point of honour that only directly affected his *erōmenos* Harmodius.[275] The death-wish can also be inspired by passionate jealousy towards one's (erstwhile) partner: hence the Macedonian Pausanias threw his life away in battle in defence of his former *erastēs*, Philip. Dover states that the willingness of loving partners to sacrifice themselves was exploited for military purposes;[276] perhaps so, but these examples show that a loving partner selfishly seeking death could do his side as a whole rather more harm than good.[277]

The potential that intensely proud, jealous homosexual relationships had to undermine an army is best illustrated by the assassination of Philip. Here then was a man, the second Pausanias, driven by passions arising out of a homosexual relationship to commit an act than which none could have been more disastrous for his army as a whole.[278] The homosexually-inspired conspiracy of the Pages against Alexander would have had an even more devastating effect, had it succeeded.

This competitiveness and selfishness of military homosexuality is fundamentally incompatible with the ideal of equality, *homoiotēs*, that underpinned the hoplite army (particularly the Spartan one), an army in which all had to act as equals.[279] This may have been less of an issue for Achilles and his fellows in the midst of the army and in the context of the tactical practices described by Homer. In this volume Hans van Wees has elucidated the individual, showy, competitive nature of Homeric battle tactics, which may indeed have been well served by homosexually driven competitiveness and selfishness. The ideal of *homoiotēs* in a hoplite army would also have been undermined by the *inequality* attributed to *erastēs* and *erōmenos* in homosexual relationships.

It is, I suppose, possible to posit a model of military homosexuality more conducive to unit cohesion: such a model would comprise a more casual, promiscuous, hedonistic practice of homosexuality within the group as a whole, such as that portrayed within the Roman unit in

Derek Jarman's film *Sebastiane*. If there was such a thing in Greek armies, there is little evidence for it; again, perhaps Episthenes in the midst of Xenophon's host of *kaloi* is the nearest we get to this. And even so, if such a practice was to contribute to the military cohesion of the unit, one would expect this to be occasioned by a celebratory pride in a sexuality that differentiated them from other people in general, or the enemy, or even the other units of their own army. However, such a pride would probably depend upon the identification of the individual soldiers as homosexual as opposed to heterosexual, and it is a difficulty that this sort of radical categorisation of individuals by sexuality (whether by themselves or others) seems not to have happened in Greece[280] (perhaps with the exception of the supposed spectacular deviance of the *kinaidos*).

Nonetheless, homosexuality does appear to have been associated in particular with élite parts of the army: the Theban Sacred Band were clearly the élite corps; the Royal Pages of Macedon may not actually have been an élite part of the army, but it was certainly a school for the training of the élite officers; Achilles and Patroclus certainly envisage themselves as the élite of the Greek army. Cartledge has argued also that pederasty was used at Sparta specifically to recruit the politico-military élite[281] (despite the fact that the entire citizen army was in many ways an élite force, Sparta also had within this an inner élite of 300.)[282] Most Greek states had some kind of military élite unit, a standing band of paid and highly trained guards,[283] and perhaps many of these employed homosexuality in their organisation: before the Sacred Band, Thebes had had an élite of 300 in 424;[284] Syracuse had a 600 in 461;[285] Argos had a 1,000 in 421–18;[286] the Arcadian League had its *Eparitoi* between 371–363;[287] Elis had élites of both 300 and 400 between 365–64.[288]

Let me repeat that this last section has only been able to focus upon the beliefs of the Greeks themselves about the efficacy of homosexuality in their armies: it has not claimed to be a sociological or psychological study. If the Greeks themselves entertained positive beliefs about the effects of homosexuality in their armies, this belief may in itself have further boosted morale, but we have seen that they also believed a great many negative things about it, and by the same token, these negative beliefs may well have undermined morale.

Appendix: Sparta and Sambia

Spartan and Cretan homosexual warrior initiation rites have been compared in passing to the customs of peoples in Papua New Guinea

(Melanesia), specifically to those of the Keraki Indians and the Marind-Anim,[289] but to my knowledge the customs of one New Guinea people in particular, the Sambia, have not yet been adduced to the issue in any detail. This society has been documented in an impressive anthropological study by Gilbert H. Herdt.[290] As a structuralist I generally distrust the comparison of institutions between societies, for I believe that an institution in society X is better understood in terms of its relationship to other institutions in society X than in terms of its relationship to ostensibly similar institutions in societies Y and Z. However, the ostensible similarities between Sambian and Spartan initiation rites (for all that the Sambians employ fellatio and not sodomy, as the Keraki Indians and Marind-Anim do) are so striking that they beg to be aired, if only for curiosity's sake. But the Sambian material does in fact raise a number of important issues for the foregoing study. The round-bracketed references in the following account are to Herdt's *Guardians of the flutes* (second ed., NY 1987).

[A] Sambian boys live with their parents until they reach the age range of 7–10. They are then taken away to live in the men's house, and will not set eyes on a woman again until marriage (3, 31). Girls will remain with their parents until marriage (31). [B] The boy then begins to undergo six stages of initiation, of which the first three are before marriage (marriage itself being the fourth), and which are undergone within a group of age-peers (54).

[C] The purpose of life in the men's house and of these initiations is the inculcation of manliness and the production of vigorous warriors, than which nothing is more prized (14, 44). [D] On first being taken into the men's house a boy is thrashed with the branches of prickly bushes until he bleeds. This is to purify his skin of the pollution he has picked up from the menstrual women around him (56, 174, 222–3). [E] The pollution of women's menstruation is particularly threatening, so much so that women must retire to a special hut when menstrual (75, 162, 182). Things female are in general the opposite of vigour (14). Women are not permitted to enter the men's portion of a family house. Women are cold and damp like the earth, with which they are identified as bearers of fruit (79), whereas men are fiery like the sun. It is women's task to grow the crops because of their affinity with plants. Sweet potatoes are the female crop par excellence (78). [F] Cowards are therefore appropriately known as 'sweet potato men' (52).

[G] In order to grow big, strong and courageous, the prepubertal boys must drink semen: it is vital if they are to become men (1, 204–5,

232–3, 236). This they do by fellating the postpubertal boys, puberty occurring around the age of 15 (2, 232). [H] The boys are taught what they must do with the aid of bamboo flutes, objects which take on great ritual significance (85, 233, 383–4). The boys are formally denied heterosexual knowledge (165). The fellatio becomes a way of daily life (234). The relationship of the postpubertal fellated to the prepubertal fellators is one of dominance, and the fellators hold the lowest status in the men's house (2, 53, 242, 288). [I] Age-peers are forbidden to be sex partners (238). As the boy reaches puberty, he has developed a pool of semen inside himself (236), and so he ceases to fellate and becomes in turn fellated by the boys of the age years below him (2). [J] But in giving his semen to help the younger boys grow, he puts his own warrior vigour at risk (233). He must replace his lost semen by drinking the milky sap of the Pandanus tree, which is believed to be the lifeblood of the tree and which resembles both breast milk and semen, and has the nourishing power of both (100, 111, 250). Boys in the men's house deny wasting their semen in masturbation (165). [K] In his years in the men's house a boy is also taught to hunt (85). The penis and the hunting stick are associated, and both called by the term *moyu* (38). The most important prey is the cassowary (whose rump is thought to resemble a woman's), and married men must abstain from sex with their wives whilst hunting it (138, 141, 146). [L] The boys display their warrior vigour by making showy raids upon the enemy (53).

At some point between the ages of 16 and 25 the man will marry an arranged bride, who is just premenarchic (3, 39). Surviving his bride's menarche constitutes the man's fifth stage of initiation (54). [M] The couple do not initially live together: the bride moves into her father-in-law's house, but the groom will continue living with the men, and only pay brief visits to his wife (177, 185). Eventually he will build a house and they will begin a joint life together (29). [N] For about a two-year period the grooms lead a bisexual existence, continuing to receive fellatio from the prepubertal boys (252). Their sexual relationship with their wife begins, as elders recommend, with the fellatio with which they are familiar, and gradually progresses to regular sex (186). Fellatio helps a woman grow strong for childbearing, and, in particular, helps her to develop breast milk (178, 186).

[O] It is a father's semen that creates and nourishes an embryo (38). [P] A man's sixth stage of initiation is the birth of his first child (34). From this point on a man should only have heterosexual sex, and the vast majority of the men lead exclusively heterosexual lives, although a few continue to display a preference for homosexuality (3, cf. 311). [Q] A man's status is transformed again after the birth of his fourth child (54). [R] Some men practice polygyny (29). [S] Women are regarded as wantonly hungry for men's semen to strengthen themselves (150, 188). Men are warned against committing adultery, but also told that if a woman invites them to it, it is unmanly to refuse (112, 167).

[T] Elders, former warriors, carry themselves with great dignity, and are held in great respect (45).

I tabulate the correspondences with Spartan society:

[A] At 7 Spartan boys were removed from their families to go to live in the men's houses (?), the *syssitia* until the age of 30, by which time they will normally have been married. Girls continued to live at home with their parents. (Xenophon *Lac.Pol.* 2–5, Plutarch *Lycurgus* 12, 16 etc.)

[B] The stages of Spartan youth were many and complex and codified to a high degree. A Spartan boy moved up through the *syssitia* system with his age-peers. (Xenophon *Lac.Pol.* 2–5, Plutarch *Lycurgus* 16–7.)

[C] The purpose of the organisation of Spartan society was conceived of as being the production of the best possible warriors. (Xenophon *Lac.Pol.* 9, Plutarch *Lycurgus* 15 etc.)

[D] Spartan youths were whipped in a cheese-stealing ritual at the altar of Artemis Orthia. (Xenophon *Lac.Pol.* 2–5, Plutarch *Lycurgus* 17–8.)

[E] The perception of women as cold and damp and allied to plants, and of men as fiery like the sun, was a general one in Greek society, though it is not specifically attested at Sparta.[291]

[F] Cowards (*tresantes*) were reviled at Sparta and compelled to shave off half their beards, apparently in recognition of their effeminacy. (Xenophon *Lac.Pol.* 9, Plutarch *Lycurgus* 20 and *Agesilaos* 30.)

[G] It is believed that Spartan boys were inseminated, usually by older boys and men, for similar reasons. (See discussion below.)

[H] The Sambian imagery of the flute is striking when we consider that the Spartan technical vocabulary of insemination speaks of 'blowing in.' (See below.)

[I] Despite my arguments that peer homosexuality did exist at Sparta as elsewhere in Greece, many scholars do believe, as we have seen, that homosexual relationships between age peers seldom occurred among any Greek peoples. (See above.)

[J] Anxiety about the waste of semen seems to have informed the various marital crimes at Sparta. (Plutarch *Lysander* 30; see below.)

[K] Hunting was often seen as the locus for homosexuality in ancient Greece. (See above: NB Crete especially.)

[L] We have investigated the links between homosexuality and competitive display in warfare in a range of Greek societies, including Sparta. (See above.)

[M] Spartan married couples began their lives apart, with the bride living in her husband's house, but the husband himself continuing to live in the men's house, and just paying her brief and surreptitious visits. (Xenophon *Lac.Pol.* 1, Plutarch *Lycurgus* 15.)

[N] It has been argued that the dressing of the Spartan bride as a man, may, in addition to marking a symmetrical-inversion *rite de passage* to womanhood for the girl, have helped to ween her husband off homosexuality. (Xenophon *Lac.Pol.* 1, Plutarch *Lycurgus* 15.)[292]

[O] The ideology of childmaking at Sparta implies that the Spartans (as indeed most Greeks) considered that semen alone made children. (Critias DK 88, Xenophon *Lac.Pol.* 1, Plutarch *Lycurgus* 15.)[293]

[P] Childless men at Sparta were ritually humiliated, hence the birth of his first child either positively transformed a man's status or precluded a negative transformation of it. (Xenophon *Lac.Pol.* 9, Plutarch *Lycurgus* 15, *Lysander* 30.7.)

[Q] Spartan men with three children were exempted from military service: their semen had done its work. (Aristotle *Politics* 1270b1–4.)

[R] The Spartans were formally polyandrous, but not polygynous; however, they had an elaborate system of wife-swapping practices. (Xenophon *Lac.Pol.* 1, Polybius 12.6, Plutarch *Lycurgus* 7 and 15; see below.)

[S] Other Greeks used to contemplate the 'licence' of Spartan women. (Aristotle *Politics* 1269b19–23, Plutarch *Lycurgus* 15).

[T] The Spartans were famously reverential of age. (E.g. Xenophon *Lac.Pol.* 5, 9–10, Plutarch *Lycurgus* 20.)

The chief point that I wish to draw from this elaborate Sambian parallel is the absolute interdependence of the warrior ideal, separation from women, and an extreme homosexual lifestyle. This raises the possibility, if no more, that these three factors were similarly interdependent at Sparta. The Sambian material interestingly suggests that a complete transition to heterosexuality is indeed perfectly possible for most individuals, but that a bisexual transitional period of readjustment is needed. Thus it would be theoretically possible to argue that while Greek males were socialised to homosexuality as boys whilst training to be warriors, there was nonetheless not much homosexuality within the actual armies of adult males themselves. My view is, however, that the positive Greek evidence for homosexuality within adult Greek armies is too strong for us to be able to apply such a hypothesis to them very successfully.

Insemination at Sparta

A prime interest of the Sambian material lies in the fact that it raises the possibility that the Spartan terms of homosexuality, *eispnēlas*, 'blower in' (?), *eispnein*, *empnein*, 'blow in', and *aïtas*, a word used to denote the *erōmenos* of which the derivation is obscure, relate similarly to fellatio, and to the metaphor of the flute.

The common understanding, which derives ultimately from Bethe, and which employs the Keraki and Marind-Anim parallels, is that the Spartan term denoting the *erastēs*, *eispnēlas*, read as literally meaning 'blower in', metaphorically describes his anal insemination of the *erōmenos*.[294] Scrutiny of the evidence for these terms, however, which is mainly lexicographical, suggests that the Sambian flute/fellatio metaphor may be more appropriate to the interpretation of this and related terms.

Eispnēl-as/-ēs/-os, eispnilos or ispnil-ēs/-os

It is clear that *eispnēlas* was a Spartan term denoting an *erastēs*. Callimachus tells of a lad (*kouros*) drawing the attention of *eispnēlai*.[295] [Theocritus] speaks of a loving couple, telling that one of them would have been called an *eispnēlos* in the Amyclaean (i.e. Spartan) dialect, and the other an *aïtēs* in the Thessalian.[296] There is no doubt, as we shall see, that *aïtēs* always denoted the *erōmenos*, which means that *eispnēlos* must be a term denoting the *erastēs*. The scholiast to the passage confirms this, as do Choeroboscus commenting on Theodosius, and, at one point, Eustathius commenting on Homer and, at one point, the *Etymologicum magnum*.[297] At other points, however, Eustathius and the *Etymologicum magnum* respectively explain *eispnilos* and *eispnēlēs* with *erōmenos*. This is almost certainly wrong, not least because the *Etymologicum magnum* cites the passage of Callimachus mentioned above to justify this meaning.[298]

But what does *eispnēlas* actually mean? Its derivation is clear enough, if a little odd: it is built on *eispneo*, 'blow in(to)', using the productive adjectival ending -*los*.[299] This does not really give us much of a clue as to whether the *erastēs* thus denoted 'blows in' or 'is blown into.' While it has been generally assumed that he 'blows in', the only ancient evidence explicit on the matter, the scholiast to [Theocritus], is on the other side: he is 'blown into'.[300]

Eispnein, eispneisthai, empnein and empneisthai
Aelian tells us that *eispnein* is an item of Spartan homosexual vocabulary, and the scholiast to [Theocritus] that *empnein* is likewise.[301] The concomitant of the belief that *eispnēlas* means 'blower in' as opposed to 'one that is blown into' is that *empnein* and *eispnein*, 'blowing in', are held to be what the *erastēs* does to the *erōmenos*. Again though, much of the evidence is on the other side: we are told a number of times that 'blowing in' is what the *erōmenos* does to the *erastēs*.[302]

But there is some evidence that takes *eispnein*, 'blowing in', as something that the *erastēs* does to the *erōmenos*: Aelian tells that beautiful boys in Sparta require their *erastai* to *eispnein* them,[303] *Etymologicum magnum* glosses *eispnein* with *eran*, the action of an *erastēs*, and Hesychius and the the scholiast to [Theocritus] likewise gloss *empnein* with *eran*.[304] We should count here also Eustathius's application of the passive form *pneisthai* to the *erōmenos*.[305]

It is not always clear therefore whether, when the form *empneisthai* or *eispneisthai* is applied to *erastai*, it should be read as middle or passive,[306] but the *Etymologicum magnum* does twice use *eispneisthai* in a clearly passive sense.[307] Interestingly, the scholiast to Theocritus speaks of a loving couple 'blowing (*epneusan*) mutual love to each other.'[308]

aïtas, aïtēs, aeitas or aeitēs
The sources are unanimous that *aïtas* etc. is a term describing an *erōmenos*.[309] Although no source actually says it is a Spartan term, and

indeed the passage of [Theocritus] referred to above might even be taken to imply that it is not one,[310] the fact that the feminine equivalent, *aïtis* (on which see below) was used by Alcman strongly suggests that it was indeed a Spartan term.[311] The etymology is obscure. It is apparently understood today to derive from *aïo*, 'hear', and to mean 'listener'; this derivation is, however, only remotely plausible (linguistic difficulties aside) if one accepts an active meaning of the type 'inspirer' for *eispnēlas*, and Chantraine is right to distance himself from this explanation.[312] The ancients derived the term from *aēmi*, 'blow', and understood it to mean 'one that blows in.' If a verb *aïo* is indeed acceptable as the etymology of *aïtas*, it would seem far preferable to relate the term to the homonymous *aïo*, 'breathe out', found once in Homer's *Iliad*, and probably related to *aēmi*.[313]

'Blowing in'

The bulk of this evidence therefore associates the act of 'blowing in' primarily with the *erōmenos*, not the *erastēs*, but the latter can not be separated entirely from active 'blowing in.' What did 'blowing in' mean in each case? In the case of the *erastēs*, one thinks first of the Homeric usage of *empnein*, with *menos* or *tharsos*, 'to inspire with courage';[314] this is, after all, what a good *erastēs* was supposed to do to the *erōmenos* under his charge. But it could equally well mean 'inseminate', particularly since Aristotle equated the action of ejaculation with blowing.[315] In the case of the *erōmenos*, the sources as a whole clearly understand 'blowing in' to mean, 'inspire love in an *erastēs*.' But is there a meaning to correspond to 'inseminate'? It could possibly mean 'give a blow job'. It is particularly interesting here that Antipater uses *empnein* of blowing a flute.[316] It is conceivable, then, that the Sambian parallel is closer to Sparta in this distinctive respect too than at first appears. It is worth recalling also Plutarch's remarks on the development of homosexuality at Thebes, which are prefaced with a seemingly irrelevant sentence upon the introduction of the flute (*aulos*) into all aspects of Theban life.[317] Did the flute occupy a symbolic significance at Thebes similar to that which it occupies among the Sambia?

The Spartans certainly did develop elaborate ideas about the role of sperm – 'noble seed', in Plutarch's phrase – in the begetting of children.[318] They clearly believed that the warrior-vigour of their nation was passed on in their seed; it was therefore imperative that all should pass on their seed: hence childmaking (*teknopoiia*) was a duty,[319] and there were punishments and humiliations for the unmarried.[320] It was also believed that the sperm of two fathers could mingle in the womb and jointly engender a child: hence Zeus and Amphitryon jointly begat Heracles (with Alcmene), Zeus and Tyndareus jointly begat the Dioscuri and Helen and Clytemnestra (with Leda), and Astrabacus and Ariston perhaps jointly begat Demaratus (with Ariston's wife).[321] No doubt both these beliefs underpinned the practice of polyandry at Sparta.[322] It was further believed that sperm gave the father's contingent properties to his child as inherent ones: hence old men were discouraged from marrying,[323] cowards (*tresantes*) could not find wives,[324] and the criterion of porphyrogenesis was used in royal succession.[325]

Aïtis

There was also a feminine version of *aïtas, aïtis*:[326] is this simply a term calqued on the masculine one, for the lesbian equivalent of an *erōmenos*? Plutarch does attest such relationships between women and girls at Sparta.[327] Or is it the term for an (inevitably heterosexually) inseminated maiden? Hagnon of Tarsus tells that unmarried Spartan girls had male lovers who sodomised them.[328] This initially seems incredible. However, the main rational reason for objecting to the existence of such a custom would be the threat that it constituted to legitimacy (i.e., could the lover be trusted not to sire children after all, and did the relationship threaten to alienate the girl's affections from her future husband?), but Xenophon's, Polybius's and Plutarch's information on Spartan marital customs reveals that the Spartans had remarkably little concern for legitimacy as we or most Greeks would have understood it.[329]

Notes

1 This paper has been greatly improved by the comments of Dr James Davidson of Trinity College Oxford, but the views it expresses are not his.

2 Aristotle *Politics* 1269b23, Diodorus 5.32.7 (= Posidonius FGH 87 F116), Strabo C119, Athenaeus 603a, e. There is also homosexuality in Celtic epic narratives, particularly concerning Cu Chulainn: see J. Markale, *Women of the Celts* (London, 1975), 39, translation of *La femme Celte* (Paris, 1972), C.L. Crumley, *Celtic Social Structure: the Generation of Archaeologically Testable Hypotheses from Literary Evidence* (Michigan, 1974), 83–6 (on the sources), M. Chapman, *The Celts: the Construction of a Myth* (London, 1992), 172–3, G. Herm, *The Celts* (London, 1976), 57–8, J. Bremmer, 'An Enigmatic Indo-European Rite: Pederasty', *Arethusa* 13 (1980), 279–98 at 288, 296 nn. 84–7, F. Buffière, *Eros adolescent: la pédérastie dans la Grèce antique* (Paris, 1980), 35–7.

3 Of particular interest here are their homosexual initiation rites, details of which came out at their famous trial (they were known as 'anus-kissers'); see

M. Barber, *The Trial of the Templars* (Cambridge, 1978), 162–6, 178–82, 190–1, 223, and index s.v. 'homosexuality'.

4 An interesting development of which is discussed by T.D. Moodie et al., 'Migrancy and Male Sexuality on the South African Gold Mines', in M.B. Duberman et al. (eds), *Hidden from History: Reclaiming the Gay and Lesbian Past* (London, 1989), 411–25.

5 Buffière op. cit. (n. 2) 17.

6 See B.R. Burg's enchantingly titled *Sodomy and the Pirate Tradition* (New York and London, 1984). Surprisingly, there is no good evidence for homosexuality on board Greek ships. There is the mythical relationship between the Argonauts Heracles and Hylas as portrayed in Theocritus 13 and Apollonius *Argonautica* 1. In Xenophon of Ephesus's *Ephesiaca*, the pirate Corymbus falls in love with the hero Habrocomes, who is old enough to have a fiancée, Anthia (1.14.7); the pirate finds that his ardour increases owing to their common life on board ship (1.16.4); however, it is not possible to take this episode as evidence that homosexuality was the typical mode of gratification for Greek pirates, since Corymbus's fellow pirate, Euxinus, equally and oppositely falls in love with the heroine Anthia. Cf. Buffière op. cit. (n. 2) 378–382, 627.

7 Some of the societies just listed are sometimes referred to as 'warrior societies'; this is a term I regard as problematic, and so have avoided. Ancient Greece too is often regarded as a series of 'warrior societies': see the views recorded, and partly challenged, by W.R. Connor, 'Early Greek Land Warfare as Symbolic Expression', *Past and Present* 119 (1988), 3–29. Undoubtedly there were *parts* of ancient Greek societies which would have to be called 'warrior (sub-) societies', whatever the term was supposed to mean: the Theban Sacred Band, the Spartan *syssitia* etc.

8 No apology is needed for making repeated reference in what follows to two studies in particular: firstly K.J. Dover's *Greek Homosexuality* (London, 1978), which remains the authoritative foundation for the study of the subject, as noted by M. Golden, 'Thirteen Years of Homosexuality (and Other Recent Work on Sex, Gender and the Body in Ancient Greece', *EMC/CV* n.s. 10 (1991), 327–40 and D. Cohen, 'Sex, Gender and Sexuality in Ancient Greece', *CP* 87 (1992), 145–60; and secondly to Buffière's exhaustive *Eros adolescent* (cited at n. 2). In researching this article it has become apparent to me that the intersection between homosexuality and warfare is covered rather better by the homosexuality specialists than by the warfare ones (who indeed rarely even mention it). Whatever this may indicate about the relative horizons of the two groups, the immediate result is that most of the secondary material pertinent to the study of this topic is to be found in the works of the former group, as the notes to this article will make clear.

9 H.-I. Marrou, *History of Education in Antiquity* (third edn, London, 1956), 26–9, translation of *Histoire de l'éducation dans l'antiquité* (Paris, 1948).

10 Thus Bremmer op. cit. (n. 2) 279 and Dover op. cit. (n. 8) 201 n. 10, although Dover does himself toy with the idea that the constant state of warfare which city-state organisation imposed on the Greeks may have occasioned the idolisation of the all-important up-coming warriors, and that this

may have favoured the development of pederasty (201–2). Buffière op. cit. (n. 2) 5, however, does see warfare and the inculcation of valour as an important aspect of pederasty in many Greek states.

11 See, e.g., J.J. Winkler, *The Constraints of Desire* (NY and London, 1990).

12 D.M. Halperin, *One Hundred Years of Homosexuality* (NY and London 1990), esp. 15–53.

13 Witness, above all, the title of Buffière's massive work (n. 2), and cf., e.g., P. Cartledge, 'The Politics of Spartan Pederasty', *PCPS* 27 (1981), 17–36 at 17: 'For "homosexuality" in ancient Greece, therefore, we can normally read "pederasty" '; Dover op. cit. (n. 8) 16: 'the reciprocal desire of partners belonging to the same age-category is virtually unknown in Greek homosexuality'; Bremmer op. cit. (n. 2) 279: 'socially approved homosexuality in Greece was virtually restricted to paederasty' (the qualification renders the last assertion more plausible).

14 In what follows I adopt the usual terminology to define the sodomiser and sodomised within the loving pair: see, e.g., Dover (n. 8) 16. A useful summary of the 'pederasty model' may be found at Halperin op. cit. (n. 12) 130–1.

15 The ideal age-range for an *erōmenos* is argued to be 12–17 in an epigram of the Hadrianic Straton of Sardis, *Palatine Anthology* 12.4, followed strongly by E. Cantarella, *Bisexuality in the Ancient World* (New Haven, 1992), 36–44, translation of *Secondo natura* (Rome, 1988). Other sources place the acme of desirability at 18, or at the age when the beard begins to grow: cf. Buffière op. cit. (n. 2) 566, 606, 609–11.

16 Unsurprisingly, this particular point has been the subject of much debate in the history of the scholarship of the topic. There are contradictory indications about the anality of homosexuality both at Athens and at Sparta. For example, on the Athenian side, vase paintings of pederastic couples only depict intercrural copulation (except for a few black figure vases made for the Etruscan market), whereas Aristophanes exclusively talks of sodomy as the mode of homosexual gratification: see Dover op. cit. (n. 8) 98–100, importantly qualified by G. Vlastos, 'Socratic Irony', *CQ* 37 (1987), 79–96 at 96; cf. also R.F. Sutton, 'Pornography and Persuasion on Attic Pottery', in A. Richlin ed., *Pornography and Representation in Greece and Rome* (Oxford, 1992), 3–35 at 13, H.A. Shapiro, 'Eros in Love: Pederasty and Pornography in Greece' in Richlin op. cit. (this note), 53–72 at 57, Buffière op. cit. (n. 8) 123–48, Golden op. cit. (n. 8) 332. On the Spartan side Xenophon's and Plutarch's testimonies to the chastity of Spartan homosexual relationships (Xenophon *Lac.Pol.* 2.13, Plutarch *Moralia* 237bc) conflict with a variety of other evidence (including Plato *Laws* 636b and 836a–c; see below for further discussion on Sparta). It is also possible that Aristotle *Politics* 1269b26 attempts to sweep the practice of homosexuality at Sparta in general under the carpet in implicitly contrasting the Spartan warrior-race with the Celts and other warrior-races that 'give public honour to relationships with men.' For anal sex at Crete, see *Palatine Anthology* 12.38 (Rhianos); Bremmer op. cit. (n. 2) 281, 287; Dover op. cit. (n. 8) 189.

17 The theory of such a progression through sexual phases strongly tied to

age is classically stated by G. Devereux, 'Greek "Pseudo-homosexuality" and the Greek Miracle', *SO* 42 (1967), 69–92. Cf. also, e.g., Bremmer op. cit. (n. 2) 287, Cartledge op. cit. (n. 13) 21–2, Sutton op. cit. (n. 16) 13, Dover op. cit. (n. 8) 171, Buffière op. cit. (n. 2) 21, 560, 605–13, Cantarella op. cit. (n. 15) 40–1. This theory does gain some support from pottery illustrations, but as the anal sex problem demonstrates, pottery need not give a complete picture.

18 Cf. Buffière op. cit. (n. 2) 631–4. A common though not universal view. The distinction between gifts of money and objects was and is a fine one.

19 Cf. especially Bremmer op. cit. (n. 2), H. Patzer, *Die griechische Knabenliebe* (Wiesbaden, 1982), B. Sergent, *Homosexuality in Greek Myth* (London, 1987), translation of *L'homosexualité dans la mythologie grecque* (Paris, 1984), K.J. Dover, 'Greek Homosexuality and Initiation', in K.J. Dover, *The Greeks and their Legacy* (Oxford, 1988), 115–34 (summarised in the postscript to the second edition of Dover op. cit. [n. 8]), Golden op. cit. (n. 8), with further bibliography.

20 Timarchus is accused of having been a prostitute man and boy (see Aeschines 1.157; cf. Dover op. cit. [n. 8] 29, 39); and the Sausage-seller at Aristophanes's *Knights* 1242 is said to have earned his money by being sodomised as an adult.

21 The *kinaidos* is an eager adult pathic, effeminate both because of his habitual role as the penetrated (the role which is the only one a woman can take on), and because he has lost control over his desires (the state of '*akrasia*', similarly regarded as typical of women). Aeschines 1.185 seems to be thinking of a *kinaidos* when he talks of a man that is physically male, but a woman by his ignominies. [Aristotle] *Physiognomonica* 808a12–6 describes the *kinaidos* as follows: 'The signs of the *kinaidos* are an unsteady eye [a sign of cowardice at 808a7–11] and knock-knees [all female animals have knock-knees at 809b8] and he inclines his head to the right; he gestures with his palms up and his wrists loose; he has two styles of walking – either waggling his hips or keeping them under control. He tends to look around in all directions. Dionysius the sophist would be an instance of this type.' See Winkler op. cit. (n. 11) 45–7, 50–4, 67 (and see index s.v.), to whom belong the *Physiognomonica* translation and notes given, Halperin op. cit. (n. 12) 133, M.W. Gleason, 'The Semiotics of Gender: Physiognomy and Self-fashioning in the Second Century C.E.', in D.M. Halperin et al. (eds), *Before Sexuality* (Princeton, 1990), 389–416 at 396–9, Dover op. cit. (n. 8) 75; Buffière op. cit. (n. 2) 435–49, 602, 617.

On *akrasia* see Aristotle *Nicomachean Ethics* 1145a–1152a, and M. Foucault, *The Use of Pleasure* (NY, 1985), part 1 chapter 3, translation of *L'usage des plaisirs* (Paris, 1984), J.J. Walsh, *Aristotle's Concept of Moral Weakness* (NY, 1964), G.S. Shrimpton, *Theopompus the Historian* (Montreal, 1991), 136–156.

22 However Dover op. cit. (n. 8) 201 n. 10 concedes, rather against the model with which he works for the most part, that there could indeed have been *erōmenoi* in Athenian armies.

23 The phrase comes from Plato *Gorgias* 494e.

24 See Golden op. cit. (n. 8) 337, H. Mommsen, *Der Affecter* (Mainz, 1975), 56–60, C.A.M. Huppperts, 'Greek Love: Homosexuality or Pederasty? Greek Love in Black Figure Vase Painting' in J. Christiansen et al. (eds), *Proceedings*

of the Third Symposium on Ancient Greek and Related Pottery (Copenhagen, 1988), 255–68. The odd Affecter's pots were destined, as were many others, for the odd Etruscan market.

25 Dover op. cit. (n. 8) 193, Buffière op.cit. (n. 2) 558–9, Cartledge op. cit. (n. 13) 32 n. 24; cf. Golden op. cit. (n. 8) 333.

26 Aeschines 1.49, 136; cf. N.H. Demand, *Thebes in the Fifth Century* (London, 1982), 158 n. 52, Dover op. cit. (n. 8) 42.

27 Athenaeus 603f–604d; cf. Plutarch *Pericles* 8; see Cantarella op. cit. (n. 15) 41–2.

28 Lysias 3.5; Cantarella op. cit. (n. 15) 41–2.

29 Plato *Protagoras* 315e; cf. Xenophon *Symposium* 8.32.

30 Dover op. cit. (n. 8) 84, cf. 144. Of course, it must be remembered that Plato often makes chronological fudges.

31 Plutarch *Moralia* 770c; at Aelian *Varia Historia* 13.5 the two are shown as lovers at the end of Euripides's life, in Macedon, and Euripides defends his love by saying 'the Spring of Beauty is splendid; the Autumn too' (cf. here the Hadrianic Straton's poem, *Palatine Anthology* 12.78, 'the setting sun is still the sun'); Buffière op. cit. (n. 2) 613, Golden op. cit. (n. 8) 337, Cantarella op. cit. (n. 15) 39, 42.

32 W.M. Ellis, *Alcibiades* (London, 1989), 20; Cantarella op. cit. (n. 15) 39.

33 Athenaeus 563e (= *SVF* i p.247), Antigonus of Carystus *Life of Zeno* p.117 Wilam.; cf. Buffière op. cit. (n. 2) 476–7, 614.

34 Xenophon *Anabasis* 2.6.28; cf. Buffière op. cit. (n. 2) 217.

35 Xenophon *Symposium* 2.3, 4.12–6.

36 Cf., importantly, Buffière op. cit. (n. 2) 440–3.

37 For courtesans on the anabasis see Curtius 5.7.2 and Plutarch *Alexander* 38.1–2, and for wives and children generally Justin 12.3–4, Diodorus 94.4, Arrian *Anabasis* 6.25.4–5, 7.4.8. It seems that, in first allowing, and then ultimately encouraging campfollowers, Alexander's behaviour was unusual in its time, and conditioned by the distance, spatial and temporal, from home. Philip had forbidden wives and women to accompany the army (Athenaeus 557b). Alexander initially continued the ban, since he sent recently-married troops back home to join their wives (Arrian *Anabasis* 1.24.1). By the time he got to Hyrcania he allowed his troops to marry captive women to stop them wanting to go home (Justin 12.3–4). See D.W. Engels, *Alexander the Great and the Logistics of the Macedonian Army* (Berkeley, 1978), 11–3. There was perhaps an increase in the phenomenon of campfollowers in the hellenistic period; for some of the evidence, see W.K. Pritchett, *The Greek State at War* (5+ vols, California 1971–), v 173–4 sub c. *aposkeuē*. M. Launey, *Recherches sur les armées hellénistiques* (2 vols, Paris 1987), 802 notes, with exhaustive references, the tendency of soldiers in New Comedy to be keen always to spend their money on courtesans (NB in particular Pyrgopolynices and Philocomasium and Acroteleutium in Plautus's *Miles Gloriosus*, and Polymachaeroplagides and Phoenicium in his *Pseudolus*).

38 Theopompus FGH 115 F213 (Athenaeus 532b–d).

39 Cf. on this passage Dover op. cit. (n. 8) 135, G.F. Pinney, 'For the Heroes are at Hand', *JHS* 104 (1984), 181–3; cf. also Buffière op. cit. (n. 2) 17 for the

presumption that men deprived of women, as in the field, turn to homosexual solace. Opponents of the idea of Greek military homosexuality might retort by quoting another comedy, Aristophanes's *Lysistrata*, in which the men away in the field become sexually frustrated when their wives (who are not present) begin to withhold sex. This might be taken to imply that soldiers in the field did not seek homosexual relief. But the entire premiss of the play is of course illogical: men away in the field have no access to their wives in any case and can hardly therefore be affected by a sex strike; and the plot equally excludes the possibility of relief through masturbation: see further Dover op. cit. (n. 8) 148, J. Henderson, *Aristophanes: Lysistrata* (Oxford, 1987), p. 33.

40 Buffière op. cit. (n. 2) 11–3.

41 Buffière op. cit. (n. 2) 97, 101, 192–3 asserts that Theban homosexuality ('pederasty') appears to have a military origin.

42 The earliest dateable battle in which the band is said to have participated is that of Tegyra in 376/7 (Plutarch *Pelopidas* 16–7, Diodorus 15.37.1–2, Xenophon *Hellenica* 5.4.63). Three men appear to be credited with the formation of the band in different places: Gorgidas (here, and cf. 19.3), Epaminondas (Hieronymus F34 at Athenaeus 602a) and Pammenes (Plutarch again, at *Moralia* 761b, on which see below). Gorgidas seems the most likely, because he is reassuringly obscure in comparison to the great Epaminondas (and NB Epaminondas, the 'philosopher of warfare', is clearly said to have *inherited* the band at Dio Chrysostom 22.2), and because Pammenes's floruit was in the 350s (Plutarch may therefore be referring at *Moralia* 761b to a mercenary band of Pammenes's own). Gorgidas appears to have had a short floruit at the beginning of the 370s, being Boeotarch in 378, and it is in this year that K.J. Dover credits him with the formation of the band: op. cit. (n. 8) 192 and 'The Date of Plato's *Symposium*', *Phronesis* 10 (1965), 2–20 at 11–3. But we must remember that there is evidence for a Theban élite of 300 as early as 424 (discussed below in main text), and that it may therefore be the case that any one or all of these three men tinkered with something that already existed in essentials.

43 The great Theban in whose house Philip of Macedon spent his hostageship (Plutarch *Pelopidas* 26.5); Suda s.v. *Karanos* tells that Pammenes became Philip's lover. This tale of Pammenes is told by Plutarch also at *Moralia* 618d and 761b (at the latter of which he appears to credit Pammenes himself with the creation of the band: see above).

44 Homer *Iliad* 2.362–3.

45 The tale is repeated at Plutarch *Moralia* 761c.

46 Aristotle F97 Rose.

47 Cf. Plutarch *Moralia* 761de, where it is also said that Heracles was roused to the brave feat of rescuing Alcestis from Hades because he had been Admetus's *erōmenos*.

48 Plato *Symposium* 179a.

49 Cf. W.K. Pritchett, 'Observations on Chaeronea', *AJA* 62 (1958), 307–11 for the excavation of the tumulus of the Sacred Band at Chaeronea.

50 Laius is often portrayed as the inventor of homosexuality: e.g. Euripides F838 Nauck (Aelian *De Natura Animalium* 6.15); cf. Sergent op. cit. (n. 19) 59–

70, Dover op. cit. (n. 8) 199–200, Buffière op. cit. (n. 2) 95–6.

51 The mention to the flute seems bizarrely irrelevant here, unless we are to refer it to the role of the flute in Sambian homosexuality: see the appendix.

52 Cf. on this text Buffière op. cit. (n. 2) 97–101.

53 Cf. Buffière op. cit. (n. 2) 99–100.

54 Cf. Plutarch *Moralia* 761b.

55 For the classical Theban gymnasia, see Demand op. cit. (n. 26) 14.

56 Pindar F123 (the fragment for Theoxenus); cf. Demand op. cit. (n. 26) 94.

57 Xenophon *Lac.Pol.* 2.12.

58 Cf. N.G.L. Hammond and G.T. Griffith, *A History of Macedon* ii (Oxford, 1979), 204–5.

59 Plutarch *Moralia* 761bd; cf. Demand op. cit. (n. 26) 94, Bremmer op. cit. (n. 2) 285.

60 Plato *Symposium* 182b. The implication is, oddly, that the Athenians, by contrast, surround pederasty with ethical traps in order to promote the art of rhetoric.

61 Diodorus 12.70.1.

62 See Oldfather's note in the Loeb edition of Diodorus ad loc. His suggestion that the names derive from those of an original wealthy class that formerly provided their own chariots in warfare (cf. the Roman 'knights') is implausible.

63 J. Henderson, *The Maculate Muse* (second ed., Oxford, 1991), 165–6.

64 Strabo C483, on which see below.

65 Homer *Iliad* 11.102–3; cf. also, e.g., 23.132.

66 Dover op. cit. (n. 42) 13.

67 As noted by Dover op. cit. (n. 42) 12.

68 Xenophon *Lac.Pol.* 2.12, Plato *Symposium* 182b; cf. Buffière op. cit. (n. 2) 89–91.

69 Xenophon *Symposium* 8.34.

70 Xenophon *Hellenica* 7.4.13, 16, 31.

71 Athenaeus 565, 609 (including Theophrastus F111 Wimmer); cf. Buffière op. cit. (n. 2) 90–1, Dover op. cit. (n. 8) 181 and M.P. Nilsson, 'Kallisteia', *RE* x (1919), 1674.

72 Theocritus 12.30–7, with scholiast; cf. Buffière op. cit. (n. 2) 92.

73 Plutarch *Moralia* 760e–761b; cf. Buffière op. cit. (n. 2) 104–5.

74 It is unclear whether Plutarch refers to the great Aristotle or to the lesser Aristotle of Chalcis (FHG ii p.141); cf. Dover op. cit (n. 8) 191–2, Buffière op. cit. (n. 2) 102.

75 Cf. Buffière op. cit. (n. 2) 105–6.

76 Hesychius s.v.; Buffière op. cit. (n. 2) 103–4.

77 Plutarch *Moralia* 761c.

78 Plutarch *Moralia* 761d.

79 The ancient sources (and indeed modern scholars) often compare Cretan and Spartan customs: cf., e.g., Aristotle *Politics* 1271b40.

80 Cf. Dover op. cit. (n. 8) 192, Buffière op. cit. (n. 2) 62, 644.

81 Ephorus FGH 70 F149, apud Strabo C483. For these Cretan customs as

initiation see Dover op. cit. (n. 19) 115–34, Bremmer op. cit. (n. 2) 284–7, Sergent op. cit. (n. 19) passim, esp. 7–39, Cantarella op. cit. (n. 15) 3–8, K.M.T. Chrimes, *Ancient Sparta* (Manchester, 1949), 224–5.

Aristotle *Politics* 1272a25 tells that homosexuality was instituted by a Cretan lawgiver in order to control the birthrate; see Dover op. cit. (n. 8) 186 for other sources asserting that the Cretans invented homosexuality, and Buffière op. cit. (n. 2) 59–62, 351 for homosexuality in Cretan myth in general. The old thesis that there was a distinctive phenomenon of 'Dorian' homosexuality in Greece (of which the strong form claims that the Dorians 'introduced' pederasty to the rest of Greece; cf. Plato's assertion at *Protagoras* 342bc that the Spartans introduced pederasty to Athens) is still favoured by Buffière op. cit. (n. 2) 49–57 (cf. 75–6).

82 *Harpagē* was apparently a technical term for the seizure of *erōmenoi*, for the term is used also of Laius's seizure of Chrysippus and Zeus's seizure of the Cretan Ganymede (e.g. Athenaeus 601–3 and esp. 603a [cf. Plato *Laws* 636d], Ibycus F289P; cf. Bremmer op. cit. [n. 2] 285, with further references). It is also the technical term used by the Spartans for the seizure of their wives (e.g. Herodotus 6.65.2, Plutarch *Lycurgus* 15.4, Athenaeus 555bc), which is the reason this Cretan rite is sometimes seen as a kind of homosexual 'marriage': cf. D.M. MacDowell, *Spartan Law* (Edinburgh, 1986), 78–81, Cartledge op. cit. (n. 13) 100–1, Buffière op. cit. (n. 2) 55–6.

83 See Aristotle *Politics* 1272a12, 26 for a comparison of Cretan and Spartan dining in the men's messes.

84 See below on Sparta and Athens. Also, the pursuit of the *erōmenos* by the *erastēs* is often represented in terms of images and metaphors drawn from hunting: e.g. *Palatine Anthology* 12.92 (Meleager); cf. Dover op. cit. (n. 8) 81–91, esp. 87–8, Buffière op. cit. (n. 2) 310–2, A. Schnapp, 'Eros the Hunter', in C. Bérard, ed., *A City of Images* (Princeton, 1989), 71–88, translation of *Cité d'images* (Paris, 1984), H. Lloyd-Jones, Review of K.J. Dover op. cit. (n. 19), *CR* 39 (1989), 370–2 at 372.

85 Cf. on this text Bremmer op. cit. (n. 2) 284–5, Dover op. cit. (n. 8) 189–90, H. Jeanmaire, *Couroi et Courètes. Essai sur l'éducation spartiate et sur les rites d'adolescence dans l'antiquité grecque* (Paris, 1939), 450–5, R.F. Willetts, *Ancient Crete: a Social History* (London, 1965), 116.

86 Cf. Bremmer op. cit. (n. 2) 285–7 for the significance of the cloak and the cup (a particularly interesting discussion of the latter). In all probability the boys had already undertaken the role of wine-pourers within the men's houses of which they had not yet been members: see J. Bremmer, 'Adolescents, *Symposion*, and Pederasty', in O. Murray, ed., *Sympotica* (Oxford, 1990), 135–148.

87 Bremmer op. cit. (n. 2) 287 presses Aelian *De Natura Animalium* 4.1 too hard in his attempt to establish that only young men (*neaniai*) could be lovers in Crete.

88 Athenaeus 561ef; cf. Buffière op. cit. (n. 2) 87.

89 Plutarch *Pelopidas* 18.

90 Buffière op. cit. (n. 2) 52–3, 56–9.

91 For *agōgē* as the basis for Spartan pederasty, see Dover op. cit. (n. 8) 192–

4 (with important references), P. Cartledge op. cit. (n. 13) 18, 26, 'Hoplites and Heroes: Sparta's Contribution to the Technique of Ancient Warfare', *JHS* 79 (1977), 11–27 at 16–7, Bremmer op. cit. (n. 2) 282, A. Brelich, *Paides e parthenoi* (Rome, 1969), i 120–1, 158, 184, 198–9, Buffière op. cit. (n. 2) 24 ('military pederasty'), 50, 65–76, 88. Cartledge op. cit. (n. 13) is the most convenient treatment of homosexuality at Sparta specifically.

92 Cf. Dover op. cit. (n. 8) 186.

93 Plutarch *Lycurgus* 17–18; cf. Cartledge op. cit. (n. 13) 21–2, and esp. 27 for the Spartan gymnasium as a prime institution of homosexuality. Cf. below for the Athenian gymnasium.

94 Cf. Cartledge op. cit. (n. 13) 22.

95 Xenophon *Symposium* 8.35; the implication of this phrase is misread by Cartledge op. cit. (n. 13) 22; cf. also Dover op. cit. (n. 8) 192.

96 Athenaeus 561ef; J. Lazenby, 'The Killing Zone', in V.D. Hanson, ed., *Hoplites: the Classical Greek Battle Experience* (London, 1991), 87–109 at 107, Buffière op. cit. (n. 2) 87.

97 Xenophon *Hellenica* 4.8.39; cf. Dover op. cit. (n. 8) 192.

98 Xenophon *Hellenica* 5.4.25; cf. Cartledge op. cit. (n. 13) 22, 29, 32 n. 31, 36 n. 79. Cartledge refers to this case as the 'locus classicus' of Spartan pederasty; cf. also Buffière op. cit. (n. 2) 81–2.

99 Thus Cartledge op. cit. (n. 13) 32 n. 24, Dover op. cit. (n. 8) 193, Buffière op. cit. (n. 2) 78, and cf., importantly, 558–9.

100 Xenophon, doubtless under the influence of Plato's ideals as expressed in the *Symposium*, implausibly denies that homosexuality at Sparta involved sodomy (*Lac.Pol.* 2.12–3) and [Plutarch] *Moralia* 237bc, building on the fallacious trend, actually claims that sodomising *erastai* were deprived of citizen rights at Sparta; but Plato at *Laws* 836a–c (cf. 636b) admits that sodomy was widely practised at Sparta and in Crete, and Athenian comedians saw Spartans as fond of sodomy (it was probably a comic poet that coined the term *kysolakōn*, 'arse-Spartan', found at Hesychius s.v.): see Henderson op. cit. (n. 63) 218 n. 37, Bremmer op. cit. (n. 2) 283, Cartledge op. cit. (n. 13) 19–20, Dover op. cit. (n. 8) 187–9, 194, Buffière op. cit. (n. 2) 69–73.

101 Cf. Dover op. cit. (n. 8) 195 n. 20.

102 Plutarch *Agesilaus* 34.8–9; cf. Buffière op. cit. (n. 2) 83–4.

103 Aelian *Varia Historia* 3.10,12; Cartledge op. cit. (n. 13) 21. We are reminded of the penalties for refusing to marry: in both cases the posterity of the community is deprived of the warrior-vigour transmitted by seed.

104 Plutarch *Lycurgus* 18.

105 Plutarch *Lycurgus* 18.

106 Cartledge op. cit. (n. 13) 21.

107 Cartledge op. cit. (n. 13) 23.

108 Cf. Brelich op. cit. (n. 91) i 156–7, with testimonia printed at n. 33, Sergent op. cit. (n. 19) 225–6, Schnapp op. cit. (n. 84).

109 Cartledge op. cit. (n. 13) 34.

110 Similar sentiments in Theopompus FGH 115 F225 version b (Athenaeus 260d–261a), with the more usual form *chamaitypai* (first declension); cf. Shrimpton op. cit. (n. 21) 119, 157–171, esp. 164–7 on this passage,

Daniel Ogden

and also Dover op. cit. (n. 8) 194.

111 On which see Hammond and Griffith op. cit. (n. 58) 154, 401–2, H. Berve, *Das Alexanderreich auf prosopographischer Grundlage* (2 vols, Munich, 1926), i 37–9.

112 Arrian *Anabasis* 4.13.1, Aelian *Varia Historia* 14.48; cf. Hammond and Griffith op. cit. (n. 58) 168 n. 1, 401, A.B. Bosworth, *Conquest and Empire* (Cambridge, 1988) 7.

113 Served king at table: e.g. Curtius 5.1.42. Guarded king as he slept: e.g. Arrian *Anabasis* 4.13, Curtius 8.6.13–5; see generally Curtius 8.6.2–6, 8.8.3, Diodorus 17.65.1; cf. Hammond and Griffith op. cit. (n. 58) 396.

114 Arrian *Anabasis* 4.13.1 (*therapeia basileōs*), Curtius 8.6.2 (*servilibus ministeriis*), and cf. Curtius 8.6.5, 19.

115 Hammond and Griffith op. cit. (n. 58) 401.

116 Cf. Hammond and Griffith op. cit. (n. 58) 401.

117 Hammond and Griffith op. cit. (n. 58) 154, 505.

118 Curtius 8.6.3.

119 Curtius 8.6.6 cf. 5.1.42; cf. Hammond and Griffith op. cit. (n. 58) 401, N.G.L. Hammond and F.W. Walbank, *A History of Macedon* iii (Oxford, 1988) 13.

120 Hammond and Walbank op. cit. (n. 119) 13.

121 Diodorus 16.93–4.

122 Other sources: Justin 9.6.4–8, Plutarch *Alexander* 10.6, Aristotle *Politics* 1311b; cf. J.R. Ellis, *Philip II and Macedonian Imperialism* (London, 1976), 223–7, Hammond and Griffith op. cit. (n. 58) 684–5, Buffière (n. 2) 227–9.

123 Arrian *Anabasis* 4.13, Plutarch *Alexander* 55, Curtius 8.6–8. See Bremmer op. cit. (n. 2) 289 for an argument about pederasty in Macedon based upon a comparative reading of the boar-hunting custom; cf., in general, Schnapp op. cit. (n. 84).

124 *Hybris* is a notoriously difficult concept to define (see most recently N.R.E. Fisher, *Hybris* (Warminster, 1992); a good shorter treatment is that of D.M. MacDowell, 'Hybris in Athens', *G&R* 23 (1976), 14–31, esp. 30. Fisher's definition (p. 1): 'Hybris is essentially the serious assault on the honour of another, which is likely to cause shame, and lead to anger and attempts at revenge...often...an act of violence...essentially deliberate activity, and the typical motive for such infliction of dishonour is the pleasure of expressing a sense of superiority...often seen to be characteristic of the young and/or of the rich and/or upper classes...often associated with drunkenness.' MacDowell 30 concludes 'it is having energy or power and misusing it self-indulgently.' In this case it seems to describe the action of an *erastēs* on an *erōmenos* when he sodomises without giving anything, or without giving sufficiently, spiritually or materially, in return: reciprocity is the key. For hybris in a sexual context, see Fisher 13–4, 27–9, 63–4, 107–11, 458–76, 485–8, and 29 for the Crateuas incident in particular.

125 Aristotle *Politics* 1311b8–35; on this episode, cf. Buffière op. cit. (n. 2) 225–7, Hammond and Griffith op. cit. (n. 58) 154, 167–8, with other references.

126 Aristotle *Politics* 1311b4; Hammond and Griffith op. cit. (n. 58) 170.

127 Berve op. cit. (n. 111) i 39.

128 Arrian *Anabasis* 3.13.3 (*hēlikiōtēn*).

129 Arrian *Anabasis* 4.13.7.

130 Herodotus 5.20.

131 Suda s.v. *Karanos*.

132 Justin 8.6.4–8; Hammond and Griffith op. cit. (n. 58) 505.

133 See Berve op. cit. (n. 111) i 10–1 and W.W. Tarn, *Alexander the Great* (2 vols, Cambridge, 1948), ii appendix 18 for unconvincing arguments that Alexander did not have any homosexual partners.

134 Athenaeus 434–5. But Athenaeus also here tells that Carystius of Pergamum told that Alexander was impotent due to drunkenness.

135 Athenaeus 303b.

136 Berve op. cit. (n. 111) no. 357.

137 Curtius 3.12.16 (*cum ipso pariter educatus*), Pseudo-Callisthenes 1.18, Julius Valerius 1.10; cf. Berve op. cit. (n. 111) ii p. 169.

138 Aelian *Varia Historia* 12.7; cf. Justin 12.12.11, who tells that Hephaestion was dear to Alexander because of his *pueritia* – which implies Hephaestion was both younger than Alexander and his *erōmenos*, although, as we have said, there can not have been any effective age-difference between the two. On the other side, some have argued, on the analogy between Alexander and Hephaestion and Achilles and Patroclus, that since Patroclus was the elder in his pair, so too must Hephaestion have been, and that he must therefore have been the *erastēs*, but this is to explain *obscurum per obscurius* (see below); cf. Buffière op. cit. (n. 2) 231; R. Lane Fox, *Alexander the Great* (London, 1973), 56–62, 64–7, 112–5, 510.

139 Arrian *Anabasis* 7.14–15.1 (the comparison is explicit), Aelian *Varia Historia* 8.8, Plutarch *Pelopidas* 34.2, *Alexander* 72; further references at Berve op. cit. (n. 111) ii p.174; cf. Buffière op. cit. (n. 2) 231–2.

140 Arrian *Anabasis* 7.14.6.

141 Diodorus 17.37.5–6.

142 Hammond and Walbank op. cit. (n. 119) 14, cf. 28.

143 Curtius 7.9.19. There is little agreement in the MSS about the exact form of the name.

144 On whom see E. Badian, 'The Eunuch Bagoas', *CQ* 8 (1958), 144–57. Bagoas was a former favourite of Darius given to Alexander by Narbazanes, one of Darius's assassins, in the hope that the eunuch would intercede for his life (Curtius 6.5.22–3). Bagoas persuaded Alexander to put Orxines to death for the plunder of Cyrus's tomb because Orxines had given presents to all of Alexander's friends except him (Curtius 10.1.22). Alexander repeatedly kissed Bagoas in the theatre at Gedrosia, for his dancing (Plutarch *Alexander* 67.3, Athenaeus 603b, quoting Dicaearchus).

An apologetic tradition also arose that emphasised Alexander's self restraint (*enkrateia*) in matters homosexual: Plutarch tells that he refused an offer to be bought pretty boys (*Alexander* 22, cf. 21), and that he was courteous to everyone except pretty boys (*Moralia* 338d), Athenaeus that he refused a kiss from a pretty boy (603b), and Curtius that there was nothing improper in his relationship with Bagoas (10.5.32).

145 Arrian *Indica* 18.8.

146 For Greek (and ancient) eunuchism in general, see Buffière op. cit. (n. 2) 30–4, who treats the practice as a variation of pederasty.

147 e.g. Arrian *Anabasis* 6.25.4–5, 7.4.8; cf. above for campfollowers.

148 Plautus *Pseudolus* 1180–1; P. Perdrizet and G. Lefèbvre, *Les graffites grecs du Memnonion d' Abydos* (Nancy, 1919), no. 910; Launey op. cit. (n. 37) ii 802.

149 Xenophon *Symposium* 8.31 is the only firm ancient assertion that they were not partners (this is part of a blanket denial of homosexuality in a series of heroic pairs; we are already familiar from the Spartan material with Xenophon's tendency to deny physical homosexuality). Many believed that they were, e.g. Aeschylus F135 Nauck, Plato *Symposium* 179e–180b, Aeschines 1.142–50 and the many other sources quoted at W.M. Clarke, 'Achilles and Patroclus in Love', *Hermes* 106 (1978), 381–97 at 381 n. 1, and Sergent op. cit. (n. 19) 310 n. 3; cf. Buffière op. cit. (n. 2) 367–74. Clarke 381–3 and Sergent 310 n. 4 review earlier modern scholarship on the issue. Dover op. cit. (n. 8) 194, 196 and Buffière op. cit. (n. 2) 369, 372 deny homosexuality in Homer.

150 The (unrelated) Patroclus is dearer to Achilles even than the members of his own family: Homer *Iliad* 19.321, 21.46–7.

151 Cf. Sergent op. cit. (n. 19) 205–15, 250–1, who argues that while Homer's reference to Zeus and Ganymede (Homer *Iliad* 22.230–35) contains no explicit reference to homosexuality, the episode makes no sense unless we accept that it is there; cf. also Shapiro op. cit. (n. 16) 58, Buffière op. cit. (n. 2) 351–7, 373; Bremmer op. cit. (n. 86) 141–3.

152 Clarke op. cit. (n. 149); cf. Sergent op. cit. (n. 19) 250–7. Dover op. cit. (n. 8) 197–8, Buffière op. cit. (n. 2) 373–4, Cartledge op. cit. (n. 13) 35 n. 62 and E. Keuls, *The Reign of the Phallus* (Berkeley, 1985), 287–9 deny the homosexuality of the relationship.

153 Homer *Iliad* 16.97–100.

154 Homer *Iliad* 24.6–9.

155 Homer *Iliad* 24.128–132.

156 Clarke's interpretation of this line, op. cit. (n. 149) 386–7.

157 e.g. C.W. MacLeod, *Homer: Iliad book xxiv* edited with an introduction and commentary (Cambridge, 1982) and N. Richardson (G.S. Kirk, general ed.), *The Iliad: a Commentary vol. vi, books 21–4* (Cambridge 1993) ad loc. Both insist that the *per* be taken with the phrase as a whole, rather than with *gynaiki* in particular, citing J.D. Denniston, *The Greek Particles* (second ed., Oxford, 1952) 482 s.v. Denniston does not however record any such usage of *per*, while his own interpretation of the particle in this phrase is odd: 'a grim hint that this intercourse will not continue for much longer.'

158 Homer *Iliad* 19.4. Cf. Clarke op. cit. (n. 149) 393. On the passages discussed here see also Sergent op. cit. (n. 19) 255–6.

159 Homer *Odyssey* 24.76–9; cf. Buffière op. cit. (n. 2) 373.

160 e.g. Homer *Iliad* 8.568–9; cf. Clarke op. cit. (n. 149) 390–1.

161 Homer *Iliad* 9.590–9; cf. Clarke op. cit. (n. 149) 394.

162 Apollodorus *Bibliotheca* 3.13.6–8; cf. Sergent op. cit. (n. 19) 253 and above on Macedon.

163 Homer *Iliad* 11.786–7.

164 e.g. Homer *Iliad* 11.648–54, 16.140–4.

165 Homer *Iliad* 23.90, 17.271, 18.152. Thus Aeschines 1.132–3, 142–50 argues that Achilles was *erastēs* and Patroclus *erōmenos*, because, for example, Achilles promises Menoetius that he will look after his son, whereas Plato *Symposium* 179e–180b argues (against Aeschylus) that Patroclus was the lover and Achilles the beloved, who nonetheless avenged Patroclus's death out of love.

166 Xenophon *Symposium* 8.31; Sergent op. cit. (n. 19) 251.

167 Homer *Odyssey* 3.397–401, 4.302–5 and 15.4–5.

168 See Clarke op. cit. (n. 149) 383, Sergent op. cit. (n. 19) 29, Buffière op. cit. (n. 2) 373–4, G. Koch-Harnak, *Erotische Symbole* (Berlin, 1989) 142, W. Poole, 'Male Homosexuality in Euripides', in A. Powell, ed., *Euripides, Women and Sexuality* (London, 1990), 108–50 at 129–131. (However, we may think that Pisistratus is the *erōmenos* in the light of Bremmer's observation about the role of wine-pourers at symposia: op. cit. [n. 86] esp. 137).

169 Buffière op. cit. (n. 2) 197 explicitly distinguishes Athenian homosexuality from, e.g., Spartan, as *not* being militarily based.

170 Eubulus F18 K–A.

171 Plutarch *Moralia* 760e, including Sophocles F44 Radt.

172 Xenophon *Anabasis* 7.4.7.

173 This may be the same man as the 'Amphipolitan' Episthenes who made an *erōmenos* of the hostage-son of a village-chieftain at Xenophon *Anabasis* 4.6.3 (however, the MSS are divided as to whether this man was called Episthenes, Pleisthenes or Cleisthenes); cf. Buffière op. cit. (n. 2) 621.

174 See Dover op. cit. (n. 42), but NB the qualifications below.

175 Cf. on this passage Dover op. cit. (n. 8) 191, Buffière op. cit. (n. 2) 403–4. Cf. also, for homosexual love and the inculcation of virtue, Xenophon *Symposium* 8.38 (discussed below), Plutarch *Moralia* 760.

176 Plato *Symposium* 182b.

177 Xenophon *Symposium* 8.34.

178 K.J. Dover op. cit. (n. 42) 9–16, op. cit. (n. 8) 51, 192, *Plato: Symposium* edited with introduction and commentary (Cambridge, 1980), 10; contra, H.B. Mattingly, 'The Date of Plato's *Symposium*', *Phronesis* 3 (1958), 31–9.

179 Athenaeus 216e–f and Dover op. cit. (n. 42) 9 think Plato's *Symposium* the earlier of the two.

180 It could of course be the case that Plato phrases himself hypothetically here, despite the known existence of a homoerotic Theban élite force, because he is (for once!) trying to preserve the integrity of the dramatic date of his dialogue (416); cf. Dover op. cit. (n. 42) 14–5. However, as we have seen, the Theban élite seems to have been organised homoerotically even before this (from at least 424; incidentally, this also allows the integrity of the dramatic date of Xenophon's *Symposium*, 422, to be preserved). And even if he did compose before the institution of a homoerotic Theban élite, he did not *have* to write hypothetically, for he could easily have referred to Xenophon's experiment some twenty years earlier.

181 Plato *Republic* 468b; cf. Buffière op. cit. (n. 2) 425; admittedly, the context here is not exclusively homosexual.

182 Plato *Symposium* 217a–219e. Alcibiades's assertions about the nature of his relationship with Socrates here are made very much under the pressure of the argument Plato has in hand. Other Platonic contexts are less coy: at *Gorgias* 481d Socrates calls himself Alcibiades's *erastēs*; at *Protagoras* ad init. Socrates is shown to chase the youthful beauty of Alcibiades; in *Alcibiades i* Socrates describes himself as the first of Alcibiades's lovers. Cf. Ellis op. cit. (n. 32) 20, Dover op. cit. (n. 8) 153, R.J. Littman, 'The Loves of Alcibiades', *TAPA* 101 (1970), 263–76, Buffière op. cit. (n. 2) 161–78 (esp. 168–74), 430–2.

183 The tale reveals clearly that Alcibiades did indeed serve as a hoplite at one point, for all that he enjoyed the wealth of a knight; cf. Buffière op. cit. (n. 2) 172.

184 They are already portrayed as a couple in the *Protagoras* (ad init.), which has a dramatic date of *c.* 435; they are lovers also in *Alcibiades i*, which has a dramatic date of 432, the same year as Potidaea. There are some chronological difficulties with having Alcibiades and Socrates together at Potidaea: see Dover op. cit. (n. 8) 158, op. cit. (n. 178) 165, Ellis op. cit. (n. 32) 26–7. The principal difficulty is that Alcibiades seems rather young to be a hoplite in 432, since he is thought to have been born close to 450 (see Ellis op. cit. (n. 32) 1, 20, J.K. Davies, *Athenian Propertied Families* (Oxford, 1971), 18. Buffière op. cit. (n. 2) 172 puts Alcibiades's birth in 452 and thus squeaks him into the hoplites at the minimum age of 20.

185 Plato *Symposium* 219e.

186 Plato *Symposium* 220b.

187 Plato *Symposium* 221bc; Plutarch *Alcibiades* 7 tells that Alcibiades, now a knight, was able to return Socrates's favour by coming on horseback to the aid of the embattled hoplite.

188 For Thucydides's attitude to women see T. Wiedemann, *'Elachiston en tois arsesi kleos*: Thucydides, Women and the Limits of Rational Analysis', *G&R* 30 (1983) 163–70, D. Harvey, 'Women in Thucydides', *Arethusa* 18 (1985) 67–90, N.S.R. Hornblower, *Thucydides* (London 1987), 14–5, 42 and 148.

189 Thucydides 1.132.

190 Thucydides 6.53–9.

191 For Aspasia's alleged role in driving Pericles to declare war, see Plutarch *Pericles* 30. Cf. N.S.R. Hornblower, *Thucydides: a Historical Commentary* (Oxford, 1991) on Thucydides 1.67.4 (i.111).

192 Glossed over at Thucydides 8.12.2, despite the fact that it ultimately revived Athens' fortunes by sending Alcibiades back into the Athenian camp; contrast Plutarch *Agesilaus* 3, *Alcibiades* 23; cf. Harvey op. cit. (n. 188) 78–80.

193 See R.T. Ridley, 'The Hoplite as Citizen', *Antiquité classique* 48 (1979) 508–48, Pritchett op. cit. (n. 37) ii 213–9, J. Delorme, *Gymnasion* (Paris, 1960), 275–6 (for the epigraphic evidence for sport as preparation for warfare).

194 Aristophanes *Peace* 355–6, with scholiast; Suda, Hesychius, Photius s.v. *Lykeion*; cf. C.A. Forbes, 'Expanded Uses of the Greek Gymnasium', *CP* 40 (1945) 32–42 at 37–9, with many references. Note that in 410 Thrasybulus used the Lyceum as a base against the Spartans (Xenophon *Hellenica* 1.1.33), and in 405 the Spartans under Pausanias camped in the Academy (Xenophon *Hellenica* 2.2.8). Also, Agesilaus used the gymnasium in Ephesus to train his

soldiers (Xenophon *Hellenica* 3.4.16, *Agesilaos* 1.25). Dio Chrysostom 23.3 says that a general goes to the gymnasium to improve his knowledge of tactics.

195 Plato *Protagoras* 326b.

196 Plato *Republic* 404a: *polemikois athlētais.*

197 Euripides *Autolycus* F284 Nauck.

198 Plutarch *Moralia* 639e.

199 Thus Philostratus *On gymnastics*: c. 3, the pentathlon was so warlike that they included the javelin in it; 4, the long race (*dolichos*) originated in Arcadian heralds running to bring the message of war (cf. the 'marathon'); 8, Boeotian and Plataean hoplites were considered the best because of the length of the race they ran; 9, Spartans developed boxing to learn how to take blows to the head, since they used not to wear helmets in battle; 11, wrestling and pankration were invented as being useful for war, as was demonstrated by Marathon and Thermopylae; 19, Spartans teach gymnasts tactics, because athletics are a preparation for war, and even exploit the dance, the mildest of peacetime occupations, for warfare, as they imitate the avoidance of missiles, or the handling of the shield, or the picking up of a weapon from the ground; 27, Lycurgus made girls exercise in order that they should bear athletes fit for war; 43 ancient athletes considered war a preparation for gymnastics, and gymnastics a preparation for warfare. A full list of citations for the associations made by Philostratus between gymnastics and warfare may be found at J. Jüthner 1909, *Philostratos über Gymnastik* edited with an introduction, translation and commentary (Leipzig and Berlin, 1909), 131 n. 1.

200 For which see Aristophanes *Birds* 291, Plato *Laws* 833, Pausanias 6.10.4, 5.12.8 and especially Plutarch *Moralia* 639e, who tells that while boxing, wrestling and running mimic and train for battle, the *hoplitodromos* was presented last at games to testify that military fitness was the aim of athletics and competition; cf. Ridley op. cit. (n. 193) 544 for the iconographic evidence.

201 Athenaeus 631bc; Ridley op. cit. (n. 192) 545–8, J.J. Winkler, 'The Ephebes' Song' in J.J. Winkler, et al. (eds), *Nothing to Do with Dionysus?* (Princeton, 1989), 55.

202 Athenaeus 628f.

203 Delorme op. cit. (n. 193) 19–20; but the introduction of the great games significantly antedates the effective introduction of hoplite warfare, according to the usual thinking: see A. Snodgrass, 'The Hoplite Reform and History', *JHS* 85 (1965), 110–22, J. Salmon, 'Political Hoplites?' *JHS* 97 (1977), 84–101.

204 e.g. A.W. Gouldner, *The Hellenic World: a Sociological Analysis* (NY, 1965), 49; cf. D.G. Kyle, *Athletics in Ancient Athens* (second edn, London, 1993), 10. O. Murray, *Early Greece* (Glasgow, 1980), 193 and Bremmer op. cit. (n. 86) 143 argue that the Greek aristocracies developed athletics in order to preserve their identities after the business of warfare had been opened up to the masses with the introduction of hoplite armour.

. 205 Note that the words 'gymnasium' and 'palaestra' appear on almost every page of Buffière's *Eros adolescent* (cited, n. 2); NB p. 199, 'schools, and above all gymnasia, were throughout Greek history the site of choice for pederasty' and pp. 561–73, 'Privileged places of love: gymnasium and palaestra.'

206 Theognis 1335–6.

207 Note the important remarks of Dover op. cit. (n. 8) 154–7 on Plato and Socrates in the gymnasium; cf. also Buffière op. cit. (n. 2) 6, 28, 76.

208 Plato *Euthydemus* 273a; cf. Buffière op. cit. (n. 2) 568–9.

209 Plato *Lysis* 203a–207b; Buffière op. cit. (n. 2) 564–6.

210 Plato *Charmides* 153d, 154d, 155cd; cf. Buffière op. cit. (n. 2) 567–8. Cf. also Vlastos op. cit. (n. 16) 96 with n. 52 for the exceptional nature of the *kalos*; note that the question 'who is the best?' played a significant role in homosexual education at Sparta (Plutarch *Lycurgus* 18), and possibly underlies Sappho's lesbian poem, F16 Voigt (the Anactoria ode).

211 Plato *Theaetetus* 162b.

212 Plato *Symposium* 217c.

213 Aristophanes *Clouds* 973–80, 1002–24; cf. Dover op. cit. (n. 8) 125.

214 Aristophanes *Birds* 136–42; cf. Dover op. cit. (n. 8) 137.

215 Aristophanes *Wasps* 1025, *Peace* 762–3.

216 Aeschines 1.135, 138, 156–7; cf. Dover op. cit. (n. 8) 69.

217 Plato *Laws* 635e–636b; cf. Plutarch *Moralia* 751f; cf. Clarke op. cit. (n. 149) 382.

218 On this institution see in particular P. Vidal-Naquet, 'The Black Hunter and the Origins of the Athenian *Ephēbeia*', in R.L. Gordon, ed., *Myth, Religion and Society: Structuralist Essays in the Classics* (Cambridge, 1981), 147–62, translation of 'Le chasseur noir', *Annales ESC* 23 (1968), 947–64, Winkler op. cit. (n. 201).

219 Buffière op. cit. (n. 2) 11 and passim in fact argues that it was to boys of ephebic age in particular that Greek *paiderastai* were attracted, and that they should really have been called therefore 'ephebophiles'.

220 See *Ath.Pol.* 42; cf. Vidal-Naquet op. cit. (n. 218) 147, Winkler op. cit. (n. 201) 26–35, Ridley op. cit. (n. 193) 531–7. See C. Pélékidis, *Histoire de l'éphébie attique* (Paris, 1962) for the problem of how and when the *ephēbeia* was organised.

221 Cf. Schnapp op. cit. (n. 84).

222 For the panoply, see *Ath.Pol.* 42.3 and cf. Aeschines 3.154; see M.H. Hansen, *The Athenian Democracy in the Age of Demosthenes* (Oxford, 1991) 89, 109, 129. See also Vidal-Naquet op. cit. (n. 218) 148 ('He both is, and is not, a member [of the *polis*]'), Winkler op. cit. (n. 201) 33. It is not clear whether, in pederastic scheme of things, they are more appropriately *erastai* or *erōmenoi*.

223 For the comparison cf. Vidal-Naquet op. cit. (n. 218) 153–4, 158.

224 Plato *Laws* 763b; Schnapp op. cit. (n. 84) 72.

225 Many similar references could be quoted from this text.

226 Cf. W.B. Tyrrell, *Amazons, a Study in Athenian Mythmaking* (Baltimore, 1984), 50–1, 64–7, 72–3, 83–5.

227 Winkler op. cit. (n. 201) 34; likewise Tyrrell op. cit. (n. 226) 72–3 notes that in terms of warrior-styles the hoplite and the ephebe were really antitheses; cf. Vidal-Naquet op. cit. (n. 218) 150, 152–4 with further references.

228 For a review of the major sources for Greek homosexuality, see Dover op. cit. (n. 8) 4–15. Of the five principal sources, the most important three are from Classical Athens: Old Comedy, especially Aristophanes; Plato, especially

the *Symposium* and the *Phaedrus*, and Aeschines 1 (*Timarchus*).

229 Thus at *Symposium* 182b–184b Plato contrasts the promiscuity of homosexual relations in other states with the elaborate set of principles (the '*nomos*') that governs them in Athens; cf. Dover op. cit. (n. 8) 81, 83, 190, Vlastos op. cit. (n. 16) 79.

230 Plutarch *Pelopidas* 18.

231 Plato *Symposium* 178e–179a.

232 Ephorus FGH 70 F149, Plutarch *Lycurgus* 17–8.

233 Plato's *Symposium* is the key text here: see Marrou op. cit. (n. 9) 29–45, Dover op. cit. (n. 8) 91, 202–3.

234 There have been some dubious attempts to find a 'sociobiological basis' for this paradigm in observed patterns of phallic display by animals for the purpose of territory protection; cf. Pinney op. cit. (n. 39) 180, W. Burkert, *Structure and History in Greek Mythology and Ritual* (Berkeley, 1979) 39–41, Dover op. cit. (n. 8) 105, Buffière op. cit. (n. 2) 518–21.

235 See Dover op. cit. (n. 8) 76, 100–9, esp. 101 and 106, 143–5, 168, 188, Foucault op. cit. (n. 21) part 4 chapter 3, Buffière op. cit. (n. 2) 179–93, 211–24, Halperin op. cit. (n. 12) 129–137, Bremmer op. cit. (n. 2) 290, Golden op. cit. (n. 8) 329–9, Cantarella op. cit. (n. 15) 42–8. The habitual pathic is represented as a woman at e.g. Aeschines 1.185, 'a man male in body, but having committed the sins of a woman'.

236 Aristophanes *Thesmophoriazusae* 59–62; cf. Dover op. cit. (n. 8) 143.

237 Aristophanes *Thesmophoriazusae* 200–1 (translation: Dover). I concede that these two paradigms, that of education and that of subjection, need not always be completely incompatible, in that the educated is properly subject to the educator; nonetheless it will become clear that they are usually very different in their significances. The two paradigms are brought together quite harshly in the bantering rustic exchange in Theocritus 5.39–43, where Lacon asks 'When can I remember learning or hearing anything good from you?' and Comatas replies 'When I went up your arse and it hurt you...' (translation: Dover op. cit. (n. 8) 104, and cf. K.J. Dover, *Theocritus: Select Poems* edited with an introduction and commentary [London, 1971], ad loc.).

238 Aristophanes *Clouds* 1083–4, *Wealth* 168, *Thesmophoriazusae* 537–8, Xenophon *Memorabilia* 2.1.5, Lucian *Peregrinus* 9, Catullus 15.19; Dover op. cit. (n. 8) 105–6. However the case is slightly complicated by the fact that it is not simply a matter of rendering the adulterer effeminate and subject to his cuckold, since adulterers were conceived of as effeminate in the first place (we think of Paris at Homer's *Iliad* 6.321–2, 503–14 and Aegisthus in Aeschylus's *Agamemnon* at, e.g. 1633–5, 1643–5; Dover op. cit. [n. 8] 106 discusses a Corinthian vase on which a fleeing adulterer is given a white skin, the tone normally reserved for women). They may be conceived of as effeminate in as much as, like women, being spectacularly lacking in sexual self–control (*akrasia*). At any rate, the *raphanidōsis* of the adulterer would appear to symbolically *recognise* a status already present in the offender, rather than simply punitively transform his status.

239 See Dover op. cit. (n. 8) 133–4. E.g. R177 (Dover's numeration): Orestes kills Aegisthus with a sword that resembles and covers his penis (cf. on

raphanidōsis above for the punishment of adulterers). R837: a spear prolongs the line of a youth's penis, and is shaped to resemble it at the tip. CW8: an arming man appears to penetrate the rear of a bending man with his spear, and Theseus's spear prolongs the line of his penis as he kills the Minotaur. B588: Iolaus holds his club as if an erect penis (cf. Aristophanes *Birds* 1253–6, where a penis is used as a battering-ram; Dover op. cit. [n. 8] 140). Dover notes that the Greeks particularly preferred straight, pointed penises that resembled swords, and that these indicated a youth's fitness to become a warrior.

240 Cf. Pinney op. cit. (n. 39) 183.

241 On this pot see K. Schauenburg, '*Eurymedōn eimi*', *Ath.Mitt.* 90 (1975) 97–121, with pl. 25, Pinney op. cit. (n. 39).

242 Thus Schauenburg op. cit. (n. 241), Dover op. cit. (n. 8) 105, 204, Winkler op. cit. (n. 11) 51, Golden op. cit. (n. 8) 329. However, a dissenting case has been put by Pinney op. cit. (n. 39). She argues that while 'I stand bent over' must inevitably be spoken by the bending figure, the preceding 'I am Eurymedon' is spoken by the running figure; the words do after all begin at his head. This in itself does not invalidate the Schauenburg/Dover interpretation – it might rather support it if the Greeks identified the river Eurymedon with themselves as victors there, rather than with the Persians as vanquished there. She also objects that the bending figure's attributes, his one-piece suit and *gorytos*, identify him as a Scythian rather than a Persian. But identification is made difficult by the loss (and purely conjectural restoration) of his head-dress, and in any case, Athenian painters did to some extent identify the attributes of Persians and Scythians, as Pinney herself explains.

Pinney further argues that the name Eurymedon, literally 'ruling widely' (*eurys*, *medōn*), should here be taken to mean more pointedly 'lording it over wide-arses', i.e., lording it over *eury-prōktoi*, excessive pathics. But I am not at all convinced that *eury-* is sufficient in itself to evoke *euryprōktos*. I agree however that the name is being used significantly here – for a kind of pun. I think, with most scholars, that the phrase 'I am Eurymedon' is indeed spoken by the bending figure (there is after all no break between this phrase and 'I stand bent over', which must be spoken by the bending figure). The second element of the name evokes *mĕd-ĕa*, 'genitals', and therefore suggests a name similar in meaning and perhaps modelled on *euryprōktos*, 'wide-genitalled' – if 'genitals' may be stretched to include 'anus.' (*Mĕdĕa*, with epsilon, and like it *mĕzĕa*, are less familiar forms of the common *mēdĕa*, with eta. The legend in fact does permit us to read eta, should we wish, since it does not differentiate between eta and epsilon, as can be seen from *hĕstēka*, written with two epsilons). The bending figure, eagerly pathic, is therefore saying 'I am wide-genitalled', and this claim is particularly well elucidated by the second phrase, '(because) I stand bent over'.

Curiously the word *kybda*, 'bent over', refers to a fellator at Archilochus F42.2 West.

243 Aristophanes *Frogs* 47–50.

244 Dover op. cit. (n. 8) 188.

245 Theopompus FGH 115 F225.

246 Cf. Winkler op. cit. (n. 11) 46–7.

247 *Kinaidoi* are the opposite of ideal citizens too: Demosthenes 22.30–1 gives us a law of Solon forbidding citizen-prostitutes to address the people; the vanquished can not be leaders; cf. Winkler op. cit. (n. 11) 55–6, 60.

248 Winkler op. cit. (n. 11) 47–8.

249 Winkler op. cit. (n. 11) 50.

250 Cf. Dover op. cit. (n. 8) 144, Winkler op. cit. (n. 11) 47.

251 Plutarch *Agesilaus* 30.3–4.

252 Plato *Timaeus* 90e. Cf. Winkler op. cit. (n. 11) 47 (and also 61, 225 n. 22). NB Hyperides F215 (only preserved in Latin): 'What then if we were conducting this case with Nature as judge – Nature who has distinguished male and female so that each performs his or her own proper duty and office – and what if I were to show that this man has misused his own body in a feminine way? Surely Nature would be shocked and astonished that any man would not think it a most blessed gift for him to have been born a man and that he had spoiled Nature's kindness to him, hastening to transform himself into a woman?'

253 Arctinus of Miletus *Aethiopis* F1 (Proclus *Chrestomathia* 2).

254 The Exekias cup is London B 210 ABV 144.7; cf. Keuls op. cit. (n. 152) 44–8 (illustrated p. 48 no. 27), Tyrrell op. cit. (n. 226) 27 with 135 n. 13.

255 Tyrrell op. cit. (n. 226) 78–81, 92; cf. N. Loraux, *Tragic Ways of Killing a Woman* (Harvard, 1987), 37–42, translation of *Façons tragiques de tuer une femme* (Paris, 1985), on the general equivalence between marriage and death for virgins.

256 Loraux op. cit. (n. 255) 37–42, 50–3, 61.

257 Lactantius *Divinae institutiones* 1.20.29–30.

258 Thus Dover op. cit. (n. 8) 193, 202, Cartledge op. cit. (n. 91) 16–7, op. cit. (n. 13) 32 n. 24.

259 Plutarch and Plato as quoted above; Xenophon *Symposium* 8.35 suggests that *erastai* and *erōmenoi* are placed side by side by the Thebans because they do not trust the *erōmenoi* to be brave without the gaze of their *erastai*.

260 Cf. Plutarch's Theban *erastēs*, who asks his enemies to kill him in a certain way for the sake of the image he will present to his *erōmenos*; Aelian *Historia Animalium* 4.1 tells a similar tale of a Cretan *erastēs* who stumbles and asks his enemies to kill him in the breast rather than the back, lest his *erōmenos* judge him a coward; cf. Bremmer op. cit. (n. 2) 287. Cf. also the tombstone of Gnathius (IG i² 920): 'Here a man in love with a boy swore an oath to join in strife and woeful war' (translation: Dover op. cit. [n. 8] 124). Plutarch *Moralia* 761c (on which see above) tells of two *erastai* competing for an *erōmenos*, of which one, Theron of Thessaly, chopped off his thumb and challenged the other to do the same; cf. Dover op. cit. (n. 8) 51 and esp. n. 23 for further similar examples.

261 Cartledge op. cit. (n. 13) 21.

262 Xenophon *Symposium* 8.32–6.

263 Plutarch *Moralia* 761c.

264 Homer *Iliad* 18.333–5; cf. Aeschines 1.145 and esp. Plato *Symposium* 179e–180a; cf. Dover op. cit. (n. 8) 41. As Buffière op. cit. (n. 2) 655 observes:

'Achilles without Patroclus would not be Achilles.'

265 Xenophon *Hellenica* 4.8.39; cf. Dover op. cit. (n. 8) 192.

266 Virgil *Aeneid* 9.176–449.

267 Virgil *Aeneid* 9.182: *his amor unus erat, pariterque in bella ruebant.*

268 Inspiration: Virgil *Aeneid* 9.194, cf. 210–8; for Euryalus as a *puer*, see 181, 216, 276; Nisus himself is a *iuvenis* at 235 (cf. 5.331, 361).

269 Virgil *Aeneid* 9.219–21, 430.

270 Virgil *Aeneid* 9.427: *in me convertite ferrum.*

271 Virgil *Aeneid* 5.294–361.

272 For a review of the scholarship on this episode, see P.G. Lennox, 'Virgil's Night-episode Re-examined (*Aeneid* ix, 176–449)', *Hermes* 105 (1977), 331–42. NB particularly the remarks of B. Otis, Review of F. Klinger, *Virgil* (1967) at *Gnomon* 41 (1969), 554–74 on the futility and recklessness of the action of Nisus and Euryalus.

273 Neanthes of Cyzicus FGH 84 F1. Cf. Dover op. cit. (n. 8) 191, Buffière op. cit. (n. 2) 117–8.

274 Plutarch *Cleomenes* 37.

275 Thucydides 6.54–9.

276 Dover op. cit. (n. 8) 51.

277 The selfish, isolationist tendency of Greek homosexuality also becomes clear in its association with marginalisation into the outlying rural areas, as in the Cretan rite and the ephebes (indeed in some respects homosexuality is paradoxically associated with the completely solitary life of the hunter; cf. Bremmer op. cit. [n. 2] 285, Schnapp op. cit. [n. 84]).

278 It was a commonplace of Greek historical writing, and, so far as we can tell, Greek culture itself, that tyrants should be assassinated by one or both partners of a loving couple; in this context, interestingly, homosexuality is strongly associated with liberty and the seizing of control over one's own destiny, and not at all with subjection: cf. Buffière op. cit. (n. 2) 119, 107–21, 345–6. See Plato *Symposium* 182c, Aristotle *Politics* 1311ab, and Plutarch *Moralia* 768f for lists of tyrants assassinated by loving pairs.

279 Cf. Winkler op. cit. (n. 11) 48 for the importance of hoplites protecting each other all alike in battle.

280 See Dover op. cit. (n. 8) 1, 62. It was however true, as Dover notes, that the Greeks could sometimes see some people as *more* homosexually inclined than others (e.g. Plato *Symposium* 189c–193d).

281 Cartledge op. cit. (n. 13) 28–9.

282 Plutarch *Lycurgus* 25, Xenophon *Lac.Pol.* 4.

283 Cf. Pritchett op. cit. (n. 49) ii 221–4.

284 Diodorus 12.70.1.

285 Diodorus 11.76.2.

286 Diodorus 12.75.7, 12.79.1, 4, 12.80.2–3, Thucydides 5.67.2.

287 Diodorus 15.62.2, 67.2, Xenophon *Hellenica* 7.4.22, 33–4, 5.3.

288 Xenophon *Hellenica* 7.4.13, 16, 31.

289 See Cartledge 1981:24–5 and Bremmer 1980:280–1, with references. For a review of anthropological work on homosexual warrior initiation in Papua New Guinea see Gilbert H. Herdt *Guardians of the Flutes: Idioms of*

Masculinity (second edn, NY 1987) xvii [second edn only], 15, 318, and the works cited there.

290 Herdt 1987: see xvii (second edn only) for further work by Herdt and others on this subject. The society has now been captured in a BBC2 documentary, *Under the Sun: Guardians of the Flutes*, broadcast Sunday 17 July 1994 10.00–10.50 pm. Herdt's work is referred to by D. Cohen, *Law, Sexuality and Society* (Cambridge, 1991), but he does not make very specific use of it.

291 See M. Detienne, *The Gardens of Adonis* (Sussex, 1977), translation of *Les jardins d'Adonis* (Paris, 1972).

292 See C. Calame, *Les choeurs de jeunes filles en Grèce archaique* (2 vols, Rome 1977), i 350–7 and P. Cartledge, 'Spartan Wives: Liberation or Licence?' *CQ* 31 (1981), 84–105 at 101.

293 Cf. W. Den Boer, *Laconian Studies* (Amsterdam, 1954), 216–8 and Cartledge op. cit. (n. 292) 89, 94–6 and 102–3.

294 See E. Bethe, 'Die dorische Knabenliebe', *RhM* 62 (1907), 438–75, Cartledge op. cit. (n. 13) 23–5, 31 n. 18, E. Bourguet, *Le dialecte laconien* (Paris, 1927), 151–2, A. Ruppersberg, *'Eispnēlas'*, *Philologus* 70 (1911), 151–4, Bremmer op. cit. (n. 2) 280–3, 293, K.J. Dover, 'Eros and Nomos', *BICS* 11 (1964), 31–42 at 42 n. 35, op. cit. (n. 8) 189 n. 12, 193, 202, Jeanmaire op. cit. (n. 85) 456–8, Buffière op. cit. (n. 2) 56–7, 70 with n. 20.

295 Callimachus F68 Pf.

296 [Theocritus] 12.12–4. Eustathius on Homer *Iliad* 9.5 also tells that *eispnilos* is a Spartan word.

297 Scholiast [Theocritus] 12.12b, Choeroboscus on Theodosius 166.33 Hilg. (*ispnil-ēs/-os*), Eustathius on Homer *Odyssey* 4.361 and *Iliad* 9.5, *Etymologicum magnum* s.v. *aïtēs*.

298 Eustathius on Homer *Iliad* 9.5, *Etymologicum magnum* s.v. *eispnēlēs*. See A.S.F. Gow, *Theocritus* (2 vols, Cambridge, 1950) ad 12.13, R. Pfeiffer *Callimachus* (Oxford, 1949–53) ad F68.

299 See P. Chantraine *Dictionnaire étymologique de la langue grecque* (4 vols, 1968–80, Paris) s.v.

300 Scholiast [Theocritus] 12.12c.

301 Aelian *Varia Historia* 3.12, scholiast [Theocritus] 12.12d.

302 Thus Xenophon *Symposium* 4.15, scholiast [Theocritus] argument and 12.12bc, *Etymologicum magnum* s.v. *aïtēs*, Eustathius on Homer *Odyssey* 4.361.

303 Aelian *Varia Historia* 3.12.

304 Hesychius s.v. *empnei mou*, scholiast [Theocritus] 12.12d.

305 Eustathius on Homer *Iliad* 9.5.

306 At Plutarch *Cleomenes* 2 *empneisthai* could be either.

307 *Etymologicum magnum* s.vv. *aïtēs* and *eispnēlēs*.

308 Scholiast [Theocritus] 12 argument.

309 Aristophanes F738, [Theocritus] 12.14, with scholiast and argument, *Etymologicum magnum* s.v. *aïtēs*, Eustathius on Homer *Odyssey* 4.361 etc.

310 [Theocritus] 12.12–4.

311 Alcman F34 Page, with scholiast [Theocritus] 12 argument.

312 Cartledge op. cit. (n. 13) 31 n. 18 takes it as 'listener'; cf. Chantraine op. cit. (n. 299) s.v. *aētas*.

313 Scholiast [Theocritus] 12 argument, Eustathius on Homer *Odyssey* 4.361 and *Iliad* 9.5; Homer *Iliad* 15.252.

314 e.g. Homer *Iliad* 20.110 and *Odyssey* 9.381.

315 See Buffière op. cit. (n. 2) 70 n. 20.

316 Antipater at *Palatine Anthology* 9.266: *empnein [sc. aulois]*.

317 Plutarch *Pelopidas* 19.

318 Plutarch *Lycurgus* 15.12.

319 Critias DK 88 F32, Xenophon *Lac.Pol.* 1.3, Plutarch *Lycurgus* 15.12–13.

320 Plutarch *Lysander* 30.7.

321 Herodotus 6.67–9.

322 Xenophon *Lac.Pol.* 1.7–9, Polybius 12.6b; cf. Plutarch *Lycurgus* 7, 15.

323 Plutarch *Lysander* 30.7.

324 Xenophon *Lac.Pol.* 9.5, Plutarch *Agesilaos* 30.4.

325 Herodotus 7.3, with the important discussion of P. Carlier, *La royauté en Grèce avant Alexandre* (Strasbourg, 1984), 240–7. See in general Den Boer op. cit. (n. 293) 216–8, Cartledge op. cit. (n. 292) 89, 94–6, 102–3, MacDowell op. cit. (n. 82) 45, 73–4, 76–7, 85–7.

326 Scholiast [Theocritus] argument, quoting Alcman F34 Page; cf. Calame op. cit. (n. 292) i 433–6, Buffière op. cit. (n. 2) 74–5, Dover op. cit. (n. 8) 193, 202.

327 Plutarch *Lycurgus* 18.

328 Hagnon of Tarsus apud Athenaeus 602d; cf. Cartledge op. cit. (n. 292) 104, MacDowell op. cit. (n. 82) 87.

329 Xenophon *Lac.Pol.* 1, Polybius 12.6b, Plutarch *Lycurgus* 15.

4

PHILIP II AND ALEXANDER THE GREAT: THE MOULDING OF MACEDON'S ARMY

Alan B. Lloyd

On November 6, 1917, the town of Passchendaele fell at last to British forces.

> The following day Lieutenant-General Sir Launcelot Kiggell paid his first visit to the fighting zone. As his staff car lurched through the swampland and neared the battleground he became more and more agitated. Finally he burst into tears and muttered, 'Good God, did we really send men to fight in that?'.
>
> The man beside him, who had been through the campaign, replied tonelessly, 'It's worse further on up.'[1]

By the time this event took place allied troops had been engaged for about fourteen weeks and sustained casualties which cannot have been far short of half a million men, of which approximately 30% will have been fatalities.[2] Furthermore, this assault had been sustained in some of the most appalling battlefield conditions in history. Passchendaele, therefore, raises in an acute form the fundamental question: 'What is it that enables men to confront, accept, and sustain the stress of battle?' It may also raise, though less imperiously, a further question: 'What determines in battle who wins and who loses?'.

In the recent past several excellent books have addressed these issues in relation to Medieval or Modern Warfare. John Keegan's *The Face of Battle* published in 1976 is of seminal importance,[3] and Richard Holmes's *Firing Line* which appeared in 1985 is also of outstanding value.[4] The results of this kind of research were subsequently taken up and applied to ancient Greek warfare by Victor Hanson in *The Western Way of War* (1989) and later work.[5] What I wish to do in this paper is to offer a preliminary study which applies the perspectives gained from such analyses to Macedonian warfare of the time of Philip II and Alexander the Great.

I should like to proceed in three stages by posing and attempting to answer three questions: i. How is an army created?; ii. Once created, how is it prevailed upon to fight?; iii. When it has engaged in battle, what determines who wins and who loses?

i. The Creation of an Army

To make an army civilians need to be militarized, i.e. they need to be converted into a group optimized for fighting. This process may involve several elements: uniform dress, initiation rituals such as swearing an oath, and training which serves to induce conformity and group solidarity at all levels, to toughen the men physically, and to create the highest possible level of skill in the use of weapons. Once created, this in-group solidarity can be enhanced in several ways, e.g. by the use of a communal language, the playing of communal games, and participation in social events, not necessarily of a very elevated kind. All these devices, if applied effectively, will create at the very least a force with considerable outward discipline, and, if the trainer is lucky, they will also provide the basis for developing the even more desirable inner discipline.[6]

Getting a force so trained to kill the enemy is a further necessary step. Killing is deprecated in most societies under normal circumstances, and means must be found to remove from the soldier or, at least, attenuate that taboo in some way. Several interrelated factors have been isolated in the literature mentioned above.[7] In the first place, an ideological or conceptual framework is generated to attenuate the guilt of killing by claiming that the war is justified. Consequently, the concept of the 'just war' is a recurrent feature in historical literature: 'We are morally right, and the enemy is in the wrong.' This conviction can be consolidated in a number of ways, e.g. the enemy can be denigrated, derided, depersonalized, dehumanized, or even unsexed. Let us now compare the evidence on the Macedonian situation with this template.[8]

The creation and training of the Macedonian army shows many of the classic features. Uniform dress was certainly employed. The clearly defined functions of the various components of the Macedonian army would in themselves have dictated that there should be consistency in weaponry, and this factor on its own would have created a high degree of uniformity in appearance within such units as the Companion Cavalry, the infantry of the phalanx, and Hypaspists. How far the Macedonians attempted to create uniformity of dress and defensive equipment in the time of Philip and Alexander is far from clear. Representational evidence is too limited to decide the point, and questions like a possible switch from the use of the Phrygian helmet to the Boeotian within the cavalry, the degree of currency of the *pilos*-helmet in the infantry, the extent of the use of the sun-burst device on shields all seem to me to be still wide open to debate.[9] At the same time there is no doubt that equipment could show unit-specific features: silver ornaments were added to the shields of the Hypaspists in 327, after which they became known as *Argyraspides*, 'Silver Shields' (D.S. XVII.57; Q.C. IV.13.27,[10] VIII.5.4; Arrian VII.11.3; Justin XII.7.5); Curtius indicates that the royal bodyguard were quite distinctive in appearance (*habitus*), though it is evident that the possession of a lance (*lancea*) was a specific feature (VII.1.18); Royal Pages, whose functions were paramilitary when they were not entirely military, may have had distinctive cloaks;[11] and the silvered helmet with horse-hair plume worn by the horseman to the left of the king in the Alexander mosaic may well have been the mark of an officer.[12] Whatever the uncertainties of detail, however, it is clear that the Macedonians were aware of and exploited uniformity of appearance as a means of enhancing *esprit de corps*. The militarization of the civilian was also promoted by a *rite de passage* in the form of an oath of allegiance sworn to the king.[13] The training programme was particularly rigorous and evidently designed to achieve all the functions described above as well as to promote operational efficiency. Philip's policy is summarized by Diodorus in the following terms:

> ... and having put their military organization on a sounder footing and equipped the men with appropriate weapons of war, he held unremitting exercises in full kit as well as competitive exercises (XVI.3).

Polyaenus expands on this illuminatingly:

> Philip used to train the Macedonians before they underwent dangers to march with full kit often three hundred stades carrying at one and the same time helmets, shields, greaves, pikes, and, as well as their weapons, provisions and utensils for their daily fare (IV.2.10).

According to Frontinus the stamina induced by such discipline and effort was quite deliberately used by Philip to wear down his opponents at Chaeronea (II.1.9). Alexander clearly followed his father's principles on training with enthusiasm: at the very beginning of his reign Diodorus describes him as submitting his army to regular manoeuvres (XVII.2.3); after the conquest of Halicarnassus and Miletus he put his force through a rigorous training programme; and, when the decision had been made to incorporate 30,000 Persian youths into the army, they too were subjected to the same medicine (Arrian VII.6;

Plu. 71). The efficacy of this régime in creating a machine-like homo-geneity of purpose and action is nowhere better described than in Curtius:

> With attention fixed on the nod of their commander, they have learned to follow the standards and keep their ranks; what is ordered they obey to a man. When it comes to standing fast, executing enveloping ma-noeuvres, running to the wing, changing battle order, the soldiers are every bit as skilled as their leaders (III.2.13–14).

At times of triumph in the course of the campaign this discipline and the sense of corporate unity which came with it were reinforced by ceremonial parades in full battle order (Arrian I.18.2 ; II.5.8; 24.6). The group's sense of solidarity was also confirmed by the use of special terms to refer to them, a point brought out in a well-known passage of Anaximenes of Lampsacus:

> Then, having accustomed those of highest distinction to function as cavalry, he (sc. Alexander)[14] called them 'Companions' (*Hetairoi*) whilst he divided the majority and infantry into companies and sections (*dekades*) and the other formations and called them 'Foot-companions' (*Pezhetairoi*) in order that both sections, by participating in companionship with the king, might continue to show the highest zeal (*FgrH* 72, F.4).

Here the emphasis of the terminology is very much on the groups' relationship to the king, but, in effect, solidarity is being affirmed at one and the same time in three separate ways: by labelling the groups, by insisting on their companionship amongst themselves, and by in-sisting upon the group solidarity with the king. Other collective nouns focusing on close proximity to the king were the terms *Philoi*, 'Friends', and *Somatophylakes*, 'Bodyguard'. Other criteria for labelling were those of equipment (Hypaspists, 'Shield-carriers'), tactics (*Hamippoi* (*dimachae*), 'infantry which mixed with cavalry'),[15] distinctive insignia (*Argyraspides*, 'Silver-shields'), and geographical origin (e.g. the 'pals' battalions called after the districts of *Elimiotis, Orestis, Lyncestis*, and *Stymphaea*, D.S. XVII.57.2: cf. Q.C. IV.13.28), though the latter crite-rion was certainly modified as joint comradeship in a great enterprise gradually overrode ties of tribal solidarity – indeed, it is evident that Alexander quite consciously ignored the territorial principle in the reorganization of his forces after the occupation of Babylon.[16]

Within the group itself language could be used in rather intriguing ways to express identity. The in-group sense of solidarity of the Mac-edonian section of the army can be confirmed by the use of the Macedonian dialect instead of the standard *koine* Greek.[17] According to

Curtius (VI.9.34–6), when Philotas was being tried before a Macedonian assembly in arms on a charge of involvement in the conspiracy of Dymnus, he was asked by Alexander if he would address them in Macedonian which is pointedly described as 'their ancestral tongue' (*patrius sermo*; at 10.23, it is called 'the native tongue', *nativus sermo*), and at 11.4, his fellow Macedonians are stated to be 'men of his own language' (*homines linguae suae*). Indeed, 11.4 seems to mean that untutored Macedonian soldiers would have found standard Greek difficult, if not impossible, to understand. Alexander's invitation to use this language is, at first sight, peculiar, since he himself, despite the fact that the context is a Macedonian assembly, had spoken to them in Greek – and evidently for the reason given by Philotas, i.e. that there were many non-Macedonians present who could not understand the Macedonian dialect. Presumably it was of critical importance to Alexander that the Greek-speaking Macedonian élite and Greek-speaking non-Macedonians should have a clear perception of what he was doing, but it was not vital that the bulk of the Macedonian army present should know. By subsequently making the proposal that Philotas should use Macedonian he was probably laying a trap into which Philotas very neatly fell whereby it was Philotas who appeared alienated from his countrymen. It is, at all events, quite clear that the employment of Macedonian is a nationalist issue and *ipso facto* bound up in this context with the identity of the Macedonian nation in arms. This in-group aspect of the Macedonian dialect fits well with Plutarch's account of the killing of Cleitus the Black (Ch. 51). This appalling episode patently had its origins in the growing alienation between the king and his Macedonian officers, and it is highly apposite that, when Alexander called his bodyguard to turn out to his assistance, he called to them in Macedonian – the spectacular evidence of the breaking of bonds of national solidarity in one relationship leads to their immediate reaffirmation in another, and it is through the language that this is done.

The Macedonian equivalents of the team games so much beloved of modern military forces are also easily found. Hunting was a great favourite: the scene of the chase in Tomb II at Vergina, probably depicting a royal lion hunt, provides a superb visual illustration of this preoccupation which can easily be supplemented from the written record:[18] the Conspiracy of the Pages arose out of an episode in a royal boar hunt (cf. Arrian IV.13); Alexander availed himself of the opportunity to hunt elephant in India (Arrian IV.30.7–8); and he won great renown from personally slaying a lion, in the narration of which episode Plutarch rightly links the ethos of the hunt with that of the warrior (ch. 40). None of this is to say that even Alexander always sought the toughest prey (Plu. 23 mentions foxes and birds as the quarry), and his Companions were perfectly capable of pursuing a mongoose for some sort of sport (id. 41)! Highly organized competitive games are also mentioned not infrequently, as we should expect, at critical junctures in the course of events where the activation of bonding mechanisms or affirmations of solidarity were a pressing psychological necessity: according to Plutarch (ch. 15), when Alexander had crossed over to Asia and visited Troy – events which were clearly of major and obvious significance both to him and his army – the king held a competitive race with his Companions in honour of Achilles; after the mutiny in India, when his army refused to proceed further, he was posed with a particularly acute problem in terms of reaffirming solidarity, and again competitive games served as part of the process for restoring harmony (e.g. Arrian V.29).[19] Even in less acute situations the bonding function will always still be present to some degree: at ch. 73 Plutarch speaks of Alexander and his Companions playing a game of ball together,[20] and it is clear that banquets could be punctuated by contests or games of a less elevated kind such as wine-drinking tournaments which many a modern barrack-block or college dining room could easily parallel (cf. Plu. 70; Q.C. VIII.6.14).

Communal drinking is also found in contexts which indicate its rôle as a means of bonding. Macedonian aristocrats were much given to it, and drinking bouts frequently feature, often at critical junctures. A clear case in point is the banquets held at the festivals of Aegae[21] and Dium before Alexander set out. Diodorus's account of the latter episode is particularly instructive:

> Having laid out a tent with one hundred couches, he entertained both his *Philoi* and the commanders, and moreover the ambassadors from the cities. In dazzling splendour he feasted large numbers and, by distributing sacrifices to all his army and the other things requisite for their good cheer, he boosted their morale (XVII.16.4).

The context here is fundamentally a major religious event celebrated at the ancient cult centre of the Macedonian people, an event motivated at the deepest level by the desire to enlist Zeus's aid in the forthcoming enterprise. At the same time it becomes an expression and a confirmation of the corporate solidarity of all those involved. The feast in the great tent brings together the *Philoi* and commanders, but even the ordinary soldier is not forgotten and is given a place in a feast embracing the entire army. A similar and better-known corporate celebration is the banquet held at Opis in 324 which served to give expression in a traditional way to Alexander's reconciliation with his troops after the mutiny of his army (Arrian VII.11.8–9). Drinking bouts with the Companions frequently punctuate our accounts of Alexander's campaigns. The Companions are specifically stated to have been involved in the notorious party which ended in the burning of the palace quarter at Persepolis. It should also be noted that Cleitus was killed at just such an event in 328 (id. IV.8). Not surprisingly, these all-lads-together debauches were a subject of adverse and caustic comment by the Greeks, and we find Demosthenes speaking with some relish of 'the licentiousness of his (Philip's) daily life, the drunkenness and lewd dancing' (*Olynthiacs* II.18).

A further issue of great importance in creating an effective fighting force is the level of its attunement to violence either through the character of the society to which it belongs or even artificial battle inoculation – necessarily, but sadly, programmed or endemic thuggery is a not uncommon concomitant of military virtue! Here the Macedonians were in a highly favourable position. At all levels of society, even in times of peace, they lived a vigorous outdoor life which was far from conducive to the development of the more delicate sensibilities, but the experience of decades of almost unremitting warfare had created a large force of battle-hardened veterans who were probably as inured to war as it is possible to get. As Demosthenes plaintively commented, 'These men had their weapons constantly in their hands' (*On the Crown*, 235).

The issue of the ideological justification for making war arises in our sources on a number of occasions. It is impossible, given the nature of our texts, to point to an explicit early Macedonian ideology of war, but we cannot be wrong in assuming that for Philip and his troops at the beginning of his reign the justification for organized slaughter of the enemy was defence of the homeland from aggressors. The long history of murderous strife with such antagonists as Illyrians and Paeonians must also have generated a deep hatred and passionate urge to vengeance which would not only have strongly fuelled Macedonian ardour when confronting them but would have been easily transferable to other enemies. The letter alleged to have been sent by Alexander to Darius after Issus neatly summarizes what were probably the main elements of his self-justification for the attack on the Persian Empire in terms which would have been heartily endorsed by all participants, Greek or Macedonian:

> Your ancestors invaded Macedonia and the rest of Greece and did us much harm, though we had previously done none to them; as for me, I

have been appointed Commander-in-Chief of the Greeks, and I have crossed over into Asia desiring to exact vengeance on Persia, but it was you who started it all. You came to the assistance of Perinthus, which wronged my father; and a force was sent into Thrace by Ochus, despite the fact that it was under our sovereignty. My father was murdered by conspirators, whom you organized, as you yourselves bragged to everyone in your letters, and you assassinated Arses with the help of Bagoas, and seized the throne unjustly and, contrary to Persian law, doing wrong to Persians; you then sent improper letters to the Greeks about me, urging them to make war upon me. You despatched sums of money to the Spartans and certain other Greeks, and, when no other city received these, save the Lacedaemonians, and when your envoys had corrupted my friends and sought to destroy the peace I had made in Greece, I took up arms against you; but it was you who started the quarrel (Arrian II.14.4–6).

Alexander's actions after Granicus are very much of a piece with his view that he was engaged in a war of retribution and, therefore, justified. According to Curtius, Alexander reminded his Greek troops before Issus of the invasions of Darius and Xerxes, the destruction of temples and capture of cities, and the violations of human and divine law which had been perpetrated (Q.C. III.10.9), i.e. the Persians were to be punished, amongst other things, for religious offences. It is, therefore, entirely consistent with this thinking that he can claim, when he burned the palace area at Persepolis:

that he wished to punish the Persians in return for the fact that they had invaded Greece, wrecked Athens, and burnt its temples, and for all the other evils which they had perpetrated against the Greeks; for this he exacted vengeance (Arrian III.18.12).

Diodorus also puts into his mouth in Asia Minor the claim that it was specifically to liberate the Greek states in the area that the war against Persia had been undertaken (XVII.24.1). The same technique of putting the enemy firmly in the moral wrong appears during the siege of Tyre (Q.C. IV.2.17).

Finally, there is the question of the image projected of the enemy. It cannot be said that the tradition preserved in our sources either depersonalizes or dehumanizes, but it certainly denigrates and can show strong sexual overtones in that the Persians can be conceptually unmanned. At one level this simply picks up a view of long-standing, e.g. Isocrates writes in 346 of 'the barbarians, whom we regard as effeminate and inexperienced in war and corrupted by luxurious living' (*Philip*, 124), but, when this theme recurs at a crucial point in Alexander's pre-battle harangue at Issus, it must surely be seen as more than a commonplace – it is a device for making the enemy seem a more tractable problem:

> their numbers will be useless to them in battle, nor are they our equals in physique or will. Macedonians, themselves now long schooled in the toils and perils of war, will engage Persians and Medes, steeped for generations in luxury, a battle, in particular, of slaves with free men...our foreign troops...will be ranged against the laziest and softest peoples of Asia (Arrian II.7.3-5).

ii. Battlefield stress

Once confronted with an enemy many factors have been claimed to assist the fighting man to hold his ground. Whatever the period, leadership is a critical consideration at all levels. The bonding of leader and led can take place in a variety of ways, e.g. the model may be paternalistic, or it may be that of comradeship. Further supports in the face of stress are a strong sense of group solidarity, particularly at small-group level, belittling the enemy, the pre-battle pep-talk, the urge to win glory, bursts of martial music, emblems such as standards, coercion, confidence in equipment, or self-confidence induced by success or experience, the impossibility of flight, patriotism or the more concrete love of home and the desire to defend it, and material rewards such as booty and decorations. Finally, the stress generated by physical confrontation of the enemy or by the trauma of engaging in battle itself needs to be attenuated – this can be done either by countering it actively, e.g. by aggression, rousing war-cries, or running; alternatively, the opposite can take place, i.e. palliation – humour, the cigarette under fire, drugs, alcohol, mental withdrawal from the situation, hard work, lucky charms, fatalism, fantasy, or religion.[22]

How did the Macedonians cope with all this? Here the pre-eminent consideration was the quality of leadership at all levels.[23] This is particularly important in the relationship between the king and his army where the bonding was intensely close. We have already discussed the fragment of Anaximenes which is particularly revealing in this respect (see above, p. 172). As for Philip, Diodorus comments:

> In association with men he was affable and strove to win over the multitudes by gifts and promises to the most fervent good will (XVI.3; cf. 35).

Alexander's leadership in battle is frequently a matter of comment and obviously a recurrent determining factor in bringing victory. His qualities in this respect make a dazzling catalogue of military virtues:

he was endowed with an audacity which at times could border on impulsiveness; he had an unshakeable confidence in success – he invaded the Persian Empire with military resources which by any prudent evaluation would have seemed totally inadequate for the job; he always led from the front where he presented his men with a superb example of a first-class fighting officer (e.g., and almost fatally, in the attack on the Mallian city in India, Arrian VI.9 ff.), and his morale was shaken seldom and never for long – indeed, it was his men who cracked in India and refused to go further; his aggressiveness in attack was unrelenting and combined with an unflinching determination to advance, an unbreakable will to succeed, and lightning rapidity of action; he was one of the greatest cavalry commanders of all time endowed with a quick eye, a sharp tactical appreciation, and the capacity to maintain total control of his horsemen in action; his flexibility of mind enabled him to change tactics with exemplary speed in any operational context; he had a keen sense of his own strengths and those of the enemy; his preparation for battle was always extremely careful; he was a master of the current technology and practice of siege warfare; he was remarkably skilful in combined operations; he had a keen sensitivity to the fighting capacity of his men, and showed remarkable solicitude for their physical welfare and the state of their morale; finally, least tangibly and most importantly, he possessed that all-important quality in a great commander – luck. All this did not simply create a commander who was virtually unbeatable; these qualities and their consequences generated in the minds of Alexander's army from the very beginning of his career a total confidence in their leader which continued experience of warfare under him served only to strengthen. This attitude is aptly described by Curtius in the words which he puts into the mouth of Craterus in an address to Alexander: 'No matter how powerful an army unites against us from all the nations of the earth, even if it were to fill the entire earth with weaponry and men or pave the seas with ships or bring strange monsters against us – *you* will make us invincible' (IX.6.7).[24]

It would, however, be a mistake to ignore the patent fact that leadership was a quality which was not simply confined to the king but was liberally spread through the entire army. Many of his officers were inherited from his father (e.g. Parmenio), and some of them had come up through the ranks (Q.C. VI.11), but, old or new, their value was often of the highest, and they were by no means all of Macedonian origin; the superb Erigyius came from Mytilene, but this did not prevent him from becoming one of the most successful and trusted of

Alexander's officers. Indeed, it is clear that Alexander had a keen appreciation of the value of choosing and treating his officers well (D.S. XVII.65.3; Q.C. V.2.2–7). Curtius aptly comments after Gaugemela:

> His officers also should not be cheated of their praise. For the wounds which each had received are witness to their valour. Hephaestion's arm was smitten by a spear; Perdiccas, Coenus, and Menidas were almost killed by arrows. And, if we want to give a just assessment of the Macedonians who lived at that time, we shall affirm both that the king was truly most worthy of such subjects and his subjects of so great a king (IV.16.31–3).

Another unsurprising factor in enabling Macedonian forces to stand was the strong sense of group bonding on which we have already commented. Here the fundamental principle is that the troops of the Macedonian army in the strict sense are the companions and comrades of the king (see above, p. 172). He must, therefore, avoid behaviour which is too 'kingly', and Curtius claims that he went to some lengths to present himself as a common soldier:

> The king, covered at once with dust and sweat, was tempted by the clear water to take a bath while his body was still warm. So he undressed in full view of his army and went down into the river, thinking that it would also increase his standing if he showed his men that he was satisfied with attention to his person which was unfussy and easy (III.5.2).

And again:

> ...leaving aside their ingrained veneration for their kings, it is far from easy for us to describe the passionate admiration and warm affection for this king...certain details, which are wont to be regarded as incidentals, are often very gratifying to a soldier: taking physical exercise amongst the troops, mode of life and appearance little removed from the ordinary, soldierly strength... (III.6.17–19).

Not surprisingly this common touch created the strongest of bonds with the common soldier which he took care to nurture by sharing their dangers and giving them rewards of many kinds. He could, therefore, even persuade them to burn their baggage for the greater good on the march to Bactriana (Q.C. VI.6.14 ff.). Perhaps, however, the most eloquent and most moving testimony to this relationship is the hysteria which accompanied the news of his demise and the determination of his men to see him on his death bed (Plu. 76).

With the Companions the bonding was also one of class. The king and they were the élite of the army and of Macedonian society. The relationship was confirmed by continuous proximity, and in some cases, e.g. Hephaestion and Ptolemy, son of Lagus, became particularly strong. Some were devoted to the king literally to the death (Q.C. VIII.2.35–9). Within the group it would also appear that homosexual relationships could be part of the bonding structure (Arrian IV.13.3; VII.27.2; Q.C. VI.7.2 ff.).[25] There were, however, rivalries within the circle (Q.C. VI.8.1 ff.), and between Alexander and this inner group there was clearly a growing tension, caused preeminently by an increasing and clearly justified perception on the part of the Macedonians that Alexander's move towards Persian ways of doing things was making him less of a *primus inter pares* and more of a Great King.

At the small-group level we should particularly emphasize the importance of the *dekas* or group of ten. On the significance of this point Holmes comments as follows:

> The importance of the primary group of up to ten, whose members were in regular face-to-face contact, was recognised long before psychologists or sociologists had turned their attention to the question of group behaviour...the pikeman fought between comrades he knew well, under the command of his file-leader and file-closer.[26]

At this level, to which our sources so rarely depress their sights, we can be sure that comradeship, mutual trust, respect, frequently affection, shared experiences – even shared trauma, and always personal honour would have created a powerful cement keeping the group together in the face of the shock or prospect of battle. One suspects that the group narcissism which surfaces strongly in our sources from time to time played an important rôle in confirming such solidarity at all levels.[27]

The pre-battle pep-talk, which could include belittling of the enemy (see above, pp. 176 f.), is another way of dealing with increased stress at the point of crisis. Philip clearly appreciated the value of this device (D.S. XVI.3–4), and it features very prominently in our tradition on Alexander. Pep-talks to officers, like those described by Arrian before the final attack on Tyre (II.23) and before Gaugamela (III.9: cf. D.S. XVII.56.4), were probably common, but we have many accounts of similar addresses to the army as a whole. We need not doubt that ancient commanders delivered pep-talks to their troops, despite the fact that many of the soldiers would have found it quite impossible to hear a word they said, as Curtius himself admits (IV.13.38 ff.). Presumably those in proximity to the leader heard and filtered back the substance of the speech with sufficient force to generate the mix of corporate solidarity and group hysteria which it was the function of such occasions to generate.[28] The details of the speeches as preserved to us are unlikely to be historically accurate, given the nature and agenda of ancient historical writing, but their general tenor is probably acceptable, focusing, as they do, on two fundamental issues: the need to test the mettle of troops at a crucial juncture (e.g. Plu. 47) and the need to put fire into the belly of soldiers about to engage in battle (e.g. Arrian II.7.3–9; note how keen the soldiers are to attack immediately after this speech).

A further inducement to stand was the desire to win personal distinction or glory. It is quite clear that Alexander himself was deeply imbued with this thinking (e.g. D.S. XVII.54.5; Plu. 4), a feature which was very much of a piece with his intense identification with Achilles and the world of the *Iliad* (see below, p. 184), but it was an aspiration much more widely current than that, e.g. Alexander played on his troops' love of honour or glory before Issus:

> In addition he reminded them of what had already been so brilliantly achieved to the common good and recalled by name any individual who had performed any distinguished and glorious deed (Arrian II.7.7).

After the battle:

> (At the funeral ceremony) he heaped with praise every man he had seen perform some distinguished deed in action or of whom he received a reliable report to that effect, and he honoured them all with commensurate rewards (id. II.12.1).

We need not doubt the claim of Curtius that after Hydaspes the army was led on to further efforts by the desire for glory as well as riches (IX.1.1). Clearly the competitive martial ethic of epic poetry was still alive and well in the Macedonian army at least!

Finally, what can we say of martial music? There is no unequivocal counterpart of the fifes and drums of later European armies which did so much to stir their soldiers onward, but it is impossible not to suspect that, when the trumpets sounded, e.g. at the opening of Alexander's assault at Granicus (Arrian I.14.7), the effect was to some degree the same.[29]

Evidence of coercion is not plentiful, in part, no doubt, because of the nature of ancient historical writing and its points of emphasis: it is more interested in high-ranking heroes than the antics of squaddies! Nevertheless, superb though the quality of the Macedonian army was, there are clear signs that by no means all of the troops were equally keen to fight. Curtius puts into the mouth of Amyntas the claim that draft-dodging had been a problem in Macedonia (VII.1.37), and we find Plutarch speaking of a certain Eurylochus of Aegae as faking sick (ch. 41). Occasional instances of coercion are not, therefore, very surprising. Frontinus describes a case where Philip placed his cavalry behind the infantry in battle to prevent them taking to their heels (*Stratagems*, II.8.14), whilst Alexander's campaigns throw up several forms of coercion: Plutarch speaks of his rigorous discipline which led to severe punishment, in two specific cases execution, for dereliction of duty (ch. 57); we are also informed that he created a regiment out of malcontents which was separated off from the army and, therefore, disgraced. This made of them a crack unit since they were determined to restore their standing in the eyes of their comrades (D.S. XVII.80.4; Q.C. VII.2.36 ff.; Justin XII.5);[30] he is also alleged to have deprived his army on two occasions of the opportunity of flight to ensure that they fought the harder (D.S. XVII.23.1–2; Curtius claims that he told his army before Gaugamela that flight was impossible, IV.14.7). A further stiffener which occurs in our texts is the high level of self-confidence possessed by the Macedonian forces, based, as it was, on an extraordinary level of success and their very considerable experience of battle (cf. Arrian I.15; II.7).

Another inducement to fight was that, in specific actions, such as the attack on the Aornos mountain, the Macedonians got themselves into a position where the only way to avoid disaster was to advance (Q.C. VIII.11.13), but a particularly prominent imperative in our sources is the rewards of success. Philip's generosity in giving cities to sack as well as gifts in abundance is claimed to have been a powerful encouragement to his troops (D.S. XVI.75), and Alexander followed this lead with something to spare: officers and Friends could be rewarded with estates and even governorships (Plu. 34: cf. Q.C. III.10.5 ff.), but all ranks received money and precious objects on a very considerable scale as booty (Arrian V.26.8; Plu. 20; Q.C. VIII.1.34; D.S. XVII.94.4). Other forms of reward were pay bonuses (D.S. XVII.64.6; Q.C. V.1.45), pay differentials (Arrian VI.9; VII.23), promotions (Arrian VI.28), gifts for specific services (Plu. 39; D.S. XVII.89.3), gratuities at the end of a soldier's service (Plu. 42.71) or discharging of debts (Plu. 70). We even hear of pensions to war orphans (Plu. 71). We should also note that not the least of the inducements offered by these military operations was the opportunities for sexual indulgence, frequently forceful (Q.C. III.11.21). This must often have happened in such contexts as the storming of cities, but the many female prisoners-of-war acquired were evidently regarded as being generally available to the troops (Arrian VII.12.2; D.S. XVII.110.3: cf. Q.C.

V.1.6). Decorations, or the ancient equivalent thereof, could also be used as a stimulus to martial endeavour. Arrian informs us of an episode at the end of Alexander's life where gold crowns were allocated to certain of his officers for conspicuous gallantry (VII.5: cf. also 10 which is surely exaggerated, like much in this speech). Elsewhere we are told that time-expired veterans were to be given at home the best seats at public contests and festivals and the right to wear garlands (Plu. 71).[31] Arrian describes a Macedonian equivalent of the posthumous Victoria Cross when Alexander arranged for the Companion fatalities at Granicus to be commemorated by bronze statues executed by Lysippus (I.16.4: cf. Plu.16).

At the point of engaging with the enemy we find evidence of very much the same processes as those identified by research into more modern conflicts. Proactive counteraction of immediate pre-battle stress could take the form of aggression,[32] and there can be little doubt that the speed and violence of a Macedonian assault under Alexander would have been a significant asset here. Clearly since speed is part of his stock-in-trade, it is impossible to be sure that this factor is at issue in any specific case, but it must be suspected as an ingredient in the situation in some cases, e.g. the advance at the gallop at Issus (Arrian II.10.3); the vigour of the cavalry attack at the crossing of the Tigris (Q.C. IV.9.24); and the rapid advance to contact at Gaugamela (if Plutarch can be trusted, ch. 33); and Alexander's lightning assault on the Persian lines in the course of the battle is also described as being swift (Arrian III.14.2). Stress could also be alleviated by the battle-cry of which we hear on many occasions: Diodorus describes with typical enthusiasm the Macedonian battle-cry before Issus (XVII.33.4), and Arrian puts into Alexander's mouth the following instruction before Gaugamela:

> ...to give a resounding cheer, when the time was ripe to cheer, and the most fearsome battle-cry, when the time was ripe to shout it (III.9.7–8; Q.C. IV.12.23; cf. Plu. 33 – the enemy does likewise at ch. 16).[33]

Palliation is equally present: battlefield narcosis does not seem to appear explicitly as a device for steeling men to face the trauma of battle, but there are enough hints to justify the strong suspicion that it was not unknown: the army is mentioned as being ordered to take breakfast before Gaugamela (Q.C. IV.13.20; Plu. 32), and this cannot have failed to involve a certain amount of imbibing. Two other episodes point in the same direction: both Arrian (I.21) and Diodorus (XVII.25.5) describe an episode at the siege of Halicarnassus where

some troops of Perdiccas got themselves drunk and attacked the citadel, and Curtius informs us that on the march to Sogdiana a severe
shortage of water led the troops to consume the wine which they had
and quickly reduce themselves to a state of incapacity (VII.5.7–8).

Even fantasy can appear as a factor attuning and motivating people
to battle. Whatever the distortions inherent in our sources, it is indis-
putably there in Alexander. The recurrent obsession with Achilles and
the *Iliad* is a clear case in point (Arrian I.11.7–8; 12.1–2). We are told
that he desired to go to Siwa because Perseus and Herakles had done it
(Arrian III.3.1–2), and he was allegedly inspired to attack the rock of
Aornos by the desire to enter into rivalry with Herakles who had
attempted to besiege it and failed. Arrian also speaks of a desire to
surpass the achievements of such heroic figures as Cyrus and
Semiramis (VI.24.2–3: cf. 29.4–11). How far such or similar fantasies
extended downwards in the army we do not have the evidence to say
for certain, but it would be surprising if they did not.

Of all the factors which steeled the Macedonians to battle by far the
most prominent in our sources is religion. The most meticulous meas-
ures were taken to generate the conviction that the gods were on their
side. The body of concepts within which this thinking operated was
very much the traditional thought-world of Greek religion according
to which action was perceived to take place on two interpenetrating
planes, the human and the divine. Therefore, human activity and
circumstance were not necessarily experienced as autonomous phenomena but frequently as manifestations of divine will. The gods may,
therefore, guide, orientate, thwart, or punish human activities. Consequently it was of cardinal importance to establish what their views or
intentions were in specific cases, and the Greeks and Macedonians
were convinced that it was possible to do so by such institutions as
oracles or through the expert interpretation of signs sent by the gods
to give men indications, usually ambiguous, of what was in the offing
or at least what the divine perspective on events might be. In such a
conceptual world it was inevitably of great importance to feel that
projected actions had divine approval so that at any critical point in an
enterprise the participants, particularly the leaders, would be acutely,
even desperately, anxious to conciliate the good will of the gods and
establish their attitudes or intentions. At such psychological crises
there would also be a heightened mental or psychic attunement to pick
up any hints which the gods might send on the future course of events
so that oracles, dreams, omens, and portents tend to cluster thickly in
our tradition about such points. It follows that, if success is ultimately

achieved, those who benefit from it will express gratitude for the divine assistance received in the fullest and most generous manner possible.

One of the most striking features to emerge from all our major sources is Alexander's intense religious devotion.[34] To take a few typical examples: beginnings are clearly critical and become foci of intense ritual activity. It is highly significant that, before leaving for Asia, Alexander celebrated the great national festivals at Aegae and Dium (see above, p. 174). Diodorus gives us the following description of ritual events at the latter:

> Having, therefore, instructed them (sc. the Greeks) concerning what was advantageous to them and having encouraged them verbally to the war, he offered splendid sacrifices to the gods in Dium in Macedonia as well as dramatic performances for Zeus and the Muses which Archelaus, a previous king, had first established. He celebrated the festival for nine days, allocating to each of the Muses a day which was called after her (XVII.16.3–4).

At the very start of the assault on the Persian Empire after landing in Asia he sacrificed to Athena at Troy and made libations to the local heroes including Achilles and Ajax. At the same juncture Diodorus describes the following event:

> When the king had set out from the Troad and had come to the sacred enclosure of Athena, the sacrificer Aristander[35] spotted before the temple a statue of Ariobarzanes, a former governor of Phrygia, lying on the ground, and, when certain other auspicious omens had manifested themselves, he approached the king and affirmed that he would win a great cavalry battle and particularly if he fought in Phrygia. He added also that he would slay in battle with his own hands a distinguished general of the enemy in the course of the action; for this was indicated to him by the gods and, above all, Athena who would even assist him in his successful enterprise (XVII.17.6–7).

Once the expedition was under way, revelations and ritual activity came thick and fast: whilst Alexander was still in Lycia, a tablet was discovered which prophesied Greek victory over the Persians and allegedly much boosted Alexander's morale (Plu. 17). In the build-up to Issus he made sacrifice to the local gods (Q.C. III.8.22), and before the battle commenced he explicitly claimed, according to Arrian, that the army was under the protection of the gods:

> ...god played the general more effectively for them by putting it into Darius's mind to cram his force into a confined space, leaving the open ground (II.7).

At Tyre Alexander's dreams were interpreted on several occasions to the advantage of the Macedonians (Plu. 24), and one of the portents, according to Curtius, was consciously used by Alexander to encourage his troops:

> But he, being far from unsubtle in dealing with the psychology of his troops, informed them that a vision of Hercules had appeared to him in his sleep, holding out his right hand; guided by him and with him opening it up, he dreamt that he entered the city (IV.2.17).

At Gaza whilst Alexander was offering sacrifice a portent occurred which was successfully given a favourable interpretation by his most trusted seer Aristander (Arrian II.26; Q.C. IV.6.10 ff.; Plu. 25.4). Before Gaugamela several sources inform us that Alexander and Aristander spent the night before his tent and 'performed certain mysterious and sacred ceremonies and offered sacrifice to the god "Fear" ' (Plu. 31; Curtius describes the focus as the deities Zeus and Athena Nike (lit. Jupiter and Minerva Victoria, IV.13.15 ff.). A little later Alexander is presented as calling on the gods for help before the battle and claiming that, since he was the son of Zeus, they should assist the Greeks. We are also told that Aristander spotted an eagle (the bird of Zeus) flying over Alexander's head and then flying towards the Persian lines. This was pointed out to the Macedonian army and acted as an immediate inspiration to them (Plu. 33; cf. Q.C. IV.15.26 ff.). When Alexander suffered a serious setback in trying to force the Susian Gates, he immediately sought divine help (Q.C. V.4.1), and before the invasion of India several portents are said to have given considerable ground for concern, one of which, at least, was success-fully interpreted to the ultimate advantage of the Macedonians. Sig-nificantly, in the accompanying debates Alexander is alleged to have expressed the view that the dispensation of power lay with the gods (Plu. 57). Of a piece with all this is the religious activity surrounding termini: after the triumph at Issus sacrifices of gratitude for aid were immediately offered (D.S. XVII.40.1); the same phenomenon occurs after the capture of Tyre (D.S. XVII.46.6); and, finally, on the point of turning back from India we predictably find Alexander inaugurating a splendid series of thank-offerings to the gods (Arrian V.29.1–2).

A further point to emphasize in the religious area is the careful treatment of the dead which must have gone some way towards recon-ciling his men to the perils of battle.[36] All the Macedonian fatalities of Chaeronea were buried together, in a mass grave, and Alexander's scrupulous treatment of his dead is mentioned by all sources (e.g. Arrian I.23; Q.C. III.12.13; D.S. XVII.89.3). After Granicus we read:

And on the day after the battle Alexander buried all the dead with their arms and other equipment, and he granted their parents and children immunity from local taxes and all forms either of personal service or property taxes. And for the wounded he showed much concern (Arrian I.16.5).

Curtius explicitly points up the great importance placed by Macedonians on this matter even in the difficult circumstances of the storming of the Susian Gates: 'The king's conscience would not permit him to leave his men unburied; for by Macedonian custom there is hardly any duty in military life as binding as the burial of one's dead' (V.4.3). Diodorus probably defines the conscious motivation rather well when he comments on the aftermath of Granicus: 'After the battle the king gave the dead a splendid burial, being anxious through this honour to make the soldiers more zealous for the perils of battle' (XVII.21.6).

iii. Who wins and why?

One army engages another in order to defeat it, and defeat takes place either when a force loses the will to continue the struggle or when it is deprived of the means to do so. Usually, it is the first that happens so that the collapse of the opponent becomes in essence a moral collapse. The factors discussed in the previous two sections contribute to the will to fight and the morale to sustain the struggle once initiated, but what precisely is it that determines who wins and who loses? Battle is a complex business, and factors can interact in an intricate way to bring about a result, but a modern historian would point to several issues which over and over again have proved demonstrably crucial.

(a) Leadership

The leader may simply exercise his rôle in battle by example, and he may win simply because he maintains the will in himself and his forces to slog it out longer than the opposition. Alternatively, superior tactical skill may be deployed which permits a preponderance of force to be brought to bear to a critical degree at a critical point, e.g. he may open a killing-zone before the enemy does or a killing-zone wider than that of the enemy. However, the relationship between leader and led is not indissoluble: it is based fundamentally on a tacit contract, and, if that contract is broken, a sense of betrayal will be generated which may lead at least to passive resistance within the army and, at worst, to active mutiny. It is of cardinal importance that commanders – and indeed officers at all levels – should be seen to be keeping their side of this tacit contract.[37]

Alan B. Lloyd

(b) Superior battle discipline
This is created pre-eminently by experience and training and results in greater controllability and willingness to fight in available military forces.

(c) Superior will to win
This can yield victory against forces which are numerically superior and better equipped, but even in the best troops it is not inexhaustible. It is ultimately a function of the physical and moral state of the army which can be sapped insidiously but inevitably by such factors as tiredness, hunger, disease, and heavy casualties, particularly if they are recurrent. However, such stresses are not necessarily decisive; superior discipline and superior will can tip the balance.

(d) Superior weaponry
This amounts to an ability either to outreach the enemy or to maintain a higher kill-rate once contact has been made.

(e) Superior numbers
Military history abounds with cases of superior numbers being defeated by highly motivated and efficient smaller forces, but, where morale, leadership, fighting quality, and tactical skill are approximately equal, the victory more often than not will go to the big battalions.[38]

If we apply this yardstick to the Macedonian context, we find that all of it has a direct relevance. The quality of leadership is almost beyond reproach. The hold which Philip and Alexander had over their men, as already indicated, was, in part, institutionally determined (see above, pp. 177 f.), but it was greatly strengthened by the care which they both took to foster links. Our accounts of Alexander's career are full of examples of this phenomenon, e.g.

> When the armies were almost in contact, Alexander rode right along the line and exhorted them all to be brave men, not only recalling the names of officers with fitting distinction but also the names of commanders of squadrons and companies, also those of the mercenaries who were distinguished in rank or valour (Arrian II.10: cf. III.7, 9, 10; V.16).

As a tactician Philip was superlatively original and effective, adapting to the Macedonian context the principle of concentration of force at one point on the line which had been developed so brilliantly at Thebes by Pelopidas and Epaminondas.[39] The fine detail of what

Philip himself did is not entirely clear, but the results are indisputable. He had available the excellent Macedonian cavalry, the *Hetairoi* or 'Companions', who had for centuries formed the backbone of the military establishment (cf. D.S. XVI.4).[40] When we can see their structure clearly, they are made up of eight squadrons, which were recruited by districts. They were 200 strong each, with the exception of the Royal Squadron which apparently had 300. The Royal Squadron was presumably the one with which the king fought and which constituted a royal bodyguard (*agema*). It should, however, be remembered that, in the absence of stirrups and the modern style of saddle, charging with couched spear was not an option available to these troops and that, in consequence, the weight of their charge would have been noticeably less than that of a force of comparable size in modern times.[41] Their impact was achieved either on a moral basis or by the horsemen insinuating themselves into gaps which appeared in enemy forces and prizing them apart. It was the corps of élite heavy cavalry which constituted the Macedonian equivalent of the striking wing of Epaminondas, and it was they who were intended to apply the heavy concentrated punch which would shatter the enemy line.

The main force of Macedonian infantry was known as the *Pezhetairoi* or 'Foot-companions'. It follows from what has just been said that they were subordinated to the cavalry and did not occupy the pre-eminent tactical position of the traditional Greek hoplite infantry. Defensive equipment consisted of a helmet and small shield not much more than half a metre in diameter, sometimes, at least, decorated with a device in the middle. Their function was to act as a holding force, and this tactical rôle is reflected in their equipment (for which see below, p. 193).

The effectiveness of Philip's tactical concept and its related equipment emerges clearly at the very beginning of his reign in combat with the Illyrians:

> ...Philip, who was in command of the right wing with the best of the Macedonians under his command, ordered his cavalry to ride past the barbarians and take them in the flank, while he himself fell on the enemy in a frontal assault and began a vigorous engagement. The Illyrians, having formed themselves into a square, valiantly confronted the danger...later, as the cavalry exerted pressure from the flank and rear and Philip with his crack troops fought with true heroism, the mass of the Illyrians was forced to take to its heels (XVI.4.5–6).

Here Philip, in command of the infantry, pins the Illyrian force down and the key offensive thrust was put in by the cavalry.[42] Whatever the problems of working out the details may be, it is evident that all Alexander's major field actions worked essentially with the same tactical principle.

The tactical and technical expertise of Philip and Alexander were not confined to general field actions such as Chaeronea and Issus. Their grasp of the most modern technology of siege warfare and its application are amongst the most startling features of their military operations. Of critical importance in numerous cases was the effectiveness of Macedonian missile warfare either to destroy enemy defences or to suppress/impair enemy resistance at crucial points. Philip's operations against Amphipolis and Perinthus, though not consistently successful, are a case in point.[43]

The effectiveness of this force was greatly enhanced by its battle discipline and the effectiveness of its control in action. Curtius gives it the following accolade in words which are worth quoting in full:

> But the Macedonian battle-line is indeed wild and rough, yet it protects behind its spears wedges of tough, densely packed soldiers who cannot be budged. They themselves call it a phalanx, an infantry column that holds its ground. Man is locked to man, arms to arms. Attention fixed on their commander's signal, they have been trained to follow the standards and hold formation. Whatever is commanded, they obey (Q.C. III.2.13–14).

The controllability and speed of response of such troops are illustrated time and time again in our sources. According to Curtius, Alexander kept a firm hold on the advance to contact at Issus by riding in front of the army and continually motioning them to slow down (III.10.3), but its discipline appears nowhere more strikingly than at Gaugamela: the infantry was easily able to readjust its lines to counter the Persian chariots (Arrian III.13.6; cf. D.S. XVII.57.6); Alexander achieved a quick realignment of the cavalry and part of the phalanx to take advantage of a gap in the Persian line; and a little later in the thick of battle he was able to orchestrate a speedy and effective response to the crisis on the Macedonian left wing (Arrian III.14–15; cf. D.S. XVII.60.5 ff.). Not infrequently the control was exercised through trumpet signals which were evidently coded so that they might indicate, e.g., the need to prepare for battle (e.g. Q.C. IV.13.22), a summons to the royal quarters (VIII.1.47), or the order to begin an action (e.g. D.S. XVII.11.3; 33.4; 86.5).[44]

The importance of superiority in will emerges in the graphic account of the clash between the Scythian and Macedonian cavalry at Gaugamela:

And Alexander's troops suffered the heavier casualties under pressure from the superior numbers of the barbarians and because the Scythians themselves and their horses were better equipped with armour. But, even so, their attacks were held by the Macedonians, and by repeated violent assaults, squadron by squadron, they shattered their formation (Arrian III.13.4).

The mechanisms by which such moral strength is eroded are complex and delicate but easily illustrated: the collapse of leadership will frequently disseminate downwards to create a general collapse (D.S. XVII.60.8); bad news from another part of the battlefield can have a serious effect (Q.C. IV.16.4 ff.); the disintegration of one force in the army may precipitate a general dissolution which leads to the 'collapse from the rear' phenomenon graphically described by Keegan (D.S. XVII.21.5; 60.3);[45] severe physical difficulties or discomfort can swiftly wear down an army's will to fight (Q.C. V.4.12 ff.; VII.5.6); the sheer difficulty of continuing resistance can erode the will to resist any more (Q.C. VIII.10.10); battle fatigue eventually destroys the capacity to sustain the struggle (Q.C. IX.4.16) and can often only be alleviated by frequent rests (e.g. Arrian III.10.1; IV 18.2) and regular reinforcement by fresh troops (cf. Q.C. V.1.39 ff.; 7.12; VII.1.37 ff.; D.S. XVII.95.4; they could even turn the tide of battle, D.S. XVII.27.1–3) – it was Alexander's unwillingness to face the realities of battle fatigue which eventually precipitated mass mutiny in his army. In the course of this event Coenus complained:

> For you yourself see the number of Greeks and Macedonians who started upon this campaign with you, and how many of us are left...some have perished in battle, others, disabled by wounds, have been left behind in various parts of Asia, and more still have died of disease, and few from that great army remain, and these bereft of their erstwhile strength of body and in spirit yet more exhausted...you will never find the same appetite for danger (Arrian V.27.4–7).

Moral collapse can also be activated by ignorance of the nature of the enemy (Q.C. IX.8.4 ff.) or when the level of fear rises to an unsustainable point: the sight of Alexander bearing down upon them created panic amongst the Persians surrounding Darius at Gaugamela, and they broke (Plu. 33: cf. Arrian I.27.3; IV.6.4; V.15.2); panic assailed the Great King at Issus with disastrous consequences (Q.C. III.11.11); it is also alleged to have afflicted the Persians before Issus (Q.C. III.8.25–6, 30) and in the action at the Susian Gates (Q.C. V.4.30). Surprise is frequently a major trigger in this respect inducing first a mind-numbing confusion which, in turn, destroys the ability to mount an effective resistance, e.g. Philip's capture of Elateia in 338 (D.S. XVI.84: cf. Arrian IV.16.7; 19.4; VI.6.3; 21.3; Q.C. III.8.24–6; V.3.10; V.4.27–8; VI.6.21–2; D.S. XVII.67.5; 68.6; 84.2) – and even Macedonians could fall victim to this (Q.C. IV.15.3 ff.; VIII.1.3 ff.; D.S. XVII.59.6). Demonstrations of sheer military efficiency, intended or incidental, can have a similar effect (Arrian I.4.3; 6.1–4). Alexander was also capable of calculated frightfulness in order to weaken an enemy's resolve:

> Having commanded Craterus to follow with the phalanx, he led forth the cavalry and the light-armed troops and those who confronted him he bundled in a brisk action into the nearest city. Craterus had already arrived. And so, in order that right at the beginning he might strike terror into the hearts of a nation as yet without experience of Macedonian arms, he instructed his men to spare no-one, having set fire to the fortifications of the city which he was besieging. But, while he was riding to the walls, he was hit by an arrow. However, he took the city, and having massacred all the inhabitants, he even vented his spleen on the houses (Q.C. VIII.10.4–6).

In the same vein Alexander is alleged to have decided to annihilate Thebes 'pour encourager les autres' (D.S. XVII.9.4), and the terror tactics used in Oreitis are another case in point (D.S. XVII.104.7; cf. Q.C. IX.10.7).

A factor which gave the Macedonians a definite edge in their military confrontations with the Persian army was the superiority of their equipment. The cavalry were ideally armed to fulfil their purpose: for defensive purposes they were equipped with helmets which were at least in some cases of the Boeotian type to give the best possible vision, as Xenophon himself recommended (*Eq.* XII.3), and they also wore breastplates of metal which imitated the contours of the body. Whether they normally carried shields is not entirely clear; Alexander is certainly not using one in the famous battle mosaic, but the reliability of that source for such details must be debatable[46] and should be set against the clear evidence that Alexander used a shield in the cavalry charge at Granicus (D.S. XVII.21.2; Plu. 16). The main weapon of offence was a long cornel-wood spear (*xyston*) whose employment is graphically described by Arrian in his account of Granicus:

> And a cavalry struggle arose with one force trying to get out of the water, the other striving to prevent them, and a rain of javelins flew from the Persians whilst the Macedonians fought with their long spears (I.15.2).

and again:

> And from this point Alexander's men began to gain the upper hand by
> reason of their strength and experience and because they fought with
> long cornel-wood spears against lances (I.15.5).

The all-important tactical fact of the superior reach of the Macedonian
cavalry spear here emerges very clearly, i.e. it opens up a killing-zone
which is markedly deeper than that of the opposition. Indeed,
Diodorus states that Darius increased the length of the swords and
spears of his own cavalry before Gaugamela because he regarded the
length of Macedonian weapons as critical in the Persian defeat at
Granicus (XVII.53.1).

Infantry equipment was equally well thought out: the main offensive
weapon was the *sarissa*, a long pike which in Alexander's time could be
as much as 5.5 m long.[47] The effectiveness of this weapon is a subject of
comment on several occasions by Diodorus (XVII.84.4; 88.2), and
Curtius emphasizes its value in dealing with Porus's elephants
(VIII.14.16). It should perhaps be noted, however, that it was very
much the weapon of a packed mass of infantry; the duel between the
Macedonian Koragos/Horratas[48] and the Athenian Dioxippus, which
the latter easily won, strikingly illustrates the vulnerability of the solitary *sarissa*-armed infantryman (D.S. XVII.100.6; Q.C. IX.7.16–22;
Aelian, *VH* X.22). However, in a general action the only solution to the
reach of the *sarissa* was something which neutralized its length, and
this Onomarchus seems to have devised at an early stage in Philip's
career when we find the Phocian general using field artillery against
Philip to open up a killing zone for his own troops which the Macedonians were unable to close down (Polyaenus II.38.2).[49] However, the
lesson of the value of field artillery was well learned by the Macedonians, and we find Alexander exploiting its long-range potential with
lethal effect on more than one occasion (Arrian I.6.8; IV.4.4).

As we should expect, artillery was used to particularly good effect in
siege warfare where its reach and the relatively high velocity of its
projectiles were at a premium. At Tyre the critical factors in the
ultimate success of the Macedonian assault were the effectiveness of
Alexander's ship-borne artillery in knocking down the wall at the point
of assault and the confusion caused by bringing down fire at all possible points on the wall (Arrian II.22–3). This made it feasible to create a
breach into which the infantry could be poured in force. Again at Gaza
artillery played a decisive rôle. The city was first ringed by an earth-
work and then the artillery was mounted on that. From this vantage
point, and with the assistance of saps, it became possible to cast down a
section of the wall whilst fire-power swept the defenders from the

battlements (Arrian II.26–7). In the extraordinary action to take Mt Aornos artillery was also critically involved (Arrian IV.28–30).

Finally, numbers. Alexander's campaign against the Persian Empire provides the example *par excellence* of the principle that morale and quality of troops can get the better of armies many times their size in number. Nevertheless, it is worth remembering that even Macedonians, when confronted with good troops, could be overwhelmed and put to flight by superior numbers (D.S. XVI.35.2: cf. XVII.59.8).

What can we read from this analysis? Ancient historians have grown accustomed, quite rightly, to insisting that in our study of ancient societies we should take them on their own terms. Certainly there is much which is fundamental that is time- and culture-specific, but we must not forget our common humanity with our ancient forebears. In many crises their psychological reactions were not particularly different from our own. No doubt, the short-term close-range butchery of ancient battle differed in important respects from the temporally extended missile-dominated conflicts of the twentieth century, but it is abundantly clear from the preceding analysis that the ancient soldier in the stress of war and battle was subject to many of the same imperatives and mobilized much the same psychological mechanisms as his modern counterpart. However, though our sources tell us much, and let us sense even more, they do not take us to the human depths of the following passage, one of the most moving I know:

> As the moment of attack approached, men's thoughts branched out away from the apprehension of the night. Heath recalled the radiance of Captain Neville one hour before his death in the great first attack on the Somme. Maze writes of the slightly hysterical jokes. Carrington was astonished by Corporal Weller, invariably coarse of speech, singing a hymn to the Virgin in Latin. More often all would stand silent, dry lips twisting, furtive glances at photos and letters. Grant wrote:
>> I gave the men a good look. They seemed more or less in a trance. Their eyes were glassy and their faces white as chalk. But the way their mouths were set gave me confidence. One or two shook hands. An old private, lying down by a very young corporal, suddenly kissed him on the cheek and then lay down again flat. My orderly behind me tugged at my ankle. I could see he had something to say but the din was terrific. He looked very excited. I noticed the beads of sweat all over his face. Putting his mouth to my ear, he yelled, 'Till the very last, Lieutenant.' I remember patting him on the shoulder.[50]

Something like this there must have been from time to time, even amongst the battle-hardened veterans of one of the finest military machines in history.

Notes

1 L. Wolff, *In Flanders' Fields* (London, 1961), 268.

2 Op. cit., 274 ff.

3 J. Keegan, *The Face of Battle* (Harmondsworth, 1978).

4 R. Holmes, *Firing Line* (London, 1985).

5 V. Hanson, *The Western Way of War. Infantry Battle in Classical Greece* (New York, 1989); (ed.), *Hoplites: the Classical Greek Battle Experience* (London and New York, 1991).

6 Holmes, op. cit., 19 ff.

7 Keegan, op.cit., 45 ff., 114 ff.; Holmes, op. cit., 365, 376 ff.

8 Sources are relatively plentiful by the standards of Ancient History. The narrative sources on which most of this study is based are Diodorus Siculus, XVI–XVII (abbreviated D.S.), Quintus Curtius Rufus (abbrev. Q.C.); Arrian, *Anabasis*; Plutarch, *Alexander* (abbrev. Plu.); and Justin, *Epitoma Historiarum Philippicarum*, VII–XII. Arrian's narrative is based on Ptolemy and Aristobulus, two sources contemporary with Alexander. The others mainly reflect the so-called vulgate tradition of which the main exponent was Cleitarchus. For a good modern commentary on Diodorus on Alexander see P. Goukowsky, *Diodore de Sicile. Bibliothèque historique. Livre XVII* (Paris, 1976); for Rufus see H. Bardon, *Quinte-Curce. Histoires*, I–II (Paris, 1947–8); for Arrian see A.B. Bosworth, *A Historical Commentary on Arrian's History of Alexander*, I (Oxford, 1980); for Plutarch see J.R. Hamilton, *Plutarch, Alexander: A Commentary* (Oxford, 1969); for Justin see M.C.J. Miller, *M. Junianus Justinus. Epitoma Historiarum Philippicarum Book VII–XII. Excerpta de Historia Macedonica* (Chicago, 1992). The merits and demerits of these authors are well discussed by E. Badian, 'Alexander the Great, 1948-67', *The Classical World* 65(2) (1971), 37–42; N.G.L. Hammond, *Three Historians of Alexander the Great: the so-called Vulgate Authors, Diodorus, Justin and Curtius* (Cambridge, 1983); id., *Sources for Alexander the Great. An Analysis of Plutarch's* Life *and Arrian's* Anabasis Alexandrou (Cambridge, 1993). It is not practicable for me to justify in every case my reliance on given passages. Suffice it to say that in all cases I have carefully considered the agenda of each writer and the intrinsic plausibility of what is stated and have never used a passage of whose essential truth I was not convinced.

9 Useful recent discussions of the uniform aspects of equipment of the Macedonian army are N. Sekunda, *The Army of Alexander the Great* (London, 1984) and A. Devine, in General Sir John Hackett (ed.), *Warfare in the Ancient World* (London, 1989), 104–29.

10 Both Diodorus and Curtius use the term anachronistically in these passages, but this is irrelevant in the present context.

11 There is evidence that purple cloaks became standard for the king's Companions (D.S. XVII.77.5: cf. Q.C. VI.6.7; Justin XII.3.9).

12 Sekunda, op. cit., 16.

13 N.G.L. Hammond, *The Macedonian State. The Origins, Institutions and History* (Oxford, 1989), index. s.v. oath of allegiance.

14 Which Alexander is meant has been a matter of much debate. Momigliano argued for Alexander Philhellene (*Filippo il Macedone: saggio sulla*

storia greca del IV secolo A.C. (Florence, 1934), 8) and the claims of Alexander II and Alexander III have also been canvassed. Most recently E. Borza has come down strongly in favour of the latter (*In the Shadow of Olympus. the Emergence of Macedon* (Princeton, 1990), 125). See also R. Milns, in *Alexandre le Grand* (Entretiens Hardt 22) (Vandoeuvres-Geneva, 1976), 92. For my purposes the issue is of no relevance, though I do not find it inconceivable that Alexander Philhellene should have introduced hoplite-style infantry into his army under a general programme of hellenization, and, if that did take place, the introduction of the term *Pezhetairoi* would have had a plausible context.

15 See Hammond, *State*, 111 ff.

16 For these locally based contingents see A. von Domaszewski, *Die Phalangen Alexanders und Cäsars Legionen* (Sitz. Heid. Ak. Phil.-hist. Kl. 1925–6, 1), 42–9; F. Granier, *Die Makedonische Heeresversammlung: ein Beitrag zum antiken Staatsrecht* (Münchener Beiträge zur Papyrusforschung 13) (Munich, 1931), 11–12; A.R. Burn, 'The Generalship of Alexander', *Greece and Rome* 12 (1965), 141–4.

17 The question of what precisely Macedonian was continues to excite debate. Hammond argues that it was an Aeolian Greek dialect (op. cit., 12–15: cf. J.R. Ellis in D.M. Lewis and others (eds), *Cambridge Ancient History*, VI (Cambridge, 1994), 730 n. 4), but the *caveats* of Borza are shrewdly argued (op. cit., 90–4). For the purposes of this paper the only issue of importance is the existence of a clearly definable linguistic entity which could act as an index or symbol of ethnicity.

18 M. Andronikos, *Vergina. The Royal Tombs and the Ancient City* (Athens, 1987), 100–19. Whether Tomb II is that of Philip II excites growing doubts (Borza, op. cit., 260–6, 299 f.). These doubts I share, but this point is not an issue which is relevant to the present enquiry.

19 Games are mentioned at important points on many occasions in Arrian: II.24.6 (after the capture of Tyre); III.1.4 (after the capture of the Egyptian capital of Memphis); III.16.9 (after the capture of Susa); III.25.1 (on taking Zadracarta, the main city of Hyrcania); IV.4.1 (at the foundation of a new city); V.8.3 (at the major city of Taxila); V.20.1 (after the Battle of Hydaspes); VI.28.3 (on deliverance from Gedrosia); VII.14.1 (at Ecbatana); VII.14.10 (at Hephaestion's funeral).

20 See Hamilton, *Plutarch, Alexander*, 103. On ball games in general see E.N. Gardiner, *Athletics of the Ancient World* (Oxford, 1930), 230 ff.; H.A. Harris, *Sport in Greece and Rome* (London and Southampton, 1972), 83 ff.

21 Arrian I.11.1.

22 Keegan, op. cit., 114 ff., 139 ff., 173 ff., 183 ff., 220 ff., 241, 245, 274 ff.; Holmes, op. cit., 138, 216, 229, 233 ff., 246, 254 ff., 270 ff., Hanson, op.cit., 96 ff., 107 ff., 117 ff., 135 ff.

23 On the critical importance of leadership in war see, e.g., Keegan, op. cit., 114, 173 ff., 187 ff., 277 ff.; Holmes, op. cit., 27, 206 ff., 257, 276, 284, 340 ff.; Hanson, op. cit., 107 ff. In a recent study of the Battle of the Bulge we read: 'Why were the Germans better than we were?... Man for man, the typical German soldier was not smarter, braver, stronger, or more highly motivated than was the American soldier. But their leaders were, for the most part, more

professional' (T.N. Dupuy et al., *Hitler's Last Gamble* (New York, 1994), 500).

24 On Alexander's qualities as a commander see J.F.C. Fuller, *The Generalship of Alexander the Great* (London, 1958); A.R. Burn, 'The Generalship of Alexander', *Greece and Rome* 12 (1965), 140 ff.; E.W. Marsden, *The Campaign of Gaugamela* (Liverpool, 1964); Hammond, *Alexander the Great: King, Commander and Statesman* (London, 1981).

25 On this factor in Greek warfare see Hanson, op. cit., 124 ff., and Ogden, this volume, p. 107 ff.

26 Op. cit., 293. The *dekas* has increased to sixteen men in Arrian, VII.23.3.

27 Holmes, op. cit., 311–12. His thinking on this issue draws on the work of E. Fromm, *The Anatomy of Human Destructiveness* (London, 1977).

28 Pre-battle harangues have recently been discussed for the Greek context by M.H. Hansen, 'The Battle Exhortation in Ancient Historiography. Fact or Fiction', *Historia* 42 (1993), 161 ff.

29 Cf. Holmes, op. cit., 164.

30 For an eighteenth-century parallel see Holmes, op. cit., 49.

31 Hamilton, *Plutarch*, 199.

32 This apparent contradiction is aptly described by Holmes (op. cit., 230) as a 'flight to the front'.

33 Holmes comments: 'War cries are a time-honoured means of boosting one's own fighting spirit and attempting to diminish the enemy's... Grunts and growls have both psychological and physiological motives, as professional tennis-players know. Not only do they help to unsettle an opponent, but they also accompany the expulsion of air by the diaphragm at a moment of intense muscular effort, thus fixing the chest wall and co-ordinating the movement' (op. cit., 164–5).

34 On the religious obligations of Macedonian kings see Borza, op. cit., 238; Hammond, *State*, 21–2.

35 All MSS read *Alexandros*, but Goukowsky plausibly emends *Aristandros* (op. cit., 179).

36 For a detailed discussion see Hammond, *State*, 24–6.

37 Holmes is most illuminating on this contractual element of the relationship between leader and led (op. cit., 321 ff.).

38 For leadership see above, pp. 177 ff., 187 ff. On the other factors see Keegan, op. cit., 104 ff., 150 f., 232 ff., 274 ff.; Holmes, op. cit., 331 ff.; Hanson, op. cit., 107 ff.

39 G.L. Cawkwell, 'Epaminondas and Thebes', *CQ* n.s. 22 (1972), 254 ff.; Borza, op. cit., 203; Hanson, 'Epameinondas, the Battle of Leuctra (371 BC), and the "Revolution" in Greek Battle Tactics', *ClAnt* 7 (1988), 190 ff.

40 On the cavalry see Hamilton, 'The Cavalry Battle at the Hydaspes', *JHS* 76 (1956), 26 ff.; P.A. Brunt, 'Alexander's Macedonian Cavalry', ibid. 83 (1963), 27 ff.; Griffith, in Hammond and G.T. Griffith, *A History of Macedonia: II: 550–336 B.C.* (Oxford, 1979), 408 ff.; Borza, op. cit., 202 ff.; Hammond, *State*, 104 ff.; Ellis, op. cit., 687 ff.

41 J.K. Anderson, *Ancient Greek Horsemanship* (Berkeley, 1961), 106 ff.; Hammond, l.c.

42 For discussions of this important action see Borza, op. cit., 202 ff.;

Hammond, *State*, 106 ff.

43 Marsden, *Greek and Roman Artillery. Historical Development* (Oxford, 1969), 58 ff., 100 ff., 116 ff.; Griffith, in Hammond and Griffith, op. cit., II, 445 ff.; Hammond, *State*, 109 ff.

44 For a recent discussion of this signalling aid in hoplite warfare see P. Krentz, 'The *Salpinx* in Greek Warfare', in Hanson (ed.), op. cit., 110 ff.

45 Op. cit., 173.

46 e.g. we cannot accept that Alexander was not wearing a helmet in this battle. He is presumably depicted without it because the artist wants maximum scope to portray his subject's head.

47 On this formidable weapon and its use see M. Andronicus, 'Sarissa', *BCH* 94 (1970), 91 ff.; M.M. Markle, 'The Macedonian Sarissa, Spear, and Related Armor', *AJA* 81 (1977), 323 ff.; id., 'The Use of the Sarissa by Philip and Alexander of Macedon', ibid. 82 (1978), 483 ff.

48 P. Perdrizet proposed the reading Corratas to reconcile the variants ('Etudes amphipolitaines', *BCH* 46 (1922), 50).

49 For discussions of this action see Marsden, op. cit, 59; Hammond, *State*, 112 ff.

50 D. Winter, *Death's Men. Soldiers of the Great War* (Harmondworth, 1979), 176.

5

MORALE AND THE ROMAN EXPERIENCE
OF BATTLE

A.D. Lee

The strikingly successful record of the Roman army in battle over many centuries is a phenomenon which has engaged the interest of historians since antiquity itself. Explanations of that success have, however, tended by and large to focus on organisational features of the army which are more readily susceptible to analysis. There has been much less willingness on the part of modern scholars to venture into questions of morale and mental toughness in the face of battle. This is certainly not to deny that the researches of Roman military historians into various facets of the army provide valuable material which can contribute towards an investigation of such questions – the references in the notes accompanying this paper testify to that – but there does seem to have been a reluctance to tackle these issues head on.[1] Presumably it is the implicit psychological dimension, with its overtones of subjectivity, which has been in large part responsible for historians' shying away from these areas.

While acknowledging the risks involved, there are good grounds for trying to grapple with these matters, even if the results require qualifications and caveats. At a very general level, there is much to be said for the view that a proper understanding of historical phenomena should include an empathetic element, some sense of 'what it was like' for those involved.[2] At the more specific level of military history, it can be argued that any explanation of the success of an army will be incomplete without some attempt to address questions relating to morale.[3] Finally, the recent work of Victor Hanson and others on hoplite warfare in ancient Greece shows the value of such an exercise in the particular context of ancient military history, despite the apparent limitations of the ancient evidence.[4] What is surprising is that Roman military historians have not thus far attempted to follow Hanson's lead.

The present paper constitutes a preliminary foray into this area, rather than a full-scale campaign. It begins with some consideration of the battle-conditions experienced by Roman soldiers, before turning to its central concern, the factors influencing discipline and morale in the Roman army. In terms of personnel, the focus is primarily on the legionary at the expense of cavalry or light infantry, while at the risk of underplaying the impact of important changes in the organisational character of the Roman army between Republic and Principate, and Principate and Late Empire, I have opted to draw on evidence across a wide chronological spectrum, from the second century BC through to the fourth century AD. The entire period of Roman military supremacy in the ancient Mediterranean is thereby encompassed, while two particularly valuable contemporary observers, Polybius and Ammianus Marcellinus, can be exploited in addition to more obvious 'central' sources such as Caesar, Josephus and Tacitus.[5] The broad spread may also enable us to detect underlying continuities and changes.

The 'face of battle' in the Roman period

We begin, then, with some consideration of the conditions of battle experienced by the Roman soldier. One of the features of hoplite warfare which has received emphasis in recent discussions is the sheer burden of arms and armour which men had to shoulder.[6] There is no doubt that Roman legionaries were also required to bear a considerable weight of equipment – for example, estimates of probable shield weight make the Roman *scutum* heavier than the hoplite shield;[7] and the legionary's helmet and body-armour, being made of iron rather than bronze, may well also have been more burdensome than the hoplite equivalent.

There were, however, offsetting advantages: iron was a better defence than bronze against enemy blows; and the oblong shape of the Roman shield gave better protection. Moreover, the design of Roman armour minimised some of the unfortunate side-effects experienced by hoplites. By the first century AD, if not earlier, Roman helmets had padding to help cushion blows to the head, and they had cut-outs for the ears,[8] which must have made hearing easier and reduced the sense of stifling claustrophobia thought to have been typical of the hoplite experience. Likewise, Roman body armour, whether of the ring-mail, scaled, or segmentary type, must have been more comfortable for a man to wear than a hoplite breastplate, by virtue of its greater flexibility and scope for ventilation.

For all these improvements, the legionary who managed to avoid death in battle nevertheless remained susceptible to serious woundings. Their precise nature will obviously have varied according to the weaponry of their opponents, but two episodes from Caesar's writings may serve to illustrate. During one desperate encounter in Gaul, one centurion 'had both his thighs pierced by a spear', while the commanding officer 'was wounded by a sling-stone which struck him full in the face' – a not uncommon injury.[9] A few years later during the civil war, when Caesar was attempting to hem Pompey's forces in near Dyrrhachium, one part of Caesar's army, comprising at least 1,000 men, came under very heavy fire from Pompey's archers, so that not a single soldier escaped being wounded, and four centurions lost their eyes; another centurion in this engagement later presented to Caesar his shield in which were found 120 holes.[10] Clearly, the face and eyes were particularly vulnerable: to add two further examples, the Republican general-turned-rebel, Sertorius, was well known for having lost the sight of one of his eyes as a result of a wound received during the Social War in 90 BC, while one of Caesar's leading centurions, Crastinus, died at Pharsalus as a result of a sword thrust in the face.[11]

In addition to these obvious hazards, there was the stress likely to be induced by the circumstances under which battles were fought, circumstances by no means unique of course to the Roman experience. High levels of noise is an obvious aspect (even if some of it was self-generated in the hope of disconcerting the enemy[12]): in the Roman engagement with the Macedonians at Cynoscephalae in 197 BC, for example, 'the encounter of the two armies was accompanied by deafening shouts and cries, both of them uttering their war-cry and those outside the battle also cheering the combatants',[13] while in Caesar's final encounter with the Pompeian forces at Munda in 45 BC, 'when shouting, mingled with groans and the clash of swords, was borne to their ears, the minds of the inexperienced were numbed with fear'.[14] In such circumstances it is not surprising to find officers having to shout and use hand-signals to convey orders in the thick of battle.[15]

Clouds of dust were another frequent concomitant of battle: 'once the troops moved into action [against the Cimbri at Vercellae in 101 BC], *as was to be expected*, a huge cloud of dust was raised and enveloped the two armies';[16] similarly in Julian's encounter with the Alamanni at Strasbourg in AD 357, 'at the very crisis of the battle, when our cavalry were bravely regrouping and the infantry were stoutly protecting their flanks with a wall of serried shields, thick clouds of dust arose'.[17] Battles fought at the height of summer also sometimes involved extremes of heat, such as was the case at the Muthul in 109 BC, at

Pharsalus in 48 BC, and at Adrianople in AD 378; in this last case, the effects were exacerbated for the Romans' troops by their being parched with thirst after marching eight miles in the middle of the day before the battle and by the Goths' calculated firing of the surrounding countryside.[18]

Once near the enemy forces, troops needed to be able to stand firm in the face of the showers of missiles which usually marked the commencement of the battle, after which came the sheer exertion of pushing and weapon-wielding required of infantry when the battle lines met. Consider the following accounts of, first, the encounter of Roman auxiliary forces with the Caledonians ('Britons') at Mons Graupius in AD 84, in which Roman superiority quickly became apparent, and secondly, the more closely contested battle with the Alamanni at Strasbourg in AD 357, in which the confusion of battle and the fragility of morale is well conveyed:

> The battle began with fighting at long range; the Britons, with their long swords and small shields, showed determination and skill in evading or brushing aside the Roman missiles, while they themselves poured on us a dense shower of spears. Then Agricola ordered four cohorts of Batavians and two of Tungrians to bring matters to a decision by close fighting with swords... The Batavians began to close with the enemy, striking them with the bosses of their shields, stabbing them in the face, and pushing their line uphill; thereupon the other cohorts joined with eager rivalry in cutting down all the nearest enemy... Everywhere there were weapons, corpses, mangled limbs, and blood-soaked earth.[19]

> After a short exchange of missiles, the Germans rushed forward... At one moment our men stood firm, at the next they gave way, and some of the most experienced fighters among the barbarians tried to force their foes backward by the pressure of their knees. Obstinately they struggled, hand to hand and shield to shield; the sky rang with the shouts of the victors and the screams of the wounded. But while our left wing, moving in close order, had thrown back the opposition...our cavalry on the right unexpectedly gave way in disorder... What caused this incident was that the horsemen saw their commander slightly wounded and one of their comrades slipping over the neck of his horse, which sank under the weight of his armour. They then began to scatter in whatever direction they could, and would have created total confusion by trampling on their own infantry, had not the latter held their ground... Elsewhere the hail of darts and javelins and the volleys of iron-tipped arrows did not slacken, although blade was clashing on blade in hand-to-hand conflict and breastplates were split asunder by sword-blows... Some had their heads severed by huge pikes...others...slipped in the blood of their comrades on the muddy and treacherous ground...[20]

Factors influencing discipline and morale

The aim of this paper thus far has been to provide a composite picture of the conditions Roman soldiers would be likely to confront in battle. In the light of this, we now turn to consider the central question of discipline and morale. Given the evident stresses of battle, what factors persuaded Roman soldiers to stand and fight, rather than turning and running?

Honour, fear and shame

Writing in the mid second century BC, Polybius had a particular interest in trying to understand why Roman military power had proved so irresistible during recent decades. One important feature of Roman military practice to which he drew attention was the system of punishments and rewards through which discipline was instilled – a subject of obvious relevance to the concerns of this paper.

In Polybius's day, there was an array of punishments which could be invoked against a Roman soldier who failed in his duty. Less serious penalties existed in the form of the withholding of pay, and flogging, though Polybius does not specify the circumstances in which these might be applied. Understandably, he concentrates on the ultimate penalty, which took the brutal form of the *fustuarium*, i.e. being beaten to death with cudgels or clubs. This could be invoked for falling asleep on guard duty at night, for lying to an officer about one's achievements in battle with a view to obtaining a reward, for throwing away any weapon on the battlefield, and for deserting one's post as part of a covering force out of fear. Polybius goes on to observe that 'for this reason men who have been posted to a covering force are often doomed to certain death...because they will remain at their posts even when overwhelmingly outnumbered on account of their dread of the punishment that awaits them.'[21]

In the case of whole units deserting their position under pressure from the enemy, the principle of decimation was implemented – i.e., one-tenth of their number was selected by lot and clubbed to death; it has been suggested by one scholar that 'there is something of a purification rite here'.[22] The remainder of the disgraced unit was subjected to various forms of public humiliation: they had their rations of wheat replaced by barley – a grain normally reserved for slaves and animals; and they were required to make their quarters outside the camp, a symbolic statement of their marginalisation and exclusion, which at the same time had the practical consequence of placing them in an exposed and dangerous position. Again, as Polybius noted,

203

the danger and fear of drawing the fatal lot threatens every man equally, and since there is no certainty on whom it may fall, and the public disgrace of receiving rations of barley is shared by all alike, the Romans have adopted the best possible practice both to inspire terror and to repair the harm done by any weakening of their warlike spirit.[23]

A number of considerations helped to make the threat of such severe punishment more bearable.[24] One was the fact that these punishments applied as much to officers as to the rank-and-file.[25] Another, well appreciated by Polybius, was the fact that these penalties were balanced by the prospect of rewards for the display of courage in battle.[26] There will be more to say about this important aspect shortly, but first some comments on military discipline during the centuries after Polybius.

Commanders can certainly be found imposing punishments such as decimation both during and after Polybius's day. What is of interest, however, is the fact that the instances of which we know, mostly relate to the first century BC, with few occurrences after the reign of Augustus. Augustus himself imposed the punishment of decimation on a unit in 34 BC;[27] yet when, some sixty years later during Tiberius's reign, a general imposed the same penalty, it was regarded as being quite exceptional and a case of harking back to old traditions.[28] And indeed there seems to be only one further instance of decimation after this time (by the emperor Galba).[29] Similarly, it was regarded as exceptional when Nero's general, Corbulo, had the death penalty enforced for desertion, without allowing offenders a second chance.[30]

The legal compilation known as the *Digest*, which reflects Roman law as it had developed by the early third century AD, contains a chapter on military discipline which tends to confirm the impression conveyed by the other sources. The regulations generally seem to have lost their uncompromising character to a significant degree. There is no longer any reference to decimation, and although being beaten with cudgels is specified as a punishment for anyone deserting the ranks, demotion to another part of the army is also given as an alternative, nor is it certain that the beating was intended to be fatal anymore.[31] Losing one's weapons was now also punishable either by death *or* by demotion,[32] and concessions were made to the inexperience of new recruits.[33]

One can suggest various explanations for this apparent relaxation of standards – the fact that the army was less consistently engaged in fighting during the first two centuries AD, the way in which the citizen army of Polybius's day has now become a thoroughly professionalised institution,[34] the need for emperors to ensure the loyalty of troops[35]; but this relaxation need not necessarily have meant that troops were less disciplined in battle. This would be very difficult to prove conclusively anyway, and even if narrative accounts of battles during this period were to suggest less resolution on the part of soldiers, this could still be explained in other ways, such as the fact that the army was fighting less frequently during these years. Moreover, the regulations contained in the *Digest* make a clear distinction between times of war and times of peace, with greater scope for leniency during the latter. Capital punishment still remains the only penalty for certain fundamental offences with a critical bearing in the context of a battle – failing to obey an order in wartime, taking flight during battle, malingering out of fear of the enemy.[36] During the siege of Jerusalem in the late 60s AD, a Jewish raid on the Roman camps was only foiled by the staunch resistance of the Roman sentries; for what it is worth, the explanation for their steadfastness offered by the historian Josephus was in terms of their 'coming under a severe Roman law that he who quits his post under any pretext whatsoever dies. These men, preferring an heroic death to capital punishment, stood firm.'[37]

As already noted, Polybius also emphasises the positive side of the coin – the incentive of winning rewards for courage in battle. Polybius conveys very forcefully the importance of these rewards:

> The Romans also have an excellent method of encouraging young soldiers to face danger. Whenever any have especially distinguished themselves in battle, the general assembles the troops and calls forward those whom he considers to have shown exceptional courage. He praises them first for gallantry in action...then he distributes gifts such as the following: for a man who has wounded one of the enemy, a spear; to one who has killed and stripped an enemy, a cup if he is in the infantry, or horse-trappings if in the cavalry... And so by means of such incentives even those who stay at home feel the impulse to emulate such achievements in the field no less than those who are present and see and hear what takes place. For the men who receive these trophies not only enjoy great prestige in the army and soon afterwards in their homes, but they are also singled out for precedence in religious processions when they return. On these occasions nobody is allowed to wear decorations, save those who have been honoured for their bravery by the consuls, and it is the custom to hang up the trophies they have won in the most conspicuous places in their houses, and to regard them as proofs and visible symbols of their valour.[38]

The rewards noted here by Polybius gradually developed over the centuries into a more differentiated and systematised range of military decorations, a thorough survey of which can be found in Valerie Maxfield's study.[39] The essential point remains, however, the one emphasised by Polybius: the very public nature of the rewards, and the way in which they encouraged soldiers to outdo one another in their exploits on the battlefield.[40] Roman generals clearly appreciated the value of such exercises. Thus, following his successful storming of New Carthage in 209, Scipio Africanus 'gave rewards to his soldiers for bravery, the largest to the one who first scaled the wall, half as much to the next, one-third to the next, and to the others according to their merit', while after his victory at Thapsus in 46 BC, Caesar 'assembled the troops in the sight of the townsfolk, praised them, gave cash gratuities to all the veterans, and from his tribunal issued decorations to all those who had rendered conspicuously good service'.[41] At the end of the siege of Jerusalem in AD 70, Titus 'gave orders to the appointed officers to read out the names of all who had performed any brilliant feat during the war. Calling up each by name he applauded them as they came forward...and placed crowns of gold upon their heads...'[42] And following the capture of a fort in the course of his Persian expedition in AD 363, the emperor Julian saw to it that 'those who had shown heroism received the distinction of a siege crown and were commended in the presence of the assembled army, in accordance with ancient usage.'[43]

Closely allied to the role of military decorations in motivating soldiers was the prospect of booty. Although during the Republican period the ultimate discretion as to how booty was distributed lay with the victorious general,[44] it was usual for troops to receive a portion; generals who failed to give it invariably engendered strong resentment against themselves.[45] The lucrative campaigns in the eastern Mediterranean during the first half of the second century BC meant that soldiers received increasingly large sums,[46] so that, for example, the prospect of booty was believed to have been responsible for inducing many to serve in the Third Macedonian War against Perseus in 171.[47] There does, however, seem to have been a significant change in practice after the end of the Republic. Although distribution of booty to the rank-and-file was not unknown even as late as the fourth century AD,[48] it appears to have been displaced to a large degree by cash handouts from the emperor at his accession and on special occasions.[49] This may be significant from our point of view, because it meant that financial reward became increasingly divorced from performance in battle, but it is difficult to demonstrate any clear consequences in terms of fighting effectiveness.

206

Group identity and cohesion

The importance of material rewards and punishments in the maintenance of morale is matched, if not surpassed, by the need to establish
and maintain a soldier's sense of identification with and commitment
to the army in general, and especially to the particular unit of which he
is a part, for this plays a crucial role in the ability of soldiers to
withstand the stresses of battle and to fight effectively.[50] The first step
in the creation of this sense of identification comprises the various
rituals of initiation into the army. In the case of the Roman army this
involved swearing an oath of allegiance.[51] According to Polybius, the
soldier swore that 'he will obey his officers and execute their orders as
far as is in his power'; Livy describes its content a little differently: 'that
they will not abandon their ranks for flight or fear, but only to take up
or seek a weapon, either to smite the enemy or to save a fellow-
citizen.'[52] Vegetius, author of a military treatise in the fourth century
AD, describes the military oath of his day in a way which combines
Polybius and Livy and shows its essential continuity throughout the
centuries we are considering: 'The soldiers swear to do all that they are
called upon to do by the Emperor to the best of their ability; never to
desert the colours; never to refuse to meet death for the Roman
state.'[53] It is tempting to minimise the significance of this apparent
formality, but that would be a mistake on two counts. In the first place,
the Latin term for the military oath was *sacramentum*, which implies
that the oath was instilled with religious meaning for those swearing it
– a consideration which will have served to increase its efficacy. Secondly, it is evident that even for soldiers in 20th century armies, whose
oaths have no religious connotations, the swearing of an oath of loyalty
nevertheless retains 'considerable moral authority'.[54]

Drill is another means by which group identity can be built up. Of
course it serves other, more immediately obvious purposes as well,
such as developing physical stamina, giving proficiency in weapons-
handling and maintaining formation, and instilling the habit of obedience to orders – all of which undoubtedly have important contributions to make on the battlefield. But these more obvious benefits make
it easy to overlook the fact that 'drill has an important ritualistic and
morale-building role... [It] binds a unit together in a way which even
unwilling soldiers may find to be curiously pleasurable... Not only
does it make men look like soldiers, but, far more important, it makes
them feel like soldiers.'[55] The Romans certainly appreciated the value
of training, as reflected in Vegetius's devotion of a whole book (I) of
his treatise to the subject, explicitly justified as being the explanation

for Roman military success. There are, moreover, clear indications in the sources that this appreciation extended to recognition of its importance with respect to morale, as in Josephus's comment that 'by their military exercises the Romans prepare not only robust bodies but also strong souls.'[56]

Identification with one's specific unit is facilitated in a very obvious way by distinctive features in one's uniform and equipment. In the Roman context, this can be observed most readily in shield-patterns. Although there is a major question-mark over the accuracy of the shield designs preserved in the late Roman administrative document known as the *Notitia Dignitatum*,[57] the historian Ammianus Marcellinus makes it clear that individual units did have distinctive patterns on their shields in the fourth century AD, and there is evidence indicating that this was the case in earlier centuries as well.[58]

Of paramount importance in promoting unit-identity was the military standard. These originally involved representations of a range of creatures besides the eagle – such as the wolf, the minotaur, the horse, the bull – and it has been suggested that they began as 'animal totems, reflecting the religious beliefs of an agricultural society'.[59] Until the Christianisation of the army during the fourth century AD, they continued to be an object of veneration, with their own shrine in the camp and associated religious ceremonies,[60] and as such they played an important role as a focus for the *esprit de corps* of a unit. When a whole unit was collectively honoured for bravery in battle, a token symbolising this was usually attached to the standard,[61] while, conversely, the loss of a standard to the enemy was regarded as the ultimate disgrace. The standards lost by Crassus to the Parthians and by Varus to the Germans are the best known instances of this, to which can be added less momentous incidents such as the standard-bearer in one of Caesar's legions whose final deed, when caught in a Gallic ambush outside his camp, was to hurl the standard back over the rampart to safety.[62] The devotion of men to their standard was such that unit commanders were sometimes able to exploit it in very practical ways, in order to resolve deadlock in a battle, as illustrated by the following incident. The context is the Roman campaigns against the Gauls of northern Italy during the 190s BC; in this particular instance the Gauls were trying to force their way into a Roman camp:

> For a long time the fighting raged in these confined spaces, and it was not sword-arms and swords which were engaged but rather shields and bodies, and the combatants pushed with all their might, the Romans striving to force their way out with the standards, the Gauls trying to

force their way into the camp, or at least prevent the Romans from issuing from it. In fact the opposing troops were unable to make head-way in either direction until Q. Victorius, a senior centurion of the 2nd legion, and C. Atinius, a military tribune of the 4th, had recourse to a device often tried in bitterly contested engagements. Snatching the standards from their bearers, they threw them into the enemy ranks; and the men of the 2nd legion, in their eagerness to recover their standard, were the first to hurl themselves through the gate.[63]

Although this scene may strike us as somewhat improbable, Livy claims that it was a ploy often used, and there are certainly other attested cases from the Republican period.[64]

A further factor which has been recognised by both military histori-ans and psychologists as playing a vital role, in determining whether soldiers stand and fight or turn and run, is the character of relations between soldiers at the level of the smallest unit, 'the primary group of up to ten, whose members [are] in regular face-to-face contact'.[65] If the men in units at this level are well known to one another, as one would normally expect to be the case, then two considerations will tend to create a willingness to face death – on the one hand, loyalty to com-rades, and on the other, personal honour:

Numberless soldiers have died, more or less willingly, not for country or honour or religious faith or for any other abstract good, but because they realised that by fleeing their posts and rescuing themselves, they would expose their companions to greater danger. Such loyalty to the group is the essence of fighting morale.[66]

When a soldier is unknown to the men around him he has relatively little reason to fear losing the one thing he is likely to value more highly than life – his reputation as a man among other men. It is the man whose identity is well known to his fellows who has the main chance of being effective in battle.[67]

Perhaps the most important contribution of MacMullen's article lies here, in his awareness of these conclusions and appreciation of their relevance to the Roman legion, for he rightly emphasises the ties of solidarity between Roman soldiers at the smallest organisational levels implicit in such terms as *contubernales* ('tent-mates') and *commilitones* ('fellow-soldiers'). To this and the other evidence of which he gives a masterly exposition, I would simply add two further interesting items which suggest Roman consciousness of the importance of this factor. The first is an episode during the Roman campaigns in northern Italy in the 190s BC:

Next day the consul crossed the river and encamped about half a mile from the enemy. From this position he defended the allies' territory from plundering raids by fighting a number of skirmishes; but he did not risk coming out in battle array with troops newly enlisted, collected from many peoples, and not yet well enough acquainted with one another to feel confidence in their fellow soldiers.[68]

The second is Livy's description of the military camp as 'the soldier's second homeland (*patria altera*) – its rampart serves as his city walls, and his tent is the soldier's hearth and home (*domus ac penates*)'.[69]

Leadership

The character of leadership also has a very important part to play in the maintenance of morale, and is the final area to be investigated. After describing the way in which Marius gained the devotion of his soldiers by showing that he was willing to endure their hardships, Plutarch goes on to generalise in the following terms:

> What a Roman soldier likes most to see is his commanding officer eating his ration of bread with the rest, or sleeping on an ordinary bed, or joining in the work of digging a trench or raising a palisade. The commanders they respect are not so much those who distribute honours and money as those who take a share in their hardships and dangers.[70]

So it was that before one of his first battles in Gaul, Caesar 'had all the horses – starting with his own – sent away out of sight, so that everyone might stand in equal danger and no one have any chance of flight.'[71] Likewise, there are frequent references to commanders taking up arms to fight alongside their men with a view to strengthening their morale, such as the following incident when one of Caesar's legions found itself hard-pressed:

> Caesar had gone to right wing where he found the troops in difficulties. The cohorts of the 12th legion were packed together so closely that the men were in one another's way and could not fight properly. All the centurions of the 4th cohort, as well as the standard-bearer, were killed, and the standard was lost; nearly all the centurions of the other cohorts were either killed or wounded... The men's movements were slow, and some in the rear, feeling themselves abandoned, were retiring from the fight and trying to get out of range. Caesar snatched a shield from a soldier in the rear, made his way to the front line, addressed each centurion by name, and shouted encouragement to the rest of the troops, ordering them to push forward and open out their ranks, so that they could use their swords more easily. His coming gave them fresh heart and hope; each man wanted to do his best under the eyes of his commander-in-chief, however desperate the peril, and the enemy's assault was slowed down a little.[72]

Close involvement of this sort could of course cut both ways and have adverse consequences. 'The trick is...for a commander to get the balance right, and to intervene personally when his presence is genuinely required, but not to risk his neck when he does not need to do so.'[73] The wounding of a commander was invariably the signal for panic among the ranks. We have already seen it in the reaction of the cavalry in the battle of Strasbourg (above p. 202); the response was the same when Vespasian was wounded during the siege of Jotapata in Judaea, and when Civilis was thrown from his horse during a battle in AD 69.[74] In this latter case, Tacitus says 'a report that he had been either wounded or slain gained belief throughout both armies, spreading incredible panic among his own troops, and giving great encouragement to their opponents.' The case of the emperor Julian in AD 363 well illustrates the disastrous effects on an army's cohesion if such a wound should prove fatal.[75] In the light of all this, Scipio must score highly for his ingenious solution, during the siege of New Carthage (209 BC), to the problem of maximising the advantages of personal involvement while minimising its risks:

> Scipio by no means remained aloof from the fighting, but had also taken precautions for his safety. He had with him three men carrying large shields, which they held so as to cover him completely on the side which was exposed to the wall, and thus protected him from missiles. In this way he could...not only see how the battle was developing, but the fact that he was in full view of his men inspired them to fight with redoubled spirit.[76]

Consideration of leadership ought also to include the vital role of officers at levels below that of the commander. Clear evidence of this is understandably harder to come by, but the passage from Caesar's *Gallic War* quoted above (p. 210) provides a good illustration: what is striking here is the number of centurions who are dead or wounded, and it seems a reasonable deduction that this high toll was the result of their efforts to give the lead to their wavering men. One is reminded of the disproportionately high numbers of officers killed on the Western Front during the Great War.[77]

A final aspect of leadership requiring some comment is the commander's exhortation to his troops immediately prior to battle. Accounts of battle in the ancient sources are of course replete with such speeches, but as Mogens Hansen has recently and forcefully reminded us, the texts of the speeches 'preserved' in the histories must largely be the work of the historians themselves rather than an accurate record of what a general actually said. Nevertheless, Hansen does not deny that 'a general usually said *something* to his men before a battle'; it must, however, have taken the form of 'a few apophthegms that could be shouted by the general as he traversed the line or of a speech made to the officers only who passed it on to the soldiers.'[78] Hansen's argument is incontrovertible, but he is hard-pressed to find detailed examples of what actually happened in the evidence from the Classical period on which he concentrates. Had he ventured into the late Roman period, he would have found an excellent illustration of his point in Julian's behaviour before the battle of Strasbourg, as reported by an historian who had himself been a professional soldier:[79]

> He could not address them in a body because of the wide extent of the front and the large numbers involved... So without a thought for his own safety, he flew along the lines within range of the enemy and encouraged his men, known and unknown alike, to deeds of valour with words like these: 'Now, comrades, the moment to fight has come, the moment to which you clamoured to be brought just now, when you impatiently called for battle.' Similarly, when he came to those who were posted behind the standards in the extreme rear, he shouted, 'Companions in arms, the long-hoped-for day is here when we must all wipe out previous stains and restore its proper glory to the majesty of Rome. These are the barbarians whose rage and unbridled folly have led them to meet our forces in an encounter which must end in their destruction'... With frequent repetition of words of this kind he deployed the greater part of his army...

Epilogue: The Roman army in the fourth century AD

Having considered the role of morale and discipline in the success of the Roman army across many centuries, it is natural to wonder whether there was perhaps some diminution in these qualities during the period of the empire's so-called 'decline'. This is a complex subject to which it is impossible to do justice in a brief epilogue,[80] but certainly the detailed evidence of Ammianus Marcellinus provides no support for the conclusion that battlefield discipline underwent any serious deterioration during the mid fourth century down to the battle of Adrianople in AD 378 (at which point his history concludes). At the battle of Strasbourg, it was certainly the case that cavalry units on the Roman right wing panicked and broke ranks when their commander was wounded, but this incident cannot be used to support a more generalised thesis of a decline of discipline in the fourth century: panic by individual units was hardly a phenomenon without precedent in Roman history, and the potentially disastrous consequences on this occasion were forestalled by the discipline of adjacent infantry regiments which held steady in spite of the danger of their being trampled underfoot by the retreating cavalry.[81] Moreover, although Ammianus's detailed account of this battle fails to explain precisely why, after a long and hard-fought contest, the Romans finally achieved such a decisive victory, the outcome seems to have hinged on the simple inability of the Alamanni to break the Roman centre, in spite of being superior in numbers.[82]

But what about the great military disasters of the fourth century – Julian's Persian expedition, and Adrianople? The outcome of the former was not in fact determined by a major set-piece battle, since the Persians preferred to wage a very effective campaign of attrition and harassment. The débâcle is explicable in terms not of poor battlefield discipline, but rather of planning and execution – such as the failure of the second Roman army to appear, and not anticipating the willingness of the Persians to hamper the Roman advance through the destruction of irrigation canals and dykes.[83] As for Adrianople, the Roman line did eventually break, but only, according to Ammianus, under the pressure of overwhelming numbers and after the Roman front-line troops had fought ferociously in utter disregard of their personal safety.[84] Errors of judgement on the part of the emperor Valens provide a more persuasive explanation for this defeat than deficiencies in discipline or courage.[85]

The army of the fourth century was of course differently organised from the army of earlier centuries, in so far as it now comprised two broad categories of troops, namely the élite units of the central field armies, the so-called *comitatenses*, and the forces usually referred to as the *limitanei*, mostly stationed in the frontier provinces of the empire. It was the field armies which fought at Strasbourg and Adrianople, so it is even more difficult to judge the quality of the *limitanei*. It is, however, important to draw attention to a common misconception about this category of troops. They have often been portrayed as farmer-soldiers or a type of peasant militia, who cultivated land allotted to them by the government and performed guard duties in recompense, with the implication that they were only part-time soldiers and therefore of poor quality. This view has not been accepted by all scholars, and in his recent careful re-evaluation of the evidence, Benjamin Isaac has confirmed the conclusion that the *limitanei* of the fourth century were not farmers.[86] Indeed, our final glimpse of them in the West, in Noricum in the years immediately prior to 476, suggests devotion to duty until the bitter end. Troops here continued endeavouring to fulfil their responsibilities to the best of their abilities in spite of shortages of arms and pay, and it was only when it became clear that no more resources could be expected from a bankrupt government in Italy that the regiments in the region finally dispersed for good.[87]

Notes

1 An impressive exception, to which this paper is much indebted, is Ramsay MacMullen's pioneering article, 'The legion as a society', *Historia* 33 (1984), 440–56, reprinted in his *Changes in the Roman Empire* (New Haven, 1990). References to this paper will be by the original pagination. Also worth noting is M.C. Bishop, 'On parade: status, display, and morale in the Roman army', in H. Vetters and M. Kandler (eds), *Akten des 14. Internationalen Limeskongresses 1986 in Carnuntum* (Vienna, 1990), 21–30 (though he makes no reference to MacMullen's article).

2 For detailed theoretical discussion of this point, see W.G. Runciman, *A Treatise on Social Theory* vol. I (Cambridge, 1983), 15–26, 223 ff.

3 See especially John Keegan, *The Face of Battle* (London, 1976) and Richard Holmes, *Firing Line* (London, 1985).

4 V.D. Hanson, *The Western Way of War: Infantry Battle in Classical Greece* (London, 1989); V.D. Hanson (ed.), *Hoplites: the Classical Greek Battle Experience* (1993).

5 MacMullen's paper concentrates on the period from Caesar to the late second century AD.

6 Hanson, *Western Way of War*, chap. 6.

7 *Pace* Hanson (ibid. 68), who elsewhere (65) cites an estimate of 16 lb for the hoplite shield, whereas the estimated weight of a Roman shield is put at 22 lb: M.C. Bishop and J.C.N. Coulston, *Roman Military Equipment* (London, 1993), 59.

8 Ibid. 93.

9 Caesar *Gallic War* 5.35.6–8 (tr. Handford and Gardner). Cf. Livy 22.49.1 for another slingstone in the face.

10 Caesar *Civil War* 3.53.3–4. The figure of 1,000 is deduced from the fact that Caesar talks of the four centuries as coming from one cohort, implying the presence of at least one other cohort.

11 Plutarch *Sertorius* 4; Caesar *Civil War* 3.99.1. The apparently high quality of Roman medical care for soldiers is worth noting at this point (see R.W. Davies, 'The Roman military medical service' in his *Service in the Roman Army* (Edinburgh, 1989), chap. 10) – it must have had a positive impact on morale.

12 Cf. Caesar *Civil War* 3.92.5; [Caesar] *Spanish War* 31.2.

13 Polybius 18.25.1 (tr. Paton).

14 [Caesar] *Spanish War* 31.6 (tr. Handford and Gardner). Cf. Plutarch *Antony* 39.

15 As in Ammianus Marcellinus 24.6.13.

16 Plutarch *Marius* 26 (tr. Warner). We may well doubt the consequence which Plutarch, on the authority of Sulla, attributes to the dust – that Marius's

first charge missed the enemy completely – without doubting the cloud of dust itself.

17 Ammianus Marcellinus 16.12.37 (tr. Hamilton). Cf. Plutarch *Sulla* 19.

18 Sallust *Jugurtha* 51.3; Caesar *Civil War* 3.95.2; Ammianus Marcellinus 31.12.11–13.

19 Tacitus *Agricola* 36.1–2, 37.3 (tr. Hutton and Ogilvie with modifications).

20 Ammianus Marcellinus 16.12.36 ff. (tr. Hamilton). For a good discussion of Ammianus's battle descriptions and the problem of literary conventions, see J. Matthews, *The Roman Empire of Ammianus* (London, 1989), 295–301.

21 Polybius 6.37.12 (tr. Scott-Kilvert), with an actual example at 1.17.12. Cf. the observation of Frederick the Great that 'the common soldier must fear his officer more than the enemy' (quoted in Holmes, *Firing Line*, 336).

22 A.W. Lintott, *Violence in Republican Rome* (Oxford, 1968), 42.

23 Polybius 6.38 (tr. Scott-Kilvert).

24 Cf. C. Nicolet, *The World of the Citizen in Republican Rome* (London, 1980), 106–8.

25 Contrast the situation during the reign of Valentinian I in the fourth century AD, where officers were exempted from punishment, leading to dissatisfaction in the ranks: Ammianus Marcellinus 27.9.4.

26 Cf. Josephus *Jewish War* 3.103 ('the high honours with which they reward the brave prevent the offenders whom they punish from regarding themselves as treated cruelly' (tr. Thackeray)).

27 Dio Cassius 49.38.4.

28 Tacitus *Annals* 3.21.1.

29 Suetonius *Galba* 12.2. The emperor Julian's misunderstanding of decimation – he had a total of ten men executed rather than one in every ten (Ammianus Marcellinus 24.3.2) – confirms that the practice had long fallen out of use before the fourth century.

30 Tacitus *Annals* 13.35.9.

31 *Digest* 16.3.16. The same expression (*fustibus caeditur*) is used at one other point in this chapter (16.4.11), where the context implies that it was viewed as a lesser penalty than being exiled and having one's property confiscated; this suggests that it was not intended to be a form of capital punishment.

32 Ibid. 16.3.13.

33 e.g., ibid. 16.3.19; 16.14.1. On the specific issue of leave and absenteeism, see M.P. Speidel, 'Furlough in the Roman army', *YCS* 28 (1985), 283–93.

34 G.R. Watson, *The Roman Soldier* (London, 1969), 118.

35 J.B. Campbell, *The Roman Emperor and the Army 31 BC – AD 235* (Oxford, 1984), chap. 7.

36 *Digest* 49.16.3.15; 16.6.3,5. Cf. also Josephus *Jewish War* 3.102 f.

37 Josephus *Jewish War* 5.482–3 (tr. Thackeray).

38 Polybius 6.39 (tr. Scott-Kilvert).

39 V.A. Maxfield, *The Military Decorations of the Roman Army* (London, 1981).

40 Cf. MacMullen, 'Legion as society', 449; Bishop, 'On parade'.

41 Appian *Spanish Wars* 23 (tr. White); [Caesar] *African War* 86.3 (tr. Handford and Gardner).

42 Josephus *Jewish War* 7.13–14 (tr. Thackeray).

43 Ammianus Marcellinus 24.4.24 (tr. Hamilton, with modifications). In fact, the mural crown was the appropriate decoration in this instance, which may have been a one-off revival anyway (Maxfield, *Decorations*, 251).

44 I. Shatzman, 'The Roman general's authority over booty', *Historia* 21 (1972), 177–205.

45 F.W. Walbank, *A Historical Commentary on Polybius* vol. I (Oxford, 1957), 217.

46 Nicolet, *World of the Citizen*, 120.

47 Livy 42.32.6.

48 Ammianus Marcellinus 24.4.26.

49 Maxfield, *Decorations*, 59–60. Cf. Campbell, *Emperor and Army*, chap. 3. This is a point apparently overlooked by MacMullen, 'Legion as society' (at 449–50: the evidence cited all derives from the Late Republic).

50 Cf. Holmes, *Firing Line*, chaps. 2 and 7.

51 In the Principate this was further preceded by a four-month period of basic training designed to test the suitability of recruits (see Davies, *Service in the Roman Army*, chap. 1). Vegetius (*Epitome of Military Science* 1.8, 2.5) also talks about soldiers being tattooed at the time when they swear the oath, but as with much of his treatise, it is unclear whether he is referring only to fourth-century practice or to earlier periods as well.

52 Polybius 6.21.1; Livy 22.38.3.

53 Vegetius *Epitome of Military Science* 2.5.

54 Holmes, *Firing Line*, 33 (with intriguing illustrative material).

55 Ibid. 42–3.

56 *Jewish War* 3.102, with valuable discussion in Y. le Bohec, *The Imperial Roman Army* (London, 1994), chap. 4.

57 R. Grigg, 'Inconsistency and lassitude: the shield emblems of the *Notitia Dignitatum*', *JRS* 73 (1983), 132–42.

58 Ammianus 16.12.6; Tacitus *Histories* 3.23; and the references and observations of MacMullen, 'Legion as society', 446.

59 L. Keppie, *The Making of the Roman Army* (London, 1984), 67.

60 Watson, *Roman Soldier*, 127–30. This is not to say that the standard lost its importance as a focus of unit pride in the fourth century: cf. Ammianus Marcellinus 27.1.6.

61 Maxfield, *Decorations*, chap. 11.

62 Caesar *Gallic War* 5.37.5.

63 Livy 34.46.10–13 (tr. Bettenson).

64 Plutarch *Aemilius Paullus* 20.1; Frontinus *Strategemata* 2.8.1–5. Cf. also Caesar *Gallic War* 4.25.3–5, Dio 74.6.6.

65 Holmes, *Firing Line*, 293.

66 J.G. Gray, *The Warriors: Reflections on Men in Battle* (London, 1970), quoted in Holmes, *Firing Line*, 300.

67 S.L.A. Marshall, *Men Under Fire* (New York, 1947), quoted in MacMullen, 'Legion as society', 448.

68 Livy 35.3.3–4 (tr. Bettenson).

69 Livy 44.39.5 (tr. Bettenson) – part of a speech Livy places in the mouth of Aemilius Paullus.

70 Plutarch *Marius* 7.4–5 (tr. Warner). Cf. the emperor Julian in the fourth century AD who 'contented himself with the cheap food of the common soldiers' (Ammianus Marcellinus 16.5.3).

71 Caesar *Gallic War* 1.25.1 (tr. Handford and Gardner).

72 Ibid. 2.25 (tr. Handford and Gardner). Cf. Livy 44.41, Tacitus *Agricola* 36, Dio 75.6.7, for other commanders getting involved, and [Caesar] *African War* 16.4 for soldiers looking for leadership in a tight situation.

73 Holmes, *Firing Line*, 347.

74 Josephus *Jewish War* 3.236–8; Tacitus *Histories* 4.34. Cf. also Livy 22.6; 25.34.

75 Ammianus Marcellinus 25.3 ff.

76 Polybius 10.13.1–5 (tr. Scott-Kilvert). This final remark about the effect of Scipio's presence on his soldiers shows, incidentally, that the previous passage about Caesar's effect on his men ought not be disqualified just because it came from Caesar's pen. Of course, Scipio's solution would not have been easy to transfer to the context of a pitched battle.

77 See, e.g., the figures cited in Holmes, *Firing Line*, 349 (with comparable evidence from other modern conflicts).

78 M.H. Hansen, 'The battle exhortation in ancient historiography: fact or fiction?', *Historia* 42 (1993), 161–80, at 166, 179.

79 Ammianus Marcellinus 16.12.29–34 (tr. Hamilton).

80 For a more detailed consideration, see my forthcoming chapter on the army in the new edition of the *Cambridge Ancient History* vol. XIII (AD 337-425).

81 Ammianus 16.12.37–8.

82 Matthews, *Ammianus*, 298.

83 Cf. ibid. 139, 159–60. This is not to deny individual cases of cowardice or lack of discipline during the course of the expedition (e.g., Ammianus 24.3.1–2), but such incidents cannot be regarded as having had any serious influence on the overall outcome of the campaign.

84 31.13.5–7. When the *Batavi*, held in reserve, were called on to join the battle, none of them were to be found (13.9): it is possible that they had deserted, but it may equally have been that they had already 'become helplessly involved in [the battle]' (Matthews, *Ammianus*, 298).

85 Cf. G.A. Crump, *Ammianus Marcellinus as a Military Historian* (Wiesbaden, 1975), 94–6.

86 B. Isaac, 'The meaning of the terms *limes* and *limitanei*', *JRS* 78 (1988), 125–47, at 139–46.

87 Eugippius *Life of St. Severinus* 4, 20.

6

THE ROMAN ARMY AND MORALITY IN WAR

Catherine M. Gilliver

What most distinguished the warfare of the Romans from that of their contemporaries and neighbours was...its ferocity. So ferocious were the Romans of the later first millennium BC that, in broad historical perspective, their behaviour bears comparison only with that of the Monguls or Timurids 1500 years later.[1]

Morality in war, and conduct in war, are issues of great concern today. Allegations of atrocities are frequently made in the aftermath of war, and there is probably no such thing as a conflict in which violations of international law, or internationally accepted codes of behaviour, do not occur. There are often excuses for atrocities: revenge, propaganda, and the setting of an example, amongst others. Such excuses do not, of course, excuse those who commit atrocities, but they can give us some understanding of why they have been committed and it is this aspect of Roman warfare that will be considered here, not the 'just war'. What follows will be a brief survey of the rules that governed the actual waging of war in antiquity, the conduct of the Romans in war, and, when they can be ascertained, the reasons behind their conduct. Little work has been done on this subject apart from a study of atrocities in the early and mid Republic by the rather appropriately named Mars McClelland Westington.[2] Westington apologizes for discussing incidents with a frankness 'which will prove nauseating even to the most 'hard-boiled' reader.' He was writing in 1938. Although I will include a few gruesome examples, and whilst I certainly do not wish to imply that familiarity breeds insensitivity, it seems that in these days when we can sit in front of the television and watch 'live war' from the Gulf or Bosnia, accounts of Roman atrocities will have less effect on us than on Westington's readers.

There was no international law concerning the waging of war such as we have today, but there were some rules. The Fetial Code included laws concerning the declaration of war and, according to Cicero, the conduct of war.[3] There was also a series of conventions and unwritten laws covering warfare,[4] and advice is given by a number of writers, including Polybius and the military theorist and philosopher Onasander, which may be considered as describing established military conventions rather than laws. Indeed, in his Στρατηγικός of the mid first century AD, Onasander seems almost more concerned with the character and behaviour of the general in war than with what strategies and tactics he should be employing. His list of the characteristics required of a 'good' general may be compared with those Cicero associated with Pompey for the purposes of his speech in favour of the latter's appointment to the Eastern command.[5] Cicero gives some general advice on behaviour and morality here and in the *De Officiis*.[6] A general should control his troops strictly, not let them plunder for his personal gain, and should show mercy to those who surrender.[7] Protection (presumably from Roman soldiers) must be granted to those who surrender; in the destruction and plundering of cities nothing should be done without good cause or with excess cruelty, and it was the general's duty to punish only the guilty and spare the rest.[8] Connected with this is a statement that those who have not been cruel and barbarous in the conduct of war should be spared.

Onasander puts forward several points on the subject, some of which echo Cicero's comments: the besieged were more likely to surrender if they knew they would not face slaughter, and generals who destroyed and massacred made the war more difficult as cities were less likely to surrender.[9] Thus acts of desperation from an enemy with nothing to lose should not be encouraged; the enemy's country should not be ravaged until the enemy had been informed of the general's intentions, to allow them time to surrender; plundering should be strictly controlled, and prisoners of war should not usually be killed while the war was still in progress, though enemy allies could be executed, if this was in the general's interest.[10] In the same way, in siege warfare, the general should prevent a massacre especially if the defenders seemed likely to hold out or seize the citadel because if they expected to be killed they would fight more fiercely and desperately.[11]

Whilst Cicero's admonishments tend to be rather abstract and sometimes of a purely moralistic nature, those of Onasander, though containing these moralizing overtones, also include suggestions for their application. He is not above the rather cold-blooded proposal that the enemy's allies could be put to death during a war if it was in the general's interest. He also advocates the starving out of the defenders during a siege, even suggesting that the besieging general aggravate the scarcity of food in the town by sending all prisoners except men of military age into the town.[12] Polybius also emphasized the importance of showing generosity to the defeated, and urged that punishment should not be excessive because it was better to conquer the enemy by generosity than by force.[13] Frontinus, an experienced general and former governor of Britain, on the other hand, suggested the alternative: if the enemy was terrorized he was more likely to surrender.[14] The objective of course was to get the enemy to surrender, or to demoralize him and destroy his will to fight, but there were clearly different schools of thought on how this could be most efficiently and effectively achieved.

The reality lies with both: the philosopher Onasander advises the general to show mercy to the enemy but goes on to suggest that this quality should be used along with brutality when necessary. Frontinus provides examples of the use of both methods to achieve objectives. And so we find Corbulo on campaign in Armenia varying his treatment of the enemy, using the panic created by the capture and demolition of Artaxata in order to capture Tigranocerta, 'for if he destroyed it, he would increase the enemy's terror; if he spared it he would be praised as merciful.' He showed lenience to those who surrendered and harshness to those who resisted, flushing out fugitives by fire.[15] Agricola also combined the use of terror tactics with mercy during his second year of campaigning in Britain which, according to Tacitus, encouraged the surrender of many tribes who clearly preferred to experience the governor's mercy.[16]

Caesar had a wide reputation for clemency which seems to have been justified in many cases;[17] for example, he was merciful towards the Aedui who were planning to join the revolt of Vercingetorix, and when Petreius executed some of Caesar's soldiers during a period of fraternization in the civil wars, Caesar made sure that all his enemy's men were sent back unharmed.[18] Caesar claims that it was his reputation for mercy that encouraged the surrender of enemy forces and cities in Africa following the defeat of Cato.[19] He makes no comment on the effect his victory over Cato, and his reputation as a general, might have had. Whatever Caesar's reputation, however, he does not seem to have been particularly concerned about humanitarian issues in war, and his use of *clementia* reflects Onasander's suggestions rather than those of Cicero. He was merciful when it was to his advantage to be merciful, and when it was in his interests, he could also be very brutal. He did not punish the Aedui who had been planning to join the revolt because he wanted to retain the tribe as an ally;[20] and because he sent Petreius's men back unharmed, several of the latter's officers deserted to Caesar. I shall return to this incident later.

Having a reputation for mercy or cultivating one was not the only method of encouraging the enemy to surrender. Magnanimous behaviour and various forms of psychological warfare are suggested by Frontinus and well illustrated by the author and by other historians. The tale of the schoolmaster of Falerii is frequently quoted not only by historians as an example of traditional Roman magnanimity, but also by military writers, to illustrate the effect such behaviour might have.[21] Frontinus included in his book one of his own stratagems which also illustrates the usefulness of this kind of behaviour: during the revolt of Civilis in Gaul, a city of the Lingones had gone over to the rebels; as Frontinus advanced with his army, the citizens feared that their land would be plundered; when the inhabitants remained unharmed and lost none of their property, they went over to the Romans and handed over a large number of armed men.[22]

Frontinus, who suggested the use of brutality in warfare as well as mercy, also advocated the use of psychological warfare in the form of terror tactics, giving several examples of their effectiveness.[23] Sulla is supposed to have broken the resistance of the besieged at Praeneste in 82 BC by fastening on spears the heads of Praenestine generals who had been killed in battle and displaying them to the defenders, and after defeating Hasdrubal at the Metaurus in 207 BC, Gaius Claudius Nero ordered his opponent's head to be flung into Hannibal's camp to demoralize the Carthaginians.[24] Decapitation and mutilation of the dead seem to have occurred fairly frequently, and these atrocities were committed not just by Rome's 'barbarian' enemies but also by the Romans.[25] The practice was still carried out in the second century AD by Rome's auxiliaries in the Dacian wars, and Trajan's Column illustrates the soldiers displaying their trophies to the emperor.[26] Corbulo, a paragon of military discipline, encouraged the Armenian city of Tigranocerta to surrender in a more dramatic fashion: he executed a captured Armenian noble and shot his head out of a catapult into the town. It fell in the middle of a council meeting and at the sight of it the besieged immediately surrendered.[27] Severity, however, could be taken too far, the dangers of which are considered below.

Surrendered and captured cities

Military textbooks advise the general to encourage the city he is besieging, or about to besiege, to surrender. This was important particularly before or during a long or hard siege, because if a city did surrender, that could prevent loss of life and waste of time and supplies. Thus when Julian wished to avoid spending time and losing lives besieging the Persian fortress of Anatha in AD 363, he persuaded the defenders to surrender, thereby avoiding, according to Ammianus, a dangerous siege. The fortress was destroyed but the defenders were treated well.[28] Titus made several attempts to persuade the defenders at Jerusalem to surrender, making one particularly impassioned effort when he had failed to take the strongest parts of the city by storm and was about to resort to circumvallation and blockade, and similarly Severus offered the Hatrenes the opportunity to surrender after his troops had breached the outer of Hatra's two walls.[29] Invitations such as these were often made after the failure of the initial assault, particularly when the attackers were barbarians who did not have the comparatively advanced siege equipment that the Romans and Persians used.[30] However, there is little evidence of any formal conventions on invitations to surrender before the late empire; they were rarely made at the first approach of the objective, and then only when the attacker had been frustrated in the initial assault. It seems that under most circumstances, the initiative was expected to come from the besieged rather than the besieger.

By the fourth century AD, however, the matter of invitations to surrender seems to have become more formalized, at least between Rome and Persia, and the different sides in civil wars. The defenders were usually invited to surrender at the beginning of a siege, and sometimes given several days to think about it. No doubt the preparations of siege equipment and so forth by the enemy army would have given the defenders even more to think about. Sapor seems to have believed that the Romans at Amida would be so terrified by the sight of his army approaching that they would immediately surrender, and at the very least would do so when invited.[31] However, these requests to surrender at the start of a siege seem to have been as much a formality as a realistic expectation: the fourth-century wars between Rome and Persia involved a great deal of siege warfare and although the cities and forts were usually asked to surrender, they rarely did so.[32]

It is easy to understand why the besiegers, or at least their commander, wanted the defenders to surrender. For the defenders and entire population of a town, however, the question of whether to surrender was an extremely important matter, for siege warfare is the oldest form of total war.[33] Surrender could involve the possibility of being raped, brutalized and enslaved, but also offered a greater likelihood of survival. There are, of course, exceptions, but on the whole, cities which surrendered at whatever stage of a siege usually fared much better at the hands of their captors than those taken by storm. This seems to have been one of the unwritten rules of warfare and is mentioned by Livy when describing the capture of the rebel Latin colony of Pometia in 502 BC.[34] The colony surrendered just as the Romans were about to storm it, but its fate, according to Livy, 'was no less horrible than if it had been taken by storm.' He spells this out again when describing the capture of Phocaea in 190 BC.[35] The soldiers wished to sack the town even though it had surrendered, and the praetor, Aemilius Regillus, ordered them not to, since 'cities were sacked after capture, not after surrender.' It is this convention on the treatment of surrendered cities, rather than any reputation a particular general might have had for mercy, that is likely to have encouraged cities to surrender.

The timing of the surrender seems also to have been important with regard to this convention on the treatment of cities. When Caesar was besieging the Gallic tribe of the Atuatuci in 57 BC, during the siege the defenders enquired about terms of surrender. Caesar replied that he would be merciful provided that they surrendered *before* the battering ram touched the wall of the *oppidum*.[36] Josephus mentions the despair of the Jews when the Romans brought their rams to bear on the walls of Jerusalem for the first time,[37] and although various skirmishes had taken place previously, this seems to represent the moment when the siege proper started. The implication is that there may have been some kind of formal convention concerning this matter, and this is confirmed by the humanitarian plea by Cicero that mercy should be shown to those who have surrendered 'even though the battering ram has hammered at their walls.'[38]

Theoretically, then, once the siege had formally begun, the general may have been entitled to treat the city however he wanted, whether or not it surrendered. In practice, though, because it was usually in the general's, or Rome's, interest to be merciful and so encourage other places to surrender, most cities which surrendered, at whatever stage of a siege, fared far better than those taken by assault. This is the case usually even with cities that had revolted or during civil wars when the treatment of defeated enemies was likely to be harsher and more violent, though of course there were exceptions. One interesting example is the treatment of Capsa, a town that surrendered to the Romans in the Jugurthine war. Despite surrendering, the town was fired, the men massacred and the rest of the population sold into slavery. Sallust describes this as a violation of the rules of war, but he does explain why Marius was prepared to violate these rules, a matter I shall discuss below.[39]

Cities which were taken by storm almost invariably fared badly. The assault was usually followed by the indiscriminate slaughter of the population, though occasionally this was confined primarily to men of military age.[40] However, in the confusion following the storming of a city, it is arguable how discriminating the victorious soldiers would have been. Those who managed to escape the slaughter might be sold into slavery or simply released depending on circumstances. The treatment of the different groups of prisoners at Cartagena by Scipio is interesting: citizens of the city were released, artisans were reduced to slavery for the duration of the war, and male non-citizens and slaves were sent to the fleet.[41] Very occasionally the defenders of a town might be spared even though it was taken by storm. At Syracuse, Marcellus allowed his soldiers to plunder the city but ordered them not to kill any of the free inhabitants. Archimedes is the only reported casualty, but again, one wonders how strictly Marcellus's order was enforced.[42]

In his description of the capture of Cartagena, Polybius suggests another possible convention of Roman warfare. Here the Carthaginian general Mago attempted to defend the citadel and only surrendered when he realized that the city had been completely overrun. Until this final surrender the Roman soldiers had been carrying out an indiscriminate massacre of the population on the orders of Scipio.[43] When the citadel surrendered, Scipio sounded the order to stop the slaughter and turn to plunder. Polybius claims that this was the Roman custom and was to inspire terror on the taking of a town by storm through the indiscriminate slaughter of both inhabitants and animals. In the case of Cartagena it was also no doubt intended to encourage those in the citadel to surrender as well as to terrorize the population, and allow the soldiers to sate their blood lust. This treatment contradicts Onasander's advice about showing mercy to the population if the defenders seemed likely to hold out in the citadel,[44] but there is a clear implication in Polybius that once the citadel surrendered the massacre would stop. This may have been considered as effective as the use of mercy in inducing the surrender of defenders.

This passage of Polybius is discussed in a recent article by Ziolkowski who provides plenty of evidence for both the massacre of defenders on the capture of a city, and of soldiers being given a signal to start looting once the general was confident that resistance had been crushed.[45] Ziolkowski also gives examples of how difficult it could be to control soldiers following battle or during the sack of a city, particularly when it came to the acquisition of loot. These difficulties are illustrated by Livy in his description of Gracchus's defeat of Hanno at Beneventum in 214 BC.[46] Gracchus had promised freedom to all the soldiers of servile origin who produced an enemy head. The best Roman soldiers then spent so long mutilating the bodies of the Carthaginian dead, cutting off their heads, that only the cowardly soldiers were left in the battle. Gracchus had to order his men back into the fight. If discipline could be a problem in a pitched battle, there seems little doubt that there could be a similar problem following the capture of a city with all the opportunities for plunder that arose. It is unlikely there was much order at all, if any, at this point in the sack of a city. Even if individual generals or officers had the power to control their soldiers, in the sack of a city soldiers would often find themselves under the cover of buildings, concealed from the eye of authority. Some soldiers may have been interested only in slaughtering the population; probably most went round slaughtering, raping and pillaging as the opportunities arose.

Ziolkowski concludes that Polybius's model of how the Romans sacked cities was 'at best an unwarranted generalisation from a most exceptional episode', linking it with Polybius's 'textbook' description of the Roman army in Book Six and portrayal of Roman soldiers as 'robots devoid of human traits, docile executors of orders'. It is the exception, rather than the norm,[47] a conclusion that seems valid. This is the kind of 'stratagem' that Frontinus collected for his book of *exempla*, and would not be out of place in his section *de iniciendo obsessis pavore*.[48] As Onasander warns, such action on the part of the attacking army may only have served to encourage resistance rather than surrender. The decision about how to treat the occupants of a captured town when the citadel continued to resist must have belonged to the commander and probably depended on the strategic situation, both immediate and in the long term, or on other factors such as how difficult the siege was and if the enemy had committed any atrocities against the Romans. The amount of control a general had over his troops must also have been a factor. At Carthage, there was no general massacre of the population to encourage the citadel of Byrsa to surrender; that was taken by storm nearly a week later.[49] Whatever the reasons for Polybius's discussion of this 'convention', it would, perhaps, be better described as a 'stratagem' of the same genre as those listed by Frontinus.

Rebellion and revenge

In the discussion above, I have noted a number of examples of atrocities which at first glance appear exceptional, but some categories of enemy or circumstance do not seem to have been covered by any of the traditions or laws concerning the conduct of war. Firstly, there is, on the whole, a marked difference between the treatment of those who had rebelled against Rome and those newly conquered by the Romans. In the latter case, the conquered enemy would not normally be treated too harshly, but rebels were usually dealt with very severely *pour encourager les autres*. In addition, if the enemy had committed atrocities towards Romans during the course of a war, they might be treated more harshly whether they were rebels or not. Under these circumstances the distinction between those who surrendered and those defeated in battle might not be so great.

Thus, when Numantia was forced through starvation to surrender, the entire population was sold into slavery except for the few who were to appear at Scipio's triumph, and the town itself was razed to the ground,[50] a fate usually reserved for the most intractable, hated or feared of Rome's enemies, such as Carthage. This harsh treatment probably had several reasons: it had taken the Romans ten years to capture the town; it had been a hard siege in difficult circumstances; and, perhaps most significantly, the defenders were the last to hold out following the revolt of Viriathus who had inflicted a number of embarrassing defeats on the Roman army. Under these circumstances it is perhaps surprising that the defenders were not slaughtered in spite of their surrender. Scipio was acting on his own initiative here in destroying the town, and not on the orders of the Senate as he had when he destroyed Carthage, but his severity was effective. Although parts of Spain were not subjugated until the time of Augustus, there were no more great revolts in the province except for that of Sertorius, which could be classed as civil war. Like Numantia, Uxellodunum was the last stronghold to hold out following the crushing of a revolt by the Romans, this time the Gallic revolt under Vercingetorix. The population, as at Numantia, was forced to surrender by blockade. Caesar wanted to make an example of the defenders to prevent further outbreaks of rebellion in Gaul, so he had the hands of all who had carried weapons cut off, to serve as an example.[51] Aulus Hirtius stresses that the punishment is for this reason, and not because of any brutality on Caesar's part. Perhaps Hirtius, like Sallust when describing the capture of Capsa, felt the need to excuse Caesar's lack of *clementia* on this occasion.

Capua brought upon itself a wide range of punishments for its actions during the Second Punic War. After the Roman defeat at Cannae, Capua defected to Hannibal. The Capuans had immediately tortured to death the Roman garrison, shut up the Roman citizens in a bath house and suffocated them with steam.[52] Under such circumstances, Rome exacted vicious retribution when Capua was forced by blockade to make an unconditional surrender in 211 BC. Some senators committed suicide; the rest were scourged and executed, as were senators from other Campanian towns that had defected. Nobles were imprisoned or sent to Latin colonies, and most Campanian citizens were sold into slavery; only some freedmen and artisans were allowed to remain. The Romans considered destroying Capua completely, but decided against this because of the fertility of the district. Rome took possession of the land and buildings, abolished the city's constitution and sent out a prefect annually to govern it – virtually unprecedented treatment.[53] The treatment of Capua served as a very clear warning to those who contemplated revolt.

It seems to have been fairly well known that those who revolted would be treated severely; Tacitus claims that the Iceni fought with great bravery in their first revolt of AD 51 because they 'had rebellion on their consciences'.[54] They knew they could expect no mercy and so had nothing to lose. Tacitus's father-in-law, the exemplary general Agricola, is supposed to have virtually annihilated the tribe of the Ordovices in North Wales following a rebellious attack on a Roman unit stationed in their territory just before his arrival.[55] The message was fairly straightforward: revolt was not worth the reprisals that would inevitably follow.

During the Gulf War, political reasons demanded that Arab troops of the UN Coalition forces were the first to liberate Kuwait City. The Egyptian, Saudi and Kuwaiti troops had with them advisers from US Central Command. One of the responsibilities of these advisers was to ensure that no reprisals were taken against Iraqi prisoners for atrocities alleged to have been committed by Iraqi troops during the occupation of Kuwait.[56] Whatever the situation, foreign war, civil war or revolt, Roman soldiers took revenge for atrocities committed by the enemy, whether on fellow soldiers or civilians. Hence the Capuans must have known their treatment by the Romans would be merciless when they surrendered. Appian states that during the Roman siege of Carthage in 146 BC, Hasdrubal tortured and executed Roman soldiers in full view of their besieging colleagues.[57] He says this was to destroy any hopes of surrender, and also that by committing these atrocities, Hasdrubal was depriving the Carthaginians of all hope of a pardon. Hasdrubal totally alienated himself from the general population by these actions, possibly because they wished to surrender. Scipio did not slaughter the general population, and this is one of the rare occasions where a Roman commander seems to have divorced the actions of the enemy general from those of the civilian population. The clear implication, however, is that atrocities on Roman soldiers and civilians would lead to savage treatment whether the enemy surrendered or not.

The murder of Roman merchants at Cenabum encouraged the particularly bloody slaughter of Gauls during the capture of Avaricum shortly afterwards.[58] The Gauls at Avaricum were mostly Bituriges, not the Carnutes who had carried out the murders, but the Roman soldiers probably did not consider discriminating between the different tribes: they were Gauls, so legitimate targets.[59] The slaughter of the Britons following the defeat of Boudicca's army also seems to have been exacerbated by the atrocities committed by the Britons on the inhabitants of Colchester, London and St. Albans, which Dio describes in great detail and with great relish.[60] This brings us back to the actions of Petreius who had executed some of Caesar's soldiers during a period of fraternization. He did this, according to Caesar, to discourage his men from surrendering,[61] presumably on the assumption that Caesar would put them to death in retaliation. His plan, however, backfired when Caesar ensured Petreius's men were returned safely. Not only did several of Petreius's officers go over to Caesar, but it also showed Petreius's army that Caesar would not take reprisals on them for the atrocities committed by their general.

Another reason, or excuse, given for excessive violence following the defeat of an enemy army or capture of a city is the difficulty of the campaign or the siege. This factor is mentioned by Caesar who seems to have felt some necessity to explain the particularly ferocious sack of Avaricum. The soldiers were, as stated above, taking revenge for the Roman merchants of Cenabum, but the siege had also been a very difficult one, requiring the construction of massive and elaborate siege-works. The soldiers spared no one, and Caesar reports that from the population of some 40,000, barely 800 escaped to Vercingetorix.

Tacitus states that the battle resulting in the defeat of Tacfarinas's rebel army in AD 24 was particularly bloody, partly because the war had been a difficult one and the soldiers had suffered hardships,[62] but such episodes were more common in sieges after an assault. The town of Locha in Africa, like Capsa, surrendered to Scipio as the Romans were about to assault, but this time a recall was sounded. The soldiers refused to obey the signal, scaled the walls and began an indiscriminate slaughter because the siege had been a hard one.[63] Interestingly,

Scipio deprived the army of its booty, executed three (chosen by lot) of the officers who had disobeyed orders, and dismissed the survivors in safety, illustrating a severity that few generals had the authority or the foolhardiness to display.[64]

Civil War

During civil war a general or emperor, whether he held a legitimate appointment or was a usurper, *could* perceive any town or army that opposed him as rebellious. Troops could not be controlled as tightly during civil war as at other times,[65] and since during a civil war money could not be made from the ransom or sale of prisoners, the slaughter of fellow Romans following a pitched battle or the capture of a town could be particularly bloody.[66] Failure to control troops led to attacks on civilians by Otho's soldiers on the coast of Gaul and north Italy, and following Vitellius's victory at Cremona, by his triumphant troops garrisoned in towns across Italy.[67]

After Caesar's defeat of the Scipionic forces at Thapsus, his soldiers went on the rampage and massacred all their opponents despite Caesar's reported entreaties to his men to spare them.[68] One of the most famous examples of complete failure to control troops occurred following the Flavian victory at Cremona in AD 69. The victorious troops stormed the city which had supported Vitellius and sacked it for four days although it had surrendered.[69] The Flavian commander seems to have made no effort to prevent his troops from sacking the town, though in the light of Tacitus's comment on controlling troops in civil war, it was probably more than his life was worth even to try to stop them, let alone punish them afterwards. Even Caesar, who may have had the authority and popularity with his troops to take some action against them for disobeying orders, did nothing.

Treatment of captured or surrendered towns could also be severe, not because of inability to control troops but, as with towns during revolts, to serve as an example to others. The town of Gomphi in Thessaly had originally sided with Caesar during the civil war, but following his setback at Dyrrachium went over to Pompey, possibly under duress.[70] The town was rich and well supplied and would be a useful supply base for either side, particularly Caesar at this point because he was running short of supplies. Caesar took the town by storm and allowed his men to plunder it, then paraded captives before the walls of another town that had acted similarly. Caesar intended his treatment of Gomphi to act as an example and terrify the other towns in Thessaly. It seems to have worked because they all surrendered, though Caesar's actions are hardly those of a man famed for *clementia*. These towns, and many others, were in a no-win situation, forced to support particular factions in civil wars. If they were captured by an opposing force they usually paid a heavy price, and it is not difficult to understand why the Romans considered civil war the worst kind of war.

Brutality and mercy

The remainder of this paper will concentrate on the use of brutality and mercy in warfare and the circumstances under which they were employed. Treatises written by Onasander and Frontinus advocated the use of both methods in war, and there are several examples above of a general combining the use of terror tactics with clemency as a tool of conquest, to encourage surrender. By cultivating a reputation for exercising clemency to those who surrendered, a general could make the war easier, but it may also have been necessary to make an example of those who refused to surrender, to show what the alternative was.

Although it has been suggested that Roman warfare became even more brutal in the second century BC, Harris claims there is not enough evidence to support this view, and I tend to agree with him.[71] The wars in this period were more intensive than any Rome had fought before, and this may explain the number of atrocities committed, but they do not seem to be any more 'atrocious' than those of earlier wars. Paul in fact notes that from the second century BC there was an increasing tendency to treat those who surrendered more leniently, or at least to condemn those who insisted on severe punishment, and sees this in Sallust.[72] The acquittal of Servius Sulpicius Galba for the massacre of the surrendered Celtiberians in 149 BC became notorious, though as much for his appeal to the emotions of his jury as for the appalling nature of his atrocity.[73] Paul's observation would also help to explain Cicero's advocacy of merciful treatment, and the trend can be seen in his fourth Verrine oration where he accuses Verres of committing outrages that would not be done 'in these days when the city was taken (*capta*), however much the passions of war-time, military licence, the custom of war and the right of the conqueror might provoke them.'[74] The statement also suggests that, even though the treatment of captured cities might be more lenient in Cicero's day than in the past, those taken by storm (*captae*) would still suffer.

This tendency towards more merciful treatment is linked with Rome's long-term military interests and a policy of creating new provinces. The use of mercy might make the defeated better disposed towards the Romans and less likely to harbour resentment than if the campaign had been a brutal one. It might also leave the land relatively unscathed and a population that could later be taxed and provide auxiliary troops for the army that defeated them. In his speech before Mons Graupius, the British general Calgacus claims that the Romans created a desert and called it peace.[75] It was actually more in the Romans' interest to subdue the inhabitants than to destroy them.

Ziolkowski noted only three occasions when Roman generals managed to keep sacking under control following the capture of a city by storm: the outer districts of Syracuse, Cartagena, and Tigranocerta in Armenia.[76] Cartagena was the supply base for Carthaginian forces in Spain, and in order to exploit fully the capture of the city, Scipio could not afford to let his troops sack it too violently. The capture of the city opened up the whole of the Spanish peninsula for the Romans as well as providing money for the Roman treasury, supplies from the city's arsenal, and the use of the base in further campaigns. Cartagena was a key city in Spain and whoever held it had a major advantage. By controlling the sack of the city, Scipio made the most of his success, and through his treatment of the inhabitants, particularly the citizens, he won their goodwill and support. The same argument could be used for the two other examples: Syracuse may not have had the enormous strategic importance of Cartagena, but it had a good harbour and served as Scipio's headquarters prior to his invasion of Africa; Tigranocerta could also have served as a supply base for Lucullus, and it was better to have the support of the inhabitants than their opposition.

Thus by controlling the sack of a city, the general could gain maximum advantage from its capture: plunder for himself and his soldiers and/or the Roman treasury, the goodwill of the inhabitants, and a good reputation which might encourage others to surrender. Perhaps most importantly though, in the short term, the general also obtained a base which could be used as the launching point for further campaigns, particularly if it were on a route that could be easily supplied, as was Cartagena.

We can see the same considerations at work during civil war. Although Marseilles surrendered to Caesar, the inhabitants had put up a very hard fight and had broken a truce to attack Caesar's soldiers and sabotage his siege works. Under such circumstances, it would not have been surprising if Caesar had allowed his soldiers to sack the place. Caesar claims he spared the inhabitants because of the city's fame and antiquity, and not because of any utility it might have to himself.[77] Caesar's very statement suggests that the potential value of a city to the victorious general might indeed influence its fate. Caesar may be advertising his *clementia* here, but Marseilles was very important strategically as a supply and naval base, and had been one of his principal objectives at the start of the campaign. He left a fairly large garrison of two legions, and it is more likely that he spared the population to gain their goodwill in using this new base rather than through any respect for the eminence of the city.

The same considerations help to account for Marius's violation of the laws of war at Capsa during the Jugurthine war. The town surrendered to the Romans, but was sacked anyway and treated as if taken by storm. As Paul notes, Sallust felt obliged to provide an explanation for this violation.[78] Sallust claims that Marius did this 'not because of avarice or cruelty, but because the place was of advantage to Jugurtha and well protected, while the people were fickle and untrustworthy and had previously shown themselves amenable neither to kindness nor to fear.'[79] He adds that this episode increased Marius's popularity with his soldiers (not surprisingly, given the unexpected opportunity for plunder), and made the Numidians fear him. Thus the treatment of cities and their inhabitants could depend on their strategic importance to the enemy as well as to the invading force, and this concern seems usually to have had far more influence on the treatment of cities than the requirements of the laws of war or any conventions on this matter.

This line of thinking can be seen in field engagements as well as in siege warfare. At Cynoscephalae in 197 BC, the Macedonian army was comprehensively defeated by the Romans under Flamininus.[80] Towards the end of the battle a section of the Macedonians held up their spears in their gesture of surrender and when Flamininus was informed of the significance of their actions, he kept back his men, considering whether to spare the defeated enemy. While he was still making up his mind, some Roman units attacked them and cut them down; only a few escaped.[81] It is perfectly possible that Flamininus simply did not have the opportunity to order his men to stop fighting, or that his soldiers had no idea of the significance of a Macedonian holding up his spear (according to Livy, Flamininus himself was ignorant of it until informed). However, it is also possible that Flamininus was 'holding the telescope to his blind eye' in the hope that the Macedonians would be slaughtered, destroying their ability to make war, and opening up the whole of Greece to Roman intervention.

Atrocities as well as acts of humanity might be performed if the action furthered the interests of Rome, or the individual commander. The fact that an experienced general such as Frontinus advocated the use of brutality as well as mercy suggests that both were accepted means of dealing with the enemy, depending on the circumstances. In some cases, perhaps fairly frequently, a general would have to consider quite carefully whether to be merciful or brutal to the enemy to get the best advantage from the situation. He could not afford to be too ruthless, however, or too compassionate. When Ostorius Scapula threatened to wipe out the entire tribe of the Silures in South Wales, this only encouraged them to resist more strongly, and literary sources point out that generals who terrorize the enemy risk making the war harder for themselves.[82] On the other hand, Dio puts the Varian disaster down partly to Varus's lenient treatment of Germany as if it were a well established province and not recently conquered.[83]

For the most part, leniency brought greater advantages, and it is this quality of mercy that most Roman writers wished to publicize. Livy has Hasdrubal state that the Romans had enlarged their empire almost more by sparing the vanquished than by conquest, and after Cynoscephalae, Flamininus informs the defeated Greeks that 'brave men should be hard on the enemy in battle...but when they conquer, gentle and humane.'[84]

Conclusions

There were a number of formal conventions and informal traditions in the conduct of war by the Romans. Usually those who surrendered were treated comparatively well, whilst those who resisted were generally treated very harshly. Many of the exceptions to these conventions occurred during periods of civil war, rebellion, and for revenge, so under abnormal conditions. In civil war, because troops could not be as tightly controlled as at other times and prisoners were worthless, atrocities might be committed which would not happen under other circumstances. The ancient sources state clearly that neither rebels nor those who committed atrocities could expect to be treated mercifully.

There are a number of exceptions to the rules of war, however, that can be best explained in the light of Rome's, or the general's, best interests. The ancient literary sources might put acts of mercy down to purely humanitarian concerns, as Cicero encourages the general to do, but that may be for propaganda purposes, like the reasons Caesar gives for his lenient treatment of Marseilles, or to indulge in a little self-congratulation and emphasise to the Roman audience how 'civilised' they were, even in war. Marius broke the rules of war at Capsa by his harsh treatment of a surrendered city but, as Sallust explains, this was because it was in the Romans' best interests (and the best interests of Marius too). By advocating the widespread use of mercy on altruistic grounds, Cicero is probably being unrealistic. Onasander and Frontinus are far more pragmatic when they suggest the use of terror and leniency when appropriate. It may have been better to conquer the enemy by generosity than by force, but brutality and mercy were both tools of conquest.[85]

NOTES

1 J.Keegan, *A History of Warfare*, 1994.

2 *Atrocities in Roman Warfare to 133 BC*, University of Chicago private edition, 1938.

3 *Off.* I.36.

4 Cicero refers to these as the *mores belli*, *Verr.* IV.116. Sallust mentions the *ius belli*, *Iug.* 91.

5 *Leg. Man.* 10–16.

6 *Off.* I.34–36.

7 *Leg. Man.* 13.

8 *Off.* I.82.

9 *Onas.* xxxviii.

10 *Onas.* vi.

11 *Onas.* xlii. cf. Vegetius's advice concerning a fleeing enemy following a pitched battle; flight should be facilitated because an enemy who is surrounded and has nothing to lose will fight more ferociously, *Veg.* III.21.

12 A tactic actually used by the Romans; Caesar refused to allow the Mandubii through his lines at Alesia after they had been expelled from the town by the Gauls precisely because of lack of supplies, *B.Gall.* VII.78. At Cremna the leader of the defenders, Lydius, expelled the young and old from the town for the same reason, and when the Romans sent them back, hurled them into the ravines around the town to conserve supplies, Zosimus I.69.

13 Polybius V.11.5; 12.2.

14 *Str.* II.ix.2–5.

15 *Ann.* xiv.23.

16 *Agr.* 20.

17 Pliny, *N.H.* VII.94, although this *clementia* was shown primarily to Romans in civil war rather than to 'barbarians' in foreign wars. J.Collins discusses evidence for 'war crimes' and *clementia* in Caesar's commentaries, 'Caesar as Political Propagandist', *ANRW* I.1, 922–66. Collins suggests Caesar was quite open about his admissions of atrocities and felt no compunction to provide explanations in the *Bellum Gallicum*, but in the *Bellum Civile* is anxious to stress his *clementia* as opposed to the *crudelitas* of the Pompeians. Collins does not see this as propaganda, but believes that Caesar actually was more merciful than his opponents.

18 *B.Gall.* VII.40; *B.Civ.* I.75.

19 *B.Afr.* 88, 92.

20 *B.Gall.* VII.54, on the importance of retaining the loyalty of the Aedui.

21 Livy V.27; Valerius Maximus VI.5; Plut. *Cam.* 10; Frontinus *Str.* IV.iv.1; Polyaenus VIII.7. When Camillus was besieging Falerii in 394 BC a Faliscan schoolmaster led the sons of the leading citizens outside the town on some pretext, then presented them to Camillus as hostages. The upright Roman general was appalled at this treachery, and sent the boys back to Falerii with the schoolmaster as their prisoner. The Faliscans were so impressed with their enemy's action that they immediately surrendered.

22 *Str.* IV.iii.14. cf. Octavian's campaigns in Illyricum. When he captured the town of Terponus which the Iapydes had abandoned, he did not destroy it in the hope that the tribe would surrender, which it did; Appian *Ill.* 18.

23 *Str.* II.ix.2–5.

24 For Sulla, *Str.* II.ix.3, Appian *B.Civ.* I.93–4; for Claudius Nero, *Str.* II.ix.2, Livy XXVII.51.

25 Westington, op. cit., chapter v is concerned with the mutilation of the dead.

26 Scenes xxiv, lxxii; scene lvii shows Dacian heads stuck on poles whilst scene cxlvii shows the head of Decebalus being displayed to Roman troops. At Beneventum, Gracchus promised freedom to the conscripted slaves who produced heads of the enemy dead, and perhaps the auxiliaries in the Dacian campaign were as anxious as those at Beneventum to show their *virtus*, in this case displaying their trophies to the emperor in person.

27 *Str.* II.ix.4. Displaying the heads of those killed in battle or shooting them into besieged towns with slings or artillery was an aspect of psychological warfare also employed in later periods, and particularly during the crusades; Christians hurled the heads of Turks killed in battle into the town of Nicea to terrorize the garrison, *Gesta Francorum et aliorum Hierosalimitanorum* viii. Corbulo, however, seems to have gone one step further by actually executing a captive rather than simply decapitating a corpse.

28 *Amm. Marc.* xxiv.1.8.

29 Josephus, *B.Iud.* V.36 ff; Dio LXXVI.10 ff.

30 e.g. the attack by Gauls on Quintus Cicero's winter camp, *B.Gall.* V.38 ff; by the Batavians on the legionary fortress of Vetera, Tacitus, *Hist.* IV.21–4 (though here the Batavians were also employing the technical expertise of Roman deserters); by the Goths on the town of Adrianople following the battle in AD 378, *Amm. Marc.* XXXI.15. Vitruvius (*de Arch.* X.xvi.2) notes that since barbarians do not besiege towns according to Roman military theory (and their methods are therefore inept), their attacks can be easily repulsed.

31 *Amm. Marc.* XIX.13.

32 Two Roman forts, Reman and Busan, did surrender to Sapor on his approach. The Persian king treated the inhabitants well, and Ammianus notes that this was a 'pretence of mildness, assumed in the hope that those who had previously been terrified by his cruelty would forget their fear and surrender to him willingly', *Amm. Marc.* XVIII.10. Perhaps this was why Sapor was so surprised, when he arrived at his next objective, to find that Amida refused to surrender.

33 M. Welzer, *Just and Unjust Wars*, 1980, 160.

34 Livy II.17.2.

35 Livy XXXVII.32.

36 *B.Gall.* II.32, *priusquam murum aries attigisset.* Interestingly, when the Atuatuci did surrender, Caesar shut them up in their *oppidum* overnight for their own protection, presumably from his own troops; cf. Cicero, *Off.* I.82, who advocates this.

37 *B.Iud.* V.277.

38 *Off.* I.35, *quamvis murum aries percusserit.*

39 *Iug.* 91. Sallust claims the action was *contra ius belli.*

40 e.g. Volandum in Armenia, captured in a ferocious but very quick assault by Corbulo, Tac. *Ann.* XIII.39.

41 Polybius X.16, one of the very rare occasions where the Romans employed slaves or prisoners of war to help man their fleet.

42 Livy XXV.25 for Marcellus's order; for the death of Archimedes, Plut. *Marc.* 19. Westington, op. cit. 93 ff, points out that slaves were not exempt from the general's order about clemency, but how do you tell the difference between a slave and a citizen, especially in a city that has been under siege for some months?

43 Polybius X.15.

44 *Onas.* xlii.

45 A. Ziolkowski, '*Urbs direpta,* or how the Romans sacked cities', in J. Rich and G. Shipley (eds), *War and Society in the Roman World,* 1993, 69–91. Ziolkowski gives several examples from Livy of the giving of a signal as permission to turn from massacre to plunder, including Veii, New Carthage and two districts of Syracuse (Livy XXV.25.5–9).

46 Livy XXIV.15–16.

47 Ziolkowski, op. cit. 79, 87. I am also doubtful of Ziolkowski's suggestion that there would have been particular phases in the sack of any city, unless the commander had a particularly firm hold over his soldiers.

48 *Str.* III. viii.

49 Appian, *Pun.* 130.

50 Appian, *Hisp.* 98.

51 Hirtius, *B.Gall.* VIII.44.

52 Livy XXIII.7; XXVI.13.

53 Livy XXVI.16.

54 *conscientia rebellionis,* Ann. XII.31.

55 *Agric.* 18.

56 Norman Schwarzkopf, *It Doesn't Take a Hero,* 1993, 441 and 571.

57 *Pun.* 118.

58 *B.Gall.* VII.3, 17 and 28.

59 When the particular individual responsible for inciting the Gallic revolt and the massacre at Cenabum was captured, Hirtius claims that Caesar's soldiers forced him to execute the Gaul, even though he was opposed to harsh punishments, *B.Gall.* VIII.38.

60 Dio LXII.7.

61 *B.Civ.* I.75.

62 *Ann.* IV.25.

63 Appian, *Pun.* 15.

64 When Valerius Flaccus attempted to copy Scipio's action, at Byzantium in 86 BC, he was murdered by his troops who wanted to keep their booty, Dio XXXV.104.

65 Tacitus *Hist.* II.29; III.7.

66 Tacitus *Hist.* II.44; Plut. *Otho* 14. Plutarch mentions the huge pile of dead by a temple after the first battle of Bedriacum.

67 Attacks by Otho's troops, during which Agricola's mother was killed, *Agric.* 7, and by those of Vitellius, *Hist.* II.56.

68 *B.Afr.* 85.

69 Tacitus *Hist.* III.33–4.

70 *B.Civ.* III.80–1.

71 Harris, *War and Imperialism in Republican Rome*, 1985, 52.

72 G.M. Paul, *A Historical Commentary on Sallust's* Bellum Jugurthinum, ARCA Classical and Medieval Texts, Papers and Monographs 13, 1984, 226–7.

73 Cicero, *De Oratore* I.227; *Brutus* 89.

74 *Verr.* iv.116.

75 *Agric.* 30.

76 Op. cit. 86. He does not explain how the three generals involved managed to keep their soldiers under control, and the ancient sources give little information on this either.

77 *B.Civ.* II.22.

78 Op. cit. 226–7.

79 *Iug.* 91; *Id facinus contra ius belli, non avaritia neque scelere consulis admissum, sed quia locus Iugurthae opportunus, nobis aditu difficilis, genus hominum mobile, infidum, ante neque beneficio neque metu coercitum.* The treatment was also no doubt seen as revenge for the massacre of Italian traders by Jugurtha when the town of Cirta surrendered to him in the opening stages of the war, *B.Iug.* 25.

80 Polybius, XVIII.24–7, and Livy, XXXIII.7–10, both provide detailed descriptions of the battle.

81 Polybius XVIII.26; Livy XXXIII.10.

82 Tacitus, *Ann.* XII.38 for Ostorius; Onasander XXXVIII.

83 Dio LVI.19.

84 Livy XXX.42 on Hasdrubal; XXXIII.12 and Polybius XVIII.37 for Flamininus.

85 Of course, not all atrocities can be explained according to the conventions discussed above, and a particularly brutal episode occurred during minor wars in the Crimea during the reign of Claudius, described by Tacitus, *Ann.* XII.16. A Roman force was besieging the hill-town of Upse, and after initial resistance the inhabitants asked to surrender, but the Romans did not want to have to deal with prisoners because of the small size of their force. In a perverse distortion of the rules of war, because they considered it barbarous to slaughter men who had surrendered, the Romans refused to accept the surrender, stormed the town and massacred the entire population.

7

BATTLE IN ANCIENT EGYPT:
THE TRIUMPH OF HORUS OR THE CUTTING
EDGE OF THE TEMPLE ECONOMY?

Ian Shaw

Introduction

Egyptologists have taken a variety of different approaches to the study of Egyptian warfare, ranging from the analysis of battle tactics to the cataloguing of types of physical injury. In particular, the excellent preservation of military equipment, such as bows, axes and chariots, has provided the basis for numerous detailed discussions of the changing nature of Egyptian military technology.[1] However, most analyses of pharaonic warfare have tended to discuss a variety of more abstract areas such as political history, military strategy, symbolism, literary criticism and the topography and ethnography of the ancient world, often steering away from the practical questions of life, death and survival on the battlefield.[2] This situation is exacerbated by the inclination of many of the ancient textual and artistic sources to present battles not as historical events but as aspects of the myth and symbolism of the king and the gods.

Egyptologists have rarely focussed on the practical experiences of the individual Egyptians on the battlefield. This paper discusses the 'official' Egyptian view of battle and compares it with the small amount of information regarding the attitudes of individual soldiers. Since much of the analysis is based on pictorial and textual evidence, the discussion inevitably deals as much with the aims and purpose of the documents themselves as with the elusive underlying reality of Egyptian battle.

Whereas many of the other aspects of Egyptian daily life portrayed on the walls of tombs (such as agriculture or craftwork) have survived to some extent in the archaeological record at the sites of ancient towns and villages, the battle scenes have relatively few corresponding archaeological traces. The battlefield is among the most ephemeral of man-made features, and even the most famous battles of medieval and post-medieval Europe have often proved difficult to locate archaeo-logically.[3] Egypt's arid climate, however, has helped to preserve a particularly vivid record of the changing physical effects of conflict on Egyptian soldiers and their enemies. The anthropological evidence for battle in Egypt stretches back at least as far as the 12th millennium BC when struggles between bands of Palaeolithic (Qadan-culture) hunter-gatherers led to flint arrowheads becoming embedded in the bones of almost half of the individuals buried in Cemetery 117 at Jebel Sahaba, near Wadi Halfa. Michael Hoffman, however, has questioned whether this evidence of hunter-gatherer conflict can be interpreted as a full-scale pitched battle: 'Assuming...that about 40 percent of the people buried at Site 117 actually did perish from arrow or dart wounds from spear throwers (the points are clearly too small for thrusting spears), we must return to the problem of why such a hunting and gathering people were so prone to violence...the varied ages and sexes of the victims at Site 117 are better explained by conditions of endemic raiding and ambush than regular, organized warfare, which takes its highest toll in young to middle-aged adult males'.[4]

Nine thousand years later, at the end of the 3rd millennium BC, at least sixty Eleventh-Dynasty soldiers were buried in a mass grave near the tomb of Nebhepetre Mentuhotep II in western Thebes;[5] many of these have been diagnosed as suffering from severe head-wounds that are assumed to have been sustained in the course of siege warfare, and in one case an ebony-tipped arrow-head was discovered still embed-ded in the left eye socket.

In the early sixteenth century BC the Theban king Seqenenre Tao II was killed, probably during a campaign against the Hyksos rulers of Lower Egypt; his body has survived, the head still disfigured by gashes matching the dimensions of a particular type of axe blade prevalent both in Syria-Palestine and in the eastern Delta of Egypt during the Hyksos period.[6] A recent study of skulls from Giza and Kerma indi-cates that skeletal remains from a wide variety of sites and dates can provide intriguing evidence of the types of injuries inflicted on the battlefield;[7] anthropological evidence of this type is an invaluable means of verifying and complementing the details of the surviving textual and pictorial descriptions of Egyptian battle.

Decoding the evidence of art and texts

The most fundamental artistic themes of Egyptian battle were encap-sulated at a surprisingly early stage in their history. The carved reliefs on the ceremonial palettes, maceheads and knife-handles of the protodynastic period (*c.* 3000 BC) are characterized by a number of constantly repeated motifs: the king smiting foreigners,[8] the siege and capture of fortified settlements, the binding and execution of prisoners, and the offering of the spoils of war to the gods. These actions all relate to the Egyptians' subtle fusion of political and religious systems, in which the role of the pharaoh was to maintain the stability of the universe; he was thus obliged to fight battles on behalf of the gods and then to bring back prisoners and booty as votive offerings for their temples.

It is likely, however, that even at this early stage in Egyptian history the political and economic motivations for warfare – the defence of borders and the acquisition of valuable land, livestock, natural resources and slaves – were being masked, to some extent, by layers of religion and ritual, providing both moral justification and a 'universal' framework. The tradition of religious justification for war was maintained throughout the pharaonic period, and even turned against the Egyptians themselves in the case of the Victory Stele of the Nubian pharaoh Piankhi (*c.* 734 BC),[9] in which he justified his conquest of Egypt in terms of a crusade on behalf of the god Amun.

The tendency for the earliest reliefs and inscriptions to oversimplify the motivations for warfare and the nature of battle can largely be explained by the fact that such objects as palettes and ceremonial maceheads were never intended to provide historical accounts of battle. The motifs on these votive gifts were designed to function within the emerging cults of the king and the various 'local' and 'national' deities with which he associated himself, and the battlefield was merely a convenient artistic context for the depiction of ritual acts and universal truths.[10] The king is often portrayed in such bestial forms as a bull or a lion in order to emphasize his symbolic role as the protector of Egypt from the forces of chaos and evil (see Figure 1).

In the pharaonic period, the secondary sources for Egyptian warfare include massive temple reliefs depicting campaigns and battles, as well as victory stelae and the funerary decoration of such key military personalities as the Eleventh-Dynasty general Intef[11] and the early New Kingdom admiral Ahmose son of Ibana.[12] All of these were relatively public displays of the Egyptian view of battle; just as the works of Classical historians and biographers were written with particular aims and readers in mind, so the pharaonic descriptions of war and battle had their own agenda, and any study must be sensitive not only to content but also to the nuances of literary form.[13] If the paintings and reliefs depicting Egyptian battles are to be understood

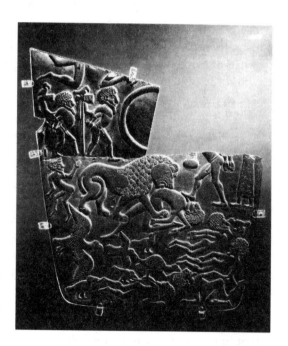

Figure 1. The 'Battlefield palette', showing enemy dead being eaten by vultures and savaged by the Egyptian king in the form of a lion; Protodynastic period (British Museum).

properly, their physical and cultural contexts must also be taken into account.

The Table on pages 253 ff. lists the major pictorial documentation for Egyptian battles, from the late prehistoric period to the end of the New Kingdom. There are clearly two major sources of information: a number of private tombs, at Deshasheh,[14] Saqqara,[15] Beni Hasan[16] and Thebes,[17] dating to the late Old Kingdom and Middle Kingdom (*c.* 2040–1782 BC), and the temple reliefs of the Ramessid period (*c.* 1293–1070 BC) at Thebes and numerous sites in Nubia, of which the most important group are those devoted to the Battle of Qadesh.[18]

Battle scenes in Old and Middle Kingdom private tombs

The earliest Old Kingdom battle scene, showing archers drawing their bows, has survived in the form of a fragment of relief from the Fourth-Dynasty mortuary complex of Khufu (the block itself having been re-used in the pyramid of Ammenemes I at Lisht).[19] The only other known royal depiction of battle in the Old Kingdom is from the funerary causeway of the Fifth-Dynasty pharaoh Unas at Saqqara, where the reliefs include fragments of a confrontation between an Asiatic soldier and Egyptians armed with daggers, bows and arrows.[20] This theme of Egyptians attacking Asiatics is repeated in two private tombs: the Sixth-Dynasty tomb of Inti at Deshasheh,[21] where there is definite evidence for the use of sophisticated siege technology (see Figure 2), and the roughly contemporary tomb of Kaemheset at Saqqara, which shows a scaling ladder on wheels being used in a siege. Both of these scenes clearly depict the sieges of Asiatic fortified towns, indicating that Egypt was already launching military campaigns into the Levant during the Old Kingdom.

Nevertheless, depictions of battles are extremely rare in the tombs of both Old and New Kingdom nobles, and it was only for a short period in the Sixth to Twelfth Dynasties that a number of officials and provincial governors appear to have regarded warfare (as well as wrestling matches) as sufficiently important aspects of their lives to have battle-scenes portrayed in their tombs.[22] It is uncertain precisely what may be deduced from the Old and Middle Kingdom battle paintings. On a broad historical level, two major historical factors seem to be at work: (1) the breakdown of order and stability at the end of the Old Kingdom, resulting in widespread conflict between the different provinces; (2) the Old Kingdom rulers' *ad hoc* system of recruiting groups of

Figure 2. Detail of a wall painting in the tomb of Inti at Deshasheh, showing the Egyptian army laying siege to an Asiatic town; Old Kingdom, Sixth Dynasty.

untrained young men as soldiers was superseded during the First Intermediate Period by the creation of small professional armies under the command of local governors, which would eventually form the nucleus of a national army in the Middle Kingdom.

Some of the surviving First Intermediate Period funerary paintings and texts, such as those in the tomb of Ankhtifi at el-Moalla[23] and the tomb of Setka at Aswan,[24] make it clear that this era was characterized by greater conflict between the individual regions of Egypt. Provincial governors continued to play a more military role in the early Middle Kingdom, and on an artistic level there must also have been a greater desire or necessity to celebrate military achievements in Middle Kingdom private tombs. The existence of the precedents described above in the late Old Kingdom tombs of Inti and Kaemheset may suggest that funerary art was already reflecting social and political change as the Old Kingdom went into decline.

Four of the tombs at Beni Hasan contain battle paintings (see Table and Figure 3); these scenes were an integral part of the funerary cult and all four were located at the bottom of the eastern wall of the main chamber. Along with the depictions of funerary offerings and such activities as dancing, hunting, fishing or agriculture, they were intended both to encapsulate the many aspects of the life of the deceased and to justify his continued existence in the afterlife. Given the tendency of Egyptian art to draw upon a reservoir of general motifs appropriate to particular circumstances, there must be some doubt as to the historicity of any battle scene on the wall of any particular tomb: the battle depicted might have been a combination of smaller

Figure 3. Detail of a mural painting in the tomb of Khety at Beni Hasan, showing an Egyptian fortified town besieged by an Egyptian army; Middle Kingdom.

skirmishes or might never have taken place, just as the deceased may never actually have speared fish from a papyrus skiff. Indeed it has been pointed out that the scenes at Beni Hasan – all depictions of the sieges of fortified towns – resemble one another sufficiently closely to suggest that none of them (or at least only the earliest of them) necessarily depicts a unique historical event. Although the three surviving Old Kingdom depictions of battles, as well as the funerary scenes of Mentuhotep II and his general, all show conflicts between Asiatics and Egyptians, the Beni Hasan scenes appear to document civil war between rival factions of Egyptians. This suggests that the content of funerary art was responding to some extent to historical events rather than endlessly repeating the same generalized motifs.

Just as the battle scenes in the Sixth-Dynasty tombs of Inti and Kaemheset appear to be echoing the appearance of similar depictions in the royal funerary complexes of Khufu and Unas, so the Beni Hasan scenes also have roughly contemporary royal counterparts in the fragments of relief surviving from the Theban mortuary temple of the Eleventh-Dynasty pharaoh Nebhepetre Mentuhotep II at Deir el-Bahari and the funerary causeways of the Twelfth-Dynasty rulers Sesostris I and III, at Lisht and Dahshur respectively.[25]

A few surviving fragments of reliefs from Mentuhotep II's temple at Deir el-Bahari, now scattered among numerous museum collections, show that it once bore scenes of battles against Egyptian or Asiatic foes. Two fragments derive from a depiction of soldiers ascending a siege ladder with enemies (Asiatics or possibly fellow-Egyptians) falling around them, pierced by arrows.[26] In the nearby Asasif region of western Thebes, the tomb of Intef, Mentuhotep II's general, also contains battle scenes, perhaps depicting the same siege.[27]

The onset of civil war and the professionalization of the army would both have conspired temporarily to raise the profile of military activities in the lives of some of the provincial governors, thus necessitating the depictions of battles on the walls of their tombs, alongside their more peaceful activities. The tomb of Mesehti at Asyut was even provided with three-dimensional models of two squads of soldiers, comprising forty Nubian archers and forty Egyptian spearmen.[28]

Alan Schulman has attempted to synthesize the various early Middle Kingdom battle scenes into a historical narrative concerning the assault on the city of Herakleopolis, which would have been the climax of Mentuhotep II's reign and the crucial battle that effectively brought an end to the First Intermediate Period.[29] However, while it is always tempting to massage the surviving pictorial and textual evidence into some kind of sequence of historical events, Schulman is clearly forced, in this instance, into far too many suppositions and imaginative links, such as the assumption that the defending Herakleopolitans included Asiatics among their ranks (in order to accommodate the fact that the reliefs from the temple of Mentuhotep II and the paintings in the tomb of his general all appear to show the siege of an Asiatic town). Conversely, he concludes his discussion with the hypothesis that depictions of the siege of Egyptian towns in the early Twelfth Dynasty – at a time when the textual and archaeological evidence increasingly suggest that the pharaohs were more likely to be attacking Asiatic towns – were simply using the archetypal image of the siege of Herakleopolis as a way of portraying any siege, even of an Asiatic town. The overall hypothesis is thus flawed by a tendency to interpret some battle scenes as mere iconography and others as depictions of historical fact, depending on whether they happen to suit the argument or not.

Having established the complexity of the possible links between the portrayals of battle and military reality in the late Old Kingdom and early Middle Kingdom, it remains to consider what light they can shed on the official and individual attitudes to battle during this period. All of the surviving Old and Middle Kingdom battle scenes in private tombs (apart from those of Ankhtifi and Setka) consist of the siege and capture of individual towns or fortresses, implying that this – rather than pitched battle in the open – was the most common form of battle during these periods.

Vincent Donohue points out that, with regard to the New Kingdom in particular, 'the climax of events upon foreign soil is typically indicated by the subjugation of a town or city, its configuration closely reflecting what is otherwise known of Near Eastern fortified architecture of the late Bronze Age.' The motif of the doomed fortress, with its inhabitants peering over crenellated battlements, was one of the most enduring images of Egyptian warfare. Initially – on protodynastic palettes and in the tomb scenes of the late Old Kingdom – the fortress was portrayed in plan-form, as if viewed from above, but from the First Intermediate Period onwards it was shown from the side. This side view, with the inhabitants either defending frantically or making pleas for mercy and elaborate gestures of surrender, is one of the principal aspects of continuity between the early Middle Kingdom portrayals of battle and the New Kingdom depictions of Ramessid campaigns in Syria–Palestine.

The battle reliefs in New Kingdom temples

The temple reliefs of the New Kingdom were inextricably linked to the religious cults that took place within their walls. Just as the iconography of battle on the protodynastic votive objects described above was already an idealization of the real situation, so it is likely that this process of over-simplification was carried over into the more elaborate arena of the pharaonic temple inscriptions and reliefs that purport to describe actual military events, such as the battles of Megiddo and Qadesh.

Since the temple reliefs were intended to illustrate basic universal concepts, such as the power of the king and the destruction or absorption of foreigners, they can rarely be relied upon to give anything more than incidental indications of the motivation and nature of Egyptian warfare. Indeed, Gaballa has argued that the various 'panoramic vistas' of the Battle of Qadesh on the temples of Ramesses II were effectively substitutes for the traditional smiting scene – in this sense he is implying that the depiction of the nitty-gritty of battle as opposed to the act of smiting was motivated primarily by artistic preference rather than by the desire to replace pure icons with real history.[30] An ostracon from the reign of Ramesses IV (Cairo, Egyptian Museum, CG 25124) bears a depiction of the king simultaneously charging in his chariot and ritually smiting the foe, surely indicating that these two standard icons of royal warfare in the New Kingdom were regarded as roughly equivalent and therefore largely interchangeable.[31]

The ideology that the New Kingdom battle reliefs express was no doubt to some extent fossilized, although it continued to be useful in the context of propaganda, and the common placement of battle reliefs in full view on the exterior walls of temples seems to make it clear that this was at least one of their aims. In the case of the Battle of Qadesh, tremendous publicity was given to this single military event in the reign of Ramesses II; it was depicted on no fewer than five of his most important temples (Luxor, Karnak, Abu Simbel, Abydos and the Ramesseum), while the literary account has also been preserved on three papyri.[32] Although the scale of the commemoration implies that it was intended to be regarded as a high point in Ramesses's reign, Hans Goedicke points out that, far from being a great victory over a foreign foe, it may actually never have developed into a full battle: 'the only major outcome of the event was a number of Pharaonic soldiers killed, not by the enemy, but by Ramesses II as punishment for the cowardliness displayed at Qadesh.'[33] Goedicke argues that the Qadesh reliefs were not so much a celebration of Egyptian military prowess as a warning to the military that cowardice would be severely punished.

Whereas the temple reliefs present battles as essential elements of the pharaohs' *res gestae*, real battles were surely being undertaken in the New Kingdom to obtain pragmatic economic and political gain rather than simply to fulfil the king's duties to the gods (although the two types of motivation were no doubt more closely linked in the cognitive scheme of the ancient Egyptians). One of the most fundamental questions in the study of Egyptian warfare is whether battles were opportunist, unpredictable affairs, or whether, like Classical Greek conflicts, there was an element of ritual not merely in the depictions of the battles but in the actual confrontations between armies.[34]

There is perhaps some evidence for a tendency towards more symbolic confrontations in the whole paraphernalia of diplomacy and agreements throughout the Near East, and Yadin and Goedicke both argue that the location and date of the Megiddo and Qadesh battles had probably been pre-arranged by the two sides.[35] Both of these battles, however, are described very much as unique and idiosyncratic historical events. Although there are certain recurring motifs (such as the heroism of the king in adversity and his tendency to advocate daring tactics in place of the cautious plans of his generals), the course of each battle was evidently spontaneous, and there is no question of anything as predictable as the clash of hoplite phalanxes. Egyptian soldiers regularly marched in formation (see Figure 4), often accompanied by a trumpeter, and there are occasional references to the importance of keeping together and preventing the enemy from breaking up the infantry, but there is no evidence for the use of a phalanx-style attack. Eugen Strouhal has pointed out that the groups of infantry sharing shields in the siege scenes at Beni Hasan are already anticipating the Roman *testudo*. In the Qadesh battle reliefs, the '*N'rn*' section of the Egyptian army is depicted marching into battle in the form of a tight formation of infantry with overlapping shields, protected by squads of archers in chariots at their rear and flanks. In pitched battle, archers – on foot from the Early Dynastic period to the end of the Middle Kingdom, but usually chariot-borne from the New Kingdom onwards – seem to have picked off the enemy from a distance,[36] allowing infantry (or the archers themselves) to move in to deliver the final blow with spear, dagger or axe at close quarters (see Figure 5).

Thus, although the time and place of crucial New Kingdom battles may have been pre-arranged, their forms were invariably

Figure 4. Detail of a relief depicting the Battle of Qadesh in the Great Temple at Abu Simbel showing a group of Egyptian soldiers marching in formation, accompanied by a trumpeter; New Kingdom, reign of Ramesses II.

Figure 5. Detail of a relief depicting the Battle of Qadesh in the Great Temple at Abu Simbel showing an Egyptian footsoldier despatching an enemy at close quarters; New Kingdom, reign of Ramesses II.

unpredictable. Goedicke makes the puzzling assertion that 'the notion of surprise as a legitimate strategic move is not an ancient Near Eastern concept', although he concedes that Egyptian siege warfare included surprise tactics.[37] There is in fact no reason to assume that the other forms of battle in the pharaonic period were not equally characterized by the use of surprise: in the depictions of the Battle of Qadesh, for instance, Clive Broadhurst has pointed out that 'Ramesses needed assistance to defeat the vast number pitted against him. In three scenes he receives it from a chariot troop...who trap the Hittites occupying the area behind the king, in one of the earliest examples of an ambush.'[38] Although the Egyptians often appear to criticise the Asiatics for their use of guerrilla tactics, this does not necessarily imply that they never used such methods themselves. The Herakleopolitan ruler Khety, in a didactic work of the First Intermediate Period (*c.* 2181–2040 BC), *The Instruction Addressed to King Merikare*,[39] complains that 'the vile Asiatic...never announces the day of combat, like a thief in a criminal gang... The Asiatic is a crocodile on the river bank: he snatches on the lonely road, (but) he will never seize at the harbour of a populous city.' Khety's criticism, however, is perhaps directed more at the Asiatics' lack of ambition or heroism than their use of unorthodox tactics.[40]

The principal differences that emerged in the battles of the New Kingdom, compared with earlier conflicts, stemmed from the

Figure 6. Detail of a relief on the outer wall of the mortuary temple of Ramesses III at Medinet Habu, depicting an Egyptian boat in the naval encounter with the Sea Peoples; New Kingdom, reign of Ramesses III.

introduction of the composite bow and the chariot (probably as a result of the Hyksos occupation of northern Egypt in the Second Intermediate Period).[41] The importance of the chariot was simply that it conferred mobility – it enabled archers to move around the battlefield more rapidly, but ultimately the battle, whether siege or open confrontation, was still considered to consist of two basic components: firstly bowmen and secondly infantry armed with spears and axes. The Medinet Habu reliefs depicting the famous naval encounter with the Sea Peoples in the reign of Ramesses III (c. 1182–1151 BC) show that the same situation applied even to sea battles – boats were used as seaborne chariots containing groups of oarsmen, archers and footsoldiers (see Figure 6). They allowed the Egyptians to encircle the enemy, while releasing hails of arrows, eventually closing in on the enemy's own boats, so that the infantry could engage in conventional hand-to-hand fighting.

The official aims and aftermath of battle in the New Kingdom

Both the protodynastic votive objects and the New Kingdom royal battle reliefs were part of the essential infrastructure of the temples and therefore inevitably reflected the religious and economic concerns of the priests. In addition, the first known hieroglyphic texts appear to have developed partly out of early Egyptian accounting systems.[42] It is not surprising therefore that later Egyptian writings sometimes retain a little of the flavour of the account book – in the case of texts and paintings evoking battles there was always the potential for an unusually economic slant. This is perhaps most vividly illustrated by a detail from the Abu Simbel reliefs of the Battle of Qadesh, showing a scribe dutifully recording the number of severed hands taken from the enemy (Figure 7). The resulting blinkered view of battle as a kind of necessary preliminary to the totting up of spoils and dead is partly a product of the predominant literary form but, for similar reasons, it must also be an accurate insight into the official Egyptian view of battle, since the art and warfare of ancient Egypt were both equally dominated by the temple-based scribal élite.

The unusually well-developed bureaucratic wing of the New Kingdom Egyptian military system probably transformed the army itself into the long arm of the Egyptian scribe, reaching out into foreign countries to obtain the materials, livestock and manpower that the maintenance of temple and state demanded. This would suggest that the heroicism of the Qadesh battle reliefs was largely an affectation, sweetening the pill of the remorseless credit and debit of the scribal account book.

Although the social and political motivation behind Egyptian warfare and 'colonization' is still not properly understood,[43] it seems likely that battle was regarded by the Egyptian state not as an opportunity for heroism or even territorial gain but as just another commercial expedient, comparable with trading or quarrying, whereby large quantities of certain commodities might be procured by force. In a recent study of the relations between Egypt and the Levant, Donald Redford provides a succinct analysis of the emerging rationale for Egyptian warfare in Syria-Palestine during the Early Dynastic period: '...cheap manpower rapidly became what Egypt expected to receive from the adjacent lands, along with booty, enforced benevolences, gifts, and raw materials, as part of their obligations to Egypt ordained by the gods. Egypt sought to ensure a regular supply, not through the establishment of an imperial infrastructure permanently subjugating foreign lands, but through intimidation and the creation of a "sphere of influence".'[44]

The Egyptians' principal motivations for attacking foreigners were the maintenance and extension of their own borders, the protection of trading and quarrying expeditions, and the acquisition of foreign goods, raw materials and extra manpower. It is evident from some of

Figure 7. Detail of a relief depicting the Battle of Qadesh in the Great Temple at Abu Simbel showing a scribe counting the severed hands of Hittites; New Kingdom, reign of Ramesses II.

the texts, however, that the Egyptian armies were often dispatched for purposes which were, in the short term at least, essentially negative and destructive – they might be sent to punish and terrify pharaoh's enemies, usually in order to maintain the 'sphere of influence'. Such acts are often described as motivated by the need to 'pacify' (*sehetep*) the 'rebels'. Barry Kemp argues that these raids were an integral part of Egyptian diplomacy: 'one might suspect that attacks on fortified towns were the shock tactics intended to force favourable alliances or even vassalage which would then be maintained or extended by diplomatic activity.'[45]

Victor Hanson quotes from the early New Kingdom *Stele of Kamose* to show Egyptian antecedents for the Classical Greeks' ravaging of the agricultural resources of defeated enemies,[46] but the history of the destruction of enemies' agricultural resources can actually be found much earlier in Egyptian history – the funerary autobiography of Weni, for instance, includes a poetic celebration of the destruction of the land and homes of the 'sand-dwellers' (a term assumed to refer to Asiatics): 'This army returned in safety, it had ravaged the sand-dwellers' land...it had flattened the sand-dwellers' land...it had sacked its strongholds...it had cut down its figs, its vines...it had thrown fire in all its [mansions]...it had slain its troops by many ten-thousands...[it had carried off] many [troops] as its captives.'[47]

A similar approach appears to have been taken to Nubian 'rebels' in the Middle Kingdom, to judge from the stele of Intefiqer, probably a high official of Amenemmes I, in which he states: 'Then I went upstream in victory, slaughtering the Nubian in his (own) land, and came back downstream stripping crops, and cutting down the rest of their trees, so that I could put fire to their homes, as is done against a rebel against the king.'[48] Redford even goes so far as to suggest that the Egyptian policy of destroying the agricultural land and fortresses of their Asiatic enemies may have contributed significantly to the decline in urbanism in post-EB III Palestine.[49]

The individual soldier's experience of battle

Whereas the official view of Egyptian battle is relatively straightforward, the experience of the individual is more difficult to elucidate. What was the role of each member of the army, whether élite *maryannu* or Nubian archer? How did individuals react to the rigours of battle and what were their rewards, if any? A reasonably clear distinction may be made between the pictorial and textual evidence: both are more concerned with the results and rewards of battles than with the battles themselves, but the pictorial evidence can at least be relied upon to provide certain details of soldiers going about their business. Virtually all texts describing warfare are largely made up of the listing of booty.

Ahmose son of Ibana, the admiral whose lifetime spanned the reigns of Ahmose, Amenophis I and Tuthmosis I, describes the major events of his career on the walls of his tomb at Elkab. The expulsion of the hated Hyksos rulers may have represented the restoration of Egyptian pride and native rule on an abstract political level, but Ahmose's summary of the campaign amounts to a personal shopping list ('Then Avaris was despoiled, and I brought spoil from there: one man, three women; total, four persons. His majesty gave them to me as slaves'), and the culmination of his career came in the form of the capture of 'a chariot, its horse and him who was on it as a living captive.' Obviously a 'funerary autobiography' of this type was designed to enumerate the virtues and possessions of the deceased, and the application of the modern term 'autobiography' is extremely misleading, decontextualizing a form of text inevitably geared more to the offering list than to the historical narrative. Ahmose's text is simply an extended version of the lists of actions and rewards recorded on private funerary stelae. Funerary narrations of military exploits are to be found on certain stelae as early as the Middle Kingdom, notably those of the general Nesumenthu (Louvre, C 1)[50] and the military official Khusobek (Manchester Museum, 3306).[51]

The ideal antidote to such eulogies of the benefits of battle, however, is to be found in Papyrus Lansing, a 'schoolbook' for scribes designed to show the superiority of their own profession by giving a jaundiced account of all other trades (hence its usual title, *Be a Scribe*). The section describing the life of the Egyptian soldier lays gleeful emphasis on the hardships endured:

> Come let me tell you the woes of the soldier... He is called up for Syria. He may not rest. There are no clothes, no sandals. The weapons of war are assembled at the fortress of Sile. His march is uphill through mountains. He drinks water every third day; it is smelly and tastes of salt. His body is ravaged by illness. The enemy comes, surrounds him with missiles and life recedes from him. He is told, 'Quick forward, valiant soldier! Win for yourself a good name!' He does not know what he is about. His body is weak, his legs fail him. When victory is won, the captives are handed over to his majesty to be taken to Egypt. The foreign woman faints on the march; she hangs herself (on) the soldier's neck. His knapsack drops, another grabs it while he is burdened with the woman... If he leaps and joins the deserters, all his people are

imprisoned. He dies on the edge of the desert, and there is none to perpetuate his name. He suffers in death as in life...[52]

This satirical account is deliberately intended to paint an exaggeratedly black picture of military life, but it does help to correct the impression given by such men as Ahmose son of Ibana that the life of the campaigning soldier was one long succession of enemy captives and severed enemy hands. With a clever insight into the travails of battle, the scribe even manages to imply not only that the acquisition of a female captive might turn out to be to the detriment of the soldier but that the all-important booty might revert to the king rather than the individual.[53] It is also interesting to note the assertion that a deserter's family would be thrown into jail – even if overstated, it suggests that desertion may have been discouraged by threats of reprisals on a man's relations.

Apart from these relatively 'formal' descriptions of battle, whether positive or negative, there is an alternative body of evidence for the soldiers' view of battle, in the form of private and official letters relating to military life, such as the Semna Dispatches,[54] some of the Amarna Letters,[55] and various items of correspondence to and from individual soldiers.[56] The forms of these texts are arguably as 'literary' as the inscriptions on the walls of temples and tombs, but it is in terms of their content that they have a greater claim to realism. They are all essentially private communications, whereas the reliefs and paintings – even of private individuals – were intended to be placed on display as integral parts of the Egyptian religious and funerary systems.

The Semna Dispatches, comprising copies of reports sent to the commander at Thebes from the Egyptian garrison at Semna in Nubia, convey something of the tedium of military life in between campaigns or battles. One, for instance, describes the routine task of desert surveillance: 'The patrol that went out to patrol the desert-edge near the fortress of Khesef-Medjau ['Repeller of the Medjay'] on the last day of the third month of spring in the third year has returned to report to me, saying "We have found the track of 32 men and 3 donkeys...".'[57] A more personal tone is struck in a letter dating to the reign of Ramesses II sent by Kenyamon the scribe to Huy the charioteer, in which he points out 'My lord's horses are in very good shape, for I am giving them grain daily.'

The essentially practical (not to say mundane) tone of these letters is echoed in some of the pictorial evidence regarding the details of New Kingdom campaigns in Nubia and the Levant. A number of reliefs from the Memphite tomb of Horemheb depict a military encampment in the reign of Tutankhamun.[58] One recently excavated fragment shows a tent already pitched and another perhaps in the process of being erected, surrounded by soldiers preparing and eating food. Three better-preserved fragments from the same tomb (now in the Berlin and Bologna museums) show boys carrying water-skins and food around the camp while the soldiers tend horses and donkeys, maintain the chariotry equipment and set up tents. Views of the tents of the army officers (including perhaps that of Horemheb himself) show that they contain stocks of food and a folding stool and are being fastidiously cleaned and dusted inside by servants. In one of these scenes a squatting scribe is shown writing instructions or perhaps a list of provisions; the presence of such scribes and servants must have considerably added to the numbers of men in the professional armies of the pharaonic period.[59]

The reliefs depicting the Battle of Qadesh incorporate similar depictions of the interior of Ramesses II's main encampment near the River Orontes.[60] The camp was surrounded by a rectangular stockade of shields and the scenes again include activities relating to the supply of food and maintenance of equipment. Among the details are ox-carts carrying supplies into the camp, a chariot in the course of being repaired, an archer re-stringing his bow, and a seated soldier whose leg-wound is in the process of being tended. Ramesses's magnificent tent is shown surrounded by the smaller tents of his officers, and there are also a number of dramatic tableaux including depictions of the seated king discussing strategy with his generals and the interrogation and beating of Hittite spies.

The evidence presented so far has principally concerned the role of individuals in the preliminaries and aftermath of battle rather than the conflict itself. However, even within the formulaic confines of the battle scenes there are scattered pieces of almost anecdotal information regarding the impact of conflict on both soldiers and civilians. In the tomb of Inti at Deshasheh, the battle in front of an Asiatic fortress (probably a fortified settlement in southern Palestine) can be broken down into three sections from top to bottom: in the upper register, a squad of Egyptian archers are assembling; in the two middle registers the Egyptian infantry armed with battle-axes are engaged in hand-to-hand combat with the defenders, some of whom are pierced by arrows. In the lowest register the Asiatics are being marched off into captivity along with their wives and children, while to the right a ladder is used to ascend the wall of the fortress, the foot of which is being mined by two soldiers with picks. In terms of the human reactions to battle the

events shown on five registers in the interior of the fortress are perhaps the most revealing, including scenes of defenders apparently
being struck by their wives (perhaps for cowardice), while in the top
register a man is breaking his bow before the gaze of his family – the
archetypal gesture of surrender. In the tomb of Kaemheset there is
also a small cameo scene of a man driving his sheep and cattle into a
wood, presumably in order to prevent their capture by the Egyptians.

The battle scene in the tomb of the nomarch Khety at Beni Hasan is
characterized by a similar combination of archers and infantry in the
attack on a fortress but with the addition of a group of men protected
by a portable roofed structure apparently advancing towards the fortress with a pole (perhaps an early battering ram). Interestingly, however, the scene is in this instance a purely military one; unlike the
Asiatic sieges in the tombs of Inti, Kaemheset and Intef, there is no
apparent pictorial reference to the panic, surrender and enslavement
of the occupants, suggesting perhaps that the civilian consequences of
wars between Egyptians were less lethal than the reprisals taken
against Asiatics.

Detailed accounts of battle have survived best in what might be
described as the purely literary record (a genre that evolved in Egypt
partly in response to the need for exercises to be repeatedly copied by
trainee scribes). One of the few surviving verbal descriptions of the
individual experience of battle is the Twelfth-Dynasty literary narrative, *The Tale of Sinuhe*. This detailed account of single-handed combat
between an Egyptian exile and his Asiatic opponent has a distinctly
Homeric ring to it, but it is also noticeable that the fundamental
aspects of the encounter are very similar to the basic elements of large-
scale battle, as portrayed in temple and tomb decoration:

> At night I strung my bow, sorted my arrows, practised with my dagger,
> polished my weapons... He came toward me while I waited, having
> placed myself near him...he <raised> his battle-axe and shield, while
> his armful of weapons fell toward me. When I had made his weapons
> attack me, I let his arrows pass by me without effect, one following the
> other. Then, when he charged me, I shot him, my arrow sticking in his
> neck; he screamed; he fell on his nose; I slew him with his axe... Then I
> carried off his goods; I plundered his cattle. What he had meant to do to
> me I did to him. I took what was in his tent; I stripped his camp. Then I
> became great, wealthy in goods, rich in herds.[61]

Sinuhe's antagonist is injured by bow and arrow from a distance and
then dispatched with an axe at close quarters – this parallels the battle
tactics depicted in late Old Kingdom and Middle Kingdom tombs,

whereby units of archers and squads of infantry armed with spears and axes were the two basic components in the army's assault. Either real-life confrontations between individuals were miniature versions of the full-scale pitched battles or the writer of *The Tale of Sinuhe* is using a formulaic battle narrative in an inappropriate context (and indeed the description of post-duel plundering sits rather oddly with the one-to-one character of the fight itself).

The description of Sinuhe's defeat of the Asiatic champion, with its inevitable echoes of David and Goliath, is a fitting comment on the Egyptian battle experience. However, this is not simply because the Egyptian hero triumphs in the traditional manner, first piercing his enemy with an arrow then dispatching him with an axe (just as the pharaoh perpetually smites the heads of Egypt's foes). Sinuhe's duel is an archetypal Egyptian battle primarily because he cannot resist concluding his description of the fight with a long description of the material benefits of the triumph, thus shifting the agenda once more away from the intangible virtues of honour, glory and heroism to the traditional economic bottom line.

Table

The major visual sources for Egyptian battles (and military manoeuvres) from the protodynastic period to the end of the New Kingdom (c. 3200–1070 BC):[62]

PREDYNASTIC/EARLY DYNASTIC PERIOD
Gebel el-Arak knife handle
> Hand-to-hand fighting and possibly the earliest depiction of a naval conflict between Egyptians and Asiatics[63]

Hierakonpolis tomb 100
> Scenes of combat and head-smiting[64]

Hunter's palette
> Row of protodynastic warriors[65]

Libyan palette
> Demolition of enemy cities[66]

Battlefield palette
> Battlefield with lion and vultures mauling the enemy dead[67]

Narmer palette
> Bull breaking down town walls; rows of beheaded corpses of enemies[68]

OLD KINGDOM

FOURTH DYNASTY
Mortuary complex of Khufu
    Fragment of battle relief: archers drawing their bows[69]

FIFTH DYNASTY
Mortuary complex of Unas
    Fighting between Egyptians and Asiatics; ships bringing Asiatics;
    text: 'smiting the [sh]asi'[70]

SIXTH DYNASTY
Tomb of Inti (Deshasheh)
    Siege and sack of an Asiatic town[71]

Tomb of Kaemheset (Saqqara)
    Siege and sack of an Asiatic town; removal of captives[72]

MIDDLE KINGDOM

ELEVENTH DYNASTY
Tomb of Ankhtifi (el-Moalla)
    Battles between armies of Egyptians[73]

Tomb of Setka (Aswan)
    Battle scene from a campaign against the Nubians[74]

Mortuary Temple of Mentuhotep II
    Siege of Asiatic(?) town[75]

Tomb of Intef (Thebes TT386)
    Siege of Asiatic town and depiction of boat filled with Egyptian
    soldiers[76]

Tomb of Baqt III (Beni Hasan 15)
    Siege of Egyptian town[77]

Tomb of Khety (Beni Hasan 17)
    Siege of Egyptian town[78]

TWELFTH DYNASTY
Tomb of Khnumhotep (Beni Hasan 14)
    Battle scene (badly preserved, but probably another siege of an
    Egyptian town)[79]

Ian Shaw

Tomb of Amenemhat (Beni Hasan 2)
  Siege of Egyptian town[80]

Causeway of Sesostris I (Lisht)
  Battle scene, including siege of town[81]

Causeway of Sesostris III (Dahshur)
  Battle scene, including siege of town[82]

NEW KINGDOM

EIGHTEENTH DYNASTY
Unknown tomb (Thebes)
  Fragment of painted relief depicting the siege of a Syro-Palestinian city[83]

Painted box of Tutankhamun (Cairo)
  One side showing the king charging Nubians in his chariot, the other showing him attacking Syrians in the same manner[84]

Speos of Horemheb (Gebel el-Silsila)
  Battle against Nubians, including scene of dying Nubian soldiers[85]

NINETEENTH DYNASTY
Seti I
Karnak
  Seti I's battles against the Shasu and various towns in Syria-Palestine; battles against Hittites and Libyans[86]

Ramesses II
Abu Simbel, Great Temple
  Battle against Nubians and Battle of Qadesh[87]

Abydos (north and south walls of the 1st Court of the temple of Seti I)
  Badly damaged scenes of battles in a Syro-Palestinian campaign[88]

Abydos (outer wall of the temple of Ramesses II)
  Siege of a Syrian fortress; Battle of Qadesh[89]

Amara West (west gate)
  King charging in chariot against the Nubians of 'Irem'[90]

Beit el-Wali
  Nubian, Syro-Palestinian and Libyan campaigns[91]

Derr
Syro-Palestinian campaign[92]

Karnak (outside of southern wall of the Great Hypostyle Hall and outside of west wall between Pylons VIII and IX)
Scenes of Ramesses II's battles in Syria-Palestine; Battle of Qadesh (later erased and replaced with scenes of battles in minor Syro-Palestinian campaigns)[93]

Luxor (western face of outer wall)
Battle of Qadesh[94]

Ramesseum (Mortuary Temple)
Campaigns in Syria-Palestine; Battle of Qadesh[95]

Deir el-Bahari (re-used block from an unknown Ramessid temple)
Fragment of painted relief depicting Asiatics killed in battle under the royal chariot (now in New York, Metropolitan)[96]

TWENTIETH DYNASTY
Ramesses III
Medinet Habu (Mortuary Temple)
Battles against Nubians and episodes in the two campaigns against the Libyans; naval battle against the Sea Peoples; sieges and battles in Syria-Palestine (possibly apocryphal)[97]

Karnak (Temple of Amun)
Battles against Libyans (probably in the second Libyan campaign)[98]

Karnak (Temple of Mut)
Battles in second campaign against the Libyans[99]

Acknowledgement
I would like to thank Professor Alan Lloyd for inviting me to contribute to the day-school on Battle in Antiquity at the University College of Wales at Swansea, thus creating the basis for this paper. I am grateful to Ann Jones for providing the line-drawings illustrating the paper. I would also like to thank the British Academy, New Hall and the Department of Archaeology at Cambridge University, and University College London, for their generous support of my research.

Abbreviations

ASAE Annales du Service des Antiquités de l'Egypte
JARCE Journal of the American Research Center in Egypt
JEA Journal of Egyptian Archaeology
JNES Journal of Near Eastern Studies
JSSEA Journal of the Society for the Study of Egyptian Antiquities
MDAIK Mitteilungen des Deutschen Archäologischen Instituts, Abteilung Kairo
WA World Archaeology

Notes

1 See, for instance, W. Wolff, *Die Bewaffnung des altägyptischen Heeres* (Leipzig, 1925); W.E. McLeod, *Composite Bows from the Tomb of Tut'ankhamun* (Oxford, 1970); A.C. Western, 'A Wheel Hub from the Tomb of Amenophis II', *JEA* 59 (1973), 91–4; M.A. Littauer and J.H. Crouwel, *Wheeled Vehicles and Ridden Animals in the Ancient Near East* (Leiden and Cologne, 1979); A.R. Schulman, 'Chariots, Chariotry and the Hyksos', *JSSEA* 10 (1980), 105–53; W.E. McLeod, *Self Bows and Other Archery Tackle from the Tomb of Tut'ankhamun* (Oxford, 1982); M.A. Littauer and J.H. Crouwel: *Chariots and Related Equipment from the Tomb of Tut'ankhamun* (Oxford, 1985); P.R.S. Moorey, 'The Emergence of the Light, Horse-drawn Chariot in the Near East *c.* 2000–1500 BC', *WA* 18/2 (1986), 196–215; W.V. Davies, *Catalogue of Egyptian Antiquities in the British Museum VII: Tools and Weapons I: Axes* (London, 1987); I. Shaw, *Egyptian Warfare and Weapons* (Princes Risborough, 1991), 31–44.

2 Two important historical analyses based largely on Egyptian textual descriptions of warfare are: C.L. Vandersleyen, *Les Guerres d'Amosis, fondateur de la XVIIIe dynastie* (Brussels, 1971), 17–87; W.J. Murnane, *The Road to Kadesh: A Historical Interpretation of the Battle Reliefs of King Sety I at Karnak* (Chicago, 1985). Notable studies concentrating on strategy and tactics include J.H. Breasted, *The Battle of Kadesh, a Study in the Earliest Known Military Strategy* (Chicago, 1903); H. Goedicke, 'Considerations on the Battle of Kadesh', *JEA* 52 (1966), 71–80; idem, 'The "Battle of Kadesh": A Reassessment', in H. Goedicke (ed.), *Perspectives on the Battle of Kadesh* (Baltimore, 1985), 77–122.

Some of the symbolic aspects of actions and gesture in depictions of Egyptian warfare, including the 'turned bow', are analysed by R. Wilkinson, *Symbol and Magic in Egyptian Art* (London, 1994), 170–3, 200–203. The use of incense burning as a symbol of surrender in New Kingdom depictions of assaults on the fortified towns of Syria-Palestine is described by V.A. Donohue, 'A Gesture of Submission', in A. Lloyd (ed.), *Studies in Pharaonic Religion and Society in Honour of J. Gwyn Griffiths* (London, 1992), 82–114.

Literary analyses include H. Grapow, *Studien zu den Annalen Thutmosis des Dritten* (Berlin, 1949); A.J. Spalinger, *Aspects of the Military Documents of the Ancient Egyptians* (Yale, New Haven, 1982); S. Morschauser, 'Observations on the Speeches of Ramesses II in the Literary Record of the Battle of Kadesh', in Goedicke, *Perspectives...*, 123–206. For topography and ethnography see A.H. Gardiner, 'The Ancient Military Road between Egypt and Palestine', *JEA* 6

(1920), 99–116; J. Simons, *Handbook for the Study of Egyptian Topographical Lists Relating to Western Asia* (Leiden, 1937); R. Giveon, *Les Bédouins Shosou des documents Egyptiens* (Leiden, 1971).

A few writers have dealt with the more practical aspects of Egyptian battle. The appendix in Murnane, *Road to Kadesh*, considering 'Movements of Armies and Timings of Travel in Egypt and the Levant' considers some important questions concerning the organization of Egyptian military campaigns, while Silvio Curto's *The Military Art of the Ancient Egyptians* (Turin, 1971) examines a number of the social and cultural aspects of Egyptian warfare, including a brief discussion of 'wartime ethics' (p. 21). In addition, Alan Schulman has made numerous substantial contributions to the study of Egyptian battle in its own right, notably in the three following papers: 'Siege Warfare in Pharaonic Egypt', *Natural History Magazine* 73/3 (March 1964), 12–21; 'The Battle Scenes of the Middle Kingdom', *JSSEA* 12 (1982), 165–83; and 'Some Observations on the Military Background of the Amarna Period', *JARCE* 3 (1964), 52–8. A detailed study of the reactions of the defeated inhabitants of Syro-Palestinian fortified towns is provided by Donohue, in Lloyd, *Studies in Pharaonic Religion and Society...*

3 See, for instance, P.J. Foss, *The Field of Redemore: The Battle of Bosworth, 1485* (Leeds, 1990) for a detailed synthesis of documentary and archaeological sources regarding the disputed location of the final battle in the Wars of the Roses. But see also D.D. Scott et al., *Archaeological Perspectives on the Battle of the Little Bighorn* (Norman and London, 1989) for a description of innovative archaeological methods for identifying and analysing American battlefields.

Donald Redford has made a pioneering attempt to reconcile the surviving archaeological landscape of Syria-Palestine with the bare textual outlines of an Egyptian campaign in the reign of Tuthmosis III (essentially a list of toponyms): D.B. Redford, 'A Bronze Age Itinerary in Transjordan (Nos. 89–101 of Tuthmosis III's List of Asiatic Toponyms)', *JSSEA* 12/2 (1982), 55–74.

4 The excavation and analysis of the late Palaeolithic cemetery at Jebel Sahaba in Lower Nubia are described in F. Wendorf (ed.), *The Prehistory of Nubia* I (Dallas, 1968), 954–9 and the results are analysed by M. Hoffman, *Egypt before the Pharaohs: The Prehistoric Foundations of Egyptian Civilization* (New York, 1979), 90–9, Tables V–IX.

5 H.E. Winlock, *The Slain Soldiers of Neb-Hepet-Re' Mentu-Hotpe* (New York, 1945).

6 M. Bietak, 'Die Totesumstände des Pharaos Seqenenre (17. Dynastie)', *Annalen des Naturhistorischen Museums Wien* 78 (1974), 29–52.

7 J.M. Filer, 'Head Injuries in Egypt and Nubia: a comparison of skulls from Giza and Kerma', *JEA* 78 (1992), 281–5.

8 E.S. Hall, *The Pharaoh Smites his Enemies*, MÄS 44 (Berlin, 1986); W. Davis, *Masking the Blow: The Scene of Representation in Late Prehistoric Egyptian Art*, California Study in the History of Art 30 (Berkeley, Los Angeles and London, 1992). For an earlier version of the head-smiting motif at Susa, see also G. LeBretton, 'The Early Periods at Susa, Mesopotamian Relations', *Iraq* 19 (1957), 79–123, fig. 18/4.

The prime importance of the acquisition of foreign captives may also be compared with the situation among the ancient Maya of Mesoamerica, where it is argued that the main cause of warfare was neither territorial expansion nor economic gain but the need to obtain sacrificial victims and thus a tendency to capture enemies alive rather than killing them. L. Schele and M.E. Miller (*The Blood of Kings: Dynasty and Ritual in Maya Art* (Fort Worth, 1986), 220) deduce that '...in the representation of warfare in their art, the Maya addressed no issues of material gain. Instead, they cast warfare and sacrifice in terms of ritual that upheld the cycle of kingship.' See note 52 below for Egyptian attitudes to captives, as revealed by the stele of Khusobek.

9 N. Grimal, *La Stèle triomphale de Pi(ankh)y au Musée du Caire* (Cairo, 1981).

10 A number of áhistorical interpretations of the protodynastic ceremonial palettes and maceheads have been put forward: R. Tefnin, 'Image et histoire: Réflexions sur l'usage documentaire de l'image égyptienne', *Chronique d'Egypte* 54 (1979), 218–44; B.J. Kemp, *Ancient Egypt, Anatomy of a Civilization* (London, 1989), 46–53; N.B. Millet, 'The Narmer Macehead and Related objects', *JARCE* 27 (1990), 53–9; Davis, *Masking the Blow*. But see also W.A. Fairservis, 'A Revised View of the Na'rmr Palette', *JARCE* 38 (1991), 1–20, who, in contrast, presents an extremely historical interpretation of the Narmer palette, suggesting that it is neither a general iconographic statement nor a simple record of the original unification of Egypt but 'a memorial to Tbwty'nh, an officer in Na'rmr's military forces who participated in the conquest of both banks of the Nile Valley south of Edfu (or Nekhen) and into Northern Nubia'.

11 The tomb of Intef was excavated in the 1960s by the German Institute of Archaeology at Cairo. The battle scenes are still only partially published, see D. Arnold and J. Settgast, 'Erster Vorbericht über die vom Deutschen Archäologischen Institut Kairo im Asasif unternommen Arbeiten', *MDAIK* 20 (1965), 47–61. See also Schulman, *JSSEA* 12, 166 n. 6.

12 Vandersleyen, *Les Guerres d'Amosis...*, 17–87; M. Lichtheim, *Ancient Egyptian Literature* II (Berkeley, 1976), 11–15.

13 See note 2 above.

14 W.M.F. Petrie, *Deshasheh* (London, 1898).

15 J.E. Quibell and A.G.K. Hayter, *Excavations at Saqqara: Teti Pyramid, North Side* (Cairo, 1927); W.S. Smith, *Interconnections in the Ancient Near East* (New Haven, 1965), fig. 85.

16 P.E. Newberry, *Beni Hasan*, 2 vols (London, 1893); G.A. Gaballa, *Narrative in Egyptian Art* (Mainz am Rhein, 1976), 39–40.

17 D. Arnold and J. Settgast, *MDAIK* 20, 47–61.

18 The Battle of Qadesh, fought between Ramesses II and the Hittite king Muwatallis in *c.* 1285 BC, has been the subject of numerous books and articles, only a few of which can be listed here: Breasted, *The Battle of Kadesh*; C. Kuentz, *La Bataille de Qadech* (Cairo, 1928–34); A.H. Gardiner, *The Kadesh Inscriptions of Ramesses II* (Oxford, 1960); C. Desroches-Noblecourt et al., *Grand Temple d'Abou Simbel: La Bataille de Qadech* (Cairo, 1971); Gaballa, *Narrative in Egyptian Art*, 113–9.

19 W.S. Smith, *Interconnections...*, fig. 187; H. Goedicke, *Re-used blocks from the Pyramid of Amenemhat I at Lisht* (New York, 1971), 74–7.

20 S. Hassan, 'Excavations at Saqqara, 1937–38', *Annales du Service des Antiquités de l'Egypte* 38 (1938), 503–21, pl. 95; idem, 'The causeway of Unis at Sakkara', *Zeitschrift für Ägyptische Sprache und Altertumskunde* 80 (1955), 138–9, fig. 2.

21 The tomb was originally dated to the late Fifth Dynasty by Petrie, *Deshasheh*, but most scholars now assign it to the Sixth Dynasty, e.g. W.S. Smith, *A History of Egyptian Sculpture and Painting in the Old Kingdom*, 2nd edn (Boston, 1949), 207, 219; Gaballa, *Narrative in Egyptian Art*, 30–1; E. Strouhal, *Life in Ancient Egypt* (Cambridge, 1992), 205–6.

22 However, a fragment of a siege scene (Berlin, Ägyptisches Museum, 21140) has survived from an unknown Theban tomb of the late Eighteenth Dynasty, see K.-H. Priese (ed.), *Ägyptisches Museum* (Mainz, 1991), 128. The Memphite tomb of Horemheb, which was decorated while he was serving as head of the armed forces under Tutankhamun, contains several scenes devoted to his military campaigns; see G.T. Martin, *The Memphite Tomb of Horemheb, Commander-in-chief of Tutankhamun* I (London, 1989).

23 J. Vandier, *Mo'alla: La Tombe d'Ankhtifi et la tombe de Sébekhotep* (Cairo, 1950), 161–242; N. Grimal, *A History of Ancient Egypt* (Oxford, 1992), 142–3.

24 The unpublished battle scenes, in the tomb of Setka at Aswan, excavated by Labib Habachi (apparently involving Nubian archers) are very briefly summarized both in H.G. Fischer, 'The Nubian Mercenaries of Gebelein', *Kush* 9, 63, fig. 5 and Schulman, *JSSEA* 12, 166 n. 9.

25 The fragment from the causeway of Sesostris I is unpublished, apart from a brief description in Fischer, *Kush* 9, 71, fig. 10. The Sesostris III fragment (Cairo Museum, JE51978) has been published by G. Jéquier, *Douze ans de fouilles dans la nécropole memphite, 1924–1936* (Neuchâtel, 1940), 136, fig. 39 and Fischer, *Kush* 9, 72–3, pl. 14c.

26 Textual evidence for Mentuhotep II's military involvement in Syria-Palestine has survived in the form of the funerary autobiography of the royal steward Henenu, who claims to have led an army against Asiatics; see W.C. Hayes, 'Career of the Great Steward Henenu under Nebhepetre' Mentuhotpe', *JEA* 35 (1949), 43–9 [pl. 4]. There is also a graffito of the Nubian soldier Tjehemau at Abisko, south of Aswan, in which he mentions his part in a battle with the Asiatics of '*D'ty*'; see G. Posener, 'A propos des graffiti d'Abisko', *Archiv Orientalni* 20 (1952), 163–6; D.B. Redford, *Egypt, Canaan and Israel in Ancient Times* (Princeton, 1992), 70. See also E. Brovarski and W.J. Murnane, 'Inscriptions from the Time of Nebhepetre Mentuhotep II at Abisko', *Serapis* 1 (1969), 11–33.

27 Arnold and Settgast, *MDAIK* 20, 47–61; Redford, *Egypt, Canaan and Israel...*, 69–70; Gaballa, *Narrative in Egyptian Art*, 38–9.

28 M. Saleh and H. Sourouzian, *Official Catalogue: The Egyptian Museum, Cairo* (Mainz, 1987), nos 72–3. A number of Middle Kingdom tombs at Asyut and Deir el-Bersheh are decorated with painted scenes of groups of soldiers in the service of the deceased; see R.O. Faulkner, 'Egyptian Military Organization', *JEA* 39 (1953), 36–9.

29 See Schulman, *JSSEA* 12, 179–83 for detailed discussion of the question of the historicity of the Middle Kingdom battle paintings.

30 Gaballa, *Narrative in Egyptian Art*, 119: 'in the battle scenes of Qadesh we find, for the first time, that what attracts the eye of the viewer is not the dominant figure of the king but the panoramic representation of the battle. In other words, the traditional theme of a pharaoh dominating and overshadowing the scene was sacrificed for the sake of an overwhelming and impressive representation of the battle as a whole.' For an unusual structuralist interpretation of the Qadesh reliefs, see R. Tefnin, 'Image, écriture, récit: A propos des représentations de la bataille de Qadesh', *Göttinger Miszellen* 47 (1981), 55–76, but see also the more conventional views of A.J. Spalinger, 'Notes on the Reliefs of the Battle of Kadesh', in H. Goedicke, *Perspectives...*, 1–42.

31 W.H. Peck, *Egyptian Drawings* (London, 1978), 154–5.

32 For the literary accounts of the Battle of Qadesh see Kuentz, *La Bataille de Qadesh*; A.H. Gardiner, *Hieratic Papyri in the British Museum*, 3rd series (London, 1935), pls 9–10; R.O. Faulkner, 'The Battle of Qadesh', *MDAIK* 16 (1958) [Appendix], 100–11; T. Von der Way, *Die Textüberlieferung Rameses' II zur Qadesh-Schlacht – Analyse und Struktur* (Hildesheim, 1984); S. Morschauser, in Goedicke, *Perspectives...*

33 Goedicke, *Perspectives...*, 112–13.

34 For the quasi-ritual nature of Classical Greek battle see V.D. Hanson, *Warfare and Agriculture in Classical Greece* (Pisa, 1983); *The Western Way of War: Infantry Battle in Classical Greece* (New York, 1989); and 'The Ideology of Hoplite Battle, Ancient and Modern', in V.D. Hanson (ed.), *Hoplites: The Classical Greek Battle Experience* (London, 1991), 3–14.

35 Y. Yadin, *The Art of Warfare in Biblical Lands* (London, 1963), 100 ff.. See also Goedicke, *Perspectives...*, 83, 90.

36 In this context the introduction of the composite bow (which had replaced the simpler self bow by the end of the Second Intermediate Period) was probably just as important as the adoption of the chariot. Thirty-two composite bows were found in the tomb of Tutankhamun, but only ten have survived from the earlier Eighteenth Dynasty. The composite bow would usually have been able to shoot arrows over distances of up to 175 metres, but if accuracy was required the distance would only have been about 50–60 metres, according to W. McLeod, 'The Range of the Ancient Bow', *Phoenix* 19 (1965), 1–14. For an experimentally-based discussion of the advantages of the composite over the wooden self bow, see R. Miller, E. McEwen and C. Bergman, 'Experimental Approaches to Ancient Near Eastern Archery', *WA* 18/2 (1986), 178–95.

37 Goedicke, *Perspectives...*, 90.

38 C. Broadhurst, 'Religious Considerations at Qadesh', in Lloyd, *Studies in Pharaonic Religion and Society...*, 78.

39 M. Lichtheim, *Ancient Egyptian Literature* I (Berkeley, 1973), 97–109.

40 For an analysis of the implications of Khety's description of the Asiatics, with regard to Egyptian involvement in Syria-Palestine in the Middle Kingdom, see D.B. Redford, *Egypt, Canaan and Israel...*, 67–8.

41 Although see Moorey, *WA* 18/2 (cited in note 1) for a discussion of the origins and spread of the chariot.

42 J.D. Ray, 'The Emergence of Writing in Egypt', *WA* 17/3 (1986), 307–16; T.G.H. James, *Pharaoh's People* (Oxford, 1985), 133–4.

43 Three alternative views on the nature and purposes of Egyptian 'imperialism' in the New Kingdom are presented by B.J. Kemp, 'Imperialism and Empire in New Kingdom Egypt', in P.D.A. Garnsey and C.R. Whittaker (eds), *Imperialism in the Ancient World* (Cambridge, 1978), 7–57; P.J. Frandsen, 'Egyptian Imperialism', in M.T. Larsen (ed.), *Power and Propaganda: A Symposium on Ancient Empires, Mesopotamia*, Copenhagen Studies in Assyriology 7 (Copenhagen, 1979), 167–92; and J. Leclant, 'Les 'empires' et l'impérialisme de l'Egypte pharaonique', in M. Duverger (ed.), *Le Concept d'Empire* (Paris, 1980), 49–68.

44 Redford, *Egypt, Canaan and Israel...*, 51.

45 B.J. Kemp, 'From Old Kingdom to Second Intermediate Period', in B.G. Trigger et al., *Ancient Egypt: A Social History* (Cambridge, 1985), 143–4.

46 Hanson, *Warfare and Agriculture...*, 4, referring to the victory stele of Kamose in the Temple of Amun at Karnak, quoting the translation given by J.B. Pritchard, *The Ancient Near East, Supplementary Texts and Pictures* (Princeton, 1969), 554.

47 Lichtheim, *Ancient Egyptian Literature* II, 20.

48 R.B. Parkinson, *Voices from Ancient Egypt: An Anthology of Middle Kingdom Writings* (London, 1991), 95.

49 Redford, *Egypt, Canaan and Israel...*, 63–4.

50 A. Gayet, *Musée du Louvre: stèles de la XIIe dynastie*, (Paris, 1886), pl. 1; K. Sethe, *Ägyptische Lesestücke zum Gebrauch im akademischen Unterricht: Texte des Mittleren Reiches* (Leipzig, 1924), 82.

51 For the original publication and translation of the Middle Kingdom stele of Khusobek, see J. Garstang, *El Arabah* (London, 1901) and T.E. Peet, *The Stela of Sebek-khu, the Earliest Record of an Egyptian Campaign in Asia* (Manchester, 1914). For a new translation and fresh analysis of the stele see J. Baines, 'The Stele of Khusobek: Private and Royal Military Narrative and Values', in M. Görg (ed.), *Form und Mass: Beiträge zur Literatur und Kunst des alten Ägypten, Festschrift für Gerhard Fecht* (Wiesbaden, 1987), 43–61. Baines summarizes the significance of the stele as follows, stressing the formulaic nature of the text: 'As in many texts recounting personal exploits, there is no neat conclusion. The structure of each episode is: context; action; reward. The reward documents the protagonist's status and his veracity' (p. 55). He notes that, as in most texts of this type, Khusobek concentrates on the rewards he achieved through battle rather than the 'historical significance of the events'. It is also suggested, somewhat tenuously perhaps, that the style of the text is sufficiently similar to the later 'royal annals' genre of the Eighteenth Dynasty to imply that it was borrowing its style from that of still-undiscovered 'royal narrative inscriptions' from Middle Kingdom temples, which would perhaps have been antecedents of the Eighteenth-Dynasty annals (pp. 57–61).

52 Lichtheim, *Ancient Egyptian Literature* II (Berkeley, 1976), 172.

53 Some support for this suggestion, concerning the claiming of credit for slaying and capturing enemies, may be gleaned from a less biased source, see Baines, op. cit. (n. 51), 56, where it is argued, with regard to the inscription on the Twelfth-Dynasty stele of Khusobek, that 'Specifically military values may be seen in the details of the capture of the Nubian and Asiatic leaders... One reason why the leaders are not indicated very clearly is probably deference to

the king, who takes the ultimate credit for all military success. It is also not stated whether the men were killed or only captured. Parallels suggest that only the king could claim in as many words that he had killed people and the reticence here might be because Khusobek did kill the men or because it would go without saying that he would not claim to have done so.'

54 P.C. Smither, 'The Semnah Despatches', *JEA* 31 (1945), 3–10; S. Quirke, *The Administration of Egypt in the Late Middle Kingdom: The Hieratic Documents* (New Malden, 1990), 191–3.

55 W.L. Moran, *The Amarna Letters* (Baltimore, 1992).

56 E. Wente, *Letters from Ancient Egypt*, SBL Writings from the Ancient World 1 (Atlanta, Georgia, 1990), 35, 114–6, 123–4, 127, 207.

57 Papyrus BM 10752, recto 3–4, see Wente, *Letters from Ancient Egypt*, 70–3; Parkinson, *Voices from Ancient Egypt...*, 93–4.

58 G.T. Martin, *The Hidden Tombs of Memphis: New Discoveries from the Time of Tutankhamun and Ramesses the Great* (London, 1991), 56–9.

59 See Faulkner, *JEA* 39 and A.R. Schulman, *Military rank, title and organization in the Egyptian New Kingdom* (Berlin, 1964).

60 A detailed analysis of the depiction of the Egyptian camp at Qadesh is given by Spalinger, in Goedicke, *Perspectives...*, 7–15.

61 Lichtheim, *Ancient Egyptian Literature* II, 222–35.

62 This table excludes such static 'post-battle' depictions as royal head-smiting scenes, tribute bearers and rows of captives (even when they were probably originally accompanied by scenes of the preceding battle that have not survived, as in the case of the 'Libyan campaign' of Sahure depicted in his mortuary temple at Abusir). It concentrates instead, as far as possible, on active scenes of episodes within the battles themselves. The Annals of Tuthmosis III in the Temple of Amon-Re at Karnak are not included because they comprise a textual, rather than visual, description of his various Asiatic campaigns, including the Battle of Megiddo. For a more detailed discussion of the visual and textual sources for the Old and Middle Kingdoms see D.B. Redford, 'Egypt and Western Asia in the Old Kingdom', *JARCE* 23 (1986), 125–43 and A.R. Schulman, *JSSEA* 12, 165–83. For these and other periods see S. Curto, *Military Art...* and Gaballa, *Narrative in Egyptian Art*.

63 G. Bénédite, 'Le Couteau de Gebel el-Arak: Etude sur un nouvel objet préhistorique acquis par le Musée du Louvre', *Fondation Eugène Piot, Monuments et Mémoires* 22 (1916), 1–34; for full bibliography see I. Shaw, 'Gebel el-Arak', *The Macmillan Dictionary of Art* (in press).

64 H. Case and J.C. Payne, 'Tomb 100: the Decorated Tomb at Hierakonpolis', *JEA* 48 (1962), 5–18; idem, 'Tomb 100: the Decorated Tomb at Hierakonpolis Confirmed', *JEA* 59 (1973), 31–5; B.J. Kemp, 'Photographs of the Decorated Tomb at Hierakonpolis', *JEA* 59 (1973), 36–43.

65 Davis, *Masking the Blow*, 93–118.

66 W.M.F. Petrie, *Ceremonial Slate Palettes and Corpus of Proto-dynastic Pottery* (London, 1953), pl. G; E.L.B. Terrace and H.G. Fisher, *Treasures from the Cairo Museum* (London, 1970), 21; Davis, *Masking the Blow*, 229–32, Figs 53–4.

67 E.J. Baumgartel, *The Cultures of Prehistoric Egypt*, 2 vols (Oxford, 1960), II 96–7; Davis, *Masking the Blow*, 119–44, Fig. 33.

68 J.E. Quibell, *Hierakonpolis* I (London, 1900), pl.XXIX; Davis, *Masking the Blow*, 161–200, Figs 38–47.

69 Smith, *Interconnections...*, Fig. 187.

70 Hassan, *ASAE* 38, pl. 95.

71 Petrie, *Deshasheh*.

72 Quibell and Hayter, *Excavations at Saqqara...*

73 Vandier, *Mo'alla*.

74 Fischer, *Kush* 9, 63–4, Fig. 5.

75 For instance, British Museum E. Naville, *The XIth Dynasty Temple at Deir el-Bahari* I (London, 1907), pls 14, 15; ibid. II (London, 1913), pl. 9; PM II 2nd edn, 383–4.

76 Arnold and Settgast, *MDAIK* 20, 47–61.

77 Newberry, *Beni Hasan*, I, 2–3.

78 Newberry, *Beni Hasan*, II, pl. 15.

79 Newberry, *Beni Hasan*, I, pl. 47.

80 Newberry, *Beni Hasan*, I, pls 14, 16.

81 Current location unknown: Fischer, *Kush* 9, 71, fig. 10.

82 Cairo, Egyptian Museum, JE51978: Jéquier, *Douze ans de fouilles...*, fig. 39.

83 Berlin, Ägyptisches Museum, 21140: Priese, *Ägyptisches Museum*, 128.

84 Cairo, Egyptian Museum, JE61467: N.M. Davies and A.H. Gardiner, *Tutankhamun's Painted Box* (Oxford, 1962).

85 W. Wreszinski, *Atlas zur altägyptischen Kulturgeschichte* II (Leipzig, 1935), pls 151–62.

86 Murnane, *Road to Kadesh*.

87 Desroches-Noblecourt et al., *Grand Temple...*

88 Wreszinski, *Atlas...* II, pl. 25; K.A. Kitchen, *Ramesside Inscriptions: Historical and Biographical* II/3 (Oxford, 1970), 187–91.

89 Wreszinski, *Atlas...* II, pls 16–25; Kuentz, *La Bataille...*, pls XVII–XXIV.

90 H.W. Fairman, 'Preliminary Report on the Excavations at Amarah West', *JEA* 34 (1948), p. 8, pl. 6:1.

91 G. Roeder, *Der Felsentempel von Beit el-Wali* (Cairo, 1938); H. Ricke, G.R. Hughes and E.F. Wente, *The Beit el-Wali Temple of Ramesses II* (Chicago, 1967), pls 7–15.

92 A.M. Blackman, *The Temple of Derr* (Cairo, 1913); Wreszinski, *Atlas...* II, pl. 168a; W.S. Smith, *The Art and Architecture of Ancient Egypt*, 2nd edn, rev. W.K. Simpson (Harmondsworth, 1981), 371–2, fig. 364.

93 Breasted, *The Battle of Kadesh*, pl. vii; G.A. Gaballa, 'Minor War Scenes of Ramesses II at Karnak', *JEA* 55 (1969), 82–8.

94 K.A. Kitchen, 'Some New Light on the Asiatic Wars of Ramesses II', *JEA* 50 (1964), 47–70, pls III–VI.

95 Wreszinski, *Atlas...* II, pls 92–106.

96 Smith, *The Art and Architecture...*, 372, fig. 365.

97 Chicago University, Oriental Institute, *Medinet Habu*, 7 vols (Chicago, 1932–63); H. Nelson, 'The Naval Battle Depicted at Medinet Habu', *JNES* 2 (1943), 40–55; N.K. Sandars: *The Sea Peoples: Warriors of the Eastern Mediterranean 1250–1150 bc* (London, 1978).

98 H.H. Nelson et al., *Reliefs and Inscriptions at Karnak* II, pls 81–2.

99 Nelson et al., *Reliefs...* II, pls 114–20.

INDEX

For most Greek terms Hellenised spelling has been used: thus 'Akhilleus', 'Khalkis', but 'Thucydides'.

Abu Simbel, 247, 249, 251, 260
Abydos (Egyptian), 247, 260
Adrianople, 202, 213
Aedui, 221
Aemilius Regillus, 224
Aeschines, 110–1
Agamemnon, 7, 23, 27, 46, 49, 52, 76 n. 121
Agathon, 110
Agricola, 202, 221, 228
Ahmose, 254
Aias, 5, 8, 18, 24, 32, 39–40, 43, 45–6, 185
Aias, son of Oileus, 26, 52
Aigai, 185
Aineias, 7, 9, 41–2
Akamas, 16
Akharnians, 97
Akhilleus, 7–8, 10, 12–14, 17–19, 24, 26–7, 32, 33, 39, 41–3, 46–7, 49, 52, 57, 76 n. 121, 100, 134, 136–7; homosexual relations with Patroklos?, 19, 123–5; Alexander's obsession with, 184–5
Alamanni, 201–2, 213
alcohol, 11, 13, 174–5, 177, 183–4
Alexander I, 121
Alexander of Epirus, 122
Alexander the Great, 120–2; ch. 4 passim
Alkibiades, 110, 127–8, 136
Amara West, 260
Amenemhat, 260
Amida, 223
Amphipolis, 190
Amphitryon, 147
Amyntas, 121

Anatha, 223
Anaxibios, 118, 137
Ankhtifi, 244, 259
Antilokhos, 19
Antiphos, 37
Aornos mountain, 182, 184, 194
Apollo, 41, 47
Archidamos (king), 97
Archidamos (son of Agesilaos), 118
Archimedes, 225
Argives, Argos, 92–3, 95, 98, 139
Argyraspides, 171–2
Aristandros, 185–6
aristeia, 24, 46, 49
Aristippos, 110
Ariston, 147
Aristophanes, 129
Arkadian League, 139
Arkhelaos, 120–1
armour, 4, 8, 12, 26, 32–4, 49, 87, 89–91, 96, 114, 130, 171, 189, 191–2; Roman, 200
artillery, 193
Asiatics (in Egyptian sources), 242–3, 245–6, 250, 252–3, 256
Asteropaios, 32, 41
Astrabakos, 147
Aswan, 244, 259
Asyut, 245
Athena, 185–6
Athenians, Athens, 92–5, 98, 101–2; and military homosexuality, 125–31
athletics, 128–9
atrocities, 192, ch. 6 passim
Attalos, 121
Atuatuci, 224

Augustus, 204
Avaricum, 229

Bagoas, 122
Baqt 111; 259
battle–cry, 183
Battlefield palette, 242, 258
battlefields, difficult to locate, 239–40
Beit el–Wali, 260
Beneventum, 225
Beni Hasan, 242, 244–5, 257, 259–60
berserkers, 47, 49
Bituriges, 229
Boiotia, Boiotians, 114, 116; *see also* 'Thebes'
booty, *see* 'plunder'
Boudicca, 229
Brasidas, 96–7
bronze, 89–90
brutality, 231–4
Byrhtnoth, earl, 35
Byrsa, 226

Caesar, Julius, 206, 210, 221, 224, 227, 229–32
Caledonians, 202
Calgacus, 232
Capsa, 224, 233–4
Capua, 227–8
Caputo, Philip, 1
Carnutes, 229
Cartagena, *see* 'Carthage, New'
Carthage, 226–8
Carthage, New, 206, 211, 225, 232
cavalry, 190–2; *see also* 'Companions'.
Celtiberians, 231
Celts, 107
Cenabum, 229
chariots, 4, 58, 190, 248, 251
chivalry, rarity of in *Iliad*, 37–44
Cicero, 220, 231, 235
Civil war, 230–1, 245
Civilis, 211
Claudius; Gaius Claudius Nero, 222
coercion, 181–2; *see also* 'discipline'
Colchester (Camulodunum), 229
'Companions' (Macedonian), 172,

174–5, 179–80, 189
comradeship, 16–21, 170, 172, 174, 179–80, 207–9
Corbulo, 204, 221–2
corpses, corpse-fights, 16, 45, 53, 55
Crastinus, 201
Cremna, 235 n. 12
Cremona, 230
Cretans, Crete, 116–7, 129–30, 132, 135
Cyrus, 184

Dacian wars, 222
Dahshur, 245, 260
Darius III, 185, 191, 193
dead, treatment of, 186, 226; *see also* 'corpses'
decimation, 203–4
decorations, 183, 206
Deiphobos, 9, 43–4
Deir el–Bahari, 245, 261
Dekamnikhos, 121
dekas, 180
Demosthenes (general), 96
Demosthenes (orator), 175
Derdas, 121
Derr, 261
Deshasheh, 242–3, 256, 259
Detienne, Marcel, 1, 42
Diomedes, 7, 10, 23, 27, 32–3, 42, 46–7, 49, 76 n. 121
Dion (Macedonia), 185
Dioskouroi, 147
Dioxippos, 193
discipline, 13, 27, 170, 172, 182, 188, 203–5
divination, 11–13, 93, 184–6
drill, *see* 'training'
drugs, 11, 177
Dyrrhachium, 201

Egypt, ch. 7 *passim*
el-Moalla, 244, 259
Elateia, 192
Elephenor, 37
Eleusis, 98
Elis, 115, 139

Elkab, 254
enemy, belittling of, 170, 176–7
Epameinondas, 152 n. 42, 188
ephebes, *ephebeia*, 129–30
Ephorus, 116–7, 131
Epimenes, 121
Episthenes, 126, 138–9
erastes, 108–10, 112–4, 116–9, 121, 132, 138, 144–6
Eretria, 95
Erigyios, 122, 178
eromenos, 108–10, 112–4, 116–21, 132, 138, 144–7
Euboulos (playwright), 111
Euphorbos, 16, 43
Euripides, 110
Euryalus, 137
Eurylokhos, 182
'Eurymedon vase', 133
Eurypylos, 7

Falerii, schoolmaster of, 222
Falklands War, 21–3, 30, 50–1, 77 n. 135
fame, *see* 'reputation'
fantasy, 184
Farnham, Lord, 58
fatalism, 11, 177
fatigue, 45, 49, 191
fear, 8–10
'Fear' (divinity), 186
Fetial Code, 219
Flamininus, T. Quinctius, 233–4
'Foot–companions', 172, 189
football, *see* 'hooligans'
Frontinus, Iulius, 221–2, 233–5

Galba, Servius Sulpicius, 231
Galba (emperor), 204
Gaugamela, 182–3, 186, 190–1, 193
Gauls, 208–9
Gawain, Sir, 35–6
Gaza, 193
Gebel el-Arak, 258
Gebel el-Silsila, 260
Glaukos, 7, 17, 32–3, 42
Gomphi, 230

Goose Green, battle of, 2, 23
Gorgidas, 111–2, 152 n. 42
Goths, 202
Gracchus, Ti. Sempronius (cos. 215 bc), 225–6
Granikos, 186, 192–3
Greek language, 172–3
Gulf War, 5, 228
gymnasium, 128–9

Halikarnassos, 183
Hamippoi, 172
Hanson, Victor, 87, 102, 169, 199
Harpalos, 122
Hasdrubal (Barca), 222,
Hasdrubal (commander in 3rd Punic War), 228
Hatra, 223
Hektor, 7–15, 17, 22–7, 40, 43, 46–7, 53–4
Helen, 147
Hellenokrates, 121
helots, 96–7
Hephaistion, 122, 180
Hephaistos, 90
Herakleopolis, 245–6
Herakles, 147, 184, 186
Hermolaos, 121
Herodotus, 88, 91, 95
Hesiod, 96, 100
Hierakonpolis, 258
Hippolytos, 130
Hitler Youth, 107
Hittites, 250, 256, 260
Homer, ch. 1, *passim*, 88, 90, 100, 136
homosexuality, 19, ch. 3 *passim*, 180; and the efficiency of warriors, 135–9
hooligans (football), 3–4, 48
hoplite warfare, ch. 2 *passim*
Horemheb, 255–6, 260
Hunter's palette, 258
hunting, 173–4
Hyksos, 251
Hypaspists, 170–2
Hysiai, 95

Iceni, 228
Idomeneus, 9, 17, 43–4, 46, 54–6
Illyrians, 189
India, 186
Intef, 245, 259
Inti, 242–4, 256, 259
Iolaos, 112, 114
Isadas, 119
Issos, 176, 183, 185–6, 190–1

Japan, medieval, 30–2, 35
Japan, modern, 58
Jebel Sahaba, 240
Jerusalem, 205, 223–4
Jews, 224
Jômyô, 35
Jotapata, 211
Julian (emperor), 206, 211–3, 223
justification, of war, 170, 175–6

Kaemheset, 243–4, 257, 259
Kallixeina, 122
Kapauku (of New Guinea), 11, 29
Karnak, 247, 260–1
Kebriones, 52
Keegan, John, 87, 169, 191
Keraki Indians (of Papua New
    Guinea), 139–40
Khaironeia, Battle of, 171, 186
Khalkis (Euboian), 95, 116
Khalkis (Thracian), 116
Kharikles, 121
Khety, 250, 257, 259
Khnumhotep, 259
Khufu, 242, 259
Khusobek, 254
Kiggell, Lt.–Gen. Sir L., 169
killing zone, 3, 187, 193
Kleitos the Black, 173, 175
Kleomakhos, 116, 137
Kleonymos, 118
Klytaimnestra, 147
Koinos, 191
Koiranos, 16
Koragos, 193
Krateros, 192
Krateuas, 121

krypteia, 130
Kuwait, 228
Kynoskephalai, 201, 233

Laios, 112–3
Laomedon (of Macedon), 122
leadership, 3–4, 14, 20, 27–9, 177–8,
    187–91, 210–2
Lelantine plain, 95
Liberia, 12
Libyan palette, 258
Libyans, 260–1
limitanei, 213–4
Lingones, 222
Lisht, 245, 260
Locha, 229
London (Londinium), 229
Lucullus, 232
Lukowiak, K, 30, 50–1
Luxor, 247, 261
Lykoorgos, 56
Lysias, 110
Lysippos, 183

Macedon, 119–23; army of, ch. 4
    passim, 233; dialect of, 172–3
madness (in *Iliad*)?, 44–50
Mae Enga (of New Guinea), 34
Mago, 225
Makhaon, 7
Maldon, Battle of, 35
manoeuvres, 172
Mantineia, 97; battle of, 97
Marcellus, M. Claudius (cos.
    222 BC), 225
Mardonius, 91–2
Marind–Anim (of Papua New
    Guinea), 139–40
Marius, C., 210, 224, 233–4
Marseilles (Massilia), 232
Medinet Habu, 250–1, 261
Megara, 115
Megiddo, battle of, 247–8
Melanion, 130
Memphis, 255
Menelaos, 9, 37
Mentuhotep II, 245, 259

mercy, 221, 231–4
Meriones, 9, 44, 54, 56
Mesehti, 245
Messenia, 98
Ministry of Defence (U.K.), 107
Mons Graupius, 202, 232
Munda, 201
music, martial, 177, 181
Muthul, 201
Mycenae, 98

Narmer palette, 258
Nearkhos, 122
Nestor, 7–8, 10, 17, 22, 26–7, 33, 56
Nesumenthu, 254
Nikias, 93
Nisus, 137
Noricum, 213
Nubia, Nubians, 253, 260–1
Numantia, 227
Numidians, 233
'nutters', 48
noise, 6, 8, 201

oath–taking, 207
Odysseus, 7, 10, 37, 45–6
Olympias, 122
Olympic Games, 94
omens, *see* 'divination'
Onasander, 220–1, 235
Onomarkhos, 193
Opis, 174
Ordovices, 228
Ostorius Scapula, 234
Otho, 230

Pages, Royal, 120–3, 139, 171;
    Conspiracy of, 121, 173
Pagondas, 100
Pammenes, 112–3, 122, 152 n.42
Pandaros, 53–4
panic, 191
Papua New Guinea, 3, 107, 139–44
Paris, 5, 8, 33, 43
Parmenion, 178
Passchendaele, 169
patriotism, 14–16, 98–101, 177

Patroklos, 6, 19, 32, 37, 46–7, 52,
    54, 76 n. 121; homosexual
    relations with Akhilleus?, 19,
    123–5
Pausanias (regent of Sparta), 128
Pausanias (Athenian), 110
Pausanias (of Macedon; *eromenos*,
    and assassin, of Philip), 121
Pausanias (of Macedon; courted by
    Philip), 121, 138
peasant farmers, 96
pederasty, as model for Greek
    homosexuality, 108–11, 113–4,
    116–7, 121–2, 124–5
Peisistratos, 125
Pelopidas, 188
Peloponnesian War, 96
Peneleos, 52
Penthesileia, 134
Perikles, 97, 99
Perinthos, 190
Persepolis, 175–6
Perseus, 184
Persian expedition, of Julian, 213,
    223
Persians, 171, 177, 191, 223
Petreius, 221, 229
Pezhetairoi, see 'Foot–companions'.
Phaidimos, 113
Pharsalus, 202
Philip of Macedon, 112–3, 120–2,
    135; ch. 4 *passim*
Philoi, 172, *174*
Philostratos, 128
Philotas, 173
Phokaia, 224
Piankhi, 241
Plato, 126–7, 129, 131–2, 135
plunder, 25–8, 55–6, 177, 181–2,
    206, 220, 225, 229–30, 254–5
Plutarch, 111–5, 131, 135–7
Polybius, 94, 203, 205, 221, 225–6
Pometia, 224
Pompey the Great, 220
Poulydamas, 53
Praeneste, 222
prostitutes, 111

Ptolemy (son of Lagos), 122, 180
punishment, *see* 'discipline'

Qadan culture, 240
Qadesh, battle of, 242, 247–51, 256,
  260–1

Ramesses II, 246–7, 250, 256, 260–1
Ramesses III, 250–1, 261
Ramesses IV, 247
Ramesseum, 247, 261
ransom, 26
rape, 182
rebellion, 226–30
religion, 184–7, 208, 241, 251; *see
  also* 'divination', 'oath–taking'
reputation, 14, 21–5, 28, 57, 99,
  181, 203
revenge, 14, 16, 27, 42, 52–3, 226–30
rewards, 182, 205; *see also* 'plunder'
Roman armies, reasons for success,
  ch. 5 *passim*; and morality, ch. 6
  passim
'rubbish men', 34

Sacred Band (Thebes), 111–5, 135,
  139
St Albans (Verulamium), 229
Sallust, 233
Sambia, 110, 139–44
samurai, 30, 35, 51–2
Sapor, 223
Saqqara, 242–3, 259
sarissa, 193
Sarpedon, 7, 10, 25, 32, 52
Sattler, German general, 58
Scipio Aemilianus, 227–30
Scipio Africanus, 206, 211, 225, 232
scribes (Egyptian), 251, 254, 256–7
Scythians, 190–I
Sea Peoples, 250–1, 261
Semiramis, 184
Semna Dispatches, 255
Seqenenre Tao II, 240
Sertorius, 201
Sesostris I, 245, 260
Sesostris III, 245, 260

Seti I, 260
Setka, 244, 259
Severus, 223
shame, *see* 'reputation'
Shasu, 260
siege, 190, 220–6, 243–6, 248
Silures, 234
Sinuhe, 257–8
Siwa, 184
social class, on the battlefield, 30–4
Socrates, 110, 127–8, 136
solidarity, *see* 'comradeship'
Somatophylakes, 172
Sophocles, 110
Sostratos, 121
Spanish Main, pirates of, 107
Sparta, Spartans, 95, 97–9, 101–2,
  109, 116–9, 129, 132, 134–5,
  137, 139, 144–7; compared with
  Sambia, 142–4
speeches, before battle, 93, 100, 103
  n. 22, 177, 180–1; 'recording' of,
  211–2
spoils, 50–6; *see also* 'plunder'
Squadron, Royal, 189
standards, military, 208
Stoics, 110
Strasbourg, battle of, 201–2, 212–3
stress, 4–8, 13, 177–87, 201. *See also*
  'fear'
Styx, River, 12
Sulla, 222
Sun, The (newspaper), 54
surrender, 220–6, 233, 257
Susian Gates, 186–7, 191
Syracuse, 92–5, 139, 225, 232
Syria–Palestine (in Egyptian sources),
  246, 252–6, 260–1

Tacfarinas, 229
Tegea, 97–8
Telemakhos, 125
Templars, 107
territory, as reason for war, 95, 252
Teukros, 52
Thapsus, 206, 230
Thebes, 111–5, 126–7, 135, 139,

146, 192
Thebes (Egyptian), 242, 260
Theopompus, 120
Theron, 116
Thersites, 134
Thessaly, 230
Thucydides, 88–9, 92, 101–2, 128
Thyreai, 95
Tigranocerta, 221–2, 232
Tigris, 183
Titus (son of Vespasian), 206, 223
training, 171–2, 207
Trajan's Column, 222
Trojan War, Troy, ch. 1 *passim; see also* 'Akhilleus'
Tutankhamun, 260
Tyndareus, 147
Tyre, 176, 186, 193
Tyrtaios, 96, 99, 119

Unas, 242, 259
uniform, 170–1, 208
Uxellodunum, 227

Valens (emperor), 213
Varus, P. Quinctilius, 234

vase painting, 92
Vegetius, 207
Vercellae, 201
Vercingetorix, 227
Vespasian (emperor), 211
victory, factors conducing to, 187–94
Vietnam, war in, 1, 47–8
Vikings, 107
Virgil, 137–8
Vitellius (emperor), 230

weapons, 2–4, 88–91, 170–1, 192–3, 239–40, 248, 251, 257
Weni, 253
wine, *see* 'alcohol'
women, 15, 29, 110, 123–4, 128, 130, 135, 140, 144, 182, 256–7
World War I, 14, 169, 211
World War II, 5, 14, 20

Xenophon, 126, 135–6

Yoshinaka, 35

Zeus, 8–9, 147, 174, 186
Zulus, 107